SIGMUND
FREUD

COLLECTED
WORKS

SIGMUND
FREUD

THE BASIS OF PSYCHOANALYTIC PSYCHOLOGY:

THE PSYCHOPATHOLOGY OF EVERYDAY LIFE

THE THEORY OF SEXUALITY

BEYOND THE PLEASURE PRINCIPLE

THE EGO AND THE ID

THE FUTURE OF AN ILLUSION

COLLECTED
WORKS

Pacific Publishing Studio

AUTHORIZED TRANSLATIONS BY

A.A. BRILL, PH.B., M.D.

ISBN is 1453640770

EAN-13 is 9781453640777

Pacific Publishing Studio books are available at discounts for volume purchases in the United States by institution, corporations, and other organizations. For information on volume or wholesale purchases, contact Pacific Publishing Studio through their website at www.PacPS.com.

CONTENTS

THE PSYCHOPATHOLOGY OF

EVERYDAY LIFE

THE THEORY OF

SEXUALITY

THE FUTURE OF AN

ILLUSION

THE PSYCHOPATHOLOGY OF
EVERYDAY
LIFE

CONTENTS

INTRODUCTION to
THE PSYCHOPATHOLOGY OF EVERYDAY LIFE

PROFESSOR FREUD DEVELOPED his system of psychoanalysis while studying the so-called borderline cases of mental diseases, such as hysteria and compulsion neurosis. By discarding the old methods of treatment and strictly applying himself to a study of the patient's life, he discovered that the hitherto puzzling symptoms had a definite meaning, and that there was nothing arbitrary in any morbid manifestation. Psychoanalysis always showed that they referred to some definite problem or conflict of the person concerned. It was while tracing back the abnormal to the normal state that Professor Freud found how faint the line of demarcation was between the normal and neurotic person, and that the psychopathologic mechanisms so glaringly observed in the psychoneuroses and psychoses could usually be demonstrated in a lesser degree in normal persons. This led to a study of the faulty actions of everyday life and later to the publication of the *Psychopathology of Everyday Life*, a book which passed through four editions in Germany and is considered the author's most popular work. With great ingenuity and penetration the author throws much light on the complex problems of human behavior, and clearly demonstrates that the hitherto considered impassable gap between normal and abnormal mental states is more apparent than real.

This translation is made of the fourth German edition, and while the original text was strictly followed, linguistic difficulties often made it necessary to modify or substitute some of the author's cases by examples comprehensible to the English-speaking reader.

New York.
A. A. Brill.

CHAPTER 1
Forgetting of Proper Names

DURING THE YEAR 1898 I published a short essay *On the Psychic Mechanism of Forgetfulness*. I shall now repeat its contents and take it as a starting-point for further discussion. I have there undertaken a psychological analysis of a common case of temporary forgetfulness of proper names, and from a pregnant example of my own observation I have reached the conclusion that this frequent and practically unimportant occurrence of a failure of a psychic function—of memory—admits an explanation which goes beyond the customary utilization of this phenomenon.

If an average psychologist should be asked to explain how it happens that we often fail to recall a name which we are sure we know, he would probably content himself with the answer that proper names are more apt to be forgotten than any other content of memory. He might give plausible reasons for this "forgetting preference" for proper names, but he would not assume any deep determinant for the process.

I was led to examine exhaustively the phenomenon of temporary forgetfulness through the observation of certain peculiarities, which, although not general, can, nevertheless, be seen clearly in some cases. In these there is not only *forgetfulness*, but also false *recollection*: he who strives for the escaped name brings to consciousness others—substitutive names—which, although immediately recognized as false, nevertheless obtrude themselves with great tenacity. The process which should lead to the reproduction of the lost name is, as it were, displaced, and thus brings one to an incorrect substitute.

Now it is my assumption that the displacement is not left to psychic arbitrariness, but that it follows lawful and rational paths. In other words, I assume that the substitutive name (or names) stands in direct relation to the lost name, and I hope, if I succeed in demonstrating this connection, to throw light on the origin of the forgetting of names.

In the example which I selected for analysis in 1898, I vainly strove to recall the name of the master who made the imposing frescoes of the "Last Judgment" in the dome of *Orvieto*. Instead of the lost name—*Signorelli*—two other names of artists—*Botticelli* and *Boltraffio*—obtruded themselves, names which my judgment immediately and definitely rejected as being incorrect. When the correct name was imparted to me by an outsider, I recognized it at once without any hesitation. The examination of the influence and association paths which caused the displacement from *Signorelli* to *Botticelli* and *Boltraffio* led to the following results:

(*a*) The reason for the escape of the name *Signorelli* is neither to be sought in the strangeness in itself of this name nor in the psychological character of the connection in which it was inserted. The forgotten name was just as familiar to me as one of the substitutive names—Botticelli—and somewhat more familiar than the other substitute—Boltraffio—of the possessor of which I could hardly say more than that he belonged to the Milanese School. The connection, too, in which the forgetting of the name took place appeared to me harmless, and led to no further explanation. I journeyed by carriage with a stranger from Ragusa, Dalmatia, to a station in Herzegovina. Our conversation drifted to travelling in Italy, and I asked my companion whether he had been in Orvieto and had seen there the famous frescoes of....

(*b*) The forgetting of the name could not be explained until after I had recalled the theme discussed immediately before this conversation. This forgetting then made itself known *as a disturbance of the newly emerging theme caused by the theme preceding it.* In brief, before I asked my travelling companion if he had been in Orvieto we had been discussing the customs of the Turks living in *Bosnia* and *Herzegovina.* I had related what I heard from a colleague who was practicing medicine among them, namely, that they show full confidence in the physician and complete submission to fate. When one is compelled to inform them that there is no help for the patient, they answer: "*Sir* (Herr), what can I say? I know that if he could be saved you would save him." In these sentences alone we can find the words and names: *Bosnia, Herzegovina,* and *Herr* (sir), which may be inserted in an association series between *Signorelli, Botticelli,* and *Boltraffio.*

(*c*) I assume that the stream of thoughts concerning the customs of the Turks in Bosnia, etc., was able to disturb the next thought, because I withdrew my attention from it before it ended. For I recalled that I wished to relate a second anecdote which was next to the first in my memory. These Turks value the sexual pleasure above all else, and at sexual disturbances merge into an utter despair which strangely contrasts with their resignation at the peril of losing their lives. One of my colleague's patients once told him: "For you know, sir (Herr), if that ceases, life no longer has any charm."

I refrained from imparting this characteristic feature because I did not wish to touch upon such a delicate theme in conversation with a stranger. But I went still further; I also deflected my attention from the continuation of the thought which might have associated itself in me with the theme "Death and Sexuality." I was at that time under the after-effects of a message which I had received a few weeks before, during a brief sojourn in *Trafoi.* A patient on whom I had spent much effort had ended his life because of an incurable sexual disturbance. I know positively that this sad event, and everything connected with it, did not come to my conscious recollection on that trip in Herzegovina. However, the agreement between *Trafoi* and *Boltraffio* forces me to assume that this reminiscence was at that time brought to activity despite all the intentional deviation of my attention.

(*d*) I can no longer conceive the forgetting of the name Signorelli as an accidental occurrence. I must recognize in this process the influence of a *motive.* There were motives which actuated the interruption in the communication of my thoughts (concerning the customs of the Turks, etc.), and which later influenced me to exclude from my consciousness the thought connected with them, and which might have led to the message concerning the incident in Trafoi—that is, I wanted to forget something, I *repressed* something. To be sure, I wished to forget something other than the name of the master of Orvieto; but this other thought brought about an associative connection between itself and this name, so that my act of volition missed the aim, and I *forgot the one against my will,* while I *intentionally* wished to forget the other. The disinclination to recall directed itself against the one content; the inability to remember appeared in another. The case would have been obviously simpler if this disinclination and the inability to remember had concerned the same content. The substitutive names no longer seem as thoroughly justified as they were before this explanation. They remind me (after the form of a compromise) as much of what I wished to forget as of what I wished to remember, and show me that my object to forget something was neither a perfect success nor a failure.

(*e*) The nature of the association formed between the lost name and the repressed theme (death and sexuality, etc.), containing the names of Bosnia, Herzegovina, and Trafoi, is also very strange. In the scheme inserted here, which originally appeared in 1898, an attempt is made to graphically represent these associations.

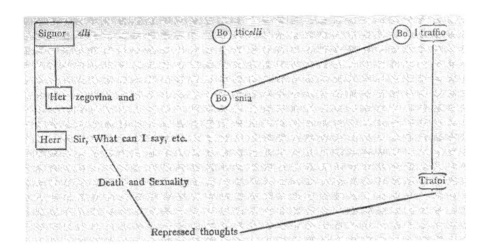

The name Signorelli was thus divided into two parts. One pair of syllables (*elli*) returned unchanged in one of the substitutions, while the other had gained, through the translation of *signor* (sir, Herr), many and diverse relations to the name contained in the repressed theme, but was lost through it in the reproduction. Its substitution was formed in a way to suggest that a displacement took place along the same associations—"Herzegovina and Bosnia"—regardless of the sense and acoustic demarcation. The names were therefore treated in this process like the written pictures of a sentence which is to be transformed into a picture puzzle (rebus). No information was given to consciousness concerning the whole process, which, instead of the name Signorelli, was thus changed to the substitutive names. At first sight, no relation is apparent between the theme that contained the name Signorelli and the repressed one which immediately preceded it.

Perhaps it is not superfluous to remark that the given explanation does not contradict the conditions of memory reproduction and forgetting assumed by other psychologists, which they seek in certain relations and dispositions. Only in certain cases have we added another *motive* to the factors long recognized as causative in forgetting names, and have thus laid bare the mechanism of faulty memory. The assumed dispositions are indispensable also in our case, in order to make it possible for the repressed element to associatively gain control over the desired name and take it along into the repression. Perhaps this would not have occurred in another name having more favorable conditions of reproduction. For it is quite probable that a suppressed element continually strives to assert itself in some other way, but attains this success only where it meets with suitable conditions. At other times the suppression succeeds without disturbance of function, or, as we may justly say, without symptoms.

When we recapitulate the conditions for forgetting a name with faulty recollection we find:

(1) a certain disposition to forget the same; (2) a process of suppression which has taken place shortly before; and (3) the possibility of establishing an *outer* association between the concerned name and the element previously suppressed. The last condition will probably not have to be much

overrated, for the slightest claim on the association is apt in most cases to bring it about. But it is a different and farther-reaching question whether such outer association can really furnish the proper condition to enable the suppressed element to disturb the reproduction of the desired name, or whether after all a more intimate connection between the two themes is not necessarily required. On superficial consideration one may be willing to reject the latter requirement and consider the temporal meeting in perfectly dissimilar contents as sufficient. But on more thorough examination one finds more and more frequently that the two elements (the repressed and the new one) connected by an outer association, possess besides a connection in content, and this can also be demonstrated in the example *Signorelli*.

The value of the understanding gained through the analysis of the example *Signorelli* naturally depends on whether we must explain this case as a typical or as an isolated process. I must now maintain that the forgetting of a name associated with faulty recollection uncommonly often follows the same process as was demonstrated in the case of *Signorelli*. Almost every time that I observed this phenomenon in myself I was able to explain it in the manner indicated above as being motivated by repression.

I must mention still another viewpoint in favor of the typical nature of our analysis. I believe that one is not justified in separating the cases of name-forgetting with faulty recollection from those in which incorrect substitutive names have not obtruded themselves. These substitutive names occur spontaneously in a number of cases; in other cases, where they do not come spontaneously, they can be brought to the surface by concentration of attention, and they then show the same relation to the repressed element and the lost name as those that come spontaneously. Two factors seem to play a part in bringing to consciousness the substitutive names: first, the effort of attention, and second, and inner determinant which adheres to the psychic material. I could find the latter in the greater or lesser facility which forms the required outer associations between the two elements. A great many of the cases of name-forgetting without faulty recollection therefore belong to the cases with substitutive name formation, the mechanism of which corresponds to the one in the example *Signorelli*. But I surely shall not venture to assert that all cases of name-forgetting belong to the same group. There is no doubt that there are cases of name-forgetting that proceed in a much simpler way. We shall represent this state of affairs carefully enough if we assert that *besides the simple forgetting of proper names there is another forgetting which is motivated by repression.*

CHAPTER 2
Forgetting of Foreign Words

THE ORDINARY VOCABULARY of our own language seems to be protected against forgetting within the limits of normal function, but it is quite different with words from a foreign language. The tendency to forget such words extends to all parts of speech. In fact, depending on our own general state and the degree of fatigue, the first manifestation of functional disturbance evinces itself in the irregularity of our control over foreign vocabulary. In a series of cases this forgetting follows the same mechanism as the one revealed in the example *Signorelli*. As a demonstration of this I shall report a single analysis, characterized, however, by valuable features, concerning the forgetting of a word, not a noun, from a Latin quotation. Before proceeding, allow me to give a full and clear account of this little episode.

Last summer, while journeying on my vacation, I renewed the acquaintance of a young man of academic education, who, as I soon noticed, was conversant with some of my works. In our conversation we drifted—I no longer remember how—to the social position of the race to which we both belonged. He, being ambitious, bemoaned the fact that his generation, as he expressed it, was destined to grow crippled, that it was prevented from developing its talents and from gratifying its desires. He concluded his passionately felt speech with the familiar verse from Virgil: *Exoriare. . .* in which the unhappy *Dido* leaves her vengeance upon *Æneas* to posterity. Instead of "concluded," I should have said, "wished to conclude," for he could not end the quotation, and attempted to conceal the open gap in his memory by transposing the words:

"*Exoriar(e) ex nostris ossibus ultor!*"

He finally became piqued and said: "Please don't make such a mocking face, as if you were gloating over my embarrassment, but help me. There is something missing in this verse. How does it read in its complete form?"

"With pleasure," I answered, and cited it correctly:

"*Exoriar(e) aliquis nostris ex ossibus ultor!*"

"It is too stupid to forget such a word," he said. "By the way, I understand you claim that forgetting is not without its reasons; I should be very curious to find out how I came to forget this indefinite pronoun '*aliquis*.'"

I gladly accepted the challenge, as I hoped to get an addition to my collection, and said, "We can easily do this, but I must ask you to tell me frankly and without any criticism everything that occurs to your mind after you focus your attention, without any particular intention, on the forgotten word."[1]

"Very well, the ridiculous idea comes to me to divide the word in the following way: *a* and *liquis*."

"What does that mean?"

"I don't know."

"What else does that recall to you?"

"The thought goes on to *reliques—liquidation—liquidity—fluid*."

"Does that mean anything to you now?"

"No, not by a long shot."

"Just go ahead."

"I now think," he said, laughing sarcastically, "of Simon of Trent, whose relics I saw two years ago in a church in Trent. I think of the old accusation which has been brought against the Jews again, and of the work of *Kleinpaul*, who sees in these supposed sacrifices reincarnations or revivals, so to speak, of the Savior."

"This stream of thoughts has some connection with the theme which we discussed before the Latin word escaped you."

"You are right. I now think of an article in an Italian journal which I have recently read. I believe it was entitled: 'What St. Augustine said Concerning Women.' What can you do with this?"

I waited.

"Now I think of something which surely has no connection with the theme."

"Oh, please abstain from all criticism, and—"

"Oh, I know! I recall a handsome old gentleman whom I met on my journey last week. He was really an *original* type. He looked like a big bird of prey. His name, if you care to know, is Benedict."

"Well, at least you give a grouping of saints and Church fathers: *St. Simon, St. Augustine,* and *St. Benedict.* I believe that there was a Church father named *Origines.* Three of these, moreover, are Christian names, like *Paul* in the name *Kleinpaul.*"

"Now I think of *St. Januarius* and his blood miracle—I find that the thoughts are running mechanically."

"Just stop a moment; both *St. Januarius* and *St. Augustine have* something to do with the calendar. Will you recall to me the blood miracle?"

"Don't you know about it? The blood of St. Januarius is preserved in a phial in a church in Naples, and on a certain holiday a miracle takes place causing it to liquefy. The people think a great deal of this miracle, and become very excited if the liquefying process is retarded, as happened once during the French occupation. The General in command—or Garibaldi, if I am not mistaken—then took the priest aside, and with a very significant gesture pointed out to him the soldiers arrayed without, and expressed his hope that the miracle would soon take place. And it actually took place.. . ."

"Well, what else comes to your mind? Why do you hesitate?"

"Something really occurred to me . . . but it is too intimate a matter to impart . . . besides, I see no connection and no necessity for telling it."

"I will take care of the connection. Of course I cannot compel you to reveal what is disagreeable to you, but then you should not have demanded that I tell you why you forgot the word '*aliquis.*'"

"Really? Do you think so? Well, I suddenly thought of a woman from whom I could easily get a message that would be very annoying to us both."

"That she missed her courses?"

"How could you guess such a thing?"

"That was not very difficult. You prepared me for it long enough. Just think of the *saints of the calendar, the liquefying of the blood on a certain day, the excitement if the event does not take place, and the distinct threat that the miracle must take place. . . .* Indeed, you have elaborated the miracle of St. Januarius into a clever allusion to the courses of the woman."

"It was surely without my knowledge. And do you really believe that my inability to reproduce the word '*aliquis*' was due to this anxious expectation?"

"That appears to me absolutely certain. Don't you recall dividing it into *a-liquis* and the associations: *reliques, liquidation, fluid*? Shall I also add to this connection the fact that St. Simon, to whom you got by way of the *reliques*, was sacrificed as a child?"

"Please stop. I hope you do not take these thoughts—if I really entertained them—seriously. I will, however, confess to you that the lady is Italian, and that I visited Naples in her company. But may not all this be coincidental?"

"I must leave to your own judgment whether you can explain all these connections through the assumption of coincidence. I will tell you, however, that every similar case that you analyze will lead you to just such remarkable 'coincidences!'"

I have more than one reason for valuing this little analysis, for which I am indebted to my traveling companion. First, because in this case I was able to make use of a source which is otherwise inaccessible to me. Most of the examples of psychic disturbances of daily life that I have here compiled I was obliged to take from observation of myself. I endeavored to evade the far richer material furnished me by my neurotic patients, because I had to preclude the objection that the phenomena in question were only the result and manifestation of the neurosis. It was therefore of special value for my purpose to have a stranger free from a neurosis offer himself as a subject for such examination. This analysis is also important in other respects, inasmuch as it elucidates a case of word-forgetting *without* substitutive recollection, and thus confirms the principle formulated above, namely, that the appearance or nonappearance of incorrect substitutive recollections does not constitute an essential distinction.[2]

But the principal value of the example *aliquis* lies in another of its distinctions from the case *Signorelli*. In the latter example the reproduction of the name becomes disturbed through the after-effects of a stream of thought which began shortly before and was interrupted, but whose content had no distinct relation to the new theme which contained the name Signorelli. Between the repression and the theme of the forgotten name there existed only the relation of temporal contiguity, which reached the other in order that the two should be able to form a connection through an outer association.[3] On the other hand, in the example *aliquis* one can note no trace of such an independent repressed theme which could occupy conscious thought immediately before and then re-echo as a disturbance. The disturbance of the reproduction proceeded here from the inner part of the theme touched upon, and was brought about by the fact that unconsciously a contradiction arose against the wish-idea represented in the quotation.

The origin must be construed in the following manner: The speaker deplored the fact that the present generation of his people was being deprived of its rights, and like Dido he presaged that a new generation would take upon itself vengeance against the oppressors. He therefore expressed the wish for posterity. In this moment he was interrupted by the contradictory thought: "Do you really wish so much for posterity? That is not true. Just think in what a predicament you would be if you should now receive the information that you must expect posterity from the quarter you have in mind! No, you want no posterity—as much as you need it for your vengeance." This contradiction asserts itself, just as in the example *Signorelli*, by forming an outer association between one of his ideation elements and an element of the repressed wish, but here it is brought about in a most strained manner through what seems an artificial detour of associations. Another important agreement with the example *Signorelli* results from the fact that the contradiction originates from repressed sources and emanates from thoughts which would cause a deviation of attention.

So much for the diversity and the inner relationship of both paradigms of the forgetting of names. We have learned to know a second mechanism of forgetting, namely, the disturbance of thought through an inner contradiction emanating from the repression. In the course of this discussion we shall repeatedly meet with this process, which seems to me to be the more easily understood.

Footnotes

[1] *This is the usual way of bringing to consciousness-hidden ideas. Cf. The Interpretation of Dreams, translated by A. A. Brill, The Macmillan Company, New York, and Allen, London.*

[2] *Finer observation reduces somewhat the contrast between the analyses of Signorelli and aliquis as far as the substitutive recollections are concerned. Here, too, the forgetting seems to be accompanied by substitutive formations. When I later asked my companion whether in his effort to recall the forgotten word he did not think of some substitution, he informed me that he was at first tempted to put an ab into the verse: nostris ab ossibus (perhaps the disjointed part of a-liquis) and that later the word exoriare obtruded itself with particular distinctness and persistency. Being skeptical, he added that it was apparently because it was the first word of the verse. But when I asked him to focus his attention on the associations to exoriare he gave me the word exorcism. This makes me think that the reinforcement of exoriare in the reproduction has really the value of such substitution. It probably came through the association exorcism from the names of the saints. However, no value need be laid upon those refinements. It seems now quite possible that the appearance of any kind of substitutive recollection is a constant sign—perhaps only characteristic and misleading—of the purposive forgetting motivated by repression. This substitution might also explain the reinforcement of an element akin to the thing forgotten, even where incorrect substitutive names fail to appear. Thus, in the example Signorelli, as long as the name of the painter remained inaccessible to me, I had more than a clear visual memory of the cycle of his frescoes, and of the picture of himself in the corner; at least it was more intensive than any of my other visual memory traces. In another case, also reported in my essay of 1898, I had hopelessly forgotten the street name and address connected with a disagreeable visit in a strange city, but—as if to mock me—the house number appeared especially vivid, whereas the memory of numbers usually causes me the greatest difficulty.*

[3] *I am not fully convinced of the lack of an inner connection between the two streams of thought in the case of Signorelli. In carefully following the repressed thought concerning the theme of death and sexual life, one does strike an idea which shows a near relation to the theme of the frescoes of Orvieto.*

CHAPTER 3
Forgetting of Names and Order of Words

EXPERIENCES LIKE THOSE mentioned concerning the process of forgetting apart of the order of words from a foreign language may cause one to wonder whether the forgetting of the order of words in one's own language requires an essentially different explanation. To be sure, one is not wont to be surprised if after awhile a formula or poem learned by heart can only be reproduced imperfectly, with variations and gaps. Still, as this forgetting does not affect equally all the things learned together, but seems to pick out there from definite parts, it may be worth our effort to investigate analytically some examples of such faulty reproductions.

Brill reports the following example:

"While conversing one day with a very brilliant young woman she had occasion to quote from Keats. The poem was entitled 'Ode to Apollo,' and she recited the following lines:

> "'In thy western house of gold
> Where thou livest in thy state,
> Bards, that once sublimely told
> Prosaic truths that came too late.'

She hesitated many times during the recitation, being sure that there was something wrong with the last line. To her great surprise, on referring to the book she found that not only was the last line misquoted but that there were many other mistakes. The correct lines read as follows:

> ODE TO APOLLO
> "'In thy western *halls* of gold
> *When* thou *sittest* in thy state,
> Bards, that *erst* sublimely told
> *Heroic deeds and sang of fate.*'

The words italicized are those that have been forgotten and replaced by others during the recitation.

"She was astonished at her many mistakes, and attributed them to a failure of memory. I could readily convince her, however, that there was no qualitative or quantitative disturbance of memory in her case, and recalled to her our conversation immediately before quoting these lines.

"We were discussing the over-estimation of personality among lovers, and she thought it was Victor Hugo who said that love is the greatest thing in the world because it makes an angel or a god out of a grocery clerk. She continued: "Only when we are in love have we blind faith in humanity; everything is perfect, everything is beautiful, and . . . everything is so poetically unreal. Still, it is a wonderful experience; worth going through, notwithstanding the terrible disappointments that usually follow. It puts us on a level with the gods and incites us to all sorts of artistic activities. We become real poets; we not only memorize and quote poetry, but we often become Apollos ourselves.' She then quoted the lines given above.

"When I asked on what occasion she memorized the lines she could not recall. As a teacher of elocution she was wont to memorize so much and so often that it was difficult to tell just when she had memorized these lines. 'Judging by the conversation,' I suggested, 'it would seem that this poem is intimately associated with the idea of over-estimation of personality of one in love. Have you perhaps memorized this poem when you were in such a state?' She became thoughtful for a while and soon recalled the following facts: Twelve years before, when she was eighteen years old, she fell in love. She met the young man while participating in an amateur theatrical performance. He was at the time studying for the stage, and it was predicated that someday he would be a matinée idol. He was endowed with all the attributes needed for such a calling. He was well built, fascinating, impulsive, very clever, and . . . very fickle-minded. She was warned against him, but she paid no heed, attributing it all to the envy of her counselors. Everything went well for a few months, when she suddenly received word that her Apollo, for whom she had memorized these lines, had eloped with and married a very wealthy young woman. A few years later she heard that he was living in a Western city, where he was taking care of his father-in-law's interests.

"The misquoted lines are now quite plain. The discussion about the over-estimation of personality among lovers unconsciously recalled to her a disagreeable experience, when she herself over-estimated the personality of the man she loved. She thought he was a god, but he turned out to be even worse than the average mortal. The episode could not come to the surface because it was determined by very disagreeable and painful thoughts, but the unconscious variations in the poem plainly showed her present mental state. The poetic expressions were not only changed to prosaic ones, but they clearly alluded to the whole episode."

Another example of forgetting the order of words of a poem well known to the person I shall cite from Dr. C. G. Jung, quoting the words of the author:

"A man wished to recite the familiar poem, 'A Pine-tree Stands Alone,' etc. In the line 'He felt drowsy' he became hopelessly stuck at the words 'with the white sheet.' This forgetting of such a well-known verse seemed to me rather peculiar, and I therefore asked him to reproduce what came to his mind when he thought of the words 'with the white sheet.' He gave the following series of associations 'The white sheet makes one think of a white sheet on a corpse—a linen sheet with which one covers a dead body—[pause]—now I think of a near friend—his brother died quite recently—he is supposed to have died of heart disease—he was also very corpulent—my friend is corpulent, too, and I thought that he might meet the same fate—probably he doesn't exercise enough—when I heard of this death I suddenly became frightened: the same thing might happen to me, as my own family is predisposed to obesity—my grandfather died of heart disease—I, also, am somewhat too corpulent, and for that reason I began an obesity cure a few days ago.'"

Jung remarks: "The man had unconsciously immediately identified himself with the pine-tree which was covered with a white sheet."

For the following example of forgetting the order of words I am indebted to my friend Dr. Ferenczi, of Budapest. Unlike the former examples, it does not refer to a verse taken from poetry, but to a self-coined saying. It may also demonstrate to us the rather unusual case where the forgetting places itself at the disposal of discretion when the latter is in danger of yielding to a momentary desire. The mistake thus advances to a useful function. After we have sobered down we justify that inner striving which at first could manifest itself only by way of inability, as in forgetting or psychic impotence.

"At a social gathering someone quoted, *Tout comprendre c'est tout pardonner*, to which I remarked that the first part of the sentence should suffice, as 'pardoning' is an exemption which must be left to God and the priest. One of the guests thought this observation very good, which in turn emboldened me to remark—probably to ensure myself of the good opinion of the well-disposed critic—that some time ago I thought of something still better. But when I was about to repeat this clever idea I was unable to recall it. Thereupon I immediately withdrew from the company and wrote my concealing thoughts. I first recalled the name of the friend who had witnessed the birth of this (desired) thought, and of the street in Budapest where it took place, and then the name of another friend, whose name was Max, whom we usually called Maxie. That led me to the word 'maxim,' and to the thought that at that time, as in the present case, it was a question of varying a well-known maxim. Strangely enough, I did not recall any maxim but the following sentence: '*God created man in His own image,*' and its changed conception, '*Man created God in his own image.* Immediately I recalled the sought-for recollection.

"My friend said to me at that time in Andrassy Street, '*Nothing human is foreign to me.*' To which I remarked, basing it on psychoanalytic experience, "You should go further and acknowledge *that nothing animal is foreign to you*"

"But after I had finally found the desired recollection I was even then prevented from telling it in this social gathering. The young wife of the friend whom I had reminded of the animality of the unconscious was also among those present, and I was perforce reminded that she was not at all prepared for the reception of such unsympathetic views. The forgetting spared me a number of unpleasant questions from her and a hopeless discussion, and just that must have been the motive of the 'temporary amnesia.'

"It is interesting to note that as a concealing thought there emerged a sentence in which the deity is degraded to a human invention, while in the sought-for sentence there was an allusion to the animal in the man. The *capitis diminutio* is therefore common to both. The whole matter was apparently only a continuation of the stream of thought concerning understanding and forgiving which was stimulated by the discussion.

"That the desired thought so rapidly appeared may be also due to the fact that I withdrew into a vacant room, away from the society in which it was censored."

I have since then analyzed a large number of cases of forgetting or faulty reproduction of the order of words, and the consistent result of these investigations led me to assume that the mechanisms of forgetting as demonstrated in the examples "*aliquis*" and "*Ode to Apollo,*" are almost of universal validity. It is not always very convenient to report such analyses, for, just as those cited, they usually lead to intimate and painful things in the person analyzed; I shall therefore add no more to the number of such examples. What is common to all these cases, regardless of the material, is the fact that the forgotten or distorted material becomes connected through some associative road with an unconscious stream of thought, which gives rise to the influence that becomes known as forgetting.

I am now returning to the forgetting of names, concerning which we have so far considered exhaustively neither the casuistic elements nor the motives. As this form of faulty acts can at times be abundantly observed in myself, I am not at a loss for examples. The slight attacks of migraine, from which I am still suffering, are wont to announce themselves hours before through the forgetting of names, and at the height of the attack, during which I am not forced, however, to give up my work, I am often unable to recall all proper names.

Still, just such cases as mine may furnish the cause for a strong objection to our analytic efforts. Should not one be forced to conclude from such observations that the causation of the forgetfulness, especially the forgetting of names, is to be sought in circulatory or functional disturbances of the brain, and spare himself the trouble of searching for psychological explanations for these phenomena? Not at all; that would mean to interchange the mechanism of a process, which is the same in all cases, with its variations. But instead of an analysis I shall cite a comparison which will settle the argument.

Let us assume that I was so reckless as to take a walk at night in an uninhabited neighborhood of a big city, and was attacked and robbed of my watch and purse. At the nearest police station I report the matter in the following words: "I was in this or that street, and was there robbed of my watch and purse by *lonesomeness* and *darkness*." Although these words would not express anything that is incorrect, I would, nevertheless, run the danger of being considered—judging from the wording of this report—as not quite right in the head. To be correct, the state of affairs could only be described by saying that, *favored* by the lonesomeness of the place and under *cover* of darkness, I was robbed of my valuables by *unknown malefactors*.

Now, then, the state of affairs in forgetting names need not be different. Favored by exhaustion, circulatory disturbances, and intoxication, I am robbed by an unknown psychic force of the disposal over the proper names belonging to my memory; it is the same force which in other cases may bring about the same failure of memory during perfect health and mental capacity.

When I analyze those cases of name-forgetting occurring in myself, I find almost regularly that the name withheld shows some relation to a theme which concerns my own person, and is apt to provoke in me strong and often painful emotions. Following the convenient and commendable practice of the Zurich School (Bleuler, Jung, Riklin), I might express the same thing in the following form: The name withheld has touched a "personal complex" in me. The relation of the name to my person is an unexpected one, and is mostly brought about through superficial associations (words of double meaning and of similar sounds); it may generally be designated as a side association. A few simple examples will best illustrate the nature of the same:

(*a*) A patient requested me to recommend to him a sanatorium in the Riviera. I knew of such a place very near Genoa, I also recalled the name of the German colleague who was in charge of the place, but the place itself I could not name, well as I believed I knew it. There was nothing left to do but ask the patient to wait, and to appeal quickly to the women of the family.

"Just what is the name of the place near Genoa where Dr. X. has his small institution in which Mrs. So-and-so remained so long under treatment?"

"Of course you would forget a name of that sort. The name is Nervi."

To be sure, I have enough to do with nerves.

(*b*) Another patient spoke about a neighboring summer resort, and maintained that besides the two familiar inns there was a third. I disputed the existence of any third inn, and referred to the fact that I had spent seven summers in the vicinity and therefore knew more about the place than he. Instigated by my contradiction, he recalled the name. The name of the third inn was "The Hochwartner." Of course, I had to admit it; indeed, I was forced to confess that for seven summers I had lived near this very inn whose existence I had so strenuously denied. But why should I have forgotten the name and the object? I believe because the name sounded very much like that of a Vienna colleague who practiced the same specialty as my own. It touched in me the "professional complex."

(*c*) On another occasion, when about to buy a railroad ticket on the Reichenhall Station, I could not recall the very familiar name of the next big railroad station which I had so often passed. I was forced to look it up in the timetable. The name was Rose home (Rosenheim). I soon discovered through what associations I lost it. An hour earlier I had visited my sister in her home near Reichenhall; my sister's name is Rose, hence also a Rose home. This name was taken away by my "family complex."

(*d*) This predatory influence of the "family complex" I can demonstrate in a whole series of complexes.

One day I was consulted by a young man, younger brother of one of my female patients, whom I saw any number of times, and whom I used to call by his fist name. Later, while wishing to talk about his visit, I forgo this first name, in no way an unusual one, and could not recall it in anyway. I walked into the street to read the business signs and recognized the name as soon as it met my eyes.

The analysis showed that I had formed a parallel between the visitor and my own brother which centered in the question: "Would my brother, in a similar case, have behaved like him or even more contrarily?" The outer connection between the thoughts concerning the stranger and my own family was rendered possible through the accident that the name of the mothers in each case was the same, Amelia. Subsequently I also understood the substitutive names, Daniel and Frank, which obtruded themselves without any explanation. These names, as well as Amelia, belong to Schiller's play *The Robbers*; they are all connected with a joke of the Vienna pedestrian, Daniel Spitzer.

(*e*) On another occasion I was unable to find a patient's name which had a certain reference to my early life. The analysis had to be followed over a long devious road before the desired name was discovered. The patient expressed his apprehension lest he should lose his eyesight; this recalled a young man who became blind from a gunshot, and this again led to a picture of another youth who shot himself, and the latter bore the same name as my first patient, though not at all related to him. The name became known to me, however, only after the anxious apprehension from these two juvenile cases was transferred to a person of my own family.

Thus an incessant stream of "self-reference" flows through my thoughts concerning which I usually have no inkling, but which betrays itself through such name-forgetting. It seems as if I were forced to compare with my own person all that I hear about strangers, as if my personal complexes became stirred up at every information from others. It seems impossible that this should be an individual peculiarity of my own person; it must, on the contrary, point to the way we grasp outside matters in general. I have reasons to assume that other individuals meet with experiences quite similar to mine.

The best example of this kind was reported to me by a gentleman named Lederer as a personal experience. While on his wedding trip in Venice he came across a man with whom he was but slightly acquainted, and whom he was obliged to introduce to his wife. As he forgot the name of the stranger he got himself out of the embarrassment the first time by mumbling the name unintelligibly. But when he met the man a second time, as is inevitable in Venice, he took him aside and begged him to help him out of the difficulty by telling him his name, which he unfortunately had forgotten. The answer of the stranger pointed to a superior knowledge of human nature: "I readily believe that you did not grasp my name. My name is like yours—Lederer!"

One cannot suppress a slight feeling of unpleasantness on discovering his own name in a stranger. I had recently felt it very plainly when I was consulted during my office hours by a man named S. Freud. However, I am assured by one of my own critics that in this respect he behaves in quite the opposite manner.

(*f*) The effect of personal relation can be recognized also in the following examples reported by Jung.

"Mr. Y. falls in love with a lady who soon thereafter marries Mr. X. In spite of the fact that Mr. Y. was an old acquaintance of Mr. X., and had business relations with him, he repeatedly forgot the name, and on a number of occasions, when wishing to correspond with X., he was obliged to ask other people for his name."

However, the motivation for the forgetting is more evident in this case than in the preceding ones, which were under the constellation of the personal reference. Here the forgetting is manifestly a direct result of the dislike of Y. for the happy rival; he does not wish to know anything about him.

(*g*) The following case, reported by Ferenczi, the analysis of which is especially instructive through the explanation of the substitutive thoughts (like '*Botticelli-Boltraffio* to *Signorelli*'), shows in a somewhat different way how self-reference leads to the forgetting of a name:

"A lady who heard something about psycho-analysis could not recall the name of the psychiatrist, Young (Jung).

"Instead, the following names occurred to her: K1. (a name)—Wilde— Nietzsche—Hauptmann.

"I did not tell her the name, and requested her to repeat her free associations to every thought.

"To K1. she at once thought of Mrs. K1., that she was an embellished and affected person who looked very well for her age. 'She does not age.' As a general and principal conception of Wilde and Nietzsche, she gave the association 'mental disease.' She then added jocosely: 'The Freudians will continue looking for the causes of mental diseases until they themselves become insane.' She continued: 'I cannot bear Wilde and Nietzsche. I do not understand them. I hear that they were both homosexual. Wilde has occupied himself with *young* people' (although she uttered in this sentence the correct name she still could not remember it).

"To Hauptmann she associated the words *half* and *youth*, and only after I called her attention to the word *youth* did she become aware that she was looking for the name Young (Jung)."

It is clear that this lady, who had lost her husband at the age of thirty-nine, and had no prospect of marrying a second time, had cause enough to avoid reminiscences recalling youth or old age. The remarkable thing is that the concealing thoughts of the desired name came to the surface as simple associations of content without any sound-associations.

(*h*) Still different and very finely motivated is an example of name-forgetting which the person concerned has himself explained.

"While taking an examination in philosophy as a minor subject I was questioned by the examiner about the teachings of Epicurus, and was asked whether I knew who took up his teachings centuries later. I answered that it was Pierre Gassendi, whom two days before while in a café I had happened to hear spoken of as a follower of Epicurus. To the question how I knew this I boldly replied that I had taken an interest in Gassendi for a long time. This resulted in a certificate with a *magna cum laude*, but later, unfortunately, also in a persistent tendency to forget the name Gassendi. I believe that it is due to my guilty conscience that even now I cannot retain this name despite all efforts. I had no business knowing it at that time."

To have a proper appreciation of the intense repugnance entertained by our narrator against the recollection of this examination episode, one must have realized how highly he prizes his doctor's degree, and for how many other things this substitute must stand.

I add here another example of forgetting the name of a city, an instance which is perhaps not as simple as those given before, but which will appear credible and valuable to those more familiar with such investigations. The name of an Italian city withdrew itself from memory on account of its far-reaching sound-similarity to a woman's first name, which was in turn connected with various emotional reminiscences which were surely not exhaustively treated in this report. Dr. S. Ferenczi, who observed this case of forgetting in himself, treated it—quite justly—as an analysis of a dream or an erotic idea.

"Today I visited some old friends, and the conversation turned to cities of Northern Italy. Someone remarked that they still showed the Austrian influence. A few of these cities were cited. I, too, wished to mention one, but the name did not come to me, although I knew that I had spent two very pleasant days there; this, of course, does not quite concur with Freud's theory of forgetting. Instead of the desired name of the city there obtruded themselves the following thoughts: 'Capua—Brescia—the lion of Brescia.' This lion I saw objectively before me in the form of a marble statue, but I soon noticed that he resembled less the lion of the statue of liberty in Brescia (which I saw only in a picture) than the other marble lion which I saw in Lucerne on the monument in honor of the Swiss Guard fallen in the Tuileries. I finally thought of the desired name: it was Verona.

"I knew at once the cause of this amnesia. No other than a former servant of the family whom I visited at the time. Her name was Veronica; in Hungarian Verona. I felt a great antipathy for her on account of her repulsive physiognomy, as well as her hoarse, shrill voice and her unbearable self-assertion (to which she thought herself entitled on account of her long service). Also the tyrannical way in which she treated the children of the family was insufferable to me. Now I knew the significance of the substitutive thoughts.

"To Capua I immediately associated *caput mortuum*. I had often compared Veronica's head to a skull. The Hungarian word *kapzoi* (greed after money) surely furnished a determinant for the displacement. Naturally, I also found those more direct associations which connected Capua and Veronaas geographical ideas and as Italian words of the same rhythm.

"The same held true for Brescia; here, too, I found concealed side-tracks of associations of ideas.

"My antipathy at that time was so violent that I thought Veronica very ugly, and have often expressed my astonishment at the fact that anyone should love her: 'Why, to kiss her,' I said, 'must provoke nausea.'

"Brescia, at least in Hungary, is very often mentioned not in connection with the lion but with another wild beast. The most hated name in this country, as well as in North Italy, is that of General Haynau, who is briefly referred to as the hyena of Brescia. From the hated tyrant Haynau one stream of thought leads over Brescia to the city of Verona, and the other over the idea of the *grave-digging animal with the hoarse voice* (which corresponds to the thought of a monument to the dead),to the skull, and to the disagreeable organ of Veronica, which was so cruelly insulted in my unconscious mind. Veronica in her time ruled as tyranically as did the Austrian General after the Hungarian and Italian struggles for liberty.

"Lucerne is associated with the idea of the summer which Veronica spent with her employers in a place near Lucerne. The Swiss Guard again recalls that she tyrannized not only the children but also the adult members of the family, and thus played the part of the 'Garde-Dame.'

"I expressly observe that this antipathy of mine against V. consciously belongs to things long overcome. Since that time she has changed in her appearance and manner, very much to her advantage, so that I am able to meet her with sincere regard (to be sure I hardly find such occasion).As usual, however, my unconscious sticks more tenaciously to those impressions; it is old in its resentment.

"The Tuileries represent an allusion to a second personality, an old French lady who actually 'guarded' the women of the house, and who was in high regard and somewhat feared by everybody. For a long time I was her *élève* in French conversation. The word *élève* recalls that when I visited the brother-in-law of my present host in northern Bohemia I had to laugh a great deal because the rural population referred to the *élèves* (pupils) of the school of forestry as *löwen* (lions). Also this jocose recollection might have taken part in the displacement of the hyena by the lion."

(*i*) The following example can also show how a personal complex swaying the person at the time being may by devious ways bring about the forgetting of a name.

Two men, an elder and a younger, who had travelled together in Sicily six months before, exchanged reminiscences of those pleasant and interesting days.

"Let's see, what was the name of that place," asked the younger, "where we passed the night before taking the trip to Selinunt? *Calatafini*, was it not?"

The elder rejected this by saying: "Certainly not; but I have forgotten the name, too, although I can recall perfectly all the details of the place. Whenever I hear someone forget a name it immediately produces forgetfulness in me. Let us look for the name. I cannot think of any other name except *Caltanisetta*, which is surely not correct."

"No," said the younger, "the name begins with, or contains, a *w*."

"But the Italian language contains no *w*," retorted the elder.

"I really meant a *v*, and I said *w* because I am accustomed to interchange them in my mother tongue."

The elder, however, objected to the *v*. He added: "I believe that I have already forgotten many of the Sicilian names. Suppose we try to find out. For example, what is the name of the place situated on a height which was called *Enna* in antiquity?"

"Oh, I know that: *Castrogiovanni*." In the next moment the younger man discovered the lost name. He cried out '*Castelvetrano*,' and was pleased to be able to demonstrate the supposed *v*.

For a moment the elder still lacked the feeling of recognition, but after he accepted the name he was able to state why it had escaped him. He thought: "Obviously because the second half, *vetrano*, suggests *veteran*. I am aware that I am not quite anxious to think of ageing, and react peculiarly when I am reminded of it. Thus, *e.g.*, I had recently reminded a very esteemed friend in most unmistakable terms that he had 'long ago passed the years of youth,' because before this he once remarked in the most flattering manner, 'I am no longer a young man.' That my resistance was directed against the second half of the name *Castelvetrano* is shown by the fact that the initial sound of the same returned in the substitutive name Caltanisetta."

"What about the name Caltanisetta itself?" asked the younger.

"That always seemed to me like a pet name of a young woman," admitted the elder.

Somewhat later he added: "The name for *Enna* was also only a substitutive name. And now it occurs to me that the name *Castrogiovanni*, which obtruded itself with the aid of a rationalization, alludes as expressly to *giovane*, young, as the last name, *Castelvetrano*, to *veteran*."

The older man believed that he had thus accounted for his forgetting the name. What the motive was that led the young man to this memory failure was not investigated.

In some cases one must have recourse to all the fineness of psychoanalytic technique in order to explain the forgetting of a name. Those who wish to read an example of such work I refer to a communication by Professor E. Jones.

I could multiply the examples of name-forgetting and prolong the discussion very much further if I did not wish to avoid elucidating here almost all the viewpoints which will be considered in later themes. I shall, however, take the liberty of comprehending in a few sentences the results of the analyses reported here.

The mechanism of forgetting, or rather of losing or temporary forgetting of a name, consists in the disturbance of the intended reproduction of the name through a strange stream of thought unconscious at the time. Between the disturbed name and the disturbing complex there exists a connection either from the beginning or such a connection has been formed—perhaps by artificial means - through superficial (outer) associations.

The self-reference complex (personal, family or professional) proves to be the most effective of the disturbing complexes.

A name which by virtue of its many meanings belongs to a number of thought associations (complexes) is frequently disturbed in its connection to one series of thoughts through a stronger complex belonging to the other associations.

To avoid the awakening of pain through memory is one of the objects among the motives of these disturbances.

In general one may distinguish two principal cases of name-forgetting; when the name itself touches something unpleasant, or when it is brought into connection with other associations which are influenced by such effects. So that names can be disturbed on their own account or on account of their nearer or more remote associative relations in the reproduction.

A review of these general principles readily convinces us that the temporary forgetting of a name is observed as the most frequent faulty action of our mental functions.

However, we are far from having described all the peculiarities of this phenomenon. I also wish to call attention to the fact that name-forgetting is extremely contagious. In a conversation between two persons the mere mention of having forgotten this or that name by one often suffices to induce the same memory slip in the other. But whenever the forgetting is induced, the sought for name easily comes to the surface.

There is also a continuous forgetting of names in which whole chains of names are withdrawn from memory. If in the course of endeavoring to discover an escaped name one finds others with which the latter is intimately connected, it often happens that these new names also escape. The forgetting thus jumps from one name to another, as if to demonstrate the existence of a hindrance not to be easily removed.

CHAPTER 4
Childhood and Concealing Memories

IN A SECOND essay, I was able to demonstrate the purposive nature of our memories in an unexpected field. I started with the remarkable fact that the earliest recollections of a person often seemed to preserve the unimportant and accidental, whereas (frequently though not universally !) not a trace is found in the adult memory of the weighty and affective impressions of this period. As it is known that the memory exercises a certain selection among the impressions at its disposal, it would seem logical to suppose that this selection follows entirely different principles in childhood than at the time of intellectual maturity. However, close investigation points to the fact that such an assumption is superfluous. The indifferent childhood memories owe their existence to a process of displacement. It is shown by psychoanalysis that in the reproduction they represent the substitute for other really significant impressions, whose reproduction is hindered by some resistance they do not owe their existence to their contents, but to an associative relation of contents to another repressed thought, deserve the title of "concealing memories" which I have designated them.

In the aforementioned essay I only touched upon, but in no way exhausted, the varieties in the relations and meanings of concealed memories. In the given example fully analyzed I particularly emphasized a peculiarity in temporal relation between the concealing and the contents of the memory concealed by it. The content of the concealing memory in that example belonged to one of the first of childhood, while the thoughts represents it which remained practically unconscious, belonged to a later period of the individual question. I called this form of displacement a retroactive or *regressive* one. Perhaps more often one finds the reversed relation—that is, an indifferent impression of the most remote period becomes a concealing memory in consciousness, which simply owes its existence to an association with an earlier experience, against whose direct reproduction there are resistances. We would call these *encroaching* or *interposing* concealing memories. What most concerns memory lies here chronologically beyond concealing memory. Finally, there may be a third possible case, namely, the concealing memory may be connected with the impression it conceals, not only through its contents, just through contiguity of time; this is the *contemporaneous,* or *contiguous* concealing memory.

How large a portion of the sum total of our memory belongs to the category of concealing memories, and what part it plays in various neurotic hidden processes, these are problems into the value of which I have neither inquired nor shall I enter here. I am concerned only with emphasizing the sameness between the forgetting of proper names with faulty recollection and the formation of concealing memories.

At first sight it would seem that the diversities of both phenomena are far more striking than their exact analogies. There we deal with proper names, here with complete impressions experienced either in reality or in thought; there we deal with a manifest failure of the memory function, here with a memory act which appears strange to us. Again, there we are concerned with a momentary disturbance—for the name just forgotten could have been reproduced correctly a hundred times before, and will be so again from tomorrow on; here we deal with lasting possession without a failure, for the indifferent childhood memories seem to be able to accompany us through a great part of life. In both these cases the riddle seems to be solved in an entirely different way. There it is the forgetting, while here it is the remembering which excites our scientific curiosity.

After deeper reflection one realizes that though there is a diversity in the psychic material and in the duration of time of the two phenomena, yet these are by far outweighed by the conformities between the two. In both cases we deal with the failure of remember what should be correctly reproduced by memory fails to appear, and instead something else comes as a substitute. In the case of getting a name there is no lack of memory function in the form of name substitution. The formation of a concealing memory depends on the forgetting of other important impressions. In both cases we are reminded by an intellectual feeling of the intervention of a disturbance, which in each case takes a different form. In the case of forgetting of names we are aware that the substitutive names are incorrect, in concealing memories we are surprised that we have them at all. Hence, if psychological analysis demonstrates that the substitutive formation in each case is brought about in the same manner—that is, through displacement of a superficial association—we are justified in saying that the diversities in material, in duration of time, and in the centering of both phenomena serve to enhance our expectation, that we have discovered something that is important and of general value. This generality purports that the stopping and straying of the reproducing function indicates more often than we suppose that there is an intervention of a tendency which favors one memory and at the same time works against another. The subject of childhood memories appears to me so important and interesting that I would like to devote to it a few additional remarks which go beyond the views expressed so far.

How far back into childhood do our memories reach? I am familiar with some investigations on this question by V. and C. Henri and Potwin. They assert that such examinations show wide individual variations, inasmuch as some trace their first reminiscences to the sixth month of life, while others can recall nothing of their lives before the end of the sixth or even the eighth year. But what connection is there between these variations in the behavior of childhood reminiscences, and what signification may be ascribed to them? It seems that it is not enough to procure the material for this question by simple inquiry, but it must be subjected to a study in which the person furnishing the information must participate.

I believe we accept too indifferently the fact of infantile amnesia—that is, the failure of memory for the first years of our lives—and fail to find in it a strange riddle. We forget of what great intellectual accomplishments and of what complicated emotions a child of four years is capable. We really ought to wonder why the memory of later years has, as a rule, retained so little of these psychic processes, especially as we have every reason for assume that these same forgotten childhood activities have not glided off without leaving a trace in the development of the person, but that they have left a definite influence for all future time. Yet in spite of this unparalleled effectiveness were forgotten! This would suggest that there are particularly formed conditions of memory (in the sense of conscious reproduction) have thus far eluded our knowledge. It is possible that the forgetting of childhood give us the key to the understanding of amnesias which, according to our newer studies, lie at the basis of the formation of all neurotic symptoms.

Of these retained childhood reminisces, some appear to us readily comprehensible, while others seem strange or unintelligible. It is not difficult to correct certain errors concerning both kinds. If the retained reminiscences of a person are subjected to an analytic test, it can be readily ascertained that a guarantee for their correctness does not exist. Some of the memory pictures are surely falsified and incomplete, or displaced in point of time and place. The assertions of persons examined that their first memories reach back perhaps to their second year are evidently unreliable. Motives can soon be discovered which explain the disfigurement and the displacement of these experiences, but they also demonstrate that these memory lapses are not the result of a mere unreliable memory. Powerful forces from a later period have molded the memory capacity of our infantile experiences, and it is probably due to these same forces that the understanding of our childhood is generally so very strange to us.

The recollection of adults, as is known, proceeds through different psychic material. Some recall by means of visual pictures—their memories are of a visual character; other individuals can scarcely reproduce in memory the most paltry sketch of an experience; we call such persons "*auditifs*" and "*moteurs*" in contrast to the "*visuels,*" terms proposed by Charcot. These differences vanish in dreams; all our dreams are preponderatingly visual. But this development is also found in the childhood memories; the latter are plastic and visual, even in those people whose later memory lacks the visual element. The visual memory, therefore preserves the type of the infantile recollections. Only my earliest childhood memories are visual character; they represent plastic depicted scenes, comparable only to stage settings.

In these scenes of childhood, whether they prove true or false, one usually sees his childish person both in contour and dress. This circumstance must excite our wonder, for adults do not see their own persons in their reflections of later experiences. It is, moreover, against our experiences to assume that the child's attention during his experiences is centered on himself rather than exclusively on outside impressions. Various sources force us to assume the so-called earliest childhood recollections are not true memory traces but later elaborate of the same, elaborations which might have been subjected to the influences of many later psychic forces. Thus the, "childhood reminiscences" of individuals altogether advance to the signification of "concealing memories," and thereby form a noteworthy analogy to the childhood remberences as laid down in the legends and of nations.

Whoever has examined mentally a number of persons by the method of psychoanalysis must have gathered in this work numerous examples of concealing memories of every description. However, owing to the previously discussed nature of the relations of the childhood reminiscences to later life, it becomes extraordinarily difficult to report such examples. For, in order to attach the value of the concealing memory to an infantile reminiscence, it would be often necessary to present the entire life history of the person concerned. Only seldom is it possible, as in the following good example, to take out from its context and report a single childhood memory.

A twenty-four-year-old man preserved the following picture from the fifth year of his life: In the garden of a summerhouse he sat on a stool next to his aunt, who was engaged in teaching him the alphabet. He found difficulty in distinguishing the letter m from n, and he begged his aunt to tell him how to tell one from the other. His aunt called his attention to the fact that the letter *m* had one whole portion (a stroke) more than the letter *n*. There was no reason to dispute the reliability of this childhood recollection; its meaning, however, was discovered only later, when it showed itself to be the symbolic representation of another boyish inquisitiveness. For just as he wanted to know the difference between *m* and *n* at that time so he concerned himself later about the difference between boy and girl, and he would have willing that just this aunt should be his teacher. He also discovered that the difference similar one; that the boy again had one portion more than the girl, and at the time of this recognition his memory awoke to the responding childish inquisitiveness.

I would like to show by one more example the sense that may be gained by a childhood reminiscence through analytic work, although it may seem to contain no sense before. In my forty-third year, when I began to interest myself in what remained in my memory of my own childhood, a scene struck me which for a long time, as I afterwards believed, had repeatedly come to consciousness, and which through reliable identification could be traced to a period before the completion of my third year. I saw myself in front of a chest, the door of which was held open by my half-brother, twenty years my senior. I stood there demanding something and screaming; my mother, pretty and slender then suddenly entered the room, as if returning from the street.

In these words I formulated this scene so vividly seen, which, however, furnished no other clue. Whether my brother wished to open or lock the chest (in the first explanation it was a "cupboard"), why I cried, and what bearing, the arrival of my mother had, all these questions were dim to me; I was tempted to explain to myself that it dealt with the memory of a hoax by my older brother, which was interrupted by my mother. Such misunderstandings of childhood scenes retained in memory are not uncommon; we recall a situation, but it is not centralized; we do not know on which of the elements to place the psychic accent. Analytic effort led me to an entirely unexpected solution of the picture. I missed my mother and began to suspect that she was locked in this cupboard or chest, and therefore demanded that my brother should unlock it. As he obliged me, and I became convinced that she was not in the chest, I began to cry; this is the moment firmly retained in the memory, which was directly followed by the appearance of my mother, who appeased my worry and anxiety.

But how did the child get the idea of looking for the absent mother in the chest? Dreams which occurred at the same time pointed dimly to a nurse, concerning whom other reminiscences were retained; as, for example, that she conscientiously urged me to deliver to her the small coins which I received as gifts, a detail which in itself may lay claim to the value of a concealing memory for later things. I then concluded to facilitate for myself this time the task of interpretation, and asked my now mother about that nurse. I found out all of things, among others the fact that this shrewd but dishonest person had committed extensive robberies during the confinement of my mother and that my half-brother was instrumental bringing her to justice. This information gave me the key to the from childhood, as through a sort of inspiration. The sudden disappearance of the nurse was a matter of indifference to me; I had just asked this brother where she was, probably because I had noticed that he had played a part in disappearance, and he, evasive and witty as he is to this day, answered that she was "boxed in." I understood this answer in the childish way, but asked no more, as there was nothing else to be discovered. When my mother left shortly thereafter I suspected that the naughty brother had treated her in the same way as he did the nurse, and therefore pressed him the chest.

I also understand now why in the translation of the visual childhood scene my mother's slenderness was accentuated; she must struck me as being newly restored. I am and a half years older than the sister born that time, and when I was three years of I was separated from my half-brother.

CHAPTER 5

Mistakes in Speech

ALTHOUGH THE ORDINARY material of speech of our mother tongue seems to be guarded against forgetting, its application, however, more often succumbs to another disturbance which is familiar to us as "slips of the tongue." What we observe in normal persons as slips of the tongue gives the gives same impression as the first step of the so-called "paraphasias" which manifest themselves under pathologic conditions.

I am in the exceptional position of being about to refer to a previous work on the subject. In the year 1895 Meringer and C. Mayer published a study on *Mistakes in Speech and Reading,* with whose viewpoints I do not agree. One of the authors, who is the spokesman in the text, is a philologist actuated by a linguistic interest to examine the rules governing those slips. He hoped to deduce from these rules the existence "of a definite psychic mechanism, whereby the Sounds of a word, of a sentence, and even the words themselves, would be associated and connected with one another in a quite peculiar manner."

The authors grouped the examples of speech mistakes collected by them first accord purely descriptive view-points, such as interchangings *(e.g.,* the Milo of Venus instead of the Venus of Milo), as anticipations (e.g., the shoes made her sorft . . . the shoes made her feet sore), echoes and post positions, as contaminations *(e.g.,* "I will soon him home," instead of I will soon go home and I will see him"), and substitutions (e.g., "he entrusted his money to a "savings crank," instead of "a savings bank.") [1] Besides these principal categories there are so others of lesser importance (or of lesser significance for our purpose). In this grouping makes no difference whether the transposition disfigurement, fusion, etc., affects single sounds of the word or syllables, or whole words of the concerned sentence.

To explain the various forms of mist speech, Meringer assumes a varied psychic value of phonetics. As soon as the innervation the first syllable of a word, or the first word of a sentence, the stimulating process immediately strikes the succeeding sounds, and the following words, and in so far as these innervations are synchronous they may effect some changes in one another. The stimulus of the psychically intensive sound "rings" before or continues echoing, and thus disturbs the less important process of innervation. It is necessary therefore to determine which are the most important sounds of a word. Meringer states: "If one wishes to know which sound of a word possesses the greatest intensity he should examine himself while searching for a forgotten word, for example, a name. That which first returns to consciousness invariably had the greatest intensity prior to the forgetting. Thus the most important sounds are the initial sound of the root-syllable and the initial sound of the word itself, as well as one or another of the accentuated vowels.

Here I cannot help voicing a contradiction. Whether or not the initial sound of the name belongs to the most important elements of the word, it is surely not true that in the case of the forgetting of the word it first returns to consciousness; the above rule is therefore of no use. When we observe ourselves during the search for a forgotten name we are comparatively often forced to express the opinion that it begins with a certain letter. This conviction proves to be as often unfounded as founded. Indeed, I would even go so far as to assert that in the majority of cases one reproduces a false initial sound. Also in our example *Signorelli* the substitutive name lacked the initial sound, and the principal syllables were lost; on the other hand, the important pair of syllables *elli* returned to consciousness in the substitutive name *Botticelli*.

How little substitutive names respect the sound of the lost names may be learned from following case. One day I found it impossible to recall the name of the small country whose capital is Monte Carlo. The substitutive names *follows: Piedmont, Albania, Montevideo, Colico.* In place of Albania *Montenegro* soon appeared and then it struck me that the syllable *Mont* (pronounced *Mon*) occurred in all but the last of the substitutive names. It thus became easy for me to find from the name of Prince Albert the forgotten name *Monaco. Colico* practically imitates the syllabic sequence and rhythm of the forgotten name.

If we admit the conjecture that a mechanism similar to that pointed out in the forgetting names may also play a part in the phenomena speech-blunders, we are then led to a better founded judgment of cases of speech-blunders. The speech disturbance which manifests a speech-blunder may in the first place be caused by the influence of another component of same speech that is, through a fore-sound or echo, or through another meaning within the sentence or context which differs from that the speaker wishes to utter. In the second place, however, the disturbance could be brought about analogously to the process in the case *Signorelli,* through influences outside this word, sentence or context, from elements which we did not intend to express, and of whose incitement we became conscious only through the disturbance. In both modes of origin of the mistake in speech the common element lies in the simultaneity of the stimulus, while the differentiating elements lie in the arrangement within or without the same sentence or context.

The difference does not at first appear as wide as when it is taken into consideration in certain conclusions drawn from the symptomatology of speech-mistakes. It is clear, however, that only in the first case is there a prospect of drawing conclusions from the manifestations of speech-blunders concerning a mechanism which connects together sounds and words for the reciprocal influence of their articulation; that is, conclusions such as the philologist hopes to gain from the study of speech-blunders. In the case of disturbance through influence outside of the same sentence or context, it would before all be a question of becoming acquainted with the disturbing elements, and then the question would arise whether the mechanism of this disturbance cannot also suggest the probable laws of the formation of speech.

We cannot maintain that Meringer and Mayer have overlooked the possibility of speech disturbance through "complicated psychic influences," that is, through elements outside of the same word or sentence or the same sequence of words. Indeed, they must have observed that the theory of the psychic variation of sounds applies, strictly speaking, only to the explanation of disturbances as well as to fore-sounds and sounds. Where the word disturbances cannot reduced to sound disturbances, as, for example, the substitutions and contaminations of words they, too, have without hesitation sought the cause of the mistake in speech outside of intended context, and proved this state of affairs by means of fitting examples. [2] According to the author's own understanding it is some similarity between a certain word in the intended sentence and some other not intended, which allows the latter to assert itself in consciousness by causing a disfigurement, a composition, or a compromise formation (contamination).

Now, in my work on the *Interpretation of Dreams* I have shown the part played by process of condensation in the origin of the called manifest contents of the dream from latent thoughts of the dream. Any similarity of objects or of word-presentations between elements of the unconscious material is taken as a cause for the formation of a third, which is a composite or compromise formation. This element represents both components in the dream content, and in view of this origin it is frequently endowed with numerous contradictory individual determinants. The formation of solutions and contaminations in speech-mistakes is, therefore, the beginning of that work of condensation which we find taking a most active part in the construction of the dream.

In a small essay destined for the general reader, [3] Meringer advanced a theory of very practical significance for certain cases of interchanging of words, especially for such cases where one word is substituted by another of opposite meaning. He says: "We may still recall the manner in which the President of the Austrian House of Deputies opened the session some time ago: 'Honored Sirs! I announce the presence of so and so many gentlemen, and therefore declare the session as closed!'" The general merriment first attracted his attention and he corrected his mistake. In the present case the probable explanation is that the President wished himself in a position to close this session, from which he had little good to expect, and the thought broke through at least partially—a frequent manifestation—resulting in his use of "closed" in place of 'opened," that is, the opposite of the statement intended. Numerous observations have taught me, however, that we frequently interchange contrasting words; they are already associated in our speech consciousness; they lie very close together and are easily incorrectly evoked.

Still, not in all cases of contrast substitution it so simple as in the example of the President as to appear plausible that the speech-mistake occurs merely as a contradiction which arises in the inner thought of the speaker opposing the sentence uttered. We have found the analogous mechanism in the analysis of the example *aliquis;* the inner contradiction asserts itself in the form of forgetting a word instead of a substitution through its opposite. But in order to adjust the difference we may remark that the little word *aliquis* is incapable of a contrast similar to "closing" and "opening," and that the word "opening" cannot be subject to forgetting on account of its being a common component of speech.

Having been shown by the last examples of Merinzer and May that speech disturbance may be caused through the influence of fore-sounds, after-sounds, words from the same sentence that were intended for expression, as well as through the effect of words outside the sentence intended, *the stimulus of which would otherwise not have been suspected,* we shall next wish to discover whether we can definitely separate the two classes of mistakes in speech, and how we can distinguish the example of the one from a case of the other class.

But at this stage of the discussion we must also think of the assertions of Wundt, who deals with the manifestations of speech-mistakes in his recent work on the development of language. [4] Psychic influences, according to Wundt, never lack in these as well as in other phenomena related to them. The uninhibited stream of *sound* and *word associations* stimulated by spoken sounds belongs here in the first place as a positive determinant. This is supported as a negative factor by the relaxation or suppression of the influences of the will which inhibit this stream, and by the active attention which is here a function of volition. Whether that play of association manifests itself in the fact that a coming sound is anticipated or a preceding sound reproduced, or whether a familiar practiced sound becomes intercalated between others, or finally, whether it manifests itself in the fact that altogether different sounds associatively related to the spoken sounds act upon these—all these questions designate only differences in the direction, and at most in the play of the occurring associations but not in the general nature of the same. In some cases it may be also doubtful to which form a certain disturbance may be attributed, or whether it would not be more correct to refer such disturbance to a concurrence of motives, *following the principle of the complication of causes* [5].

I consider these observations of Wundt as absolutely justified and very instructive. Perhaps we could emphasize with even greater firmness than Wundt that the positive factor favoring mistakes in speech (the uninhibited stream of associations, and its negative, the relaxation of the inhibiting attention) regularly attain synchronous action, so that both factors only different determinants of the same process. With the relaxation, or, more unequivocal pressed, *through* this relaxation, of the uninhibited attention the uninhibited stream of associations becomes active.

Among the examples of the mistakes in collected by me I can scarcely find one in I would be obliged to attribute the speech disturbance simply and solely to what Wundt calls "contact effect of sound." Almost invariably I discover besides this a disturbing influence something outside of the intended speech. The disturbing element is either a single unconscious thought, which comes to light through the special blunder, and can only be brought to consciousness through a searching analysis, or it is a general psychic motive, which directs against the entire speech.

(Example a) Seeing my daughter make an unpleasant face while biting into an apple, I wished to quote the following couplet:

> "The ape he is a funny sight,
> When in the apple he takes a bite."

But I began: "The apel . . ." This seems to be a contamination of "ape" and "apple" (compromise formation), or it may be also conceived as an anticipation of the prepared "apple." The true state of affairs, however, was this: I began the quotation once before, and made no mistake the first time. I made the mistake only during the repetition, which was necessary because my daughter, having been distracted from another side, did not listen to me. This repetition with the added impatience to disburden myself of the sentence I must include in the motivation of the speech-blunder, which represented itself as a function of condensation.

(b) My daughter said, "I wrote to Mrs. Schresinger." The woman's name was Schlesinger. This speech-blunder may depend on the tendency to facilitate articulation. I must state, however, that this mistake was made by my daughter a few moments after I had said *apel,* instead of *ape.* Mistakes in speech are in a great measure contagious; a similar peculiarity was noticed by Meringer and Mayer in the forgetting of names. I know of no reason for this contagiousness.

(c) "I *sut* up like a pocket-knife," patient in the beginning of treatment, in "I *shut* up." This suggests a difficulty of articulation which may serve as an excuse for interchanging of sounds. When her attention was called to the speech-blunder, she promptly replied, "Yes, that happened because you said *'earnesht'* instead of *'earnest.'* " As a of fact I received her with the remark, "Today we shall be in earnest" (because it was the last hour before her discharge from treatment), jokingly changed the word into *earnesht.* In the course of the hour she repeatedly made in mistakes speech, and I finally observed that it only because she imitated me but because she had a special reason in her unconscious to linger on the word earnest (Ernst) as a name. [6]

(d) A woman, speaking about a game invented by her children and called by them "the man in the box," said "the manx in the boc." I could readily understand her mistake. It was while analyzing her dream, in which her husband is depicted as very generous in money matters—just the reverse of reality—that she made this speech-blunder. The day before she had asked for a new set of furs, which her husband denied her, claiming that he could not afford to spend so much money. She upbraided

him for his stinginess, "for putting away so much into the strongbox," and mentioned a friend whose husband has not nearly his income, and yet he presented his wife with a *mink* coat for her birthday. The mistake is now comprehensible. The word *manx (manks)* reduces itself to the "minks" which she longs for, and the *box* refers to her husband's stinginess.

(e) A similar mechanism is shown in the mistake of another patient whose memory deserted her in the midst of a long-forgotten childish reminiscence. Her memory failed to inform her on what part of the body the prying and lustful hand of another had touched her. Soon thereafter she Visited one of her friends, with whom she discussed summer homes. Asked where her cottage in M. was located, she answered, "Near the *mountain loin*" instead of *"mountain lane."*

(f) Another patient, whom I asked at the end of her visit how her uncle was, answered: "I don't know, I only see him now *in flagranti."*

The following day she said, "I am really ashamed of myself for having given you yesterday such a stupid answer. Naturally you must have thought me a very uneducated person always mistakes the meaning of foreign words I wished to say *en passant."* We did not know at the time where she got the incorrectly used foreign words, but during the same session she reproduced a reminiscence as a continuation the theme from the previous day, in which being caught *in flagranti* played the principal part. The mistake of the previous day had therefore anticipated the recollection, which at that had not yet become conscious.

(g) In discussing her summer plans, a patient said, "I shall remain most of the summer in *Elberlon."* She noted her mistake, and asked me to analyze it. The associations to *Elberton* elicited: seashore on the Jersey coast—summer resort—vacation travelling. This recalled travelling in Europe with her cousin, a topic which we had discussed the day before during the analysis of a dream. The dream dealt with her dislike for this cousin, and she admitted that it was due to the fact that the latter was the favorite of the man whom they met together while travelling abroad. During the dream analysis she not recall the name of the city in which they met this man, and I did not make any effort time to bring it to her consciousness, as we were then engrossed in a totally different problem. When asked to focus her attention again on Elberton and reproduce her associations, she said, "It brings to mind *Elberlawn-lawn-field*-and-*Elberfield.”*

Elberleld was the lost name of the city in Germany. Here the mistake served to bring to consciousness in a concealed manner a memory which was connected with a painful feeling.

(h) A woman said to me, "If you wish to buy a carpet, go to *Merchant* (Kaufmann) in *Matthew Street* (Mathdusgasse)." I repeated, "Then at Matthew's—I mean at Merchant's—" It would seem that my repeating of one name in place of the other was simply the result of distraction. The woman's remark really did distract me, as she turned my attention to something else much more vital to me than carpet. In Matthew Street stands the house in which my wife lived as a bride, The entrance to the house was in another street, and now I noticed that I had forgotten its name and could only recall it through a roundabout method. The name Matthew, which kept only attention, is thus a substitutive name for the forgotten name of the street. It is more suitable than the name Merchant, for Matthew is exclusively the name of a person, while Merchant is lot. The forgotten street, too, bears the name of a person: *Radetzky.*

(i) A patient consulted me for the first time, and from her history it became apparent that the cause of her nervousness was largely happy married life. Without any encouragement she went into details about her marital troubles. She had not lived with her husband for about six months, and she saw him last at the theatre when she saw the play *Officer 606.* I her attention to the mistake, and she

immediately corrected herself, saying that she to say *Officer 666* (the name of a recent popular play). I decided to find out the reason for the mistake, and as the patient came for analytic treatment, I discovered that immediate cause of the rupture between herself and husband was the disease which is treated by "606." [7]

(k) Before calling on me a patient telephone for an appointment, and also wished to be informed about my consultation fee. He was told that the first consultation was ten dollars; after the examination was over he again as what he was to pay, and added: " I don't like to owe money to anyone, especially to doctors; I prefer to pay right away." Instead of he said *play*. His last voluntary remarks and his mistake put me my guard, but after a few more uncalled-for remarks he set me at ease by taking money from his pocket. He counted four paper dollars and was very chagrined and surprised because he had no more money with him, and promised to send me a check for the balance. I was sure that his mistake betrayed him, that he was only *playing* with me, but there was nothing to be done. At the end of a few weeks I sent him a bill for the balance, and the letter was returned to me by the post-office authorities marked "Not found."

(*l*) Miss X. spoke very warmly of Mr. Y., which was rather strange, as before this she had always expressed her indifference, not to say her contempt, for him. On being asked about this sudden change of heart she said: "I really never had anything against him; he was always nice to me, but I never gave him the chance to cultivate my acquaintance." She said "cuptivate." This neologism was a contamination of *cultivate* and *captivate,* and foretold the coming betrothal.

(m) An illustration of the mechanisms of contamination and condensation will be found in the following *lapsus linguæ.* Speaking of Miss Z., Miss W. depicted her as a very "straitlaced" person who was not given to levities, etc. Miss X. thereupon remarked: "Yes, that is a very characteristic description, she always appealed to me as very *'straicet-brazed.'* " Here the mistake resolved itself into *straitlaced and brazen-laced,* which corresponded to Miss W.'s opinion of Miss Z.

(n) I shall quote a number of example a paper by my colleague, Dr. W. Stekel, which appeared in the Berlin *Tageblaltt* of January 1904, entitled "Unconscious Confessions."

"An unpleasant trick of my unpleasant thoughts was revealed by the following example: To begin with, I may state that in my capacity as a physician I never consider my remuneration: but always keep in view the patient's interest only: this goes without saying. I was visiting a patient who was convalescing from a serious illness. We had passed through hard days and nights. I was happy to find her improved, and I portrayed to her the pleasures of a sojourn in Abbazia, concluding with: 'If, as I hope, you will *not* soon leave your bed.' This obviously came from an unconscious selfish motive, to be able to continue treating wealthy patient, a wish which is entirely foreign to my waking consciousness, and which I would reject with indignation."

(o) Another example (Dr. W. Stekel): My wife engaged a French governess for the afternoons, and later, coming to a satisfactory agreement, wished to retain her testimonials. The governess begged to be allowed to keep them, saying, 'Je cherche encore pour les *après-midis*—pardons, pour les *avant-midis.'* She apparently intended to seek another place which would perhaps offer more profitable arrangements—an intention which she carried out."

(p) I was to give a lecture to a woman. Her husband, upon whose request this was done, stood behind the door listening. At the end of my sermonizing, which had made a visible impression, I said: "Good-bye, sir !" To the experienced person I thus betrayed the fact that the words were directed towards the husband; that I had spoken to oblige him.

(q) Dr. Stekel reports about himself that he had under treatment at the same time two patients from Triest, each of whom he always addressed incorrectly. "Good morning, Mr. Peloni!" he would say to Askoli, and to Peloni, " Good morning, Mr. Askoli !" He was at first inclined to attribute no deeper motive to this mistake, but to explain it through a number of similarities in both persons. However, he easily convinced himself that here the interchange of names bespoke a sort of boast—that is, he was acquainting each of his Italian patients with the fact that neither was the only resident of Triest who came to Vienna in search of his medical advice.

(r) Two women stopped in front of a drugstore, and one said to her companion, "If you will wait a few *moments* I'll soon be back," but she said *movements* instead. She was on her way to buy some castoria for her child.

(s) Mr. L., who is fonder of being called on than of calling, spoke to me through the telephone from a nearby summer resort. He wanted to know when I would pay him a visit. I reminded him that it was his turn to visit me, and called his attention to the fact that, as was the happy possessor of an automobile would be easier for him to call on me. (We were at different summer resorts, separated about one half-hour's railway trip.) He gladly promised to call, and asked: "How about Labor Day (September 1st), will it be convenient for you?" When I answered affirmatively, he said, "Very well, then, put me down for *Election* Day" (November). His mistake was quite plain. He likes to visit me, but it was inconvenient to travel so far. November we would both be in the city. My analysis proved correct.

(t) A friend described to me a nervous patient, and wished to know whether I could benefit him. I remarked: "I believe that in time I can remove all his symptoms by psychoanalysis because it is a durable case" wishing to say "curable"!

(u) I repeatedly addressed my patient as Mrs. Smith, her married daughter's name, when her real name is Mrs. James. My attention having been called to it, I soon discovered that I had another patient of the same name who refused to pay for the treatment. Mrs. Smith was also my patient and paid her bills promptly.

(v) A *lapsus linguæ* sometimes stands for a particular characteristic. A young woman, who is the domineering spirit in her home, said of her ailing husband that he had consulted the doctor about a wholesome diet for himself and then added: "The doctor said that diet has nothing to do with his ailments, and that he can eat and drink what *I* want."

(w) I cannot omit this excellent and instructive example, although, according to my authority, it is about twenty years old. A lady once expressed herself in society—the very words show that they were uttered with fervor and under the pressure of a great many secret emotions: "Yes, a woman must be pretty if she is to please the men. A man is much better off. As long as he has *five* straight limbs, he needs no more !"

This example affords us a good insight into the intimate mechanisms of a mistake in speech by means of condensation and contamination. It is quite obvious that we have here a fusion of two similar modes of expression:

"As long as he has his four *straight limbs*."

" As long as he has all his *five senses*."

Or the term "straight" may be the common element of the two intended expressions:

"As long as he has his *straight* limbs."

"All five should be *straight*."

It may also be assumed that both modes of expression—viz., those of the five senses and those of the straight five—have co-operated to introduce into the sentence about the straight limbs first a number and then the mysterious five instead of the simple four. But this fusion surely would not have succeeded if it had not expressed good sense in the form resulting from the mistake; if it had not expressed a cynical truth which, naturally, could not be uttered unconcealed, coming as it did from a woman.

Finally, we shall not hesitate to call attention to the fact that the woman's saying, following wording, could just as well be an excellent witticism as a jocose speech-blunder. It is simply a question whether she uttered these words with conscious or unconscious intention. The behavior of the speaker in this case certainly speaks against the conscious intention, and thus excludes wit.

(x) Owing to similarity of material, I add here another case of speech-blunder, the interpretation of which requires less skill. A professor of anatomy strove to explain the nostril, which, as is known, is a very difficult anatomical structure. To his question whether his audience grasped his ideas he received an affirmative reply. The professor, known self-esteem, thereupon remarked: "I can hardly believe this, for the number of people who understand the nostril, even in a city of millions like Vienna, can be counted *on a finger*—pardon me, I meant to say *on the fingers* of a hand."

(y) I am indebted to Dr. Alf. Robitsek, of Vienna, for calling my attention to two speech-blunders from an old French author, which I shall reproduce in the original.

Brantôme (1527-1614), Vies des Dames galantries, Discours second: " Si ay-je cogneu une très belle et honneste dame de par le monde, qui, devisant avec un honneste gentilhomme de la cour des affaires de la guerre durant ces civiles, elle luy dit: 'J'ay ouy dire que le roy a faiet rompre tous les c— de ce pays là.' Elle vouloit dire le ponts. Pensez que, venant de coucher d'avec son mary, ou songeant à son amant, elle avoit encor ce nom frais en la bouche; et le gentil homme s'en eschauffer en amours d'elle pour ce mot.

"Une autre dame que j'ai cogneue, entretenant une autre grand dame plus qu'elle, et luy louant et exaltant ses beautez, elle luy dit après : 'Non, madame, ce que je vous en dis, ce n'est point pour vous adultérer; voulant dire adulater, comme elle le rhabilla ainsi : pensez qu'elle songeoit à adultérer."

In the psychotherapeutic procedure which I employ in the solution and removal of neurotic symptoms, I am often confronted with the task of discovering from the accidental utterances and fancies of the patient the thought contents, which, though striving for concealment, nevertheless intentionally betray themselves. In doing this the mistakes often perform the most valuable, service, as I can show through most convincing and still most singular examples.

For example, patients speak of an aunt and later, without noting the mistake, call her "my mother, or designate a husband as a "brother." In this way they attract my attention to the fact that they have "identified" these person with each other, that they have placed them same category, which for their emotional life signifies the recurrence of the same type. Or, a young man of twenty years presents himself during my office hours with these words: "I am the father of N. N., whom you have treated— pardon me, I mean the brother; why, he is four years older than I." I understand though this mistake that he wishes to express that, like the brother, he, too, is ill through the fault the father; like his brother, he wishes to be cured, but that the father is the one most need of treatment. At other times an unusual arrangement of words, or a forced expression is sufficient to disclose in the speech of the patient the participation of a repressed thought having a different motive.

Hence, in coarse as well as in finer speech disturbances, which may, nevertheless, be summed as " speech-blunders," I find that it is not the not the contact effects of the thoughts outside the intended speech, which determine the origin of the speech-blunder, and also suffice to explain the newly formed, mistakes in speech. I do not doubt the laws whereby the sounds produce changes upon one another;

but they alone do not appear to me sufficiently forcible to mar the correct execution of speech. In those cases which I have studied and investigated more closely they merely represent the preformed mechanism, which is conveniently utilized by a more remote psychic motive. The latter does not, however, form a part of the sphere of influence of these sound relations. *In a large number of substitutions caused by mistakes in talking there is an entire absence of such phonetic laws.* In this respect I am in full accord with Wundt, who likewise assumes that the conditions underlying speech-blunders are complex and go far beyond the contact effect of the sounds.

If I accept as certain "these more remote psychic influences," following Wundt's expression, there is still nothing to detain me from conceding also that in accelerated speech, with a certain amount of diverted attention, the causes of speech-blunder may be easily limited to the definite law of Meringer and Mayer. However, in a number of examples gathered by these authors a more complicated solution is apparent.

In some forms of speech-blunders we may assume that the disturbing factor is the of striking against obscene words and meanings. The purposive disfigurement and distortion of words and phrases, which is so popular with vulgar persons, aims at nothing else but the employing of a harmless motive as a reminder of the obscene, and this sport is so frequent that it would not be at all remarkable if appeared unintentionally and contrary to the will.

I trust that the readers will not depreciate the value of these interpretations, for which there no proof, and of these examples which I have myself collected and explained by means of analysis. But if secretly I still cherish the expectation that even the apparently simple of speech-blunder will be traced to a disturbance caused by a half-repressed idea cuts the intended context, I am tempted to it noteworthy observation of Meringer. This author asserts that it is remarkable that nobody wishes to admit having made a mistake in speaking. There are many intelligent and honest people who are offended if we tell them that they made a mistake in speaking. I would not risk making this assertion as general as Meringer, using the term "nobody." But the emotional trace which clings to the demonstration of the mistake, which manifestly belongs to the nature of shame, has its significance. It may be classed with the anger displayed- at the inability to recall a forgotten name, and with the surprise at the tenaciousness of an apparently indifferent memory, and it invariably points to the participation of a motive in the formation of the disturbance.

The distorting of names amounts to an insult when done intentionally, and could have the same significance in a whole series of cases where it appears as unintentional speech-blunders. The person who, according to Mayer's report, once said "Freuder" instead of "Freud," because shortly before he pronounced the name "Breuer, and who at another time spoke of the Freuer-Breudian" method, was certainly not particularly enthusiastic over this method. Later, under the mistakes in writing, I shall report a case of name disfigurement which certainly admits of no other explanation. [8]

As a disturbing element in these cases there is an intermingling of a criticism which be omitted, because at the time being it does not correspond to the intention of the speaker.

Or it may be just the reverse; the substituted name, or the adoption of the strange name, signifies an appreciation of the same. The identification which is brought about by mistake is equivalent to a recognition which for the moment must remain in the background. An experience of this kind from his schooldays is related by Dr. Ferenczi:

"While in my first year at college I obliged to recite a poem before the whole class. It was the first experience of the kind in my life, but I was well prepared. As soon as I began my recitation I was dismayed at being disturbed by an outburst of laughter. The professor later explained to me this strange reception. I started by giving the title 'From the Distance,' which was correct, but instead of giving the name of the real author, I mentioned—my own. The name of the poet is Alexander Petöfi. The identity of the first name with my own favored the interchange of names, but the real reason was surely the fact that I identified myself at that time with the celebrated poet-hero. Even consciously I entertained for him a love and respect which verged on adoration. The whole ambition-complex hides it under this faulty action."

A similar identification was reported to me concerning a young physician who timidly and reverently introduced himself to the celebrated Virchow with the following words: " I am Dr. Virchow." The surprised professor turned to him and asked, "Is your name also Virchow" I do not know how the ambitious young man justified his speech-blunder, whether he thought of the charming excuse that he imagined himself so insignificant next to this big man that his own name slipped from him, or whether I had the courage to admit that he hoped that he too would someday be as great a man Virchow, and that the professor should therefore, not treat him in too disparaging a manner. One or both of these thoughts may have put young man in an embarrassing position during the introduction.

Owing to very personal motives I must it undecided whether a similar interpretation may also apply in the case to be cited. At the International Congress in Amsterdam, in 1907 my theories of hysteria were the subject of a lively discussion. One of my most violent opponents, in his diatribe against me, repeatedly made mistakes in speech in such a manner that he put himself in my place and spoke name. He said, for example, "Breuer and I, as is well known, have demonstrated," etc., when he wished to say "Breuer and Freud." The name of this opponent does not show the slightest sound similarity to my own. From this example, as well as from other cases of interchanging names in speech-blunders, we are reminded of the fact that the speech-blunder can fully forego the facility afforded to it through similar sounds, and can achieve its purpose if only supported in content by concealed relations.

In other and more significant cases it is a self-criticism, an internal contradiction against one's own utterance, which causes the speech-blunder, and even forces a contrasting substitution for the one intended. We then observe with surprise how the wording of an assertion removes the purpose of the same, and how the error in speech lays bare the inner dishonesty. Here the *lapsus linguæ* becomes a mimicking form of expression, often, indeed, for the expression of what one does not wish to say. It is, thus a means of self-betrayal.

Brill, relates: "I had recently been consulted by a woman who showed many paranoid trends, and as she had no relatives who could co-operate with me, I urged her to enter a State hospital as a voluntary patient. She was quite willing to do so, but on the following day she told me that her friends with whom she leased an apartment objected to her going to a hospital as it would interfere with their plans, and so on. I lost patience and said: 'There is no use listening to your friends who know nothing about your mental condition; you are quite *incompetent* to take care of your own affairs.' I meant to say 'competent.' Here the *lapus linguæ* expressed my true opinion."

Favored by chance the speech material often gives origin to examples of speech-blunders which serve to bring about an overwhelming revelation or a full comic effect, as shown by the following examples reported by Brill:

"A wealthy but not very generous host invited his friends for an evening dance. Everything went well until about 11:30 P.M., when was an intermission, presumably for supper. To the great disappointment of most of the guests there was no supper; instead, they were regaled with thin sandwiches and lemonade. As it was close to Election day the conversation centered on the different candidates; and as the discussion grew warmer, one of the guests, an ardent admirer of the Progressive

Party candidate, marked to the host: 'You may say what please about Teddy, but there is one thing can always be relied upon; he always gives you *a square meal,*' wishing to say *square deal.* The assembled guests burst into a roar of laughter to the great embarrassment of the speaker and the host, who fully understood each other."

"While writing a prescription for a woman who was especially weighed down by the financial burden of the treatment, I was interested to hear her say suddenly: 'Please do not give me *big bills,* because I cannot swallow them.' Of course she meant to say *pills.*"

The following example illustrates a rather serious case of self-betrayal through a mistake in talking. Some accessory details justify, full reproduction as first printed by Dr. A. A. Brill. [9]

"While walking one night with Dr. Frink we accidentally met a colleague, Dr. P., whom I had not seen for years, and of whose private life I knew nothing. We were naturally very pleased to meet again, and on my invitation he accompanied us to a café, where we spent about two hours in pleasant conversation. To my question as to whether he was married he gave a negative answer, and added, 'Why should a man like me marry?'

"On leaving the cafe, he suddenly turned to me and said: 'I should like to know what you would do in a case like this: I know a nurse who was named as co-respondent in a divorce case. The wife sued the husband for divorce and named her as co-respondent, and *he* got the divorce.' I interrupted him, saying, 'You mean *she* got the divorce.' He immediately corrected himself, saying, 'Yes, she got the divorce,' and continued to tell how the excitement of the trial had affected this nurse to such an extent that she became nervous and took to drink. He wanted me to advise him how to treat her.

"As soon as I had corrected his mistake I asked him to explain it, but, as is usually the case he was surprised at my question. He wanted to know whether a person had no right, to make mistakes in talking. I explained to him that there is a reason for every mistake and that if he had not told me that he was unmarried, I would say that he was the hero of the divorce case in question, and that the mistake showed that he wished he had obtained the divorce instead of his wife, so as not to obliged to pay alimony and to be permitted marry again in New York State.

"He stoutly denied my interpretation, but his emotional agitation, followed by loud laughter only strengthened my suspicions. To my appeal that he should tell the truth for science sake he said, 'Unless you wish me to lie you must believe that I was never married, and hence your psychoanalytic interpretation is all wrong.' He, however, added that it was dangerous to be with a person who paid attention to such little things. Then he suddenly remembered that he had another appointment and left us.

"Both Dr. Frink and I were convinced that my interpretation of his *lapsus linguæ* was correct, and I decided to corroborate or disprove it by further investigation. The next day I found a neighbor and old friend of Dr. P., who confirmed my interpretation in every particular. The divorce was granted to Dr. P.'s wife a few weeks before, and a nurse was named as co-respondent. A few weeks later I met Dr. P., and he told me that he was thoroughly convinced of the Freudian mechanisms."

The self-betrayal is just as plain in the following case reported by Otto Rank:

A father who was devoid of all patriotic feeling and desirous of educating his children to be just as free from this superfluous sentiment, reproached his sons for participating in a patriotic demonstration, and rejected their reference to a similar behavior of their uncle with these words: "You are not obliged to imitate him; why, he is an *idiot.*" The astonished features of the children at their father's unusual tone aroused him to the fact that he had made a mistake, and he remarked apologetically, "Of course I wished to say *patriot.*" When such a speech-blunder occurs in a serious squabble and reverses the intended meaning of one of the disputants, it at once puts him at a disadvantage with his adversary a disadvantage which the latter seldom fails to utilize.

This clearly shows that although people are unwilling to accept the theory of my conception and are not inclined to forego the convenience that is connected with the tolerance of a faulty action, they nevertheless interpret speech-blunders and other faulty acts in a manner similar to the one presented in this book. The merriment and derision which are sure to be evoked at the decisive moment through such linguistic mistakes speak conclusively against the generally accepted convention that such a speech-blunder is a *lapsus lingæ* and, psychologically of no importance. It was no less a man than the German Chancellor, who endeavored to save the situation through such a protest when the wording of his defense of his Emperor (November 1907) turned into the opposite through speech-blunder.

"Concerning the present, the new epoch of Emperor Wilhelm II, I can only repeat what I said a year ago, that *it would be unfair and unjust to speak of a coterie of responsible advisers around our Emperor* (loud calls, 'Irresponsible!')—to speak of *irresponsible advisers*. Pardon the *lapsus linguæ*" (hilarity).

A nice example of speech-blunder, which aims not so much at the betrayal of the speaker as at the enlightenment of the listener outside the scene, is found in Wallenstein (*Piccolomini,* Act I, Scene 5), and shows us that the poet who here uses this means is well versed in the mechanism and intent of speech-blunders. In the preceding scene Max Piccolomini was passionately in favor of the ducal party, and was enthusiastic over the blessings of the peace which became known to him in the course of a journey while accompanying Wallenstein's daughter to the encampment. He leaves his father and the Court ambassador, Questenberg, in great consternation.

The scene proceeds as follows:

QUESTENBERG. Woe unto us! Are matters thus? Friend, should we allow him to go there with this false opinion, and not recall him at once in order to open his eyes instantly.

OCTAVIO (*rousing himself from profound meditation*). He has already opened mine, and I see more than pleases me.

QUESTENBERG. What is it, friend ?

OCTAVIO. A curse on that journey!

QUESTENBERG. Why? What is it?

OCTAVIO. Come! I must immediately follow the unlucky trail, must see with my own eyes - come— (*Wishes to lead him away.*)

QUESTENBERG. What is the matter? Where ?

OCTAVIO (*urging*). To *her!*

QUESTENBERG. To—?

OCTAVIO (*corrects himself*). To the duke! Let us go, etc.

The slight speech-blunder *to her* in place of *to him* is meant to betray to us the fact that the father has seen through his son's motive for espousing the other cause, while the courtier complains that "he speaks to him altogether in riddles."

Another example wherein a poet makes use of a speech-blunder was discovered by Otto Rank in Shakespeare. I quote Rank's report from the *Zentralblatt für Psychoanalyse,* I. 3." A poetic speech-blunder, very delicately motivated and technically remarkably utilized, which, like the one pointed out by Freud in Wallenstein (*Zur Psychopathologie des Alltagslebens,* 2nd Edition, not only shows that poets knew the mechanism and sense of this error, but also presupposes an understanding of it on the part of the hearer, can be found in Shakespeare's *Merchant of Venice* (Act Ill, Scene 2). By the will of her father's Portia was bound to select a husband through a lottery. She escaped all her distasteful suitors by lucky chance. When she finally found in Bassanio the suitor after her own heart, she had cause to fear lest he, too, should draw the unlucky lottery.' In the scene she would to tell him that even if he chose the wrong casket, he might, nevertheless, be sure of love. But she is hampered by her vow. In this mental conflict the poet puts these words in her mouth, which were directed to the welcome suitor:

> "There is something tells me (but it is not love),
> I would not lose you; and you know yourself
> Hate counsels not in such a quality.
> But lest you should not understand me well
> (And yet a maiden hath no tongue but thought),
> I would detain you here some month or two,
> Before you venture for me. I could teach you
> How to choose right, but then I am forsworn
> So will I never be; so may you miss me;
> But if you do, you'll make me wish a sin,
> That I had been forsworn. Be shrew your eyes,
> They have overlooked me, and divided me:
> *One half of me is yours, the other half yours—*
> *Mine own, I would say;* but if mine, then yours—
> And so all yours."

"Just the very thing which she would like to hint to him gently, because really she should keep it from him, namely, that even before the choice she is wholly his—that she loves him, the poet, with admirable psychological sensitiveness, allows to come to the surface in the speech-blunder. It is through this artifice that he manages to allay the intolerable uncertainty of the lover as well as the like tension of the hearer concerning the outcome of the choice."

The interest merited by the confirmation of our conception of speech-blunders through the great poets justifies the citation of a third example which was reported by Dr. E. Jones [10]

"Our great novelist, George Meredith, in his masterpiece, *The Egoist,* shows an even finer understanding of the mechanism. The plot of the novel is, shortly, as follows: Sir Willoughby Patterne, an aristocrat greatly admired by his circle, becomes engaged to a Miss Constantia Durham. She discovers in him an intense egoism, which he skillfully conceals from the world, and to escape the marriage she elopes with a Captain Oxford. Some years later Patterne becomes engaged to a Miss Middleton, and most of the book is taken up with a detailed description of the conflict that arises in her mind on also discovering his egotism. External circumstances and her conception of honor hold her to her pledge, while he becomes more and more distasteful in her eyes. She partly confided in his cousin and secretary, Vernon Whitford, the man whom she ultimately marries, but from a mixture of motives stands aloof.

"In the soliloquy Clara speaks as follows: 'If some noble gentleman could see me as I am and not disdain to aid me! Oh I to be caught out of this prison of thorns and brambles I cannot tear my own way out. I am a coward. A beckoning of a finger would change me, I believe. I could fly bleeding and through hootings to a comrade. . . . Constantia met a soldier. Perhaps she prayed and her prayer was answered. She did ill. But, oh, how I love her for it! His name was Harry Oxford. . . . She did not waver, she cut the links, she signed herself over. Oh, brave girl, what do you think of me? But I have no Harry Whitford; I am alone. . . .' The sudden consciousness that she had put another name for Oxford struck her a buffet, drowning her in crimson.

"The fact that both men's names end in 'ford' evidently renders the confounding of them more easy, and would by many be regarded as an adequate cause for this, but the real underlying motive for it is plainly indicated by the author. In another passage the same *lapsus* occurs, and is followed by the hesitation and change of subject that one is familiar with in psychoanalysis when a half-conscious complex is touched. Sir Willoughby patronizingly says of Whitford: 'False alarm. The resolution to do anything unaccustomed is quite beyond poor old Vernon.' Clara replies: 'But if Mr. Oxford—Whitford . . . your swans, coming sailing up the lake; how beautiful they look when they are indignant! I was going to ask you, surely men witnessing a marked admiration for someone else will naturally be discouraged? 'Sir Willoughby stiffened with sudden enlightenment.

In still another passage Clara, by another *lapsus,* betrays her secret wish that she was on a more intimate footing with Vernon Whitford. Speaking to a boy friend, she says, 'Tell Mr. Vernon—tell Mr. Whitford.'"

The conception of speech-blunders here defended can be readily verified in the smallest details. I have been able to demonstrate repeatedly that the most insignificant and most natural cases of speech-blunders have their good sense, and admit of the same interpretation as the more striking examples. A patient who, contrary to my wishes but with firm personal motives, decided upon a short trip to Budapest justified herself by saying that she was for only three days, but she blundered said for only three weeks. She, betrayed her secret feeling that, to spite me, she preferred spending three weeks to three days in that society which I considered unfit for her.

One evening, wishing to excuse myself for not having called for my wife at the theatre, I said: "I was at the theatre at ten minutes after ten." I was corrected: "You meant to say ten o'clock." Naturally I wanted to say before ten. After ten would certainly be no excuse. I had been told that the theatre program read, "Finished before ten o'clock." We arrived at the theatre I found the foyer dark and the theatre empty. Evidently the performance was over earlier and my wife did not wait me. When I looked at the clock it still wanted five minutes to ten. I determined to make my case more favorable at home, and say that it was ten minutes to ten. Unfortunately, the speech-blunder spoiled the intent and laid bare my dishonesty, in which I acknowledged more than there really was to confess.

This leads us to those speech disturbances which can no longer be described as speech-blunders, for they do not injure the individual word., but affect the rhythm and execution of the entire speech, as, for example, the stammering and stuttering of embarrassment. But here, as in the former cases, it is the inner conflict that is betrayed to us through the disturbance in speech. I really do not believe that anyone will make mistakes in talking in an audience with His Majesty, in a serious love declaration, or in defending one's name and honor before a jury; in short, people make no mistakes where *they are all there* as the saying goes. Even in criticizing an author's style we are allowed and accustomed to follow the principle of explanation, which we cannot miss in the origin of a single speech-blunder. A clear and unequivocal manner of writing shows us that here the author is in harmony with himself, but where we find a forced and involved expression aiming at more target, as appropriately expressed, we can thereby recognize the participation of an unfinished and complicated thought, or we can hear through it the stifle voice of the author's self-criticism. [11]

Footnotes

[1] *These examples are given by the editor.*

[2] *Those who are interested are referred to pp. 62-97 of the author's work.*

[3] *Neue Freie Presse, August 23, 1900: "Wie man sich versprechen kann."*

[4] *Völker psychologie, vol. I., pt. I., p. 371, ect., 1900*

[5] *Italics are mine.*

[6] *It turned out that she was under the influence conscious thoughts concerning pregnancy and prevention of conception. With the words "shut up like a knife," which she uttered consciously as a complaint, she meant to describe the position of the child in the womb. The word "earnest" in my remark recalled to her the name (S. Ernst) of the well-known Vienna business firm in Ka¨rthner Strasse, which used to advertise the sale of articles for the prevention of conception.*

[7] *Similar mistakes dealing with Officer 666 were reported to me by other psychoanalysts.*

[8] *It may be observed that aristocrats in particular very frequently distort the names of the physicians they consult, from which we may conclude that inwardly they slight them, in spite of the politeness with which they are wont to greet them. I shall cite here some excellent observations concerning the forgetting of names from the works of Professor E. Jones, of Toronto : Papers on Psychoanalysis, chap. iii. p. 49 :*

"Few people can avoid feeling a twinge of resentment when they find that their name has been forgotten, particularly if it is by someone with whom they had hoped or expected it would be remembered. They instinctively realize if they had made a greater impression on the person's mind he would certainly have remembered them again, for the name is an integral part of the personality. Similarly, few things are more flattering to most people than to find themselves addressed by name by a great person where they could hardly have anticipated it. Napoleon, like most leaders of men, was a master of this art. In the midst of the disastrous campaign of France in 1814, he gave a proof of his memory in this direction. When in a town near Craonne, he recollected that he had met the mayor, De Bussy, over twenty years ago in the La Fère Regiment. The delighted De Bussy at once threw himself into his service with extraordinary zeal. Conversely, there is no surer of affronting someone than by pretending to forget his name; the insinuation is thus conveyed that the person is so unimportant in our eyes that we cannot be bothered to remember his name. This device is often exploited in literature. In Turgentev's Smoke (p. 255) the following passage occurs: " 'So you still find Baden entertaining, M'sieur—Litvinov.' Ratmirov always uttered Litvinov's surname with hesitation, every time, as though he had forgotten it, and could not at once recall it. In this way, as well as by the lofty flourish of his hat in saluting him, he meant to insult his pride." The same author, in his Fathers and Children (p. 107), writes : "The Governor invited Kirsanov and Bazarov to his ball, and within a few minutes invited them a second time, regarding them as brothers, and calling them Kisarov." Here the forgetting that he had spoken to them, the mistake in the names, and the inability to distinguish between the two young men, constitute a culmination of disparagement. Falsification of a name has the same signification as forgetting it; it is only a step towards complete amnesia."

CHAPTER 6
Mistakes in Reading and Writing

THAT THE SAME view-points and observation should hold true for mistakes in reading and writing as for lapses in speech is not at all surprising when one remembers the inner relation of these functions. I shall here confine myself to the reports of several carefully analyzed examples and shall make no attempt to include all of the phenomena.

A. LAPSES IN READING

(*a*) While looking over a number of the *Leipziger Illustrierten*, which I was holding obliquely, I read as the title of the front-page picture, "A Wedding Celebration in the Odyssey." Astonished and with my attention aroused, I moved the page into the proper position only to read correctly, "A Wedding Celebration in the Ostsee (Baltic Sea)." How did this senseless mistake in reading come about?

Immediately my thoughts turned to a book by Ruth, *Experimental Investigations of "Music Phantoms*," etc., with which I had recently been much occupied, as it closely touched the psychological problems that are of interest to me. The author promised a work in the near future to be called *Analysis and Principles of Dream Phenomena*. No wonder that I, having just published an *Interpretation of Dreams*, awaited the appearance of this book with the most intense interest. In Ruth's work concerning music phantoms I found an announcement in the beginning of the table of contents of the detailed inductive proof that the old Hellenic myths and traditions originated mainly from slumber and music phantoms, from dream phenomena and from deliria. Thereupon I had immediately plunged into the text in order to find out whether he was also aware that the scene where Odysseus appears before Nausicaa was based upon the common dream of nakedness. One of my friends called my attention to the clever passage in G. Keller's *Grünem Heinrich*, which explains this episode in the Odyssey as an objective representation of the dream of the mariner straying far from home. I added to it the reference to the exhibition dream of nakedness.

(*b*) A woman who is very anxious to get children always reads *storks* instead of *stocks*.

(*c*) One day I received a letter which contained very disturbing news. I immediately called my wife and informed her that poor Mrs. Wm. H. was seriously ill and was given up by the doctors. There must have been a false ring to the words in which I expressed my sympathy, as my wife grew suspicious, asked to see the letter, and expressed her opinion that it could not read as stated by me, because no one calls the wife by the husband's name. Moreover, the correspondent was well acquainted with the Christian name of the woman concerned. I defended my assertion obstinately and referred to the customary visiting-cards, on which a woman designates herself by the Christian name of her husband. I was finally compelled to take up the letter, and, as a matter of fact, we read therein "Poor W. M." What is more, I had even overlooked "Poor Dr. W. M." My mistake in reading signified a spasmodic effort, so to speak, to turn the sad news from the man towards the woman. The title between the adjective and the name did not go well with my claim that the woman must have been meant. That is why it was omitted in the reading. The motive for this falsifying was not that the woman was less an object of my sympathy than the man, but the fate of this poor man had excited my fears regarding another and nearer person who, I was aware, had the same disease.

(*d*) Both irritating and laughable is a lapse in reading to which I am frequently subject when I walk through the streets of a strange city during my vacation. I then read *antiquities* on every shop sign that shows the slightest resemblance to the word; this displays the questing spirit of the collector.

(*e*) In his important work Bleuler relates:"While reading I once had the intellectual feeling of seeing my name two lines below. To my astonishment I found only the words blood corpuscles. Of the many thousands of lapses in reading in the peripheral as well as in the central field of vision that I have analyzed, this was the most striking case. Whenever I imagined that I saw my name, the word that induced this illusion usually showed a greater resemblance to my name than the word *blood corpuscles*. In most cases all the letters of my name had to be close together before I could commit such an error. In this case, however, I could readily explain the delusion of reference and the illusion. What I had just read was the end of a statement concerning a form of bad style in scientific works, a tendency from which I am not entirely free."

B. LAPSES IN WRITING

(*a*) On a sheet of paper containing principally short daily notes of business interest, I found, to my surprise, the incorrect date, "Thursday, October 20th," bracketed under the correct date of the month of September. It was not difficult to explain this anticipation as the expression of a wish. A few days before I had returned fresh from my vacation and felt ready for any amount of professional work, but as yet there were few patients. On my arrival I had found a letter from a patient announcing her arrival on the 20th of October. As I wrote the same date in September I may certainly have thought "X. ought to be here already; what a pity about that whole month!" and with this thought I pushed the current date a month ahead. In this case the disturbing thought can scarcely be called unpleasant; therefore after noticing this lapse in writing, I immediately knew the solution. In the fall of the following year I experienced an entirely analogous and similarly motivated lapse in writing. E. Jones has made a study of similar cases, and found that most mistakes in writing dates are motivated.

(*b*) I received the proof sheets of my contribution to the annual report on neurology and psychiatry, and I was naturally obliged to review with special care the names of authors, which, because of the many different nationalities represented, offer the greatest difficulties to the compositor. As a matter of fact, I found some strange-sounding names still in need of correction; but, oddly enough, the compositor had corrected one single name in my manuscript, and with very good reason. I had written *Buckrhard*, which the compositor guessed to be *Burckhard*. I had praised the treatise of this obstetrician entitled *The Influence of Birth on the Origin of Infantile Paralysis*, and I was not conscious of the least enmity toward him. But an author in Vienna, who had angered me by an adverse criticism of my *Traumdeutung*, bears the same name. It was as if in writing the name Burckhard, meaning the obstetrician, a wicked thought concerning the other B. had obtruded itself. The twisting of the name, as I have already stated in regard to lapses in speech, often signifies a depreciation.

(*c*) The following is seemingly a serious case of *lapsus calami*, which it would be equally correct to describe as an erroneously carried out action. I intended to withdraw from the postal savings bank the sum of 300 crowns, which I wished to send to an absent relative to enable him to take treatment at a watering place. I noted that my account was 4,380 crowns, and I decided to bring it down to the round sum of 4,000 crowns, which was not to be touched in the near future. After making out the regular check I suddenly noticed that I had written not 380 crowns, as I had intended, but exactly 438 crowns. I was frightened at the untrustworthiness of my action. I soon realized that my fear was groundless, as I had not grown poorer than I was before. But I had to reflect for quite a while in order to discover what influence diverted me from my first intention without making itself known to my consciousness.

First I got on a wrong track: I subtracted 380 from 438, but after that I did not know what to do with the difference. Finally an idea occurred to me which showed me the true connection. 438 is exactly 10 percent of the entire account of 4,380 crowns! But the bookseller, too, gives a 10 percent. discount! I recalled that a few days before I had selected several books, in which I was no longer interested, in order to offer them to the bookseller for 300 crowns. He thought the price demanded too high, but promised to give me a final answer within the next few days. If he should accept my first offer he would replace the exact sum that I was to spend on the sufferer. There is no doubt that I was sorry about this expenditure. The emotion at the realization of my mistakes can be more easily understood as a fear of growing poor through such outlays. But both the sorrow over this expense and the fear of poverty connected with it were entirely foreign to my consciousness; I did not regret this expense when I promised the sum, and would have laughed at the idea of any such underlying motive. I should probably not have assigned such feelings to myself had not my psychoanalytic practice made me quite familiar with the repressed elements of psychic life, and if I had not had a dream a few days before which brought forth the same solution.

(*d*) Although it is usually difficult to find the person responsible for printers' errors, the psychological mechanisms underlying them are the same as in other mistakes. Typographical errors also well demonstrate the fact that people are not at all indifferent to such trivialities as "mistakes," and, judging by the indignant reactions of the parties concerned, one is forced to the conclusion that mistakes are not treated by the public at large as mere accidents. This state of affairs is very well summed up in the following editorial from the *New York Times* of April 14, 1913. Not the least interesting are the comments of the keen-witted editor, who seems to share our views:

A BLUNDER TRULY UNFORTUNATE

"Typographical errors come only too frequently from even the best-regulated newspaper presses. They are always humiliating, often a cause of anger, and occasionally dangerous, but now and then they are distinctly amusing. This latter quality they are most apt to have when they are made in the office of a journalistic neighbor, a fact that probably explains why we can read with smiling composure an elaborate editorial apology which appears in the *Hartford Courant.*

"Its able political commentator tried the other day to say that, *unfortunately* for Connecticut, 'J. H. is no longer a Member of Congress. Printer and proof-reader combined to deprive the adverb of its negative particle.' At least, the able political commentator so declares, and we wouldn't question his veracity for the world; but sorrowful experience has taught most of us that it's safer to get that sort of editorial disclaimer of responsibility into print before looking up the copy, and perhaps—just perhaps— the world-enlightener, who *knows* that he wrote *unfortunate*, because that is what he intended to write, didn't rashly chance the discovery of his own guilt before he convicted the composing-room of it.

"Be that as it may, the meaning of the sentence was cruelly changed, and a friend was grieved or offended. Not so long ago a more astonishing error than this one crept into a book review of ours—a very solemn and scientific book. It consisted of the substitution of the word 'caribou' for the word 'carbon' in a paragraph dealing with the chemical composition of the stars. In that case the writer's fierce self-exculpation is at least highly plausible, as it seems hardly possible that he wrote 'caribou' when he intended to write 'carbon,' but even he was cautious enough to make no deep inquiry into the matter."

(*e*) I cite the following case contributed by Dr. W. Stekel, for the authenticity of which I can vouch: "An almost unbelievable example of miswriting and misreading occurred in the editing of a widely circulated weekly. It concerned an article of defense and vindication which was written with much warmth and great pathos. The editor-in-chief of the paper read the article, while the author himself naturally read it from the manuscript and proof-sheets more than once. Everybody was satisfied, when the printer's reader suddenly noticed a slight error which had escaped the attention of all. There it was, plainly enough: 'Our readers will bear witness to the fact that we have always acted in a *selfish* manner for the good of the community.' It is quite evident that it was meant to read *unselfish*. The real thoughts, however, broke through the pathetic speech with elemental force."

(*f*) The following example of misprinting is taken from a Western gazette: The teacher was giving an instruction paper on mathematical methods, and spoke of a plan "for the instruction of youth that might be carried out *ad libidinem*."

(*g*) Even the Bible did not escape misprints. Thus we have the "Wicked Bible," so called from the fact that the negative was left out of the seventh commandment. This authorized edition of the Bible was published in London in 1631, and it is said that the printer had to pay a fine of two thousand pounds for the omission.

Another biblical misprint dates back to the year 1580, and is found in the Bible of the famous library of Wolfenbuttel, in Hesse. In the passage in Genesis where God tells Eve that Adam shall be her master and shall rule over her, the German translation is "*Und er soll dein Herr sein.*" The word *Herr* (master) was substituted by *Narr*, which means fool. Newly discovered evidence seems to show that the error was a conscious machination of the printer's suffragette wife, who refused to be ruled by her husband.

(*h*) Dr. Ernest Jones reports the following case concerning A.A. Brill: "Although by custom almost a teetotaler, he yielded to a friend's importunity one evening, in order to avoid offending him, and took a little wine. During the next morning an exacerbation of an eyestrain headache gave him cause to regret this slight indulgence, and his reflection on the subject found expression in the following slip of the pen. Having occasion to write the name of a girl mentioned by a patient, he wrote not Ethel but Ethyl. It happened that the girl in question was rather too fond of drink, and in Dr. Brill's mood at the time this characteristic of hers stood out with conspicuous significance."

(*i*) A woman wrote to her sister, felicitating her on the occasion of taking possession of a new and spacious residence. A friend who was present noticed that the writer put the wrong address on the letter, and what was still more remarkable was the fact that she did not address it to the previous residence, but to one long ago given up, but which her sister had occupied when she first married. When the friend called her attention to it the writer remarked, "You are right; but what in the world made me do this?" to which her friend replied: "Perhaps you begrudge her the nice big apartment into which she has just moved because you yourself are cramped for space, and for that reason you put her back into her first residence, where she was no better off than yourself."

"Of course I begrudge her the new apartment," she honestly admitted. As an afterthought she added, "It is a pity that one is so mean in such matters."

(*k*) Ernest Jones reports the following example given to him by Dr. A. A. Brill. In a letter to Dr. Brill a patient tried to attribute his nervousness to business worries and excitement during the cotton crisis. He went on to say: "My trouble is all due to that d—frigid wave; there isn't even any seed to be obtained for new crops." He referred to a cold wave which had destroyed the cotton crops, but instead of writing "wave" he wrote "wife." In the bottom of his heart he entertained reproaches against his wife on account of her marital frigidity and childlessness, and he was not far from the cognition that the enforced abstinence played no little part in the causation of his malady.

Omissions in writing are naturally explained in the same manner as mistakes in writing. A remarkable example of omission which is of historic importance was reported by Dr. B. Dattner. In one of the legal articles dealing with the financial obligations of both countries, which was drawn up in the year 1867 during the readjustment between Austria and Hungary, the word "effective" was accidentally omitted in the Hungarian translation. Dattner thinks it probable that the unconscious desire of the Hungarian lawmakers to grant Austria the least possible advantages had something to do with this omission.

Another example of omission is the following related by Brill:"A prospective patient, who had corresponded with me relative to treatment, finally wrote for an appointment for a certain day. Instead of keeping his appointment he sent regrets which began as follows: 'Owing to *foreseen* circumstances I am unable to keep my appointment.' He naturally meant to write *unforeseen*. He finally came to me months later, and in the course of the analysis I discovered that my suspicions at the time were justified; there were no unforeseen circumstances to prevent his coming at that time; he was advised not to come to me. The unconscious does not lie."

Wundt gives a most noteworthy proof for the easily ascertained fact that we more easily make mistakes in writing than in speaking. He states: "In the course of normal conversation the inhibiting function of the will is constantly directed toward bringing into harmony the course of ideation with the movement of articulation. If the articulation following the ideas becomes retarded through mechanical causes, as in writing, such anticipations then readily make their appearance."

Observation of the determinants which favor lapses in reading gives rise to doubt, which I do not like to leave unmentioned, because I am of the opinion that it may become the starting-point of a fruitful investigation. It is a familiar fact that in reading aloud the attention of the reader often wanders from the text and is directed toward his own thoughts. The results of this deviation of attention are often such that when interrupted and questioned he cannot even state what he had read. In other words, he has read automatically, although the reading was nearly always correct. I do not think that such conditions favor any noticeable increase in the mistakes. We are accustomed to assume concerning a whole series of functions that they are most precisely performed when done automatically ,with scarcely any conscious attention. This argues that the conditions governing attention in mistakes in speaking, writing, and reading must be differently determined than assumed by Wundt (cessation or diminution of attention). The examples which we have subjected to analysis have really not given us the right to take for granted a quantitative diminution of attention. We found what is probably not exactly the same thing, a disturbance of the attention through a strange obtruding thought.

CHAPTER 7
Forgetting of Impressions and Resolutions

IF ANYONE SHOULD be inclined to overrate the state of our present knowledge of mental life, all that would be needed to force him to assume a modest attitude would be to remind him of the function of memory. No psychological theory has yet been able to account for the connection between the fundamental phenomena of remembering and forgetting; indeed, even the complete analysis of that which one can actually observe has as yet scarcely been grasped. Today forgetting has perhaps grown more puzzling than remembering, especially since we have learned from the study of dreams and pathologic states that even what for a long time we believed forgotten may suddenly return to consciousness.

To be sure, we are in possession of some view-points which we hope will receive general recognition. Thus we assume that forgetting is a spontaneous process to which we may ascribe a certain temporal discharge. We emphasize the fact that, just as among the units of every impression or experience, in forgetting, too, a certain selection takes place among the existing impressions. We are acquainted with some of the conditions that underlie the tenaciousness of memory and the awakening of that which would otherwise remain forgotten. Nevertheless, we can observe in innumerable cases of daily life how unreliable and unsatisfactory our knowledge of the mechanism is. Thus we may listen to two persons exchanging reminiscences concerning the same outward impressions, say of a journey that they have taken together some time before. What remains most firmly in the memory of the one is often forgotten by the other, as if it had never occurred, even when there is not the slightest reason to assume that this impression is of greater psychic importance for the one than for the other. A great many of those factors which determine the selective power of memory are obviously still beyond our ken.

With the purpose of adding some small contribution to the knowledge of the conditions of forgetting, I was wont to subject to a psychological analysis those cases in which forgetting concerned me personally. As a rule I took up only a certain group of those cases, namely, those in which the forgetting astonished me, because, in my opinion, I should have remembered the experience in question. I wish further to remark that I am generally not inclined to forgetfulness (of things experienced, not of things learned), and that for a short period of my youth I was able to perform extraordinary feats of memory. When I was a schoolboy it was quite natural for me to be able to repeat from memory the page of a book which I had read; and shortly before I entered the University I could write down practically verbatim the popular lectures on scientific subjects directly after hearing them. In the tension before the final medical examination I must have made use of the remnant of this ability, for in certain subjects I gave the examiners apparently automatic answers, which proved to be exact reproductions of the text-book, which I had skimmed through but once and then in greatest haste.

Since those days I have steadily lost control over my memory; of late, however, I became convinced that with the aid of a certain artifice I can recall far more than I would otherwise credit myself with remembering. For example, when, during my office hours, a patient states that I have seen him before and I cannot recall either the fact or the time, then I help myself by guessing—that is, I allow a number of years, beginning from the present time, to come to my mind quickly. Whenever this could be controlled by records of definite information from the patient, it was always shown that in over ten years[1] I have seldom missed it by more than six months. The same thing happens when I meet a casual acquaintance and, from politeness, inquire about his small child. When he tells of its progress I try to fancy how old the child now is. I control my estimate by the information given by the father, and at most I make a mistake of a month, and in older children of three months. I cannot state, however, what basis I have for this estimate. Of late I have grown so bold that I always offer my estimate spontaneously, and still run no risk of grieving the father by displaying my ignorance in regard to his offspring. Thus I extend my conscious memory by invoking my larger unconscious memory.

I shall report some *striking* examples of forgetting which for the most part I have observed in myself. I distinguish forgetting of impressions and experiences, that is, the forgetting of knowledge, from forgetting of resolutions, that is, the forgetting of omissions. The uniform result of the entire series of observations I can formulate as follows: *The forgetting in all cases is proved to be founded on a motive of displeasure.*

A. FORGETTING OF IMPRESSIONS AND KNOWLEDGE

(*a*) During the summer my wife once made me very angry, although the cause in itself was trifling. We sat in a restaurant opposite a gentleman from Vienna whom I knew, and who had cause to know me, and whose acquaintance I had reasons for not wishing to renew. My wife, who had heard nothing to the disrepute of the man opposite her, showed by her actions that she was listening to his conversation with his neighbors, for from time to time she asked me questions which took up the thread of their discussion. I became impatient and finally irritated. A few weeks later I complained to a relative about this behavior on the part of my wife, but I was not able to recall even a single word of the conversation of the gentleman in the case. As I am usually rather resentful and cannot forget a single incident of an episode that has annoyed me, my amnesia in this case was undoubtedly determined by respect for my wife.

A short time ago I had a similar experience. I wished to make merry with an intimate friend over a statement made by my wife only a few hours earlier, but I found myself hindered by the noteworthy fact that I had entirely forgotten the statement. I had first to beg my wife to recall it to me. It is easy to understand that my forgetting in this case may be analogous to the typical disturbance of judgment which dominates us when it concerns those nearest to us.

(*b*) To oblige a woman who was a stranger in Vienna I had undertaken to procure a small iron safe for the preservation of documents and money. When I offered my services, the image of an establishment in the heart of the city where I was sure I had seen such safes floated before me with extraordinary visual vividness. To be sure, I could not recall the name of the street, but I felt certain that I would discover the store in a walk through the city, for my memory told me that I had passed it countless times. To my chagrin I could not find this establishment with the safes, though I walked through the inner part of the city in every direction. I concluded that the only thing left to do was to search through a business directory, and if that failed, to try to identify the establishment in a second round of the city. It did not, however, require so much effort; among the addresses in the directory I found one which immediately presented itself as that which had been forgotten. It was true that I had passed the show window countless times, each time, however, when I had gone to visit the M. family, who have lived a great many years in this identical building. After this intimate friendship had turned to an absolute estrangement, I had taken care to avoid the neighborhood as well as the house, though without ever thinking of the reason for my action. In my walk through the city searching for the safe in the show window I had traversed every street in the neighborhood but the right one, and I had avoided this as if it were forbidden ground.

The motive of displeasure which was at the bottom of my disorientation is thus comprehensible. But the mechanism of forgetting is no longer so simple as in the former example. Here my aversion naturally does not extend to the vendor of safes, but to another person, concerning whom I wish to know nothing, and later transfers itself from the latter to this incident where it brings about the forgetting. Similarly, in the case of *Burckhard* mentioned above, the grudge against the one brought about the error in writing the name of the other. The similarity of names which here established a connection between two essentially different streams of thought was accomplished in the showcase window instance by the contiguity of space and the inseparable environment. Moreover, this latter case was more closely knit together, for money played a great part in the causation of the estrangement from the family living in this house.

(*c*) The B. and R. Company requested me to pay a professional call on one of their officers. On my way to him I was engrossed in the thought that I must already have been in the building occupied by the firm. It seemed as if I used to see their signboard in a lower story while my professional visit was taking me to a higher story. I could not recall, however, which house it was nor when I had called there. Although the entire matter was indifferent and of no consequence, I nevertheless occupied myself with it, and at last learned in the usual roundabout way, by collecting the thoughts that occurred to me in this connection, that one story above the floor occupied by the firm B. and R. was the *Pension Fischer*, where I had frequently visited patients. Then I remembered the building which sheltered both the company and the *pension*.

I was still puzzled, however, as to the motive that entered into play in this forgetting. I found nothing disagreeable in my memory concerning the firm itself or the *Pension Fischer*, or the patients living there. I was also aware that it could not deal with anything very painful, otherwise I hardly would have been successful in tracing the thing forgotten in a roundabout way without resorting to external aid, as happened in the preceding example. Finally it occurred to me that a little before, while starting on my way to a new patient, a gentleman whom I had difficulty in recalling greeted me in the street. Some months previously I had seen this man in an apparently serious condition and had made the diagnosis of general paresis, but later I had learned of his recovery, consequently my judgment had been incorrect. Was it not possible that we had in this case a remission, which one usually finds in *dementia paralytica*? In that contingency my diagnosis would still be justified. The influence emanating from this meeting caused me to forget the neighborhood of the B. and R. Company, and my interest to discover the thing forgotten was transferred from this case of disputed diagnosis. But the associative connection in this loose inner relation was effected by means of a similarity of names: the man who recovered, contrary to expectation, was also an officer of a large company that recommends patients to me. And the physician with whom I had seen the supposed paretic bore the name of Fischer, the name of the *pension* in the house which I had forgotten.

(*d*) Mislaying a thing really has the same significance as forgetting where we have placed it. Like most people delving in pamphlets and books, I am well oriented about my desk, and can produce what

I want with one lunge. What appears to others as disorder has become for me perfect order. Why, then, did I mislay a catalogue which was sent to me not long ago so that it could not be found? What is more, it had been my intention to order a book which I found announced therein, entitled *Ueber die Sprache*, because it was written by an author whose spirited, vivacious style I like, whose insight into psychology and whose knowledge of the cultural world I have learned to appreciate. I believe that was just why I mislaid the catalogue. It was my habit to lend the books of this author among my friends for their enlightenment, and a few days before, on returning one, somebody had said: "His style reminds me altogether of yours, and his way of thinking is identical." The speaker did not know what he was stirring up with this remark. Years ago, when I was younger and in greater need of forming alliances, I was told practically the same thing by an older colleague, to whom I had recommended the writings of a familiar medical author. To put it in his words, "It is absolutely your style and manner." I was so influenced by these remarks that I wrote a letter to this author with the object of bringing about a closer relation, but a rather cool answer put me back "in my place." Perhaps still earlier discouraging experiences conceal themselves behind this last one, for I did not find the mislaid catalogue. Through this premonition I was actually prevented from ordering the advertised book, although the disappearance of the catalogue formed no real hindrance, as I remembered well both the name of the book and the author.

(*e*) Another case of mislaying merits our interest on account of the conditions under which the mislaid object was rediscovered. A younger man narrates as follows: "Several years ago there were some misunderstandings between me and my wife. I found her too cold, and though I fully appreciated her excellent qualities, we lived together without evincing any tenderness for each other. One day on her return from a walk she gave me a book which she had bought because she thought it would interest me. I thanked her for this mark of 'attention,' promised to read the book, put it away, and did not find it again. So months passed, during which I occasionally remembered the lost book, and also tried in vain to find it.

"About six months later my beloved mother, who was not living with us, became ill. My wife left home to nurse her mother-in-law. The patient's condition became serious and gave my wife the opportunity to show the best side of herself. One evening I returned home full of enthusiasm over what my wife had accomplished, and felt very grateful to her. I stepped to my desk and, without definite intention but with the certainty of a somnambulist, I opened a certain drawer, and in the very top of it I found the long-missing, mislaid book."

The following example of "misplacing" belongs to a type well known to every psychoanalyst. I must add that the patient who experienced this misplacing has himself found the solution of it.

This patient, whose psychoanalytic treatment had to be interrupted through the summer vacation when he was in a state of resistance and ill-health, put away his keys in the evening in their usual place, or so he thought. He then remembered that he wished to take some things from his desk, where he also had put the money which he needed on the journey. He was to depart the next day, which was the last day of treatment and the date when the doctor's fee was due. But the keys had disappeared.

He began a thorough and systematic search through his small apartment. He became more and more excited over it, but his search was unsuccessful. As he recognized this "misplacement" as a symptomatic act—that is, as being intentional—he aroused his servant in order to continue his search with the help of an "unprejudiced" person. After another hour he gave up the search and feared that he had lost the keys. The next morning he ordered new keys from the desk factory, which were hurriedly made for him. Two acquaintances who had been with him in a cab even recalled hearing something fall to the ground as he stepped out of the cab, and he was therefore convinced that the keys had slipped from his pocket. They were found lying between a thick book and a thin pamphlet, the latter a work of one of my pupils, which he wished to take along as reading matter for his vacation; and they were so skillfully placed that no one would have supposed that they were there. He himself was unable to replace the keys in such a position as to render them invisible. The unconscious skill with which an object is misplaced on account of secret but strong motives reminds one of "somnambulistic sureness." The motive was naturally ill humor over the interruption of the treatment and the secret rage over the fact that he had to pay such a high fee when he felt so ill.

(*g*) Brill relates:[2] "A man was urged by his wife to attend a social function in which he really took no interest. Yielding to his wife's entreaties, he began to take his dress-suit from the trunk when he suddenly thought of shaving. After accomplishing this he returned to the trunk and found it locked. Despite a long, earnest search the key could not be found. A locksmith could not be found on Sunday evening, so that the couple had to send their regrets. On having the trunk opened the next morning the lost key was found within. The husband had absentmindedly dropped the key into the trunk and sprung the lock. He assured me that this was wholly unintentional and unconscious, but we know that he did not wish to go to this social affair. The mislaying of the key therefore lacked no motive."

Ernest Jones noticed in himself that he was in the habit of mislaying his pipe whenever he suffered from the effects of over-smoking. The pipe was then found in some unusual place where it did not belong and which it normally did not occupy.

If one looks over the cases of mislaying it will be difficult to assume that mislaying is anything other than the result of an unconscious intention.

(*h*) In the summer of 1901 I once remarked to a friend with whom I was then actively engaged in exchanging ideas on scientific questions: "These neurotic problems can be solved only if we take the position of absolutely accepting an original bi-sexuality in every individual." To which he replied: "I told you that two and a half years ago while we were taking an evening walk in Br. At that time you wouldn't listen to it."

It is truly painful to be thus requested to renounce one's originality. I could neither recall such a conversation nor my friend's revelation. One of us must be mistaken; and according to the principle of the question *cui prodest*? I must be the one. Indeed, in the course of the following weeks everything came back to me just as my friend had recalled it. I myself remembered that at that time I gave the answer: "I have not yet got so far, and I do not care to discuss it." But since this incident I have grown more tolerant when I miss any mention of my name in medical literature in connection with ideas for which I deserve credit.

It is scarcely accidental that the numerous examples of forgetting which have been collected without any selection should require for their solution the introduction of such painful themes as exposing of one's wife; a friendship that has turned into the opposite; a mistake in medical diagnosis; enmity on account of similar pursuits, or the borrowing of somebody's ideas. I am rather inclined to believe that every person who will undertake an inquiry into the motives underlying his forgetting will be able to fill up a similar sample card of vexatious circumstances. The tendency to forget the disagreeable seems to me to be quite general; the capacity for it is naturally differently developed in different persons. Certain *denials* which we encounter in medical practice can probably be ascribed to *forgetting*.[3] Our conception of such forgetting confines the distinction between this and that behavior to purely psychological relations, and permits us to see in both forms of reaction the expression of the same motive. Of the numerous examples of denials of unpleasant recollection which I have observed in kinsmen of patients, one remains in my memory as especially singular.

A mother telling me of the childhood of her nervous son, now in his puberty, made the statement that, like his brothers and sisters, he was subject to bed-wetting throughout his childhood, a symptom which certainly has some significance in a history of a neurotic patient. Some weeks later, while seeking information regarding the treatment, I had occasion to call her attention to signs of a constitutional morbid predisposition in the young man, and at the same time referred to the bed-wetting recounted in the anamnesis. To my surprise she contested this fact concerning him, denying it as well for the other children, and asked me how I could possibly know this. Finally I let her know that she herself had told me a short time before what she had thus forgotten.[4]

One also finds abundant indications which show that even in healthy, not neurotic, persons resistances are found against the memory of disagreeable impressions and the idea of painful thoughts.[5] But the full significance of this fact can be estimated only when we enter into the psychology of neurotic persons. One is forced to make such elementary defensive striving against ideas which can awaken painful feelings, a striving which can be put side by side only with the flight-reflex in painful stimuli, as the main pillar of the mechanism which carries the hysterical symptoms. One need not offer any objection to the acceptance of such defensive tendency on the ground that we frequently find it impossible to rid ourselves of painful memories which cling to us, or to banish such painful emotions as remorse and reproaches of conscience. No one maintains that this defensive tendency invariably gains the upper hand, that in the play of psychic forces it may not strike against factors which stir up the contrary feeling for other purposes and bring it about in spite of it.

As the architectural principle of the psychic apparatus we may conjecture a certain stratification or structure of instances deposited in strata. And it is quite possible that this defensive tendency belongs to a lower psychic instance, and is inhibited by higher instances. At all events, it speaks for the existence and force of this defensive tendency, when we can trace it to processes such as those found in our examples of forgetting. We see then that something is forgotten for its own sake, and where this is not possible the defensive tendency misses the target and causes something else to be forgotten—something less significant, but which has fallen into associative connection with the disagreeable material.

The views here developed, namely, that painful memories merge into motivated forgetting with special ease, merits application in many spheres where as yet it has found no, or scarcely any, recognition. Thus it seems to me that it has not yet been strongly enough emphasized in the estimation of testimony taken in court,[6] where the putting of a witness under oath obviously leads us to place too great a trust on the purifying influence of his psychic play of forces. It is universally admitted that in the origin of the traditions and folklore of a people care must be taken to eliminate from memory such a motive as would be painful to the national feeling. Perhaps on closer investigation it may be possible to form a perfect analogy between the manner of development of national traditions and infantile reminiscences of the individual. The great Darwin has formulated a "golden rule" for the scientific worker from his insight into this pain-motive of forgetting.[7]

Almost exactly as in the forgetting of names, faulty recollections can also appear in the forgetting of impressions, and when finding credence they may be designated as delusions of memory. The memory disturbance in pathologic cases (in paranoia it actually plays the role of a constituting factor in the formation of delusions) has brought to light an extensive literature in which there is no reference whatever to its being motivated. As this theme also belongs to the psychology of the neuroses it goes beyond our present treatment. Instead, I will give from my own experience a curious example of memory disturbance showing clearly enough its determination through unconscious repressed material and its connection with this material.

While writing the latter chapters of my volume on the interpretation of dreams, I happened to be in a summer resort without access to libraries and reference books, so that I was compelled to introduce into the manuscript all kinds of references and citations from memory. These I naturally reserved for future correction. In the chapter on daydreams I thought of the distinguished figure of the poor bookkeeper in Alphonse Daudet's *Nabab*, through whom the author probably described his own daydreams. I imagined that I distinctly remembered one fantasy of this man, whom I called Mr. Jocelyn, which he hatched while walking the streets of Paris, and I began to reproduce it from memory. This fantasy described how Mr. Jocelyn boldly hurled himself at a runaway horse and brought it to a standstill; how the carriage door opened and a great personage stepped from the coupé, pressed Mr. Jocelyn's hand and said: "You are my savior—I owe my life to you! What can I do for you?"

I assured myself that casual inaccuracies in the rendition of this fantasy could readily be corrected at home on consulting the book. But when I perused *Nabab* in order to compare it with my manuscript, I found to my very great shame and consternation that there was nothing to suggest such a dream by Mr. Jocelyn; indeed, the poor bookkeeper did not even bear this name—he was called Mr. Joyeuse.

This second error then furnished the key for the solution of the first mistake, the faulty reminiscence. Joyeux, of which Joyeuse is the feminine form, was the only possible word which would translate my own name *Freud* into French. Whence, therefore, came this falsely remembered fantasy which I had attributed to Daudet? It could only be a product of my own, a daydream which I myself had spun, and which did not become conscious, or which was once conscious and had since been absolutely forgotten. Perhaps I invented it myself in Paris, where frequently enough I walked the streets alone, and full of longing for a helper and protector, until Charcot took me into his circle. I had often met the author of *Nabab* in Charcot's house. But the provoking part of it all is the fact that there is scarcely anything to which I am so hostile as the thought of being some one's protégé. What we see of this sort of thing in our country spoils all desire for it, and my character is little suited to the role of a protected child. I have always entertained an immense desire to "be the strong man myself." And it had to happen that I should be reminded of such a, to be sure, never fulfilled, daydream! Besides, this incident is a good example of how the restraint relation to one's ego, which breaks forth triumphantly in paranoia, disturbs and entangles us in the objective grasp of things.

Another case of faulty recollection which can be satisfactorily explained resembles the *fausse reconnaissance* to be discussed later. I related to one of my patients, an ambitious and very capable man, that a young student had recently gained admittance into the circle of my pupils by means of an interesting work, *Der Künstler, Versuch einer Sexualpsychologie*. When, a year and a quarter later, this work lay before me in print, my patient maintained that he remembered with certainty having read somewhere, perhaps in a bookseller's advertisement, the announcement of the same book even before I first mentioned it to him. He remembered that this announcement came to his mind at that time, and he ascertained besides that the author had changed the title, that it no longer read "*Versuch*" but "*Ansätze zu einer Sexualpsychologie.*"

Careful inquiry of the author and comparison of all dates showed conclusively that my patient was trying to recall the impossible. No notice of this work had appeared anywhere before its publication, certainly not a year and a quarter before it went to print. However, I neglected to seek a solution for this false recollection until the same man brought about an equally valuable renewal of it. He thought that he had recently noticed a work on "agoraphobia" in the show window of a bookshop, and as he was now looking for it in all available catalogues I was able to explain to him why his effort must remain fruitless. The work on agoraphobia existed only in his fantasy as an unconscious resolution to write such a book himself. His ambition to emulate that young man, and through such a scientific work to become one of my pupils, had led him to the first as well as to the second false recollection. He also recalled later that the bookseller's announcement which had occasioned his false reminiscence dealt with a work entitled *Genesis, Das Gesetz der* Zeugung ("Genesis, The Law of Generation"). But the change in the title as mentioned by him was really instigated by me; I recalled that I myself have perpetrated the same inaccuracy in the repetition of the title by saying "*Ansätze*" in place of "*Versuch.*"

B. FORGETTING OF INTENTIONS

No other group of phenomena is better qualified to demonstrate the thesis that lack of attention does not in itself suffice to explain faulty acts as the forgetting of intentions. An intention is an impulse for an action which has already found approbation, but whose execution is postponed for a suitable occasion. Now, in the interval thus created sufficient change may take place in the motive to prevent the intention from coming to execution. It is not, however, forgotten, it is simply revised and omitted.

We are naturally not in the habit of explaining the forgetting of intentions which we daily experience in every possible situation as being due to a recent change in the adjustment of motives. We generally leave it unexplained, or we seek a psychological explanation in the assumption that at the time of execution the required attention for the action, which was an indispensable condition for the occurrence of the intention, and was then at the disposal of the same action, no longer exists. Observation of our normal behavior towards intentions urges us to reject this tentative explanation as arbitrary. If I resolve in the morning to carry out a certain intention in the evening, I may be reminded of it several times in the course of the day, but it is not at all necessary that it should become conscious throughout the day. As the time for its execution approaches it suddenly occurs to me and induces me to make the necessary preparation for the intended action. If I go walking and take a letter with me to be posted, it is not at all necessary that I, as a normal not nervous individual, should carry it in my hand and continually look for a letterbox. As a matter of fact I am accustomed to put it in my pocket and give my thoughts free rein on my way, feeling confident that the first letter-box will attract my attention and cause me to put my hand in my pocket and draw out the letter.

This normal behavior in a formed intention corresponds perfectly with the experimentally produced conduct of persons who are under a so-called "post-hypnotic suggestion" to perform something after a certain time.[8] We are accustomed to describe the phenomenon in the following manner: the suggested intention slumbers in the person concerned until the time for its execution approaches. Then it awakes and excites the action.

In two positions of life even the layman is cognizant of the fact that forgetting referring to intended purposes can in no wise claim consideration as an elementary phenomenon no further reducible, but realizes that it ultimately depends on unadmitted motives. I refer to affairs of love and military service. A lover who is late at the appointed place will vainly tell his sweetheart that unfortunately he has entirely forgotten their rendezvous. She will not hesitate to answer him: "A year ago you would not have forgotten. Evidently you no longer care for me" Even if he should grasp the above cited psychological explanation, and should wish to excuse his forgetting on the plea of important business, he would only elicit the answer from the woman, who has become as keen-sighted as the physician in the psychoanalytic treatment, "How remarkable that such business disturbances did not occur before!" Of course the woman does not wish to deny the possibility of forgetting; but she believes, and not without reason, that practically the same inference of a certain unwillingness may be drawn from the unintentional forgetting as from a conscious subterfuge.

Similarly, in military service no distinction is recognized between an omission resulting from forgetting and one in consequence of intentional neglect. And rightly so. The soldier dares forget nothing that military service demands of him. If he forgets in spite of this, even when he is acquainted with the demands, then it is due to the fact that the motives which urge the fulfillment of the military exactions are opposed by contrary motives. Thus the one year's volunteer[9] who at inspection pleads forgetting as an excuse for not having polished his buttons is sure to be punished. But this punishment is small in comparison to the one he courts if he admits to his superiors that the motive for his negligence is because "this miserable menial service is altogether disgusting to me." Owing to this saving of punishment for economic reasons, as it were, he makes use of forgetting as an excuse, or it comes about as a compromise.

The service of women (as well as the military service of the State) demands that nothing relating to that service be subject to forgetting. Thus it but suggests that forgetting is permissible in unimportant matters, but in weighty matters its occurrence is an indication that one wishes to treat weighty matters as unimportant: that is, that their importance is disputed.[10] The view-point of psychic validity is in fact not to be contested here. No person forgets to carry out actions that seem important to himself without exposing himself to the suspicion of being a sufferer from mental weakness. Our investigations therefore can extend only to the forgetting of more or less secondary intentions, for no intention do we deem absolutely indifferent, otherwise it would certainly never have been formed.

As in the preceding functional disturbances, I have collected the cases of neglect through forgetting which I have observed in myself, and endeavored to explain them. I have found that they could invariably be traced to some interference of unknown and unadmitted motives—or, as may be said, they were due to a counterwill. In a number of these cases I found myself in a position similar to that of being in some distasteful service: I was under a constraint to which I had not entirely resigned myself, so that I showed my protest in the form of forgetting. This accounts for the fact that I am particularly prone to forget to send congratulations on such occasions as birthdays, jubilees, wedding celebrations, and promotions to higher rank. I continually make new resolutions, but I am more than ever convinced that I shall not succeed. I am now on the point of giving it up altogether, and to admit consciously the striving motives. In a period of transition, I told a friend who asked me to send a congratulatory telegram for him, at a certain time when I was to send one myself, that I would probably forget both. It was not surprising that the prophecy came true. It is undoubtedly due to painful experiences in life that I am unable to manifest sympathy where this manifestation must necessarily appear exaggerated, for the small amount of my feeling does not admit the corresponding expression. Since I have learned that I often mistook the pretended sympathy of others for real, I am in rebellion against the conventions of expressing sympathy, the social expediency of which I naturally acknowledge. Condolences in cases of death are excepted from this double treatment; once I determine to send them I do not neglect them. Where my emotional participation has nothing more to do with social duty, its expression is never inhibited by forgetting

Cases in which we forget to carry out actions which we have promised to do as a favor for others can similarly be explained as antagonism to conventional duty and as an unfavorable inward opinion. Here it regularly proves correct, inasmuch as the only person appealed to believes in the excusing power of forgetfulness, while the one requesting the favor has no doubt about the right answer: he has no interest in this matter, otherwise he would not have forgotten it.

There are some who are noted as generally forgetful, and we excuse their lapses in the same manner as we excuse those who are short-sighted when they do not greet us in the street.[11] Such persons forget all small promises which they have made; they leave unexecuted all orders which they have received; they prove themselves unreliable in little things; and at the same time demand that we shall not take these slight offences amiss—that is, they do not want us to attribute these failings to personal characteristics but to refer them to an organic peculiarity.[12] I am not one of these people myself, and have had no opportunity to analyze the actions of such a person in order to discover from the selection of forgetting the motive underlying the same. I cannot forego, however, the conjecture *per analogiam*, that here the motive is an unusual large amount of unavowed disregard for others which exploits the constitutional factor for its purpose.[13]

In other cases the motives for forgetting are less easy to discover, and when found excite greater astonishment. Thus, in former years I observed that of a great number of professional calls I only forgot those that I was to make on patients whom I treated gratis or on colleagues. The mortification caused by this discovery led me to the habit of noting every morning the calls of the day in a form of resolution. I do not know if other physicians have come to the same practice by a similar road. Thus we get an idea of what causes the so-called neurasthenic to make a memorandum of the communications he wishes to make to the doctor. He apparently lacks confidence in the reproductive capacity of his memory. This is true, but the scene usually proceeds in this manner. The patient has recounted his various complaints and inquiries at considerable length. After he has finished he pauses for a moment, then he pulls out the memorandum, and says apologetically, "I have made some notes because I cannot remember anything." As a rule he finds nothing new on the memorandum. He repeats each point and answers it himself: "Yes, I have already asked about that." By means of the memorandum he probably only demonstrates one of his symptoms, the frequency with which his resolutions are disturbed through the interference of obscure motives.

I am touching, moreover, on an affliction to which even most of my healthy acquaintances are subject, when I admit that especially in former years I had the habit of easily forgetting for a long time to return borrowed books, also that it very often happened that I deferred payments through forgetfulness. One morning not long ago I left the tobacco-shop where I make my daily purchase of cigars without paying. It was a most harmless omission, as I am known there and could therefore expect to be reminded of my debt the next morning. But this slight neglect, the attempt to contract a debt, was surely not unconnected with reflections concerning the budget with which I had occupied myself throughout the preceding day. Even among the so-called respectable people one can readily demonstrate a double behavior when it concerns the theme of money and possession. The primitive greed of the suckling which wishes to seize every object (in order to put it in its mouth) has generally been only imperfectly subdued through culture and training.[14]

I fear that in all the examples thus far given I have grown quite commonplace. But it can be only a pleasure to me if I happen upon familiar matters which everyone understands, for my main object is to collect everyday material and utilize it scientifically. I cannot conceive why wisdom, which is, so to speak, the sediment of everyday experiences, should be denied admission among the acquisitions of knowledge. For it is not the diversity of objects but the stricter method of verification and the striving for far-reaching connections which make up the essential character of scientific work.

We have invariably found that intentions of some importance are forgotten when obscure motives arise to disturb them. In still less important intentions we find a second mechanism of forgetting. Here a counter-will becomes transferred to the resolution from something else after an external association has been formed between the latter and the content of the resolution. The following example reported by Brill illustrates this: "A patient found that she had suddenly became very negligent in her correspondence. She was naturally punctual and took pleasure in letter-writing, but for the last few weeks she simply could not bring herself to write a letter without exerting the greatest amount of effort. The explanation was quite simple. Some weeks before she had received an important letter calling for a categorical answer. She was undecided what to say, and therefore did not answer it at all. This indecision in the form of inhibition was unconsciously transferred to other letters and caused the inhibition against letter-writing in general."

Direct counter-will and more remote motivation are found together in the following example of delaying: I had written a short treatise on the dream for the series *Grenzfragen des Nerven - und Seelenlebens*, in which I gave an abstract of my book, *The Interpretation of Dreams*.[15] Bergmann, the publisher, had sent me the proof sheets and asked for a speedy return of the same as he wished to issue the pamphlet before Christmas. I corrected the sheets the same night, and placed them on my desk in order to take them to the post office the next morning. In the morning I forgot all about it, and only thought of it in the afternoon at the sight of the paper cover on my desk. In the same way I forgot the proofs that evening and the following morning, and until the afternoon of the second day, when I quickly took them to a letterbox, wondering what might be the basis of this procrastination. Obviously I did not want to send them off, although I could find no explanation for such an attitude.

After posting the letter I entered the shop of my Vienna publisher, who put out my *Interpretation of Dreams*. I left a few orders; then, as if impelled by a sudden thought, said, "You undoubtedly know that I have written the 'Dream' book a second time?"

"Ah!" he exclaimed, "then I must ask you to..."

"Calm yourself," I interposed; "it is only a short treatise for the Löwenfeld-Kurella collection." But still he was not satisfied; he feared that the abstract would hurt the sale of the book. I disagreed with him, and finally asked: "If I had come to you before, would you have objected to the publication?"

"No; under no circumstances," he answered.

Personally I believe I acted within my full rights and did nothing contrary to the general practice; still it seems certain to me that a thought similar to that entertained by the publisher was the motive for my procrastination in dispatching the proof sheets.

This reflection leads back to a former occasion when another publisher raised some difficulties because I was obliged to take out several pages of the text from an earlier work on cerebral infantile paralysis, and put them unchanged into a work on the same theme in Nothnagel's handbook. There again the reproach received no recognition; that time also I had loyally informed my first publisher (the same who published *The Interpretation of Dreams*) of my intention.

However, if this series of recollections is followed back still farther it brings to light a still earlier occasion relating to a translation from the French, in which I really violated the property rights that should be considered in a publication. I had added notes to the text without asking the author's permission, and some years later I had cause to think that the author was dissatisfied with this arbitrary action.

There is a proverb which indicates the popular knowledge that the forgetting of intentions is not accidental. It says: "What one forgets once he will often forget again."

Indeed, we sometimes cannot help feeling that no matter what may be said about forgetting and faulty actions, the whole subject is already known to everybody as something self-evident. It is strange enough that it is still necessary to push before consciousness such well-known facts. How often I have heard people remark: "Please do not ask me to do this, I shall surely forget it." The coming true of this prophecy later is surely nothing mysterious in itself. He who speaks thus perceives the inner resolution not to carry out the request, and only hesitates to acknowledge it to himself.

Much light is thrown, moreover, on the forgetting of resolutions through something which could be designated as "forming false resolutions." I had once promised a young author to write a review of his short work, but on account of inner resistances, not unknown to me, I promised him that it would be done the same evening. I really had serious intentions of doing so, but I had forgotten that I had set aside that evening for the preparation of an expert testimony that could not be deferred. After I thus recognized my resolution as false, I gave up the struggle against my resistances and refused the author's request.

Footnotes

[1] *In the course of the conference the details of the previous first visit return to consciousness.*

[2] *Brill, loc. cit., p. 197.*

[3] *If we inquire of a person whether he suffered from luetic infection ten or fifteen years ago, we are only too apt to forget that psychically the patient has looked upon this disease in an entirely different manner than on, let us say, an acute attack of rheumatism. In the anamneses which parents give about their neurotic daughters, it is hardly possible to distinguish with any degree of certainty the portion forgotten from that hidden, for anything that stands in the way of the girl's future marriage is systematically set aside by the parents, that is, it becomes repressed. A man who had recently lost his beloved wife from an affection of the lungs reported to me the following case of misleading the doctor, which can only be explained by the theory of such forgetting. "As my poor wife's pleuritis had not disappeared after many weeks, Dr. P. was called in consultation. While taking the history he asked among others the customary questions whether there were any cases of lung trouble in my wife's family. My wife denied any such cases, and even I myself could not remember any. While Dr. P. was taking leave the conversation accidentally turned to excursions, and my wife said: 'Yes, even to Landgersdorf, where my poor brother lies buried, is a long journey.' This brother died about fifteen years ago, after having suffered for years from tuberculosis. My wife was very fond of him, and often spoke about him. Indeed, I recall that when her malady was diagnosed as pleurisy she was very worried and sadly remarked: 'My brother also died of lung trouble.' But the memory was so very repressed that even after the above-cited conversation about the trip to L. she found no occasion to correct her information concerning the diseases in her family. I myself was struck by this forgetting at the very moment she began to talk about Landgersdorf." A perfectly analogous experience is related by Ernest Jones in his work. A physician whose wife suffered from some obscure abdominal malady remarked to her: "It is comforting to think that there has been no tuberculosis in your family." She turned to him very astonished and said, " Have you forgotten that my mother died of tuberculosis, and that my sister recovered from it only after having been given up by the doctors?"*

[4] *During the days when I was first writing these pages the following almost incredible case of forgetting happened to me. On the 1st of January I examined my notes so that I could send out my bills. In the month of June I came across the name M ----l, and could not recall the person to whom it belonged. My surprise increased when I observed from my books that I treated the case in a sanatorium, and that for weeks I had called on the patient daily. A patient treated under such conditions is rarely forgotten by a physician in six months. I asked myself if it could have been a man—a paretic—a case without interest? Finally, the note about the fee received brought to my memory all the knowledge which strove to elude it. M ----l was a fourteen- year-old girl, the most remarkable case of my latter years, a case which taught me a lesson I am not likely ever to forget, a case whose upshot gave me many painful hours. The child became afflicted with an unmistakable hysteria, which quickly and thoroughly improved under my care. After this improvement the child was taken away from me by the parents. She still complained of abdominal pains which had played the part in the hysterical symptoms. Two months later she died of sarcoma of the abdominal glands. The hysteria, to which she was greatly predisposed, took the tumor-formation as a provocative agent, and I, fascinated by the tumultuous but harmless manifestations of hysteria, perhaps overlooked the first sign of the insidious and incurable disease.*

[5] *A. Pick ("Zur Psychologie des Vergessens bei Geistesund Nervenkranken," Archiv. f. Kriminal- Anthropologie u. Kriminalistik, von H. Gross) has recently collected a number of authors who realize the value of the influence of the affective factors on memory, and who more or less clearly recognize that a defensive striving against pain can lead to forgetting. But none of us has been able to represent this phenomenon and its psychological determination as exhaustively, and at the same time as effectively, as Nietzsche in one of his aphorisms (Fenseits von Gut und Bosen, ii., Haupstuck 68) : "'I have done that,' says my Memory. 'I could not have done that,' says my Pride, and remains inexorable. Finally, my Memory yields."*

[6] *Cf. Hans Gross, Kriminal Psychologie, 1898.*

[7] *Darwin on forgetting. In Darwin's autobiography one finds the following passage that does equal credit to his scientific honesty and his psychological acumen: "I had during many years followed a golden rule, namely, that whenever a published fact, a new observation or thought, came across me which was opposed to my general results, to make a memorandum of it without fail and at once; for I had found by experience that such facts and thoughts were far more apt to escape from the memory than favorable ones" (quoted by Jones, loc. cit., p. 38).*

[8] *Cf. Bernheim, Neue Studien über Hypnotismus, Suggestion und Psychotherapie, 1892.*

[9] *Young men of education who can pass the examination and pay for their maintenance serve one instead of two years' compulsory service.*

[10] *In Bernard Shaw's Cæsar and Cleopatra, Cæsar's indifference to Cleopatra is depicted by his being vexed on leaving Egypt at having forgotten to do something. He finally recollected what he had forgotten—to take leave of Cleopatra—this, to be sure, is in full accord with historical truth. How little Cæsar thought of the little Egyptian princess! Cited from Jones, loc. cit., p. 50.*

[11] *Women, with their fine understanding of unconscious mental processes, are, as a rule, more apt to take offence when we do not recognize them in the street, and hence do not greet them, than to accept the most obvious explanation, namely, that the dilatory one is short-sighted or so engrossed in thought that he did not see them. They conclude that they surely would have been noticed if they had been considered of any consequence.*

[12] Dr. Ferenczi reports that he was a distracted person himself, and was considered peculiar by his friends on account of the frequency and strangeness of his failing. But the signs of this inattention have almost all disappeared since he began to practice psychoanalysis with patients, and was forced to turn his attention to the analysis of his own ego. He believes that one renounces these failings when one learns to extend by so much one's own responsibilities. He therefore justly maintains that distractedness is a state which depends on unconscious complexes, and is curable by psychoanalysis. One day he was reproaching himself for having committed a technical error in the psychoanalysis of a patient, and on this day all his former distractions reappeared. He stumbled while walking in the street (a representation of that faux pas in the treatment), he forgot his pocket book at home, he was a penny short in his car fare, he did not properly button his clothes, etc.

[13] E. Jones remarks regarding this: "Often the resistance is of a general order. Thus a busy man forgets to mail a letter entrusted to him—to his slight annoyance—by his wife, just as he may 'forget' to carry out her shopping orders.

[14] For the sake of the unity of the theme I may here digress from the accepted classification, and add that the human memory evinces a particular partiality in regard to money matters. False reminiscences of having already paid something are often very obstinate, as I know from personal experience. When free sway is given to avaricious intent outside of the serious interests of life, when it is indulged in in the spirit of fun, as in card playing, we then find that the most honorable men show an inclination to errors, mistakes in memory and accounts, and without realizing how, they even find themselves involved in small frauds. Such liberties depend in no small part also on the psychically refreshing character of the play. The saying that in play we can learn a person's character may be admitted if we can add "the repressed character." If waiters ever make unintentional mistakes they are apparently due to the same mechanism. Among merchants we can frequently observe a certain delay in the paying out of sums of money, in payments of bills and the like, which brings the owner no profit and can be only understood psychologically as the expression of a counter-will against giving out money. Brill sums it up with epigrammatic keenness: "We are more apt to mislay letters containing bills than checks" (Brill, *Psychoanalysis, its Theories and Practical Application*, p. 197).

CHAPTER 8

Erroneously Carried-Out Actions

I SHALL GIVE another passage from the above-mentioned work of Meringer and Mayer:

"Lapses in speech do not stand entirely alone. They resemble the errors which often occur in our other activities and are quite foolishly termed 'forgetfulness.'"

I am therefore in no way the first to presume that there is a sense and purpose behind the slight functional disturbances of the daily life of healthy people.[1]

If the lapse in speech, which is without doubt a motor function, admits of such a conception, it is quite natural to transfer to the lapses of our other motor functions the same expectation. I have here formed two groups of cases; all these cases in which the faulty effect seems to be the essential element—that is, the deviation from the intention—I denote as erroneously carried-out actions (*Vergreifen*); the others, in which the entire action appears rather inexpedient, I call "symptomatic and chance actions. But no distinct line of demarcation can be formed; indeed, we are forced to conclude that all divisions used in this treatise are or only descriptive significance and contradict the inner unity of the sphere of manifestation.

The psychological understanding of erroneous actions apparently gains little in clearness when we place it under the head of "ataxia," and especially under "cortical ataxia." Let us rather try to trace the individual examples to their proper determinants. To do this I shall again resort to personal observations, the opportunities for which I could not very frequently find in myself .

(*a*) In former years, when I made more calls at the homes of patients than I do at present, it often happened, when I stood before a door where I should have knocked or rung the bell, that I would pull the key of my own house from my pocket, only to replace it, quite abashed. When I investigated in what patients' homes this occurred, I had to admit that the faulty action—taking out my key instead of ringing the bell—signified paying a certain tribute to the house where the error occurred. It was equivalent to the thought "Here I feel at home," as it happened only where I possessed the patient's regard. (Naturally, I never rang my own bell.)

The faulty action was therefore a symbolic representation of a definite thought which was not accepted consciously as serious; for in reality the neurologist is well aware that the patient seeks him only so long as he expects to be benefited by him and that his own excessively warm interest for his patient is evinced only as a means of psychic treatment.

An almost identical repetition of my experience is described by A. Maeder (*"Contrib. à la psychopathologie de la vie quotidienne," Arch.de Psychol., vi., 1906*): *" Il est arrivè a chacun de sortir son trousseau, ·en arrivant à la porte d'un ami particulièrement cher, de se surprendre pour ainsi dire, en train d'ouvrir avec sa clé comme chez soi. C'est un retard, puisqu'il faut sonner malgré tout, mais c'est une preuve qu'on se sent—ou qu'on voudrait se sentir—comme chez soi, auprès de cet ami."*

Jones speaks as follows about the use of keys [2] "The use of keys is a fertile source of occurrences of this kind, of which two examples may be given. If I am disturbed in the midst of some engrossing work at home by having to go to the hospital to carry out some routine work, I am very apt to find myself trying to open the door of my laboratory there with the key of my desk at home, although the two keys are quite unlike each other. The mistake unconsciously demonstrates where I would rather be at the moment.

"Some years ago I was acting in a subordinate position at a certain institution, the front door of which was kept locked, so that it was necessary to ring for admission. On several occasions I found myself making serious attempts to open the door with my house key. Each one of the permanent visiting staff, of which I aspired to be a member, was provided with a key to avoid the trouble of having to wait at the door. My mistake thus expressed the desire to be on a similar footing and to be quite 'at home' there."

A similar experience is reported by Dr. Hans Sachs of Vienna: "I always carry two keys with me, one for the door of my office and one for my residence. They are not by any means easily interchanged, as the office key is at least three times as big as my house key. Besides, I carry the first in my trouser pocket and the other in my vest pocket. Yet it often happened that I noticed on reaching the door that while ascending the stairs I had taken out the wrong key. I decided to undertake a statistical examination; as I was daily in about the same emotional state when I stood before both doors, I thought that the interchanging of the two keys must show a regular tendency, if they were differently determined psychically. Observation of later occurrences showed that I regularly took out my house key before the office door. Only on one occasion was this reversed: I came home tired, knowing that I would find there a guest. I made an attempt to unlock the door with the, naturally too big, office key."

(*b*) At a certain time twice a day for six years I was accustomed to wait for admission before a door in the second story of the same house, and during this long period of time it happened twice (within a short interval) that I climbed a story higher. On the first of these occasions I was in an ambitious daydream, which allowed me to "mount always higher and higher." In fact, at that time I heard the door in question open as I put my foot on the first step of the third flight. On the other occasion I again went too far "engrossed in thought." As soon as I became aware of it, I turned back and sought to snatch the dominating fantasy; I found that I was irritated over a criticism of my works, in which the reproach was made that I "always went too far," which I replaced by the less respectful expression "climbed too high."

(*c*) For many years a reflex hammer and a tuning-fork lay side by side on my desk. One day I hurried off at the close of my office hours, as I wished to catch a certain train, and, despite broad daylight, put the tuning-fork in my coat pocket in place of the reflex hammer. My attention was called to the mistake through the weight of the object drawing down my pocket. Anyone unaccustomed to reflect on such slight occurrences would without hesitation explain the faulty action by the hurry of the moment, and excuse it. In spite of that, I preferred to ask myself why I took the tuning-fork instead of the hammer. The haste could just as well have been a motive for carrying out the action properly in order not to waste time over the correction.

"Who last grasped the tuning-fork?" was the question which immediately flashed through my mind. It happened that only a few days ago an idiotic child, whose attention to sensory impressions I was testing, had been so fascinated by the tuning-fork that I found it difficult to tear it away from him. Could it mean, therefore, that I was an idiot? To be sure, so it would seem, as the next thought which associated itself with the hammer was *chamer* (Hebrew for "ass").

But what was the meaning of this abusive language? We must here inquire into the situation. I hurried to a consultation at a place on the Western railroad to see a patient who, according to the anamnesis which I received by letter, had fallen from a balcony some months before, and since then had been unable to walk. The physician w ho invited me wrote that he was still unable to say whether he was dealing with a spinal injury or traumatic neurosis—hysteria. That was what I was to decide. This could therefore be a reminder to be particularly careful in this delicate differential diagnosis. As it is, my colleagues think that hysteria is diagnosed far too carelessly where more serious matters are concerned. But the abuse is not yet justified. Yes, the next association was that the small railroad station is the same place in which, some years previous, I saw a young man who, after a certain emotional experience, could not walk properly. At that time I diagnosed his malady as hysteria, and later put him under psychic treatment; but it afterward turned out that my diagnosis was neither incorrect nor correct. A large number of the patient's symptoms were hysterical, and they promptly disappeared in the course of treatment. But back of these there was a visible remnant that could not be reached by therapy, and could be referred only to a multiple sclerosis. Those who saw the patient after me had no difficulty in recognizing the organic affection. I could scarcely have acted or judged differently, still the impression was that of a serious mistake; the promise of a cure which I had given him could naturally not be kept.

The mistake in grasping the tuning-fork instead of the hammer could therefore be translated into the following words: "You fool, you ass, get yourself together this time, and be careful not to diagnose again a case of hysteria where there is an incurable disease, as you did in this place years ago in the case of the poor man !" And fortunately for this little analysis, even if unfortunately for my mood, this same man, now having a very spastic gait, had been to my office a few days before, one day after the examination of the idiotic child.

We observe that this time it is the voice of self-criticism which makes itself perceptible through the mistake in grasping. The erroneously carried-out action is specially suited to express self-reproach. The present mistake attempts to represent the mistake which was committed elsewhere.

(*d*) It is quite obvious that grasping the wrong thing may also serve a whole series of other obscure purposes. Here is a first example: It is very seldom that I break anything. I am not particularly dexterous, but by virtue of the anatomic integrity of my nervous and muscular apparatus there are apparently no grounds in me for such awkward movements with undesirable results. I can recall no object in my home the counterpart of which I have ever broken. Owing to the narrowness of my study it has often been necessary for me to work in the most uncomfortable position among my numerous antique clay and stone objects, of which I have a small collection. So much is this true that onlookers have expressed fear lest I topple down something and shatter it. But it never happened. Then why did I brush to the floor the cover of my simple inkwell so that it broke into pieces? My inkstand is made of a flat piece of marble which is hollowed out for the reception of the glass inkwell; the inkwell has a marble cover with a knob of the same stone. A circle of bronze statuettes with small terra-cotta figures is set behind this inkstand. I seated myself at the desk to write, I made a remarkably awkward outward movement with the hand holding the pen-holder, and so swept the cover of the ink-stand, which already lay on the desk, to the floor.

It is not difficult to find the explanation. Some hours before my sister had been in the room to look at some of my new acquisitions. She found them very pretty, and then remarked: "Now the desk really looks very well, only the inkstand does not match. You must get a prettier one." I accompanied my sister out and did not return for several hours. But then, as it seems, I performed the execution of the condemned inkstand.

Did I perhaps conclude from my sister's words that she intended to present me with a prettier inkstand on the next festive occasion, and did I shatter the unsightly old one in order to force her to carry out her signified intention? If that be so, then my swinging motion was only apparently awkward; in reality it was most skilful and designed, as it understood how to avoid all the valuable objects located near it.

I actually believe that we must accept this explanation of the whole series of seemingly accidental awkward movements. It is true that on the surface these seem to show something violent and irregular, similar to spastic-ataxic movements, but on examination they seem to be dominated by some intention, and they accomplish their aim with a certainty that cannot be generally credited to conscious arbitrary motions. In both characteristics, the force as well as the sure aim, they show besides a resemblance to the motor manifestations of the hysterical neurosis, and in part also to the motor accomplishments of somnambulism, which here as well as there point to the same unfamiliar modification of the functions of innervation.

In latter years, since I have been collecting such observations, it has happened several times that I have shattered and broken objects of some value, but the examination of these cases convinced me that it was never the result of accident or of my unintentional awkwardness. Thus, one morning while in my bath-robe and straw slippers I followed a sudden impulse as I passed a room, and hurled a slipper from my foot against the wall so that it brought down a beautiful little marble Venus from its bracket. As it fell to pieces I recited quite unmoved the following verse from Busch:

"Ach ! Die Venus ist perdü—[3]
Klickeradoms!—von Medici!"

This crazy action and my calmness at the sight of the damage is explained in the then existing situation. We had a very sick person in the family, of whose recovery I had personally despaired. That morning I had been informed that there was a great improvement; I know that I had said to myself, "After all she will live." My attack of destructive madness served therefore as the expression of a grateful feeling toward fate, and afforded me the opportunity of performing an "act of sacrifice," just as if I had vowed, "If she gets well I will give this or that as a sacrifice," That I chose the Venus of Medici as this sacrifice was only gallant homage to the convalescent. But even today it is still incomprehensible to me that I decided so quickly, aimed so accurately, and struck no other object in close proximity.

Another breaking, in which I utilized a penholder falling from my hand, also signified a sacrifice, but this time it was a pious offering to avert some evil. I had once allowed myself to reproach a true and worthy friend for no other reason than certain manifestations which I interpreted from his unconscious activity. He took it amiss and wrote me a letter in which he bade me not to treat my friends by psychoanalysis. I had to admit that he was right and appeased him with my answer. While writing this letter I had before me my latest acquisition-a small, handsome glazed Egyptian figure. I broke it in the manner mentioned, and then immediately knew that I had caused this mischief to avert a greater one. Luckily, both the friendship and the figure could be so cemented that the break would not be noticed.

A third case of breaking had a less serious connection; it was only a disguised "execution," to use an expression from Th. Vischer's *Auch Einer*, of an object that no longer suited my taste. For quite a while I had carried a cane with a silver handle; through no fault of mine the thin silver plate was once damaged and poorly repaired. Soon after the cane was returned I mirthfully used the handle to angle for the leg of one of my children. In that way it naturally broke, and I got rid of it.

The indifference with which we accept the resulting damage in all these cases may certainly be taken as evidence for the existence of an unconscious purpose in their execution.

(*e*) As can sometimes be demonstrated by, analysis, the dropping of objects or the overturning and breaking of the same are very frequently utilized as the expression of unconscious streams of thought, but more often they serve to represent the superstitious or odd significances connected therewith in popular sayings. The meanings attached to the spilling of salt, the overturning of a wineglass, the sticking of a knife dropped to the floor, and so on, are well known. I shall discuss later the right to investigate such superstitious interpretations ; here I shall simply, observe that the individual awkward acts do not by any means always have the same meaning, but, depending on the circumstances, they serve to represent now this or that purpose.

Recently we passed through a period in my house during which an unusual number of glass and china dishes were broken. I myself largely contributed to this damage. This little endemic was readily explained by the fact that it preceded the public betrothal of my eldest daughter. On such festivities it is customary to break some dishes and utter at the same time some felicitating expression. This custom may signify a sacrifice or express any other symbolic sense.

When servants destroy fragile objects through dropping them, we certainly do not think in the first place of a psychological motive for it; still, some obscure motives are not improbable even here. Nothing lies farther from the uneducated than the appreciation of art and works of art. Our servants are dominated by a foolish hostility against these productions, especially when the objects, whose worth they do not realize ,become a source of a great deal of work for them. On the other hand, persons of the same education and origin employed in scientific institutions often distinguish themselves by great dexterity and reliability in the handling of delicate objects, as soon as they begin to identify themselves with their masters and consider themselves an essential part of the staff.

I shall here add the report of a young mechanical engineer, which gives some insight into the mechanism of damaging things. "Some time ago I worked with many others in the laboratory of the High School on a series of complicated experiments on the subject of elasticity. It was a work that we undertook of our own volition, but it turned out that it took up more of our time than we expected. One day, while going to the laboratory with F., he complained of losing so much time, especially on this day, when he had so many other things to do at home. I could only agree with him, and he added half jokingly, alluding to an incident of the previous week, 'Let us hope that the machine will refuse to work, so that we can interrupt the experiment and go home earlier.'

"In arranging the work, it happened that F. was assigned to the regulation of the pressure valve, that is, it was his duty to carefully open the valve and let the fluid under pressure flow from the accumulator into the cylinder of the hydraulic press. The leader of the experiment stood at the manometer and called a loud 'Stop!' when the maximum pressure was reached. At this command F. grasped the valve and turned it with all his force—to the left (all valves, without any exception, are closed to the right). This caused a sudden full pressure in the accumulator of the press, and as there was no outlet, the connecting pipe burst. This was quite a trifling accident to the machine, but enough to force us to stop our work for the day and go home.

"It is characteristic, moreover, that some time later, on discussing this occurrence, my friend F. could not recall the remark that I positively remember his having made."

Similarly, to fall, to make a misstep, or to slip need not always be interpreted as an entirely accidental miscarriage of a motor action. The linguistic double meaning of these expressions points to diverse hidden fantasies, which may present themselves through the giving up of bodily equilibrium. I recall a number of lighter nervous ailments in women and girls which made their appearance after falling without injury, and which were conceived as traumatic hysteria as a result of the shock of the fall. At that time I already entertained the impression that these conditions had a different connection, that the fall was already a preparation of the neurosis, and an expression of the same unconscious fantasies of sexual content which may be taken as the moving forces behind the symptoms. Was not this very thing meant in the proverb which says, "When a maiden falls, she falls on her back!"

We can also add to these mistakes the case of one who gives a beggar a gold piece in place of a copper or a silver coin. The solution of such mishandling is simple: it is an act of sacrifice designed to mollify fate, to avert evil, and so on. If we hear a tender mother or aunt express concern regarding the health of a child, directly before taking a walk during which she displays her charity, contrary to her usual habit, we can no longer doubt the sense of this apparently undesirable accident. In this manner our faulty acts make possible the practice of all those pious and superstitious customs which must shun the light of consciousness, because of the strivings against them of our unbelieving reason.

(f) That accidental actions are really intentional will find no greater credence in any other sphere than in sexual activity, where the border between the intention and accident hardly seems discernible, That an apparently clumsy movement may be utilized in a most refined way for sexual purposes I can verify by; a nice example from my own experience. In a friend's house I met a young girl visitor who excited in me a feeling of fondness which I had long believed extinct, thus putting me in a jovial, loquacious, and complaisant mood. At that time I endeavored to find out how this came about, as a year before this same girl made no impression on me.

As the girl's uncle, a very old man, entered the room, we both jumped to our feet to bring him a chair which stood in the corner. She was more agile than I and also nearer the object, so that she was the first to take possession of the chair. She carried it with its back to her, holding both hands on the edge of the seat. As I got there later and did not give up the claim to carrying the chair, I suddenly stood directly back of her, and with both my arms was embracing her from behind, and for a moment my hands touched her lap. I naturally solved the situation as quickly as it came about. Nor did it occur to anybody how dexterously I had taken advantage of this awkward movement.

Occasionally I have had to admit to myself that the annoying, awkward stepping aside on the street, whereby for some seconds one steps here and there, yet always in the same direction as the other person, until finally both stop facing each other, that this "barring one's way" repeats an ill-mannered, provoking conduct of earlier times and conceals erotic purposes under the mask of awkwardness. From my psychoanalysis of neurotics I know that the so-called naïveté of young people and children is frequently only such a mask, employed in order that the subject may say or do the indecent without restraint.

W. Stekel has reported similar observations in regard to himself: "I entered a house and offered my right hand to the hostess. In a most remarkable way I thereby loosened the bow which held together her loose morning-gown. I was conscious of no dishonorable intent, still I executed this awkward movement with the agility of a juggler."

(g) The effects which result from mistakes of normal persons are, as a rule, of a most harmless nature. Just for this reason it would be particularly interesting to find out whether mistakes of considerable importance, which could be followed by serious results, as, for example, those of physicians or druggists, fall within the range of our point of view.

As I am seldom in a position to deal with active medical matters, I can only, report one mistake from my own experience. I treated a very old woman, whom I visited twice daily for several years. My medical activities were limited to two acts, which I performed during my morning visits: I dropped a few drops of an eye lotion into her eyes and gave her a hypodermic injection of morphine. I prepared regularly two bottles—a blue one, containing the eye lotion, and a white one, containing the morphine solution. While performing these duties my thoughts were mostly occupied with something else, for they had been repeated so often that the attention acted as if free. One morning I noticed that the automaton worked wrong; I had put the dropper into the white instead of into the blue bottle, and had dropped into the eyes the morphine instead of the lotion. I was greatly frightened, but then calmed myself through the reflection that a few drops of a *two per cent.* solution of morphine would not likely do any harm even if left in the conjunctival sac. The cause of the fright manifestly belonged elsewhere .

In attempting to analyze the slight mistake I first thought of the phrase, "to seize the old woman by mistake," which pointed out the short way to the solution. I had been impressed by a dream which a young man had told me the previous evening, the contents of which could be explained only on the basis of sexual intercourse with his own mother.[4] The strangeness of the fact that the Oedipus legend takes no offence at the age of Queen Jocasta seemed to me to agree with the assumption that in being in love with one's mother we never deal with the present personality, but with her youthful memory picture carried over from our childhood. Such incongruities always show themselves where one fantasy fluctuating between two periods is made conscious, and is then bound to one definite period.

Deep in thoughts of this kind, I came to my patient of over ninety; I must have been well on the way to grasp the universal character of the Oedipus fable as the correlation of the fate which the oracle pronounces, for I made a blunder in reference to or on the old woman. Here, again, the mistake was harmless; of the two possible errors, taking the morphine solution for the eye, or the eye lotion for the injection, I chose the one by far the least harmful. The question still remains open whether in mistakes in handling things which may cause serious harm we can assume an unconscious intention as in the cases here discussed.

The following case from Brill's experience corroborates the assumption that even serious mistakes are determined by unconscious intentions: "A physician received a telegram informing him that his aged uncle was very sick. In spite of important family affairs at home he at once repaired to that distant town because his uncle was really his father, who had cared for him since he was one and a half years old, when his own father had died. On reaching there he found his uncle suffering from pneumonia, and, as the old man was an octogenarian, the doctors held out no hope for his recovery. 'It was simply a question of a day or two,' was the local doctor's verdict. Although a prominent physician in a big city, he refused to co-operate in the treatment, as he found that the case was properly managed by the local doctor, and he could not suggest anything to improve matters.

"Since death was daily expected, he decided to remain to the end. He waited a few days, but the sick man struggled hard, and although there was no question of any recovery, because of the many new complications which had arisen, death seemed to be deferred for a while. One night before retiring he went into the sick-room and took his uncle's pulse. As it was quite weak, he decided not to wait for the doctor, and administered a hypodermic injection. The patient grew rapidly worse and died within a few hours.

There was something strange in the last symptoms, and on later attempting to replace the tube of hypodermic tablets into the case, he found to his consternation that he had taken out the wrong tube, and instead of a small dose of digitalis he had given a large dose of hyoscine.

"This case was related to me by the doctor after he read my paper on the Oedipus Complex.[5] We agreed that this mistake was determined not only by his impatience to get home to his sick child, but also by an old resentment and unconscious hostility toward his uncle (father)."

It is known that in the more serious cases of psychoneuroses one sometimes finds self-mutilations as symptoms of the disease. That the psychic conflict may end in suicide can never be excluded in these cases. Thus I know from experience, which someday I shall support with convincing examples, that many apparently accidental injuries happening to such patients are really self-inflicted. This is brought about by the fact that there is a constantly lurking tendency to self-punishment, usually expressing itself in self-reproach, or contributing to the formation of a symptom, which skillfully makes use of an external situation. The required external situation may accidentally present itself or the punishment tendency may assist it until the way is open for the desired injurious effect.

Such occurrences are by no means rare even in cases of moderate severity, and they betray the portion of unconscious intention through a series of special features—for example, through the striking presence of mind which the patients show in the pretended accidents. [6]

I will report exhaustively one in place of many such examples from my professional experience. A young woman broke her leg below the knee in a carriage accident so that she was bedridden for weeks. The striking part of it was the lack of any manifestation of pain and the calmness with which she bore her misfortune. This calamity ushered in a long and serious neurotic illness, from which she was finally cured by psychotherapy. During the treatment I discovered the circumstances surrounding the accident, as well as certain impressions which preceded it. The young woman with her jealous husband spent some time on the farm of her married sister, in company with her numerous other brothers and sisters with their wives and husbands.

One evening she gave an exhibition of one of her talents before this intimate circle; she danced artistically the "cancan," to the great delight of her relatives, but to the great annoyance of her husband, who afterward whispered to her, "Again you have behaved like a prostitute." The words took effect; we will leave it undecided whether it was just on account of the dance. That night she was restless in her sleep, and the next forenoon she decided to go out driving. She chose the horses herself refusing one team and demanding another. Her youngest sister wished to have her baby with its nurse accompany her, but she opposed this vehemently. During the drive she was nervous; she reminded the coachman that the horses were getting skittish, and as the fidgety animals really produced a momentary difficulty she jumped from the carriage in fright and broke her leg, while those remaining; in the carriage were uninjured. Although after the disclosure of these details we can hardly doubt that this accident was really contrived, we cannot fail to admire the skill which forced the accident to mete out a punishment so suitable to the crime. For as it happened "cancan" dancing with her became impossible for a long time.

Concerning self-inflicted injuries of my own experience, I cannot report anything in calm times, but under extraordinary: conditions I do not believe myself incapable of such acts. When a member of my family complains that he or she has bitten his tongue, bruised her finger, and so on, instead of the expected sympathy I put the question, "Why did you do that?" But I have most painfully squeezed my thumb, after a youthful patient acquainted me during the treatment with his intention (naturally not to be taken seriously) of marrying my eldest daughter, while I knew that she was then in a private hospital in extreme danger of losing her life.

One of my boys, whose vivacious temperament was wont to put difficulties in the management of nursing him in his illness, had a fit of anger one morning because he was ordered to remain in bed during the forenoon, and threatened to kill himself a way out suggested to him by the newspapers. In the evening he showed me a swelling on the side of his chest which was the result of bumping against the door knob. To my ironical question why he did it, and what he meant by, it, the eleven-year-old child explained, "That was my attempt at suicide which I threatened this morning." However, I do not believe that my views on self-inflicted wounds were accessible to my children at that time.

Whoever believes in the occurrence of semi-intentional self-inflicted injury—if this awkward expression be permitted—will become prepared to accept through it the fact that aside from conscious intentional suicide there also exists semi-intentional annihilation—with unconscious intention—which is capable of aptly utilizing a threat against life and masking it as a casual mishap. Such mechanism is by no means rare. For the tendency to self-destruction exists to a certain degree in many more persons than in those who bring it to completion. Self-inflicted injuries are, as a rule, a compromise between this impulse and the forces working against it, and even where it really comes to suicide the inclination has existed for a long time with less strength or as an unconscious and repressed tendency.

Even suicide consciously committed chooses its time, means, and opportunity; it is quite natural that unconscious suicide should wait for a motive to take upon itself one part of the causation and thus free it from its oppression by taking up the defensive forces of the person.[7] These are in no way idle discussions which I here bring up; more than one case of apparently accidental misfortune (on a horse or out of a carriage) has become known to me whose surrounding circumstances justified the suspicion of suicide.

For example, during an officers' horse-race one of the riders fell from his horse and was so seriously injured that a few days later he succumbed to his injuries. His behavior after regaining consciousness was remarkable in more than one way, and his conduct previous to the accident was still more remarkable. He had been greatly depressed by the death of his beloved mother, had crying spells in the society of his comrades, and to his trusted friend had spoken of the *tædium vitæ*. He had wished to quit the service in order to take part in a war in Africa which had no interest for him.[8] Formerly a keen rider, he had later evaded riding whenever possible. Finally, before the horse-race, from which he could not withdraw, he expressed a sad foreboding, which most expectedly in the light of our conception came true. It may be contended that it is quite comprehensible without any further cause that a person in such a state of nervous depression cannot manage a horse as well as on normal days. I quite agree with that, only, I should like to look for the mechanism of this motor inhibition through "nervousness" in the intention of self-destruction here emphasized.

Dr. Ferenczi has left to me for publication the analysis of an apparently accidental injury by shooting which he explained as an unconscious attempt at suicide. I can only agree with his deduction :

"J. Ad., 22 years old, carpenter, visited me on the 18th of January, 1908. He wished to know whether the bullet which pierced his left temple March 20, 1907, could or should be removed by operation. Aside from occasional, not very severe, headaches, he felt quite well, also the objective examination showed nothing besides the characteristic powder wound on the left temple, so that I advised against an operation. When questioned concerning the circumstances of the case he asserted that he injured himself accidentally. He was playing with his brother's revolver, and *believing that it was not loaded* he pressed it with his left hand: against the left temple (he is not left-handed), put his finger on the trigger, and the shot went off. *There were three bullets in the six-shooter.*

"I asked him how he came to carry the revolver, and he answered that it was at the time of his army conscription, that he took it to the inn the evening before because he feared fights. At the army examination he was considered unfit for service on account of varicose veins, which caused him much mortification. He went home and played with the revolver. He had no intention of hurting himself, but the accident occurred. On further questioning, whether he was otherwise satisfied with his fortune, he answered with a sigh, and related a love affair with a girl who loved him in return, but nevertheless left him. She emigrated to America out of sheer avariciousness. He wanted to follow her, but his parents prevented him. His lady-love left on the 20th of January, 1907, just two months before the accident.

"Despite all these suspicious elements the patient insisted that the shot was an 'accident.' I was firmly convinced, however, that the neglect to find out whether the revolver was loaded before he began to play with it, as well as the self-inflicted injury, were psychically determined. He was still under the depressing effects of the unhappy love affair, and apparently wanted 'to forget everything' in the army. When this hope, too, was taken away from him he resorted to playing with the weapon—that is, to an unconscious attempt at suicide. The fact that he did not hold the revolver in the right but in the left hand speaks conclusively in favor of the fact that he was really only 'playing'—that is, he did not wish consciously to commit suicide."

Another analysis of an apparently accidental self-inflicted wound, detailed to me by an observer, recalls the saying, "He who digs a pit for others falls in himself."[9]

"Mrs. X., belonging to a good middle-class family, is married and has three children. She is somewhat nervous, but never needed any strenuous treatment, as she could sufficiently adapt herself to life. One day she sustained a rather striking though transitory disfigurement of her face in the following manner: She stumbled in a street that was in process of repair and struck her face against the house wall. The whole face was bruised, the eyelids blue and oedematous, and as she feared that something might happen to her eyes she sent for the doctor. After she was calmed I asked her, 'But why did you fall in such a manner? She answered that just before this accident she wanted her husband, who had been suffering for some months from a joint affection, to be very careful in the street, and she often had the experience that in some remarkable way those things occurred to her against which she warned others.

"I was not satisfied with this as the determination of her accident, and asked her whether she had not something else to tell me. 'Yes, just before the accident she noticed a nice picture in a shop on the other side or the street, which she suddenly desired as an ornament for her nursery, and wished to buy it at once. She thereupon walked across to the shop without looking at the street, stumbled over a heap of stones, and fell with her face against the wall without making the slightest effort to shield herself with her hands. The intention to buy the .picture was immediately forgotten, and she walked home in haste.'

"'But why were you not more careful?' I asked.

"'Oh!' she answered, 'perhaps it was only a punishment for that episode which I confided to you!'

"'Has this episode still bothered you?'

"'Yes, later I regretted it very much; I considered myself wicked, criminal, and immoral, but at the time I was almost crazy with nervousness.'

"She referred to an abortion which was started by a quack and had to be brought to completion by a gynecologist. This abortion was initiated with the consent of her husband, as both wished, on account of their pecuniary circumstances, to be spared from being additionally blessed with children.

"She said: 'I had often reproached myself with the words, "You really had your child killed," and I feared that such a crime could not remain unpunished. Now that you have assured me that there is nothing seriously wrong with my eyes I am quite assured I have already been sufficiently punished.'

"This accident, therefore, was, on the one hand, a retribution for her sin, but, on the other hand, it may have served as an escape from a more dire punishment which she had feared for many months. In the moment that she ran to the shop to buy the picture the memory of this whole history, with its fears (already quite active in her unconscious at the time she warned her husband), became overwhelming and could perhaps find expression in words like these: 'But why do you want an ornament for the nursery?—you who had your child killed! You are a murderer! The great punishment is surely approaching!'

"This thought did not become conscious, but instead of it she made use of the situation—I might say of the psychological moment—to utilize in a commonplace manner the heap of stones to inflict upon herself this punishment. It was for this reason that she did not even attempt to put out her arms while falling and was not much frightened. The second determinant of her accident was obviously the self-punishment for her unconscious wish to be rid of her husband, who was an accessory to the crime in this affair. This was betrayed by her absolutely superfluous warning to be very careful in the street on account of the stones. For, just because her husband had a weak leg, he was very careful in walking."

If such a rage against one's own integrity and one's own life can be hidden behind apparently accidental awkwardness and motor insufficiency then it is not a big step forward to grasp the possibility of transferring the same conception to mistakes which seriously endanger the life and health of others. What I can put forward as evidence for the validity of this conception was taken from my experience with neurotics, and hence does not fully meet the demands of this situation. I will report a case in which it was not an erroneously carried-out action, but what may be more aptly termed a symbolic or chance action that gave me the clue which later made possible the solution of the patient's conflict.

I once undertook to improve the marriage relations of a very intelligent man, whose differences with his tenderly attached young wife could surely be traced to real causes, but as he himself admitted could not be altogether explained through them. He continually occupied himself with the thought of a separation, which he repeatedly rejected because he dearly loved his two small children. In spite of this he always returned to that resolution and sought no means to make the situation bearable to himself. Such an unsettlement of a conflict served to prove to me that there were unconscious and repressed motives which enforced the conflicting conscious thoughts, and in such cases I always undertake to end the conflict by psychic analysis. One day the man related to me a slight occurrence which had extremely frightened him. He was sporting with the older child, by far his favorite. He tossed it high in the air and repeated this tossing till finally he thrust it so high that its head almost struck the massive gas chandelier. Almost, but not quite, or say "just about!" Nothing happened to the child except that it became dizzy from fright. The father stood transfixed with the child in his arms, while the mother merged into an hysterical attack. The particular facility of this careless movement, with the violent reaction in the parents, suggested to me to look upon this accident as a symbolic action which gave expression to an evil intention toward the beloved child.

I could remove the contradiction of the actual tenderness of this father for his child by referring the impulse to injure it to the time when it was the only one, and so small that as yet the father had no occasion for tender interest in it. Then it was easy to assume that this man, so little pleased with his wife at that time, might have thought: "If this small being for whom I have no regard whatever should die, I would be free and could separate from my wife." The wish for the death of this much loved being must therefore have continued unconsciously. From here it was easy to find the way to the unconscious fixation of this wish.

There was indeed a powerful determinant in a memory from the patient's childhood: it referred to the death of a little brother, which the mother laid to his father's negligence, and which led to serious quarrels with threats of separation between the parents. The continued course of my patient's life, as well as the therapeutic success confirmed my analysis.

Footnotes

[1] *A second publication of Meringer has later shown me how very unjust I was to this author when I attributed to him so much understanding.*

[2] *Jones, loc. cit., p. 79.·*

[3] *Alas! the Venus of Medici is lost!*

[4] *The Oedipus dream as I was wont to call it, because it contains the key to the understanding of the legend of King Oedipus. In the text of Sophocles the relation of such a dream is put in the mouth of Jocasta (cf. The Interpretation of Dreams, pp. 222-4, etc.).*

[5] *New York Medical Journal, September, 1912. Reprinted in large form as Chapter X of Psychoanalysis, etc., Saunders. Philadelphia.*

[6] *The self-inflicted injury which does not entirely tend toward self-annihilation has, moreover, no other choice in our present state of civilization than to hide itself behind the accidental, or to break through in a simulation of spontaneous illness. Formerly, it was a customary sign of mourning, at other times it expressed itself in ideas of piety and renunciation of the world.*

[7] *The case is then identical with a sexual attack on a woman, in whom the attack of the man cannot be warded off through the full muscular strength of the woman because a portion of the unconscious feelings of the one attacked meets it with ready acceptance. To be sure, it is said that such a situation paralyses the strength of a woman; we need only add the reasons for this paralysis. Insofar the clever sentence of Sancho Panza, which he pronounced as governor of his island, is psychologically unjust (Don Quixote, vol. ii. chap. xlv). A woman hauled before the judge a man who was supposed to have robbed her of her honor by force of violence. Sancho indemnified her with a full purse which he took from the accused, but after the departure of the woman he gave the accused permission to follow her and snatch the purse from her. Both returned wrestling, the woman priding herself that the villain was unable to possess himself of the purse. Thereupon Sancho spoke: "Had you shown yourself so stout and valiant to defend your body (nay, but half so much) as you have done to defend your purse, the strength of Hercules could not have forced you."*

[8] *It is evident that the situation of a battlefield is such as to meet the requirement of conscious suicidal intent which, nevertheless, shuns the direct way. Cf. in Wallenstein the words of the Swedish captain concerning the death of Max Piccolomini: "They say he wished to die."*

[9] *"Selbstbestrafung wegen Abortus von Dr. J. E. G. van Emden," Haag (Holland), Zentralb. f. Psychoanalyse, ii, 12.*

CHAPTER 9
Symptomatic and Chance Actions

THE ACTIONS DESCRIBED so far, in which we recognize the execution of an unconscious intention, appeared as disturbances of other unintended actions, and hid themselves under the pretext of awkwardness. Chance actions, which we shall now discuss, differ from erroneously carried out actions only in that they disdain the support of a conscious intention and really need no pretext. They appear independently and are accepted because one does not credit them with any aim or purpose. We execute them "without thinking anything of them," "by mere chance," "just to keep the hands busy," and we feel confident that such information will be quite sufficient should one inquire as to their significance. In order to enjoy the advantage of this exceptional position these actions which no longer claim awkwardness as an excuse must fulfill certain conditions: they must not be striking, and their effects must be insignificant.

I have collected a large number of such "chance actions" from myself and others, and after thoroughly investigating the individual examples, I believe that the name "symptomatic actions" is more suitable. They give expression to something which the actor himself does not suspect in them, and which as a rule he has no intention of imparting to others, but aims to keep to himself. Like the other phenomena considered so far, they thus play the part of symptoms .

The richest output of such chance or symptomatic actions is above all obtained in the psychoanalytic treatment of neurotics. I cannot deny myself the pleasure of showing by two examples of this nature how far and how delicately the determination of these plain occurrences are swayed by unconscious thoughts. The line of demarcation between the symptomatic actions and the erroneously carried out actions is so indefinite that I could have disposed of these examples in the preceding chapter.

(*a*) During the analysis a young woman reproduced this idea which suddenly occurred to her. Yesterday while cutting her nails "she had cut into the flesh while engaged in trimming the cuticle." This is of so little interest that we ask in astonishment why it is at all remembered and mentioned, and therefore come to the conclusion that we deal with a symptomatic action. It was really the finger upon which the wedding-ring is worn which was injured through this slight awkwardness. It happened, moreover, on her wedding-day, which thus gives to the injury of the delicate skin a very definite and easily guessed meaning. At the same time she, also related a dream which alluded to the awkwardness of her husband and her anesthesia as a woman. But why did she injure the ring finger of her left hand when the wedding-ring is worn on the right? Her husband is a jurist, a "Doctor of Laws" (*Doktor der Rechte*, literally a Doctor of Rights), and her secret affection as a girl belonged to a physician who was jokingly called *Doktor der Linke* (literally, Doctor of Left). Incidentally a left-handed marriage has a definite meaning.

(b) A single young woman relates: "Yesterday, quite unintentionally, I tore a hundred-dollar note in two pieces and gave half to a woman who was visiting me. Is that, too, a symptomatic action?" After closer investigation the matter of the hundred-dollar note elicited the following associations: She dedicated a part of her time and her fortune to charitable work. Together with another woman she was taking care of the rearing of an orphan. The hundred dollars was the contribution sent her by that woman, which she enclosed in an envelope and provisionally deposited on her writing-desk.

The visitor was a prominent woman with whom she was associated in another act of charity. This woman wished to note the names of a number of persons to whom she could apply for charitable aid. There was no paper, so my patient grasped the envelope from her desk, and without thinking of its contents tore it in two pieces, one of which she kept, in order to have a duplicate list of names, and gave the other to her visitor.

Note the harmlessness of this aimless occurrence. It is known that a hundred-dollar note suffers no loss in value when it is torn, provided all the pieces are produced. That the woman would not throw away the piece of paper was assumed by the importance of the names on it, and there was just as little doubt that she would return the valuable content as soon as she noticed it.

But to what unconscious thought should this chance action, which was made possible through forgetfulness, give expression? The visitor in this case had a very definite relation to my patient and myself. It was she who at one time had recommended me as physician to the suffering girl, and if I am, not mistaken my patient considered herself indebted for this advice. Should this halved hundred-dollar note perhaps represent a fee for her mediation? That still remained enigmatic.

But other material was added to this beginning. Several days before a woman mediator of a different sort had inquired of a relative whether the gracious young lady wished to make the acquaintance of a certain gentleman, and that morning, some hours before the woman's visit, the wooing letter of the suitor arrived, giving occasion for much mirth. When therefore the visitor opened the conversation with inquiries regarding the health of my patient, the latter could well have thought: "You certainly found me the right doctor, but if you could assist me in obtaining the right husband (and a child) I should be still more grateful."

Both mediators became fused into one in this repressed thought, and she handed the visitor the fee which her fantasy was ready to give the other. This resolution became perfectly convincing when I add that I had told her of such chance or symptomatic actions only the previous evening. She then took advantage of the next occasion to produce an analogous action.

We can undertake a grouping of these extremely frequent chance and symptomatic actions according to their occurrence as habitual, regular under certain circumstances, and as isolated ones. The first group (such as playing with the watch-chain, fingering one's beard, and so on), which can almost serve as a characteristic of the person concerned, is related to the numerous tic movements, and certainly deserves to be dealt with in connection with the latter. In the second group I place the playing with one's cane, the scribbling with one's pencil, the jingling of coins in one's pocket, kneading dough and other plastic materials, all sorts of handling of one's clothing, and many other actions of the same order.

These playful occupations during psychic treatment regularly conceal sense and meaning to which other expression is denied. Generally the person in question knows nothing about it; he is unaware whether he is doing the same thing or whether he has imitated certain modifications in his customary playing, and he also fails to see or hear the effects of these actions. For example, he does not hear the noise which is produced by the jingling of coins, and he is astonished and incredulous when his attention is called to it. Of equal significance to the physician, and worthy of his observation, is everything that one does with his clothing often without noticing it. Every change in the customary attire, every little negligence, such as an unfastened button, every trace of exposure means to express something that the wearer of the apparel does not wish to say directly, usually he is entirely unconscious of it.

The interpretation of these trifling chance actions, as well as the proof for their interpretation, can be demonstrated every time with sufficient certainty from the surrounding circumstances during the treatment, from the themes under discussion, and from the ideas that come to the surface when attention is directed to the seeming accident. Because of this connection I will refrain from supporting my assertions by reporting examples with their analyses; but I mention these matters because I believe that they have the same meaning in normal persons as in my patients.

I cannot, however, refrain from showing by at least one example how closely an habitually accomplished symbolic action may be connected with the most intimate and important part of the life of a normal individual.[1]

"As Professor Freud has taught us, the symbolism in the infantile life of the normal plays a greater role than was expected from earlier psychoanalytic experiences. In view of this the following brief analysis may be of general interest, especially on account of its medical aspects.

"A doctor on rearranging his furniture in a new house came across a straight, wooden stethoscope, and, after pausing to decide where he should put it, was impelled to place it on the side of his writing-desk in such a position that it stood exactly between his chair and the one reserved for his patients. The act in itself was certainly odd, for in the first place the straight stethoscope served no purpose, as he invariably used a binaural one; and in the second place all his medical apparatus and instruments were always kept in drawers, with the sole exception of this one. However, he gave no thought to the matter until one day it was brought to his notice by a patient who had never seen a wooden stethoscope, asking him what it was. On being told, she asked why he kept it there. He answered in an offhand way that that place was as good as any other. This, however, started him thinking, and he wondered whether there had been an unconscious motive in his action. Being interested in the psychoanalytic method, he asked me to investigate the matter.

"The first memory that occurred to him was the fact that when a medical student he had been struck by the habit his hospital interne had of always carrying in his hand a wooden stethoscope on his ward visits, although he never used it. He greatly admired this interne, and was much attached to him. Later on, when he himself became an interne he contracted the same habit, and would feel very uncomfortable if by mistake he left the room without having the instrument to swing in his hand. The aimlessness of the habit was shown, not only by the fact that the only stethoscope he ever used was a binaural one, which he carried in his pocket, but also in that it was continued when he was a surgical interne and never needed any stethoscope at all.

"From this it was evident that the idea of the instrument in question had in some way or other become invested with a greater psychic significance than normally belongs to it—in other words, that to the subject it stood for more than it does for other people. The idea must have got unconsciously associated with some other one, which it symbolized, and from which it derived its additional fullness of meaning. I will forestall the rest of the analysis by saying what this secondary idea was—namely, a phallic one; the way in which this curious association had been formed will presently be related. The discomfort he experienced in hospital on missing the instrument, and the relief and assurance the presence of it gave him, was related to what is known as a 'castration-complex'—namely, a childhood fear, often continued in a disguised form into adult life, lest a private part of his body should be taken away from him, just as playthings so often were. The fear was due to paternal threats that it would be cut off if he were not a good boy, particularly in a certain direction. This is a very common complex, and accounts for a great deal of general nervousness and lack of confidence in later years.

"Then came a number of childhood memories relating to his family doctor. He had been strongly attached to this doctor as a child, and during the analysis long-buried memories were recovered of a double fantasy he had in his fourth year concerning the birth of a younger sister—namely, that she was the child (1) of himself and his mother, the father being relegated to the background, and (2) of the doctor and himself; in this he thus played both a masculine and feminine part.[2] At the time, when his curiosity was being aroused by the event, he could not help noticing; the prominent share taken by the doctor in the proceedings, and the subordinate position occupied by the father: the significance of this for his later life will presently be pointed out.

"The stethoscope association was formed through many connections. In the first place, the physical appearance of the instrument- - a straight, rigid, hollow tube, having a small bulbous summit at one extremity and a broad base at the other—and the fact of its being the essential part of the medical paraphernalia, the instrument with which the doctor performed his magical and interesting feats, were matters that attracted his boyish attention. He had had his chest repeatedly examined by the doctor at the age of six, and distinctly recollected the voluptuous sensation of feeling the latter's head near him pressing the wooden stethoscope into his chest, and of the rhythmic to-and-fro respiratory movement. He had been struck by the doctor's habit of carrying his stethoscope inside his hat; he found it interesting that the doctor should carry his chief instrument concealed about his person, always handy when he went to see patients, and that he only had to take off his hat (i.e., a part of his clothing) and 'pull it out.' At the age of eight he was impressed by being told by an older boy that it was the doctor's custom to get into bed with his women patients. It is certain that the doctor, who was young and handsome, was extremely popular among the women of the neighborhood, including the subject's own mother. The doctor and his 'instrument' were therefore the objects of great interest throughout his boyhood.

"It is probable that, as in many other cases, unconscious identification with the family doctor had been a main motive in determining the subject's choice of profession. It was here doubly conditioned (1) by the superiority of the doctor on certain interesting occasions to the father, of whom the subject was very jealous, and (2) by the doctor's knowledge of forbidden topics[3] and his opportunity for illicit indulgence. The subject admitted that he had on several occasions experienced erotic temptations in regard to his women patients; he had twice fallen in love with one, and finally had married one.

"The next memory was of a dream, plainly of a homosexual-masochistic nature; in it a man, who proved to be a replacement figure of the family doctor, attacked the subject with a 'sword.' The idea of a sword, as is so frequently the case in dreams, represented the same idea that was mentioned above to be associated with that of a wooden stethoscope. The thought of a sword reminded the subject of the passage in the *Nibelung Saga*, where Sigurd sleeps with his naked sword (*Gram*) between him and Brunhilda, an incident that had always greatly struck his imagination.

"The meaning of the symptomatic act now at last became clear. The subject had placed his wooden stethoscope between him and his patients, just as Sigurd had placed his sword (an equivalent symbol) between him and the maiden he was not to touch. The act was a compromise-formation; it served both to gratify in his imagination the repressed wish to enter into nearer relations with an attractive patient (interposition of phallus), and at the same time to remind him that this wish was not to become a reality (interposition of sword). It was, so to speak, a charm against yielding to temptation.

"I might add that the following passage from Lord Lytton's *Richelieu* made a great impression on the boy:

> *'Beneath the rule of men entirely great*
> *The pen is mightier than the sword,'* [4]

When I asked him what need he had of this pen, he replied in a characteristic manner, 'I have so much to express.'

"This analysis again reminds us of the profound views that are afforded us in the psychic life through the 'harmless' and 'senseless' actions, and how early in life the tendency to symbolization develops."

I can also relate an experience from my psychotherapeutic practice in which the hand, playing with a mass of bread-crumbs, gave evidence of an eloquent declaration. My patient was a boy not yet thirteen years of age, who had been very hysterical for two years. I finally took him for psychoanalytic treatment, after a lengthy stay at a hydrotherapeutic institution had proved futile. My supposition was that he must have had sexual experiences, and that, corresponding to his age, he had been troubled by sexual questions; but I was cautious about helping him with explanations as I wished to test further my assumption. I was therefore curious as to the manner in which the desired material would evince itself in him.

One day it struck me that he was rolling something between the fingers of his right hand; he would thrust it into his pocket and there continue playing with it, then would draw it out again, and so on. I did not ask what he had in his hand; but as he suddenly opened his hand he showed it to me. It was bread-crumbs kneaded into a mass. At the next session he again brought along a mass, and in the course of our conversation, although his eyes were closed, modeled a figure with an incredible rapidity which excited my interest. Without doubt it was a manikin like the crudest prehistoric idols, with a head, two arms, two legs, and an appendage between the legs which he drew out to a long point.

This was scarcely completed when he kneaded the manikin together again: later he allowed it to remain, but modeled an identical appendage on the flat of the back and on other parts in order to veil the meaning of the first. I wished to show him that I had understood him, but at the same time I wanted to deprive him of the evasion that he had thought of nothing while actively forming these figures. With this intention I suddenly asked him whether he remembered the story of the Roman king who gave his son's envoy a pantomimic answer in his garden.

The boy did not wish to recall what he must have learned so much more recently than I. He asked if that was the story of the slave on whose bald skull the answer was written. I told him, "No, that belonged to Greek history," and related the following: "King Tarquinius Superbus had induced his son Sextus to steal into a Latin city. The son, who had later obtained a foothold in the city, sent a messenger to the king asking what steps he should take next. The king gave no answer, but went into his garden, had the question repeated there, and silently struck off the heads of the largest and most beautiful poppies. All that the messenger could do was to report this to Sextus, who understood his father, and caused the most distinguished citizens of the city to be removed by assassination."

While I was speaking the boy stopped kneading, and as I was relating what the king did in his garden, I noticed that at the words "silently struck" he tore off the head of the manikin with a movement as quick as lightning. He therefore understood me, and showed that he was also understood by me. Now I could question him directly, and gave him the information that he desired, and in a short time the neurosis came to an end.

The symptomatic actions which: we observe in inexhaustible abundance in healthy as well as in nervous people are worthy of our interest for more than one reason. To the physician they often serve as valuable indications for orienting himself in new or unfamiliar conditions; to the keen observer they often betray everything, occasionally even more than he cares to know. He who is familiar with its application sometimes feels like King Solomon, who, according to the Oriental legend, understood the language of animals.

One day I was to examine a strange young man at his mother's home. As he came towards me I was attracted by a large stain on his trousers, which by its peculiar stiff edges I recognized as one produced by albumen. After a moment's embarrassment the young man excused this stain by remarking that he was hoarse and therefore drank a raw egg, and that some of the slippery white of the egg had probably fallen on his clothes. To confirm his statements he showed the eggshell which could still be seen on a small plate in the room. The suspicious spot was thus explained in this harmless way; but as his mother left us alone I thanked him for having so greatly facilitated the diagnosis for me, and without further procedure I took as the topic of our discussion his confession that he was suffering from the effects of masturbation.

Another time I called on a woman as rich as she was miserly and foolish, who was in the habit of giving the physician the task of working his way through a heap of her complaints before he could reach the simple cause of her condition. As I entered she was sitting at a small table engaged in arranging silver dollars in little piles as she rose she tumbled some of the pieces of money to the floor. I helped her pick them up, but interrupted the recitation of her misery by remarking: "Has your good son-in-law been spending so much of your money again?" She bitterly denied this, only to relate a few moments later the lamentable story of the aggravation caused by her son-in-law's extravagances. And she has not sent for me since. I cannot maintain that one always makes friends of those to whom he tells the meaning of their symptomatic actions.

He who observes his fellow-men while at table will be able to verify in them the nicest and most instructive symptomatic actions.

Dr. Hans Sachs relates the following:

"I happened to be present when an elderly, couple related to me partook of their supper. The lady had stomach trouble and was forced to follow a strict diet. A roast was put before the husband, and he requested his wife, who was not allowed to partake of this food, to give him the mustard. The wife opened the closet and took out the small bottle of stomach drops, and placed it on the table before her husband. Between the barrel-shaped mustard-glass and the small drop-bottle there was naturally no similarity through which the mishandling could be explained; yet the wife only noticed the mistake after her husband laughingly called her attention to it. The sense of this symptomatic action needs no explanation."

For an excellent example of this kind which was very skillfully utilized by the observer, I am indebted to Dr. Bernh. Dattner (Vienna):

"I dined in a restaurant with my colleague H., a doctor of philosophy. He spoke about the injustice done to probationary students, and added that even before he finished his studies he was placed as secretary to the ambassador, or rather the extraordinary plenipotentiary Minister to Chili [sic]. 'But,' he added, 'the minister was afterwards transferred, and I did not make any effort to meet the newly appointed.' While uttering the last sentence he was lifting a piece of pie to his mouth, but he let it drop as if out of awkwardness. I immediately grasped the hidden sense of this symptomatic action, and remarked to my colleague, who was unacquainted with psychoanalysis, 'You really allowed a very choice morsel to slip from you.' He did not realize, however, that my words could equally refer to his symptomatic action, and he repeated the same words I uttered with a peculiarly agreeable and surprising vividness, as if I had actually -taken the words from his mouth: 'It was really a very choice morsel that I allowed to get away from me.' He then followed this remark with a detailed description of his clumsiness, which has cost him this very remunerative position.

"The sense of this symbolic action becomes clearer if we remember that my colleague had scruples about telling me, almost a perfect stranger, concerning his precarious material situation, and his repressed thought took on the mask of symptomatic action which expressed symbolically what was meant to be concealed, and the speaker thus got relief from his unconscious."

That the taking away or taking along things without any apparent intention may prove to be senseful [*sic*] may be shown by the following examples .

1. Dr. B. Dattner relates: "An acquaintance paid the first after-marriage visit to a highly regarded lady friend of his youth. He told me of this visit and expressed his surprise at the fact that he failed in his resolution to visit with her only a short time, and then reported to me a rather strange faulty act which happened to him there.

"The husband of this friend, who took part in the conversation, was looking for a box of matches which he was sure was on the table when he came there. My acquaintance, too, looked through his pockets to ascertain whether he had not put it in his pocket, but without avail. Sometime later he actually found it in his pocket, and was struck by the fact that there was only one match in the box.

"A dream a few days later showing the box symbolism in reference to the friend of his youth confirmed my explanation. With the symptomatic action my acquaintance meant to announce his priority-right and the exclusiveness of his possession (it contained only one match)."

Dr. Hans Sachs relates the following: "Our cook is very fond of a certain kind of pie. There is no possible doubt about this, as it is the only kind of pastry which she always prepares well. One Sunday she brought this pie to the table, took it off the pie-plate, and proceeded to remove the dishes used in the former course, but on the top of this pile she placed the pie, and disappeared with it into the kitchen.

We first thought that she had something to improve on the pie, but as she failed to appear my wife rang the bell and asked, 'Betty, what happened to the pie?' to which the girl answered, without comprehending the question, 'How is that?' We had to call her attention to the fact that she carried the pie back to the kitchen. She had put it on the pile of dishes, taken it out, and put it away 'without noticing it.'

"The next day, when we were about to consume the rest of the pie, my wife noticed that there was as much of it as we had left the day before—that is, the girl had disdained to eat the portion of her favorite dish which was rightly hers. Questioned why she did not eat the pie, she answered, somewhat embarrassed, that she did not care for it.

"The infantile attitude is distinctly noticeable on both occasions—first the childish insatiableness in refusing to share with anybody the object of her wishes, then the reaction of spite which is just as childish: 'If you grudge it to me, keep it for yourself, I want nothing of it.' "

Chance or symptomatic actions occurring in affairs of married life have often a most serious significance, and could lead those who do not concern themselves with the psychology of the unconscious to a belief in omens. It is not an auspicious beginning if a young woman loses her wedding-ring on her wedding-tour, even if it were only mislaid and soon found.

I know a woman, now divorced, who in the management of her business affairs frequently signed her maiden name many years before she actually resumed it.

Once I was the guest of a newly married couple and heard the young woman laughingly relate her latest experience, how, on the day succeeding her return from the wedding tour she had sought out her single sister in order to go shopping with her as in former times, while her husband was attending business. Suddenly she noticed a man on the opposite side of the street; nudging her sister she said, "Why, that is surely Mr. L." She forgot that for some weeks this man had been her husband. I was chilled at this tale, but I did not dare draw any inferences. The little story came back to me only several years later, after this marriage had ended most unhappily .

The following observation, which could as well have found a place among the examples of forgetting, was taken from a noteworthy work published in French by A. Maeder.[5]

"Une dame nous racontait récemment qu'elle avait oublie d'essayer sa robe de noce et s'en souvint la veille du marriage, à huit heur du soir, la couturière désespérait de voir sa cliente. Ce détail suffit à montrer que la fiancée ne se sentait pas très hereuse de porter une robe d'épouse, elle cherchait à oublier cette représentation pénible. Elle est aujourd 'hui . . . divorcée."

A friend who has learned to observe signs related to me that the great actress Eleanora Duse introduces a symptomatic action into one of her roles which shows very nicely from what depth she draws her acting. It is a drama dealing with adultery; she has just been discussing with her husband and now stands soliloquizing before the seducer makes his appearance. During this short interval she plays with her wedding-ring, she pulls it off, replaces it, and finally takes it off again. She is now ready for the other.

I know of an elderly man who married a young girl, and instead of starting at once on his wedding tour he decided to spend the night in a hotel. Scarcely had they reached the hotel, when he noticed with fright that he was without his wallet, in which he had the entire sum of money for the wedding tour; he must have mislaid or lost it. He was still able to reach his servant by telephone; the latter found the missing article in the coat discarded for the travelling clothes and brought it to the hotel to the waiting bridegroom, who had thus entered upon his marriage without means.

It is consoling to think that the "losing of objects" by people is merely an unsuspected extension of a symptomatic action, and is thus welcome at least to the secret intention of the loser. Often it is only an expression of slight appreciation of the lost article, a secret dislike for the same, or perhaps for the person from whom it came, or the desire to lose this object was transferred to it from other and more important objects through symbolic association. The loss of valuable articles serves as an expression of diverse feelings; it may either symbolically represent a repressed thought—that is, it may bring back a memory which one would rather not hear—of it may represent a sacrifice to the obscure forces of fate, the worship of which is not yet entirely extinct even with us. [6]

The following examples will illustrate these statements concerning the losing of objects:

Dr. B. Dattner states: "A colleague related to me that he lost his steel pencil which he had had for over two years, and which, on account of its superior quality, was highly prized by him. Analysis elicited the following facts: The day before he had received a very disagreeable letter from his brother-in-law, the concluding sentence of which read: 'At present I have neither the desire nor the time to assist you in your carelessness and laziness.' The effect connected with this letter was so powerful that the next day he promptly sacrificed the pencil which was a present from this brother-in-law in order not to be burdened with his favors."

Brill reports the following example: "A doctor took exception to the following statement in my book, 'We never lose what we really want' (*Psychoanalysis, its Theories and Practical Application*). His wife, who is very interested in psychological subjects, read with him the chapter on "Psychopathology of Everyday Life "; they were both very much impressed with the novelty of the ideas, and so on, and were very willing to accept most of the statements. He could not, however, agree with the above-given statement because, as he said to his wife, 'I surely did not wish to lose my knife.' He referred to a valuable knife given to him by his wife, which he highly prized, the loss of which caused him much pain.

"It did not take his wife very long to discover the solution for this loss in a manner to convince them both of the accuracy of my statement. When she presented him with this knife he was a bit loath to accept it. Although he considered himself quite emancipated, he nevertheless entertained some superstition about giving or accepting a knife as a gift, because it is said that a knife cuts friendship. He even remarked this to his wife, who only laughed at his superstition. He had the knife for years before it disappeared.

"Analysis brought out the fact that the disappearance of the knife was directly connected with a period when there were violent quarrels between himself and his wife, which threatened to end in separation. They lived happily together until his step-daughter (it was his second marriage) came to live with them. His daughter was the cause of many misunderstandings, and it was at the height of these quarrels that he lost the knife.

"The unconscious activity is very nicely shown in this symptomatic action. In spite of his apparent freedom from superstition, he still unconsciously believed that a donated knife may cut friendship between the persons concerned. The losing of it was simply an unconscious defense against losing his wife, and by sacrificing the knife he made the superstitious ban impotent."

In a lengthy discussion and with the aid of dream analysis[7] Otto Rank made clear the sacrificial tendency with its deep-reaching motivation. It must be said that just such symptomatic actions often give us access to the understanding of the intimate psychic life of the person.

Of the many isolated chance-actions, I will relate one example which showed a deeper meaning even without analysis. This example clearly explains the conditions under which such symptoms may be produced most casually, and also shows that an observation of practical importance may be attached to it. During a summer tour it happened that I had to wait several days at a certain place for the arrival of my travelling companions. In the meantime I made the acquaintance of a young man, who also seemed lonely and was quite willing to join me. As we lived at the same hotel it was quite natural that we should take all our meals and our walks together.

On the afternoon of the third day he suddenly informed me that he expected his wife to arrive on that evening's express train. My psychological interest was now aroused, as it had already struck me that morning that my companion rejected my proposal to make a long excursion, and in our short walk he objected to a certain path as too steep and dangerous. During our afternoon walk he suddenly thought that I must be hungry and insisted that I should not delay my evening meal on his account, that he would not sup before his wife's arrival. I understood the hint and seated myself at the table while he went to the station.

The next morning we met in the foyer of the hotel. He presented me to his wife, and added, "Of course, you will breakfast with us? " I had to attend first to a small matter in the next street, but assured him that I would return shortly. Later, as I entered the breakfast-room, I noticed that the couple were at a small table near the window, both seated on the same side of it. On the opposite side there was only one chair, which was covered, however, with a man's large and heavy coat. I understood well the meaning of this unintentional, none the less expressive, disposition of the coat. It meant this: "There is no room for you here, you are superfluous now."

The man did not notice that I remained standing before the table, being unable to take the seat, but his wife noticed it, and quickly nudged her husband and whispered: "Why, you have covered the gentleman's place with your coat."

These as well as other similar experiences have caused me to think that the actions executed unintentionally must inevitably become the source of misunderstanding in human relations. The perpetrator of the act, who is unaware of any associated intention, takes no account of it, and does not hold himself responsible for it. On the other hand, the second party, having regularly utilized even such acts as those of his partner to draw conclusions as to the purpose and meaning, recognizes more of the stranger's psychic processes than the latter is ready either to admit or believe that he has imparted. He becomes indignant when these conclusions drawn from his symptomatic actions are held up to him; he declares them baseless because he does not see any conscious intention in their execution, and complains of being misunderstood by the other. Close examination shows that such misunderstandings are based on the fact that the person is too fine an observer and understands too much. The more "nervous" two persons are the more readily will they give each other cause for disputes, which are based on the fact that one as definitely denies about his own person what he is sure to accept about the other.

And this is, indeed, the punishment for the inner dishonesty to which people grant expression under the guise of "forgetting," of erroneous actions and accidental emotions, a feeling which they would do better to confess to themselves and others when they can no longer control it. As a matter of fact it can be generally affirmed that everyone is continually practicing psychoanalysis on his neighbors, and consequently learns to know them better than each individual knows himself. The road following the admonition leads through study of one's own apparently casual commissions and omissions.

Footnotes

[1] *"Beitrag zur Symbolik im Alltag von Ernest Jones," Zentralb. f. Psychoanalyse, i. 3, 1911.*

[2] *Psychoanalytic research, with the penetration of infantile amnesia, has shown that this apparent precocity is a less abnormal occurrence than was previously supposed.*

[3] *The term " medical questions" is a common periphrasis for " sexual questions."*

[4] *Cf. Oldham's "I wear my pen as others do their sword."*

[5] *Maeder, "Contribution a la psychologie de la vie quotidienne," Arch. des psychologie, T. vi. 1906.*

[6] *Here is another small collection of various symptomatic actions in normal and neurotic persons. An elderly colleague who does not like to lose at cards had to pay one evening a large sum of money in consequence of his losses; he did this without complaint, but with a peculiar constrained temper. After his departure it was discovered that he had left at this place practically everything he had with him, spectacles, cigar-case, and handkerchief. That would be readily translated into the words: "You robbers, you have nicely plundered me." A man who suffers from occasional sexual impotence, which has its origin in the intimacy of his infantile relations to his mother,*

relates that he is in the habit of embellishing pamphlets and notes with an S, the initial of his mother's name. He cannot bear the idea of having letters from home come in contact with other unsanctified correspondence, and therefore finds it necessary to keep the former separate. A young woman suddenly flings open the door of the consulting-room while her predecessor is still present. She excused herself on the ground of "thoughtlessness"; it soon came to light that she demonstrated her curiosity which caused her at an earlier time to intrude into the bedroom of her parents. Girls who are proud of their beautiful hair know so well how to manipulate combs and hairpins, that in the midst of conversation their hair becomes loosened. During the treatment (in a reclining position) some men scatter change from their pockets and thus pay for the hour of treatment; the amount scattered is in proportion to their estimation of the work. Whoever forgets articles in the doctor's office, such as eye-glasses, gloves, handbags, generally indicates that he cannot tear himself away and is anxious to return soon. Ernest Jones says: "One can almost measure the success with which a physician is practicing psychotherapy, for instance, by the size of the collection of umbrellas, handkerchiefs, purses, and so on, that he could make in a month. The slightest habits and acts performed with a minimum of attention, such as the winding of a clock before retiring to sleep, the putting out of lights before leaving the room, and similar actions, are occasionally subject to disturbances which clearly demonstrate the influence of the unconscious complex, and what is thought to be the strongest "habits." In the journal Coenobium, Maeder relates about a hospital physician who, on account of an important matter, desired to get to the city that evening, although he was on duty and had no right to leave the hospital. On his return he noticed to his surprise that there was a light in his room. On leaving the room he had forgotten to put it out, something that had never happened before. But he soon grasped the motive of this forgetting. The hospital superintendent who lived in the same house must have concluded from the light in the room that he was at home. A man overburdened with worries and subject to occasional depressions assured me that he regularly forgot to wind his watch on those evenings when life seemed too hard and unfriendly. In this omission to wind his watch he symbolically expressed that it was a matter of indifference to him whether he lived to see the next day. Another man who was personally unknown to me wrote: "Having been struck by a terrible misfortune, life appeared so harsh and unsympathetic, that I imagined that I had not sufficient strength to live to see the next day. I then noticed that almost every day I forgot to wind my watch, something that I never omitted before. I had been in the habit of doing it regularly before retiring in an almost mechanical and unconscious manner. It was only very seldom that I thought of it, and that happened when I had something important for the next day which held my interest. "Should this be considered a symptomatic action? I really cannot explain it." Whoever will take the trouble, like Jung (The Psychology of Dementia Præcox, translated by Peterson and Brill), or Maeder ("Une voie nouvelle en Psychologie—Freud et son ecole," Coenobium, Lugano, 1906), to pay attention to melodies which one hums to himself aimlessly and unconsciously, will regularly discover the relation of the melody's text to a theme which occupies the person at that time.

[7] Das Verlieren als Symptom-handlung," Zentralb. f. Psychoanalyse, i. 10-11.

CHAPTER 10

Errors

ERRORS OF MEMORY are distinguished from forgetting and false recollections through one feature only, namely, that the error false recollection) is not recognized as such but finds credence. However, the use of the expression "error" seems to depend on still another condition. We speak of "erring." instead of "falsely recollecting where the character of the objective reality is emphasized in the psychic material to be reproduced—that is, where something other than a fact of my own psychic life is to be remembered, or rather something that may be confirmed or refuted through the memory of others. The reverse of the error in memory in this sense is formed by ignorance.

In my book *The Interpretation of Dreams,* [1] I was responsible for a series of errors in historical, and above all, in material facts, which I was astonished to discover after the appearance of the book. On closer examination I found that they did not originate from my ignorance, but could be traced to errors of memory explainable by means of analysis.

(*a*) I indicated as *Schiller's* birthplace the city of *Marburg*, a name which recurs in *Styria*. The error is found in the analysis of a dream during a night journey from which I was awakened by the conductor calling out the name of the station *Marburg*. In the contents of the dream inquiry is made concerning a book by *Schiller*. But *Schiller* was not born in the university town of *Marburg* but in the Swabian city *Marbach*. I maintain that I always knew this.

(*b*) *Hannibal's* father is called *Hasdrubal*. This error was particularly annoying to me, but it was most corroborative of my conception of such errors. Few readers of the book are better posted on the history of the *Barkides* than the author who wrote this error and overlooked it in three proofs. The name of Hannibal's father was *Hamilcar Barkas*; *Hasdrubal* was the name of *Hannibal's* brother as well as that of his brother-in-law and predecessor in command.

(*c*) I assert that *Zeus* emasculates his father *Kronos*, and hurls him from the throne. This horror I have erroneously advanced by a generation; according to Greek mythology it was *Kronos* who committed this on his father *Uranos*.[2]

How is it to be explained that my memory furnished me with false material on these points, while it usually places the most remote and unusual material at my disposal, as the readers of my books can verify? And, what is more, in three carefully executed proof-readings I passed over these errors as if struck blind.

Goethe said of Lichtenberg: "Where he cracks a joke, there lies a concealed problem." Similarly we can affirm of these passages cited from my book: back of every error is a repression. More accurately stated: the error conceals a falsehood, disfigurement which is ultimately based on repressed material. In the analysis of the dreams there reported, I was compelled by the very nature of the theme to which the dream thoughts related, on the one hand, to break off the analysis in some places before it had reached its completion, and on the other hand, to remove an indiscreet detail through a slight disfigurement of its outline. I could not act differently, and had no other choice if I was at all to offer examples and illustrations. My constrained position was necessarily brought about by the peculiarity of dreams, which give expression repressed thoughts, or to material which is incapable of becoming conscious. In spite of this it is said that enough material remained to offend the more sensitive souls. The disfigurement or concealment of the continuing thoughts known to me could not be accomplished without leaving some trace. What I wished to repress has often against my will obtruded itself on what I have taken up, and evinced itself in the matter as an unnoticeable error. Indeed, each of the three examples given is based on the same theme: the errors are the results of repressed thoughts which occupy themselves with my deceased father.

(*ad a*) Whoever reads through the dream analyzed previously will find some parts unveiled; in some parts he will be able to divine through allusions that I have broken off the thoughts which would have contained an unfavorable criticism of my father. In the continuation of this line of thoughts and memories there lies an annoying tale, in which books and a business friend of my father, named *Marburg*, play a part; it is the same name the calling out of which in the southern railway-station had aroused me from sleep. I wished to suppress this Mr. *Marburg* in the analysis from myself and my readers: he avenged himself by intruding where he did not belong, and changed the name of Schiller's birthplace from *Marbach* to *Marburg*.

(*ad b*) The error *Hasdrubal* in place of *Hamilcar*, the name of the brother instead of that of the father, originated from an association which dealt with the Hannibal fantasies of my college years and my dissatisfaction with the conduct of my father towards the "enemies of our people." I could have continued and recounted how my attitude toward my father was changed by a visit to England, where I made the acquaintance of my half-brother, by a previous marriage of my father. My brother's oldest son was my age exactly. Thus the age relations were no hindrance to a fantasy which may be stated thus: how much pleasanter it would be had I been born the son of my brother instead of the son of my father! This suppressed fantasy then falsified the text of my book at the point where I broke off the analysis, by forcing me to put the name of the brother for that of the father.

(*ad c*) The influence of the memory of this same brother is responsible for my having advanced by a generation the mythological horror of the Greek deities. One of the admonitions of my brother has lingered long in my memory. " Do not forget one thing concerning your conduct in life," he said: " you belong not to the second but really to the third generation of your father." Our father had remarried at an advanced age, and was therefore an old man to his children by the second marriage. I commit the error mentioned where I discuss the piety between parents and children.

Several times friends and patients have called my attention to the fact that in reporting their dreams or alluding to them in dream analyses, I have related inaccurately the circumstances experienced by us in common. These are also historic errors. On re-examining such individual cases I have found that my recollection of the facts was unreliable only where I had purposely disfigured or concealed something in the analysis. Here again we have *an unobserved error as a substitute for an intentional concealment or repression.*

From these errors, which originate from repression, we must sharply distinguish those which are based on actual ignorance. Thus, for example, it was ignorance when on my excursion to Wachau I believed that I had passed the resting-place of the revolutionary leader Fischof. Only the name is common to both places. *Fischof's Emmersdorf* is located in Kärnthen. But I did not know any better.

Here is another embarrassing but instructive error, an example of temporary ignorance if you like. One day a patient reminded me to give him the two books on Venice which I had promised him, as he wished to use them in planning his Easter tour. I answered that I had them ready and went into the library to fetch them, though the truth of the matter was that I had forgotten to look them up, since I did not quite approve of my patient's journey, looking upon it as an unnecessary interruption to the treatment, and as a material loss to the physician. Thereupon I made a quick survey of the library for the books.

One was *Venedig als Kunststätte*, and besides this I imagined I had an historic work of a similar order. Certainly there was *Die Mediceer* (*The Medicis*); I took them and brought them in to him, then, embarrassed, I confessed my error. Of course I really knew that the Medicis had nothing: to do with Venice, but for a short time it did not appear to me at all incorrect. Now I was compelled to practice justice; as I had so frequently interpreted my patient's symptomatic actions I could save my prestige only by, being honest and admitting to him the secret motives of my averseness to his trip.

It may cause general astonishment to learn how much stronger is the impulse to tell the truth than is usually supposed. Perhaps it is a result of my occupation with psychoanalysis that I can scarcely lie any more. As often as I attempt a distortion I succumb to an error or some other faulty act, which betrays my dishonesty, as was manifest in this and in the preceding examples.

Of all faulty actions the mechanisms of the error seems to be the most superficial. That is, the occurrence of the error invariably indicates that the mental activity concerned had to struggle with some disturbing influence, although the nature of the error need not be determined but the quality of the disturbing idea, which may have remained obscure. It is not out of place to add that the same state of affairs may be assumed in many simple cases of lapses in speaking and writing. Every time we commit a lapse in speaking or writing we may conclude that through mental processes there has come a disturbance which is beyond our intention. It may be conceded, however, that lapses in speaking and writing often follow the laws of similarity and convenience, or the tendency to acceleration, without allowing the disturbing element to leave a trace of its own character in the error resulting from the lapses in speaking or writing. It is the responsiveness of the linguistic material which at first makes possible the determination of the error, but it also limits the same.

In order not to confine myself exclusively to personal errors I will relate a few examples which could just as well have been ranged under "Lapses in Speech" or under "Erroneously Carried-out Actions," but as ah these forms of faulty action have the same value they may as well be reported here.

(*a*) I forbade a patient to speak on the telephone to his lady-love, with whom he himself was willing to break off all relations, as each conversation only renewed the struggling against it. He was to write her his final decision, although there were some difficulties in the way of delivering the letter to her. He visited me at one o'clock to tell me that he had found a way of avoiding these difficulties, and among other things he asked me whether he might refer to me in my professional capacity.

At two o'clock while he. was engaged in com- posing the letter of refusal, he interrupted himself suddenly, and said to his mother, "Well, I have forgotten to ask the Professor whether I may use his name in the letter." He hurried to the telephone, got the connection, and asked the question, "May I speak to the Professor after his dinner?" In answer he got an astonished "Adolf, have you gone crazy I " The answering voice was the very voice which at my command he had listened to for the last time. He had simply "made a mistake," and in place of the physician's number had called up that of his beloved.

(*b*) During a summer vacation a school-teacher, a poor but excellent young man, courted the daughter of a summer resident, until the girl fell passionately in love with him, and even prevailed upon her family to countenance the matrimonial alliance in spite of the difference in position and race. One day, however, the teacher wrote his brother a letter in which he said: "Pretty, the lass is not at all, but she is very amiable, and so far so good. But whether I can make up my mind to marry a Jewess I cannot yet tell." This letter got into the hands of the fiancée, who put an end to the engagement, while at the same time his brother was wondering at the protestations of love directed to him. My informer assured me that this was really an error and not a cunning trick.

I am familiar with another case, in which a woman who was dissatisfied with her old physician, and still did not openly wish to discharge him, accomplished this purpose through the interchange of letters. Here, at least, I can assert confidently that it was error and not conscious cunning that made use, of this familiar comedy-motive.

(c) Brill[3] tells of a woman who, inquiring about a mutual friend, erroneously called her by her maiden name. Her attention having been directed to this error, she had to admit that she disliked her friend's husband and had never been satisfied with her marriage.

Maeder[4] relates a good example of how a reluctantly repressed wish can be satisfied by means of an "error." A colleague wanted to enjoy his day of leave of absence absolutely undisturbed, but he, also felt that he ought to go to Lucerne to pay a call which he did not anticipate with any pleasure. After long reflection, however, he concluded to go. For pastime on the train he, read the daily newspapers. He journeyed from Zurich to Arth Goldau, where he changed trains for Lucerne, all the time engrossed in reading. Presently the conductor informed him that he was in the wrong train—that is, he had got into the one which was returning from Goldau to Zurich, whereas his ticket was for Lucerne.

A very similar trick was played by me quite recently. I had promised my oldest brother to pay him a long-due visit at a sea-shore in England; as the time was short I felt obliged to travel by the shortest route and without interruption. I begged for a day's sojourn in Holland, but he thought that I could stop there on my return trip. Accordingly I journeyed from Munich through Cologne to Rotterdam—Hook of Holland—where I was to take the steamer at midnight to Harwich. In Cologne I had to change cars; I left my train to go into the Rotterdam express, but it was not to be found. I asked various railway employees, was sent from one platform to another, got into an exaggerated state of despair, and could easily reckon that during this fruitless search I had probably missed my connection.

After this was corroborated, I pondered whether or not I should spend the night in Cologne. This was favored by a feeling of piety, for according to an old family tradition, my ancestors were once expelled from this city during a persecution of the Jews. But eventually I came to another decision; I took a later train to Rotterdam, where I arrived late at night and was thus compelled to spend a day in Holland. This brought me the fulfillment of a long-fostered wish—the sight of the beautiful Rembrandt paintings at The Hague and in the Royal Museum at Amsterdam. Not before the next forenoon, while collecting my impressions during the railway journey in England, did I definitely remember that only a few steps from the place where I got off at the railroad station in Cologne, indeed, on the same platform, I had seen a large sign, "Rotterdam—Hook of Holland." There stood the train in which I should have continued my journey.

If one does not wish to assume that, contrary to my brother's orders, I had really resolved to admire the Rembrandt pictures on my way to him, then the fact that despite clear directions I hurried away and looked for another train must be designated as an incomprehensible "blinding." Everything else—my well-acted perplexity, the emergence of the pious intention to spend the night in Cologne—was only a contrivance to hide my resolution until it had been fully accomplished.

One may possibly be disinclined to consider the class of errors which I have here explained as very numerous or particularly significant. But I leave it to your consideration whether there is no ground for extending the same points of view also to the more important errors of judgment, as evinced by people in life and science. Only for the most select and most balanced minds does it seem; possible to guard the perceived picture of external reality against the distortion to which it is otherwise subjected in its transit through the psychic individuality of the transit through the psychic individuality of the one perceiving it.

Footnotes

[1] *Translated by A. A. Brill. The Macmillan Company, New York; George Allen Company, London.*
[2] *This is not a perfect error. According to the orphic version of the myth the emasculation was performed by Zeus on his father Kronos.*
[3] *Loc. cit., p. 191.*
[4] *Nouvelles contributions, etc., Arch. de Psych., vi. 1908·*

CHAPTER 11

Combined Faulty Acts

TWO OF THE last-mentioned examples, my error which transfers the Medici to Venice and that of the young man who knew how to circumvent a command against a conversation on the telephone with his lady love, have really not been fully discussed, as after careful consideration they may be shown to represent a union of forgetting with an error. I can show the same union still more clearly in certain other examples.

(*a*) A friend related to me the following experience: "Some years ago I consented to be elected to the committee of a certain literary; society, as I supposed the organization might sometime be of use to me in assisting me in the production of my drama. Although not much interested, I attended the meetings regularly every Friday. Some months ago I was definitely assured that one of my dramas would be presented at the theatre in F., and since that time it regularly happened that I forgot the meeting of the association. As I read their program announcements I was ashamed of my forgetfulness. I reproached myself, feeling that it was certainly rude of me to stay away now when I no longer needed them, and determined that I would certainly not forget the next Friday. Continually I reminded myself of this resolution until the hour came and I stood before the door of the meeting-room. To my astonishment it was locked; the meeting: was already over. I had mistaken my day; it was already Saturday!"

(*b*) The next example is the combination of a symptomatic action with a case of mislaying; it reached me by, remote byways, but from a reliable source.

A woman travelled to Rome with her brother-in-law, a renowned artist. The visitor was highly honored by the German residents of Rome, and among other things received a gold medal of antique origin. The woman was grieved that her brother-in-law did not sufficiently appreciate the value of this beautiful gift. After she had returned home she discovered in unpacking that—without knowing how—she had brought the medal home with her. She immediately notified her brother-in-law of this by letter, and informed him that she would send it back to Rome the next day. The next day, however, the medal was so aptly mislaid that it could not be found and could not be sent back, and then it dawned on the woman what her "absent-mindedness" signified—namely, that she wished to keep, the medal herself.

(*c*) Here are some cases in which the falsified action persistently repeats itself, and at the same time also changes its mode of action:

Due to unknown motives, Jones I left a letter[1] for several days on his desk, forgetting each time to post it. He ultimately posted it, but it was returned to him from the Dead-letter Office because he forgot to address it. After addressing and posting it a second time it was again returned to him, this time without a stamp. He was then forced to recognize the unconscious opposition to the sending of the letter.

(*d*) A short account by Dr. Karl Weiss (Vienna) [2] of a case of forgetting impressively describes the futile effort to accomplish something in the face of opposition. "How persistently the unconscious activity can achieve its purpose if it has cause to prevent a resolution from being executed, and how difficult it is to guard against this tendency, will be illustrated by the following incident: An acquaintance requested me to lend him: a book and bring it to him the next day. I immediately promised it, but perceived a distinct feeling of displeasure which I could not explain at the time. Later it became clear to me: this acquaintance had owed me for years a sum of money which he evidently had no intention of returning. I did not give this matter anymore thought, but I recalled it the following: forenoon with the same feeling of displeasure, and at once said to myself: 'Your unconscious will see to it that you forget the book, but you don't wish to appear unobliging and will therefore do everything not to forget it.' I came home, wrapped the book in paper, and put it near me on the desk while I wrote some letters.

"A little later I went away, but after a few steps I recollected that I had left on the desk the letters which I wished to post. (By, the way, one of the letters was written to a person who urged me to undertake something disagreeable.) I returned, took the letters, and again left. While in the street-car it occurred to me that I had undertaken to purchase something for my: wife, and I was pleased at the thought that it would be only a small package. The association 'small package,' suddenly recalled 'book'—and only then I noticed that I did not have the book with me. Not only had I forgotten it when I left my home the first time, but I had overlooked it again when I got the letters near which it lay."

(*e*) A similar mechanism is shown in the following fully analyzed observation of Otto Rank[3]:

"A scrupulously orderly and pedantically precise man reported the following occurrence, which he considered quite remarkable: One afternoon on the street wishing to find out the time, he discovered that he had left his watch at home, an omission which to his knowledge had never occurred before. As he had an engagement elsewhere and had not enough time to return for his watch, he made use of a visit to a woman friend to borrow her watch for the evening. This was the most convenient way out of the dilemma, as he had a previous engagement to visit this lady the next day. Accordingly, he promised to return her watch at that time.

"But the following day when about to consummate this he found to his surprise that he had left the watch at home; his own watch he had with him. He then firmly, resolved to return the lady's property that same afternoon, and even followed out his resolution. But on wishing to see the time on leaving her he found to his chagrin and astonishment that he had again forgotten to take his own watch.

"The repetition of this faulty action seemed so pathologic to this order-loving man that he was quite anxious to know its psychological motivation, and when questioned whether he experienced anything disagreeable on the critical day of the first forgetting, and in what connection it had occurred, the motive was promptly found. He related that he had conversed with his mother after luncheon, shortly before leaving the house. She told him that an irresponsible relative, who had already caused him much worry and loss of money, had pawned his (the relative's) watch, and, as it was needed in the house, the relative had asked for money to redeem it. This almost "forced" loan affected our man very painfully and brought back to his memory all the disagreeable episodes perpetrated by this relative for many years.

"His symptomatic action therefore proves to be manifoldly determined. First, it gives expression to a stream of thought which runs perhaps as follows: 'I won't allow my money to be extorted this way, and if a watch is needed I will leave my own at home.' But as he needed it for the evening to keep his appointment, this intention could only be brought about on an unconscious path in the form of a symptomatic action. Second, the forgetting expresses a sentiment something like the following: "This everlasting sacrificing of money for this good-for-nothing is bound to ruin me altogether, so that I will have to give up everything.' Although the anger, according to the report of this man, was only momentary, the repetition of the same symptomatic action conclusively shows that in the unconscious it continued to act more intensely, and may be equivalent to the conscious expression: 'I cannot get this story out of my head.[4] That the lady's watch should later meet the same fate will not surprise us after knowing this attitude of the unconscious.'

"Yet there may be still other special motives which favor the transference on the 'innocent' lady's watch. The nearest motive is probably that he would have liked to keep it as a substitute for his own sacrificed watch, and that hence he forgot to return it the next day. He also might have liked to possess this watch as a souvenir of the lady. Moreover, the forgetting of the lady's watch gave him the excuse for calling on the admired one a second time; for he was obliged to visit her in the morning in reference to another matter, and with the forgetting of the watch he seemed to indicate that this visit for which an appointment had been made so long ago was too good for him to be used simply for the return of a watch.

"Twice forgetting his own watch and thus making possible the substitution of the lady's watch speaks for the fact that our man unconsciously endeavored to avoid carrying both watches at the same time. He obviously thought of avoiding the appearance of superfluity which would have stood out in striking contrast to the want of the relative; but, on the other hand, he utilized this as a self-admonition against his apparent intention to marry this lady, reminding himself that he was tied to his family (mother) by indissoluble obligations.

"Finally, another reason for the forgetting of the lady's watch may be sought in the fact that the evening before he, a bachelor, was ashamed to be seen with a lady's watch by his friends, so that he only looked at it stealthily, and in order to evade the repetition of this painful situation he could not take the watch along. But as he was obliged to return it, there resulted here, too, an unconsciously performed symptomatic action which proved to be a compromise formation between conflicting emotional feelings and a dearly bought victory of the unconscious instance."

In the same discussion Rank has also paid attention to the very interesting! relation of "faulty actions and dreams," which cannot, however, be followed here without a comprehensive analysis of the dream with which the faulty action is connected. I once dreamed at great length that I had lost my pocket-book. In the morning while dressing I actually missed it; while undressing the night before the dream I had forgotten to take it out of my trousers pocket and put it in its usual place, This forgetting was therefore not unknown to me; probably it was to give expression to an unconscious thought which was ready to appear in the dream content.

I do not mean to assert that such cases of combined faulty actions can teach anything new that we have not already seen in the individual cases. But this change in form of the faulty action, which nevertheless attains the same result, gives the plastic impression of a will working towards a definite end, and in a far more energetic way contradicts the idea that the faulty action represents something: fortuitous and requires no explanation. Not less remarkable is the fact that the conscious intention thoroughly fails to check the success of the faulty, action. Despite all, my friend did not pay his visit to the meeting of the literary society, and the woman found it impossible to give up the medal. That unconscious something which worked against these resolutions found another outlet after the first road was closed to it. It requires something other than the conscious counter-resolution to overcome the unknown motive ; it requires a psychic work which makes the unknown known to consciousness.

Footnotes

[1] Loc. cit., p. 42.

[2] Zentralb.f. Psychoanalyse, ii. 9.

[3] Zentralb. f. Psychoanalyse, ii. 5.

[4] This continued action in the unconscious manifested itself once in the form of a dream which followed the faulty action, another time in the repetition of the same or in the omission of a correction.

CHAPTER 12

Determinism, Chance, and Superstitious Beliefs

AS THE GENERAL result of the preceding separate discussions we must put down the following principle: *Certain inadequacies of our psychic capacities—whose common character will soon be more definitely determined—and certain performances which are apparently unintentional prove to be well motivated when subjected to the psychoanalytic investigation, and are determined through the consciousness of unknown motives.*

In order to belong to this class of phenomena thus explained a faulty psychic action must satisfy the following conditions:

(*a*) It must not exceed a certain measure which is firmly established through our estimation, and is designated by the expression "within normal limits."

(*b*) It must evince the character of the momentary and temporary disturbance. The same action must have been previously performed more correctly or we must always rely on ourselves to perform it more correctly; if we are corrected by others we must immediately recognize the truth of the correction and the incorrectness of our psychic action.

(*c*) If we at all perceive a faulty action, we must not perceive in ourselves any motivation of the same, but must attempt to explain it through "inattention" or attribute it to an "accident."

Thus there remain in this group the cases of forgetting and the errors, despite better knowledge, the lapses in speaking, reading, writing, the erroneously carried-out actions, and the so-called chance actions. The explanations of these so definite psychic processes are connected with a series of observations which may in part arouse further interest.

I. By abandoning a part of our psychic capacity as unexplainable through purposive ideas we ignore the realms of determinism in our mental life. Here, as in still other spheres, determinism reaches farther than we suppose. In the year 1900 I read an essay published in the *Zeit* written by the literary historian R. M. Meyer, in which he maintains, and illustrates by examples, that it is impossible to compose nonsense intentionally and arbitrarily, For some time I have been aware that it is impossible to think of a number, or even of a name, of one's own free will. If one investigates this seeming voluntary formation, let us say, of a number of many digits uttered in unrestrained mirth, it always proves to be so strictly determined that the determination seems impossible. I will now briefly discuss an example of an "arbitrarily chosen" first name, and then exhaustively analyze an analogous example of: a "thoughtlessly uttered" number.

While preparing the history of one of my patients for publication I considered what first name I should give her in the article. There seemed to be a wide choice; of course, certain names were at once excluded by me, in the first place the real name, then the names of members of my family to which I would have objected, also some female names having an especially peculiar pronunciation. But, excluding these, there should have been no need of being puzzled about such a name. It would be thought, and I myself supposed, that a whole multitude of feminine names would be placed at my disposal. Instead of this only one sprang up, no other besides it; it was the name Dora.

I inquired as to its determination: "Who else is called Doral?" I wished to reject the next idea as incredulous; it occurred to me that the nurse of my sister's children was named Dora. But I possess so much .self-control, or practice in analysis, if you like, that I held firmly to the idea and proceeded. Then a slight incident of the previous evening soon flashed through my mind which brought the looked-for determination. On my sister's dining-room table I noticed a letter bearing the address, "Miss Rosa W." Astonished, I asked whose name this was, and was informed that the right name of the supposed Dora was really Rosa, and that on accepting the position she had to lay; aside her name, because Rosa would also refer to my sister. I said pityingly, "Poor people! They cannot even retain their own names!" I now recall that on hearing this I became quiet for a moment and began to think of all sorts of serious matters which merged into the obscure, but which I could now easily bring; into my consciousness. Thus when I sought a name for a person *who could not retain her own name* no other except "Dora" occurred to me. The exclusiveness here is based, moreover, on firmer internal associations, for in the history of my patient it was a stranger in the house, the governess, who exerted a decisive influence on the course of the treatment.

This slight incident found its unexpected: continuation many years later. While discussing in a lecture the long-since published history; of the girl called Dora it occurred to me that one of my two women pupils had the very name Dora which I was obliged to utter so often in the different associations of the case. I turned to the young student, whom I knew personally, with the apology that I had really not thought that she bore the same name, and that I was ready to substitute it in my lecture by another name.

I was now confronted with the task of rapidly choosing another name, and reflected that I must not now choose the first name of the other woman student, and so set a poor example to the class, who were already quite conversant with psychoanalysis. I was therefore well pleased when the name "Erna" occurred to me as the substitute for Dora, and Erna I used in the discourse. After the lecture I asked myself whence the name "Erna" could possibly have originated, and had to laugh as I observed that the feared possibility in the choice of the substitutive name had come to pass, in part at least. The other lady's family name was Lucerna, of which Erna was a part.

In a letter to a friend I informed him that I had finished reading the proof-sheets of *The Interpretation of Dreams*, and that I did not intend to make any further changes in it, "even if it contained *2,467* mistakes." I immediately attempted to explain to myself the number, and added this little analysis as a postscript to the letter. It will be best to quote it now as I wrote it when I caught myself in this transaction:

"I will add hastily another contribution to the Psychopathology of Everyday Life. You will find in the letter the number 2,467 as a jocose and arbitrary estimation of the number of errors that may be found in the dream-book. I meant to write: no matter how large the number might be, and this one presented itself. But there is nothing arbitrary or undetermined in the psychic life. You will therefore rightly suppose that the unconscious hastened to determine the number which was liberated by consciousness. Just previous to this I had read in the paper that General E. M. had been retired as Inspector-General of Ordnance. You must know that I am interested in this man. While I was serving as military medical student he, then a colonel, once came into the hospital and said to the physician: 'You must make me well in eight days, as I have some work to do for which the Emperor is waiting.'

"At that time I decided to follow this man's career, and just think, today (1899) he is at the end of it—Inspector-General of Ordnance and already retired. I wished to figure out in what time he had covered this road, and assumed that I had seen him in the hospital in 1882. That would make 17 years. I related this to my wife, and she remarked, 'Then you, too, should be retired.' And I protested, 'The Lord forbid!' After this conversation I seated myself at the table to write to you. The previous train of thought continued, and for good reason. The figuring was incorrect; I had a definite recollection of the circumstances in my mind. I had celebrated my coming of my *24th* birthday, in the military prison (for being absent without permission). Therefore I must have seen him in 1880, which makes it 19 years ago. You then have the number 24 in 2,467! Now take the number that represents my age, 43, and add 24 years to it and you get *67*! That is, to the question whether I wished to retire I had expressed the wish to work 24 years more. Obviously I am annoyed that in the interval during which I followed Colonel M. I have not accomplished much myself, and still there is a sort of triumph in the fact that he is already finished, while I still have all before me. Thus we may justly say that not even the unintentionally thrown-out number 2,467 lacks its determination from the unconscious."

Since this first example of the interpretation of an apparently arbitrary choice of a number I have repeated a similar test with the same result; but most cases are of such intimate content that they do not lend themselves to report .

It is for this reason that I shall not hesitate to add here a very interesting analysis of a "chance number" which Dr. Alfred Adler (Vienna) received from a "perfectly healthy" man.[1] A. wrote to me: "Last night I devoted myself to the *Psychopathology of Everyday Life*, and I would have read it all through had I not been hindered by a remarkable coincidence. When I read that every number that we apparently conjure up quite arbitrarily in our consciousness has a definite meaning, I decided to test it. The number 1,734 occurred to my mind. The following associations then came up: $1,734 \div 17 = 102$; $102 \div 17 = 6$. I then separated the number into 17 and 34. I am 34 years old. .. I believe that I once told you that I consider 34 the last year of youth, and for this reason I felt miserable on my last birthday. The end of my 17th year was the beginning of a very nice and interesting period of my development. I divide my life into period of 17 years. That do the divisions signify? The number 102 recalls the fact that volume 102 Of the Reclam Universal Library is Kotzebue's play *Menschenhass und Reue* (*Human Hatred and Repentance*).

"My present psychic state is 'human hatred and repentance.' No. 6 of the U. L. (I know a great many numbers by heart) is Mullner's 'Schuld' (Fault). I am constantly annoyed at the thought that it is through my own fault that I have not become what I could have been with my abilities.

"I then asked myself, 'What is No. 17 of U. L.?' But I could not recall it. But as I positively knew it before, I assumed that I wished to forget this number. All reflection was in vain. I wished to continue with my reading, but I read only mechanically without understanding a word, for I was annoyed by the number 17. I extinguished the light and :continued my search. It finally came to me that number 17 must be a play by Shakespeare. But which one! I thought of Hero and Leander. Apparently a stupid attempt of my will to distract me. I finally arose and consulted the catalogue of the U. L. Number 17 was *Macbeth*! To my surprise I had to discover that I knew nothing of the play, despite the fact that it did not interest me any less than any other Shakespearean drama. I only thought of murder, Lady Macbeth, witches, 'nice is ugly,' and that I found Schiller's version of *Macbeth* very nice. Undoubtedly I also wished to forget the play. Then it occurred to me that 17 and 34 may be divided by 17 and result in 1 and 2. Numbers 1 and 2 of the U. L. is Goethe's *Faust*. Formerly I found much of Faust in me."

We must regret that the discretion of the physician did not allow us to see the significance of ideas. Adler remarked that the man did not succeed in the synthesis of his analysis. His association would hardly be worth reporting unless their continuation would bring out something that would give us the key to the understanding of the number 1,734 and the whole series of ideas.

To quote further: "To be sure this morning I had an experience which speaks much for the correctness of the Freudian conception. My wife, whom I awakened through my getting up at night, asked me what I wanted with the catalogue of the U. L. I told her the story. She found it all pettifogging but—very interesting;. *Macbeth*, which caused me so much trouble, she simply passed over. She said that nothing came to her mind when she thought of a number. I answered, 'Let us try; it.' She named the number 117· To this I immediately; replied: '17 refers to what I just told you; furthermore, I told you yesterday that if a wife is in the 82nd year and the husband is in the 35th year it must be a gross misunderstanding.' For the last few days I have been teasing my wife by maintaining that she was a little old mother of 82 years. 82 + 35 = 117."

The man who did not know how to determine his own number at once found the solution when his wife named a number which was apparently arbitrarily chosen. As a matter of fact, the woman understood very well from which complex the number of her husband originated, and chose her own number from the same complex, which surely common it, both, as it dealt in his case with their relative ages. Now, we find it easy to interpret the number that occurred to the man. As Dr, Adler indicates, it expressed 'a repressed wish of the husband which, fully developed, would read: "For a man of 34 years as I am, only a woman of 17 would be suitable."

Lest one should think too lightly of such "playing," I will add that I was recently informed by Dr. Adler that a year after the publication of this analysis the man was divorced from his wife.[2]

Adler gives a similar explanation for the origin of obsessive numbers. Also the choice of so-called "favorite numbers" is not without relation to the life of the person concerned, and does not lack a certain psychological interest. A gentleman who evinced a particular partiality for the numbers 17 and 19 could specify, after brief reflection, that at the age of 17 he attained the greatly longed-for academic freedom by having been admitted to the university, that at 19 he made his first long journey, and shortly thereafter made his first scientific discovery. But the fixation of this preference followed later, after two questionable affairs, when the same numbers were invested with importance in his "love-life."

Indeed, even those numbers which we use in a particular connection extremely often and with apparent arbitrariness can be traced by analysis to an unexpected meaning. Thus, one day it struck one of my patients that he was particularly fond of saying, "I have already told you this from 17 to 36 times." And he asked himself whether there was any motive for it. It soon occurred to him that he was born on the 27th day of the month, and that his younger brother was born on the 26th day of another month, and he had grounds for complaint that Fate had robbed him of so many of the benefits of life only to bestow them on his younger brother. Thus he represented this partiality of Fate by deducting 10 from the date of his birth and adding it to the date of his brother's birthday. I am the elder and yet am so "cut short."

I shall tarry a little longer at the analysis of chance numbers, for I know of no other individual observation which would so readily demonstrate the existence of highly organized thinking processes of which consciousness has no knowledge. Moreover, there is no better example of analysis in which the suggestion of the position, a frequent accusation, is so distinctly out of consideration. I shall therefore report the analysis of a chance number of one of my patients (with his consent), to which I will only add that he is the youngest of many children and that he lost his beloved father in his young years.

While in a particularly happy mood he let the number *426,718* come to his mind, and put to himself the question, "Well, what does it bring to your mind?" First came a joke he had heard: "If your catarrh of the nose is treated by a doctor it lasts 42 days, if it is not treated it lasts—6 weeks." This corresponds to the first digit of the number (42 = 6 x 7). During the obstruction that followed this first solution I called his attention to the fact that the number of six digits selected by him contains all the first numbers except 3 and 5. He at once found the continuation of this solution:

"We were altogether 7 children, I was the youngest. Number 3 in the order of the children corresponds to my sister A., and 5 to my brother L.; both of them were my enemies. As a child I used to pray to the Lord every night that He should take out of my life these two tormenting spirits. It seems to me that I have fulfilled for myself this wish: '3' and '5,' the *evil* brother and the hated sister, are omitted."

"If the number stands for your sisters and brothers, what significance is there to 18 at the end? You were altogether only 7."

"I often thought if my father had lived longer I should not have been the youngest child. If one more would have come, we should have been 8, and there would have been a younger child, toward whom I could have played the role of the older one."

With this the number was explained, but we still wished to find the connection between the first part of the interpretation and the part following it. This came very readily from the condition required for the last digits—if the father had lived longer. 42 = 6 x 7 signifies the ridicule directed against the doctors who could not help the father, and in this way expresses the wish for the continued existence of the father. The whole number really corresponds to the fulfillment of his two wishes in reference to his family circle—namely, that both the evil brother and sister should die and that another little child should follow him. Or, briefly expressed: *If only these two had died in place of my father!*[3]

Another analysis of numbers I take from Jones.[4] A gentleman of his acquaintance let the number 986 come to his mind, and defied him to connect it to anything of special interest in his mind. "Six years ago, on the hottest day he could remember, he had seen a joke in an evening newspaper, which stated that the thermometer had stood at 98.6 degrees F., evidently an exaggeration of 98.6 degrees F.[*sic*] We were at the time seated in front of a very hot fire, from which he had just drawn back, and he remarked, probably quite correctly, that the heat had aroused his dormant memory. However, I was curious to know why this memory had persisted with such vividness as to be so readily brought out, for with most people it surely would have been forgotten beyond recall, unless it had become associated with some other mental experience of more significance .

"He told me that on reading: the joke he had laughed uproariously, and that on many subsequent occasions he had recalled it with great relish. As the joke was obviously of an exceedingly tenuous nature, this strengthened my expectation that more lay behind. His next thought was the general reflection that the conception of heat had always greatly impressed him, that heat was the most important thing in the universe, the source of all life, and so on. This remarkable attitude of a quite prosaic young man certainly needed some explanation, so I asked him to continue his free associations. The next thought was of a factory stack which he could see from his bedroom window. He often stood of an evening watching the flame and smoke issuing out of it, and reflecting on this deplorable waste of energy. Heat, flame, the source of life, the waste of vital energy issuing from an upright, hollow tube—it was not hard to divine from such associations that the ideas of heat and fire were unconsciously linked in his mind with the idea of love, as is so frequent in symbolic thinking, and that there was a strong masturbation complex present, a conclusion that he presently confirmed."

Those who wish to get a good impression of the way the material of numbers becomes elaborated in the unconscious thinking, I refer to two papers by Jung[5] and Jones.[6]

In personal analysis of this kind two things were especially striking. First, the absolute somnambulistic certainty with which I attacked the unknown objective point, merging into a mathematical train of thought, which later suddenly extended to the looked-for number, and the rapidity with which the entire subsequent work was performed. Secondly, the fact that the numbers were always at the disposal of my unconscious mind, when as a matter of fact I am a poor mathematician and find it very difficult to consciously recall years, house numbers, and the like. Moreover, in these unconscious mental operations with figures I found a tendency to superstition, the origin of which had long remained unknown to me.

It will not surprise us to find that not only numbers but also mental occurrences of different kinds of words regularly prove on analytic investigation to be well determined.

Brill relates: "While working on the English edition of this book I was obsessed one morning with the strange word 'Cardillac.' Busily intent on my work, I refused at first to pay attention to it, but, as is usually the case, I simply could not do anything else. 'Cardillac' was constantly in my mind. Realizing that my refusal to recognize it was only a resistance, I decided to analyze it. The following associations occurred to me: *Cardillac, cardiac, carrefour, Cadillac.*

"*Cardiac* recalled cardalgia—heartache—a medical friend who had recently told me confidentially that he feared that he had some cardiac affection because he had suffered some attacks of pain in the region of his heart. Knowing him so well, I at once rejected his theory, and told him that his attacks were of a neurotic character, and that his other apparent physical ailments were also only the expression of his neurosis.

"I might add that just before telling me of his heart trouble he spoke of a business matter of vital interest to him which had suddenly come to naught. Being a man of unbounded ambitions, he was very depressed because of late he had suffered many similar reverses. His neurotic conflicts, however, had become manifest a few months before this misfortune. Soon after his father's death had left a big business on his hands. As the business could be continued only under my friend's management, he was unable to decide whether to enter into commercial life or continue his chosen career. His great ambition was to become a successful medical practitioner, and although he had practiced medicine successfully for many years, he was not altogether satisfied with the financial fluctuations of his professional income. On the other hand, his father's business promised him an assured, though limited, return. In brief, he was 'at a crossing and did not know which way to turn.'

"I then recalled the word *carrefour*, which is the French for 'crossing,' and it occurred to me that while working in a hospital in Paris I lived near the 'Carrefour St. Lazarre.' And now I could understand what relation all these associations had for me.

"When I resolved to leave the State Hospital I made the decision, first, because I desired to get married, and, secondly, because I wished to enter private practice. This brought up a new problem. Although my State hospital service was an absolute success, judging by promotions and so on, I felt like a great many others in the same situation, namely, that my training was ill suited for private practice. To specialize in mental work was a daring undertaking for one without money and social connections. I also felt that the best I could do for patients should they ever come my way would be to commit them to one of the hospitals, as I had little confidence in the home treatment in vogue. In spite of the enormous advances made in recent years in mental work, the specialist is almost helpless when he is confronted with the average case of insanity. This may be partially attributed to the fact that such cases are brought to him after they have fully developed the psychosis when hospital treatment is imperative. Of the great army of milder mental disturbances, the so-called border-line cases, which make up the bulk of clinic and private work and which rightfully belong to the mental specialist, I knew very little, as those patients rarely, or never, came to the State hospital, and what I did know concerning the treatment of neurasthenia and psychasthenia was not conducive to make me more hopeful of success in private practice.

"It was in this state of mind that I came to Paris, where I hoped to learn enough about the psychoneuroses to enable me to continue my specialty in private practice, and yet feel that I could do something for my patients. What I saw in Paris did not, however, help to change my state of mind. There, too, most of the work was directed to dead tissues. The mental aspects, as such, received but scant attention. I was, therefore, seriously thinking of giving up my mental work for some other specialty. As can be seen, I was confronted with a situation similar to the one of my medical friend. I, too, was at a crossing and did not know which way to turn. My suspense was soon ended. One day, I received a letter from my friend Professor Peterson, who, by the way, was responsible for my entering the State hospital service. In this letter he advised me not to give up my work, and suggested the psychiatric clinic of Zurich, where he thought I could find what I desired.

"But what does *Cadillac* mean? Cadillac is the name of a hotel and of an automobile. A few days before in a country place my medical friend and I had been trying to hire an automobile, but there was none to be had. We both expressed the wish to own an automobile—again an unrealized ambition. I also recalled that the 'Carrefour St. Lazarre' always impressed me as being one of the busiest thoroughfares in Paris. It was always congested with automobiles. Cadillac also recalled that only a few days ago on the way to my clinic I noticed a large sign over a building which announced that on a certain day 'this building was to be occupied by the Cadillac,' etc. This at first made me think of the Cadillac Hotel, but on second sight I noticed that it referred to the Cadillac motorcar. There was a sudden obstruction here for a few moments. The word Cadillac reappeared and by sound association the word *catalogue* occurred to me. This word brought back a very mortifying occurrence of recent origin, the motive of which is again blighted ambition.

"When one wishes to report any auto-analysis he must be prepared to lay bare many intimate affairs of his own life. Anyone reading carefully Professor Freud's works cannot fail to become intimately acquainted with him and his family. I have often been asked by persons who claim to have read and studied Freud's works such questions as: 'How old is Freud?' 'Is Freud married?' 'How many children has he?' etc. Whenever I hear these or similar questions I know that the questioner has either lied when he made these assertions, or, to be more charitable, that he is a very careless and superficial reader. All these questions and many more are answered in Freud's works. Auto-analyses are autobiographies *par excellence*; but whereas the autobiographer may for definite reasons consciously and unconsciously hide many facts of his life, the auto-analyst not only tells the truth consciously, but perforce brings to light his whole intimate personality. It is for these reasons that one finds it very unpleasant to report his own auto-analyses. However, as we often report our patients' unconscious productions, it is but fair that we should sacrifice ourselves on the altar of publicity when occasion demands. This is my apology for having thrust some of my personal affairs on the reader, and for being obliged to continue a little longer in the same strain.

"Before digressing with the last remarks I mentioned that the word *Cadillac* brought the sound association catalogue. This association brought back another important epoch in my life with which Professor Peterson is connected. Last May I was informed by the secretary of the faculty that I was appointed chief of clinic of the department of psychiatry. I need hardly say that I was exceedingly pleased to be so honored—in the first place because it was the realization of an ambition which I dared entertain only under special euphoric states; and, secondly, it was a compensation for the many unmerited criticisms from those who are blindly and unreasonably opposing some of my work. Soon thereafter I called on the stenographer of the faculty and spoke to her about a correction to be made in my name as it was printed in the catalogue. For some unknown reason (perhaps racial prejudice) this stenographer, a maiden lady, must have taken a dislike to me. For about three years I repeatedly requested her to have this correction made, but she had paid no attention to me. To be sure she always promised to attend to it, but the mistake remained uncorrected.

"When I saw her last May I again reminded her of this correction, and also called her attention to the fact that as I had been appointed chief of clinic I was especially anxious to have my name correctly printed in the catalogue. She apologized for her remissness and assured me that everything should be as I requested. Imagine my surprise and chagrin when on receiving the new catalogue I found that while the correction had been made in my name I was not listed as chief of clinic. When I asked her about this she was quite puzzled; she said she had no idea that I had been appointed chief of clinic. She had to consult the minutes of the faculty, written by herself, before she was convinced of it. It should be noted that as recorder to the faculty it was her duty to know all these things as soon as they transpired.[7] When she finally ascertained that I was right she was very apologetic and informed me that she would at once write to the superintendent of the clinic to inform him of my appointment, something which she should have done months before. Of course I gained nothing by her regrets and apologies. The catalogue was published and those who read it did not find my name in the desired place. I am chief of clinic in fact but not in name. Moreover, as the appointments are made only for one year, it is quite likely that my great ambition will never be actually realized.

"Thus the obsessive neologism *cardillac*, which is a condensation of *cardiac*, *Cadillac*, and *catalogue*, contains some of the most important efforts of my medical experience. When I was almost at the end of this analysis I suddenly recalled a dream containing this neologism cardillac in which my wish was realized. My name appeared in its rightful place in the catalogue. The person who showed it to me in the dream was Professor Peterson. It was when I was at the first 'crossing' after I had graduated from the medical college that Professor Peterson urged me to enter the hospital service. About five years later while I was in the state of indecision which I have described, it was Professor Peterson who advised me to go to the clinic of psychiatry at Zurich where through Bleuler and Jung I first became acquainted with Professor Freud and his works, and it was also through the kind recommendation of Dr. Peterson that I was elevated to my present position." I am indebted to Dr. Hitschman for the solution of another case in which a line of poetry repeatedly obtruded itself on the mind in a certain place without showing any trace of its origin and relation.

Related by Dr. E.: "Six years ago I travelled from Biarritz to San Sebastian. The railroad crosses over the Bidassao—a river which here forms the boundary between France and Spain. On the bridge one has a splendid view, on the one side of the broad valley and the Pyrenees and on the other of the sea. It was a beautiful, bright summer day; everything was filled with sun and light. I was on a vacation and pleased with my trip to Spain. Suddenly the following words came to me: '*But the soul is already free, floating on a sea of light.*'

"At that time I was trying to remember where these lines came from, but I could not remember; judging by the rhythm, the words must be a part of some poem, which, however, entirely escaped my memory. Later when the verse repeatedly came to my mind, I asked many people about it without receiving any information.

"Last year I crossed the same bridge on my return journey from Spain. It was a very dark night and it rained. I looked through the window to ascertain whether we had already reached the frontier station and noticed that we were on the Bidassao bridge. Immediately the above cited verse returned to my memory and again I could not recall its origin.

"At home many months later I found Uhland's poems. I opened the volume and my glance fell upon the verse: '*But the soul is already free, floating on a sea of light*,' which were the concluding lines of the poem entitled 'The Pilgrim.' I read the poem and dimly recalled that I had known it many years ago. The scene of action is in Spain, and this seemed to me to be the only relation between the quoted verse and the place on the railroad journey described by me. I was only half satisfied with my discovery and mechanically continued to turn the pages of the book. On turning the next page I found a poem the title of which was '*Bidassao Bridge*.'

"I may add that the contents of this poem seemed even stranger to me than that of the first, and that its first verse read:

"'On the Bidassao bridge stands a saint grey with age, he blesses to the right the Spanish mountain, to the left he blesses the French land.'"

II. This understanding of the determination of apparently arbitrarily selected names, numbers, and words may perhaps contribute to the solution of another problem. As is known, many persons argue against the assumption of an absolute psychic determinism by referring to an intense feeling of conviction that there is a free will. This feeling of conviction exists, but is not incompatible with the belief in determinism. Like all normal feelings, it must be justified by something. But, so far as I can observe, it does not manifest itself in weighty and important decisions; on these occasions one has much more the feeling of a psychic compulsion and gladly falls back upon it. (Compare Luther's "Here I stand, I cannot do anything else.")

On the other hand, it is in trivial and indifferent decisions that one feels sure that he could just as easily have acted differently, that he acted of his own free will, and without any motives. From our analyses we therefore need not contest the right of the feeling of conviction that there is a free will. If we distinguish conscious from unconscious motivation we are then informed by the feeling of conviction that the conscious motivation does not extend over all our motor resolutions. *Minima non curat prætor.* What is thus left free from the one side receives its motive from the other side, from the unconscious, and the determinism in the psychic realm is thus carried out uninterruptedly.[8]

III. Although conscious thought must be altogether ignorant of the motivation of the faulty actions described above, yet it would be desirable to discover a psychologic proof of its existence; indeed, reasons obtained through a deeper knowledge of the unconscious make it probable that such proofs are to be discovered somewhere. As a matter of fact phenomena can be demonstrated in two spheres which seem to correspond to an unconscious and hence to a displaced knowledge of these motives.

(*a*) It is a striking and generally to be recognized feature in the behavior of paranoiacs, that they attach the greatest significance to the trivial details in the behavior of others. Details which are usually overlooked by others they interpret and utilize as the basis of far-reaching conclusions. For example, the last paranoiac seen by me concluded that there was a general understanding among people of his environment, because at his departure from the railway-station they made a certain motion with one hand. Another noticed how people walked on the street, how they brandished their walking-sticks, and the like.[9]

The category of the accidental, requiring no motivation, which the normal person lets pass as a part of his own psychic activities and faulty actions, is thus rejected by the paranoiac in the application to the psychic manifestations to others. All that he observes in others is full of meaning, all is explainable. But how does he come to look at it in this manner? Probably here as in so many other cases, he projects into the mental life of others what exists in his own unconscious activity. Many things obtrude themselves on consciousness in paranoia which in normal and neurotic persons can only be demonstrated through psychoanalysis as existing in their unconscious.[10] In a certain sense the paranoiac is here justified, he perceives something that escapes the normal person, he sees clearer than one of normal intellectual capacity, but his knowledge becomes worthless when he imputes to others the state of affairs he thus recognizes. I hope that I shall not be expected to justify every paranoid interpretation. But the point which we grant to paranoia in this conception of chance actions will facilitate for us the psychological understanding of the conviction which the paranoiac attaches to all these interpretations. *There is certainly same truth to it*; even our errors of judgment, which are not designated as morbid, acquire their feeling of conviction in the same way. This feeling is justified for a certain part of the erroneous train of thought or for the source of its origin, and we shall later extend to it the remaining relationships.

(*b*) The phenomena of superstition furnish another indication of the unconscious motivation in chance and faulty actions. I will make myself clear through the discussion of a simple experience which gave me the starting-point to these reflections .

Having returned from vacation, my thoughts immediately turned to the patients with whom I was to occupy myself in the beginning of my year's work. My first visit was to a very old woman (see above) for whom I had twice daily performed the same professional services for many years. Owing to this monotony unconscious thoughts have often found expression on the way to the patient and during my occupation with her. She was over ninety years old; it was therefore pertinent to ask oneself at the beginning of each year how much longer she was likely to live.

On the day of which I speak I was hurry and took a carriage to her house. Every coachman at the cabstand near my house knew the old woman's address, as each of them had often driven me there. This day it happened that the driver did not stop in front of her house, but before one of the same number in a near-by and really similar-looking parallel street. I noticed the mistake and reproached the coachman, who apologized for it.

Is it of any significance when I am taken to a house where the old woman is not to be found? Certainly not to me; but were I *superstitious*, I should see an omen in this incident, a hint of fate that this would be the last year for the old woman. A great many omens which have been preserved by history have been founded on no better symbolism. Of course, I explain the incident as an accident without further meaning. The case would have been entirely different had I come on foot and, "absorbed in thought "or "through distraction," I had gone to the house in the parallel street instead of the correct one. I would not explain that as an accident, but as an action with unconscious intent requiring interpretation. My explanation of this "lapse in walking" would probably be that I expected that the time would soon come when I should not meet the old woman any longer.

I therefore differ from a superstitious person in the following manner:

I do not believe that an occurrence in which my mental life takes no part can teach me anything hidden concerning the future shaping of reality; but I do believe that an unintentional manifestation of my own mental activity surely contains something concealed which belongs only to my mental life—that is, I believe in outer (real) chance, but not in inner (psychic) accidents. With the superstitious person the case is reversed: he knows nothing of the motive of his chance and faulty actions; he believes in the existence of psychic contingencies; he is therefore inclined to attribute meaning to external chance, which manifests itself in actual occurrence, and to see in the accident a means of expression for something hidden outside of him. There are two differences between me and the superstitious person: first, he projects the motive to the to the outside, while I look for it in myself; second, he explains the accident by an event which I trace to a thought. What he considers hidden corresponds to the unconscious with me, and the compulsion not to let chance pass as chance, but to explain it as common to both of us. Thus I admit that this conscious ignorance and unconscious knowledge of the motivation of psychic accidentalness is one of the psychic roots of superstition. *Because* the superstitious person knows nothing of the motivation of his own accidental actions, and because the fact of this motivation strives for a place in his recognition, he is compelled to dispose of them by displacing them into the outer world. If such a connection exists it can hardly be limited to this single case. As a matter of fact, I believe that a large portion of the mythological conception of the world which reaches far into the most modern religions *is nothing but psychology projected into the outer world.* The dim perception (the endo-psychic perception, as it were) of psychic factors and relations[11] of the unconscious was taken as a model in the construction of a *transcendental reality,* which is destined to be changed again by science into *psychology of the unconscious.*

It is difficult to express it in other terms; the analogy to paranoia must here come to our aid. We venture to explain in this way the myths of paradise and the fall of man, of God, of good and evil, of immortality, and the like—that is, to transform *metaphysics* into *meta-psychology.* The gap between the paranoiac's displacement and that of superstition is narrower than appears at first sight. When human beings began to think, they were obviously compelled to explain the outer world in an anthropomorphic sense by a multitude of personalities in their own image; the accidents which they explained superstitiously were thus actions and expressions of persons. In that regard they behaved just like paranoiacs, who draw conclusions from insignificant signs which others give them, and like all normal persons who justly take the unintentional actions of their fellow-beings as a basis for 'the estimation of their characters. Only in our modern philosophical, but by no means finished, views of life does superstition seem so much out of place: in the view of life of prescientific times and nations it was justified and consistent.

The Roman who gave up an important undertaking because he sighted an ill-omened flock of birds was relatively right; his action was consistent with his principles. But if he withdrew from an undertaking because he had stumbled on his threshold (*un Romain retournerait*), he was absolutely superior even to us unbelievers. He was a better psychologist than we are striving to become. For his stumbling could demonstrate to him the existence of a doubt, an internal counter-current the force of which could weaken the power of his intention at the moment of its execution. For only by concentrating all psychic forces on the desired aim can one be assured of perfect success. How does Schiller's Tell, who hesitated so long to shoot the apple from his son's head, answer the bailiff's question why he had provided himself with a second arrow!

"*With the second arrow I would have pierced you had I struck my dear child—and; truly, I should not have failed to reach you.*"

IV. Whoever has had the opportunity of studying the concealed psychic feelings of persons by means of psychoanalysis can also tell something new concerning the quality of unconscious motives, which express themselves in superstition. Nervous persons afflicted with compulsive thinking and compulsive states, who are often very intelligent, show very plainly that superstition originates from repressed hostile and cruel impulses. The greater part of superstition signifies fear of impending evil, and he who has frequently wished evil to others, but because of a good bringing-up has repressed the same into the unconscious, will be particularly apt to expect punishment for such unconscious evil in the form of a misfortune threatening him: from without.

If we concede that we have by no means exhausted the psychology of superstition in these remarks, we must, on the other hand, at least touch upon the question whether real roots of superstition should be altogether denied, whether there are really no omens, prophetic dreams, telepathic experiences, manifestations of supernatural forces, and the like. I am now far from willing to repudiate without anything further all these phenomena, concerning which we possess so many minute observations even from men of intellectual prominence, and which should certainly form a basis for further investigation. We map even hope that some of these observations will be explained by our present knowledge of the unconscious psychic processes without necessitating radical changes in our present aspect. If still other phenomena, as, for example, those maintained by the spiritualists, should be proven, we should then consider the modification of our "laws" as demanded by the new experience, without becoming confused in regard to the relation of things of this world.

In the sphere of these analyses I can only answer the questions here proposed subjectively—that is, in accordance with my personal experience. I am sorry to confess that I belong to that class of unworthy individuals before whom the spirits cease their activities and the supernatural disappears, so that I have never been in position to experience anything personally that would stimulate belief in the miraculous. Like everybody else, I have had forebodings and experienced misfortunes; but the two evaded each other, so that nothing followed the foreboding, and the misfortune struck me unannounced. When as a young man I lived alone in a strange city I frequently heard my name suddenly pronounced by an unmistakable, dear voice, and I then made a note of the exact moment of the hallucination in order to inquire carefully of those at home what had occurred at that time. There was nothing to it. On the other hand, I later worked among my patients calmly and without foreboding while my child almost bled to death. Nor have I ever been able to recognize as unreal phenomena any of the forebodings reported to me by my patients.

The belief in prophetic dreams numbers many adherents, because it can be supported by the fact that some things really so happen in the future as they were previously foretold by the wish of the dream. But in this there is little to be wondered at, as many far-reaching deviations may be regularly demonstrated between a dream and the fulfillment which the credulity of the dreamer prefers to neglect.

A nice example, one which may be justly called prophetic was once brought to me for exhaustive analysts by an intelligent and truth-loving patient. She related that she once dreamed that she had met a former friend and family physician in front of a certain store in a certain street, and next morning when she went down town she actually met him at the place named in the dream. I may observe that the significance of this wonderful coincidence was not proven to be due to any subsequent event—that is, it could not be justified through future occurrences.

Careful examination definitely established the fact that there was no proof that the woman recalled the dream in the morning following the night of the dream—that is, before the walk and before the meeting. She could offer no objection when this state of affairs was presented in a manner that robbed this episode of everything miraculous, leaving only an interesting psychological problem. One morning she had walked through this very street, had met her old family physician before that certain store, and on seeing him received the conviction that during the preceding night she had dreamed of this meeting at this place.

The analysis then showed with great probability how she came to this conviction, to which, in accordance with the general rule, we cannot deny a certain right to credence. A meeting at a definite place following a previous expectation really describes the fact of a rendezvous. The old family physician awakened her memory of old times, when meetings with a third person, also a friend of the physician, were of marked significance to her. Since that time she had continued her relations with this gentleman, and the day before the mentioned dream she had waited for him in vain. If I could report in greater detail the circumstances here before us, I could easily show that the illusion of the prophetic dream at the sight of the friend of former times is perchance equivalent to the following speech: "Ah, doctor, you now remind me of bygone times, when I never had to wait in vain for N. when we had arranged a meeting."

I have observed in myself a simple and easily explained example, which is probably a good model for similar occurrences of those familiar "remarkable coincidences" wherein we meet a person of whom we were just thinking. During a walk through the inner city a few days after the title of "Professor" was bestowed on me, which carries with it a great deal of prestige even in monarchical cities, my thoughts suddenly merged into a childish revenge-fantasy against a certain married couple. Some months previous they had called me to see their little daughter who suffered from' an interesting compulsive manifestation following the appearance of a dream. I took a great interest in the case, the genesis of which I believed I could surmise, but the parents were unfavorable to my treatment, and gave me to understand that they thought of applying to a foreign authority who cured by means of hypnotism. I now fancied that after the failure of this attempt, the parents begged me to resume my treatment, that they now had full confidence in me, etc. But I answered: "Now that I have become a professor, you have confidence in me. The title has made no change in my ability; if you could not use me when I was instructor you can get along without me now that I am! a professor." At this point my fantasy was interrupted by a loud "Good evening, Professor!" and as I looked up there passed me the same couple on whom I had just taken this imaginary vengeance.

The next reflection destroyed the semblance of the miraculous. I was walking towards this couple on a straight, almost deserted street; glancing up hastily at a distance of perhaps twenty steps from me, I had spied and realized their stately personalities; but this perception, following the model of a negative hallucination, was set aside by certain emotionally accentuated motives and then asserted itself in the apparently spontaneous emerging fantasy.

A similar experience is related by Brill, which also throws some light on the nature of telepathy.

"While engrossed in conversation during our customary Sunday evening dinner at one of the large New York restaurants, I suddenly stopped and irrelevantly remarked to my wife, 'I wonder how Dr. R. is doing in Pittsburg.' She looked at me much astonished and said: 'Why, that is exactly what I have been thinking for the last few seconds! Either you have transferred this thought to me or I have transferred it to you. How can you otherwise explain this strange phenomenon?' I had to admit that I could offer no solution. Our conversation throughout the dinner showed not the remotest association to Dr. R., nor, so far as our memories went, had we heard or spoken of him for some time. Being a skeptic, I refused to admit that there was anything mysterious about it, although inwardly I felt quite uncertain. To be frank, I was somewhat mystified.

"But we did not remain very long in this state of mind, for on looking toward the cloak-room we were surprised to see Dr. R. Though closer inspection showed our mistake, we were both struck by the remarkable resemblance of this stranger to Dr. R. From the position of the cloak-room we were forced to conclude that this stranger had passed our table. Absorbed in our conversation, we had not noticed him consciously, but the visual image had stirred up the association of his double, Dr. R. That we should both have experienced the same thought is also quite natural. The last word from our friend was to the effect that he had taken up private practice in Pittsburg, and, being aware of the vicissitudes that beset the beginner, it was quite natural to wonder how fortune smiled upon him.

"What promised to be a supernatural manifestation was thus easily explained on a normal basis; but had we not noticed the stranger before he left the restaurant, it would have been impossible to exclude the mysterious. I venture to say that such simple mechanisms are at the bottom of the most complicated telepathic manifestations; at least, such has been my experience in all cases accessible to investigation."

Another "solution of an apparent foreboding " was reported by Otto Rank[12]:

"Some time ago I had experienced a remarkable variation of that peculiar coincidence wherein one meets a person who has just been occupying one's thoughts. Shortly before Christmas I went to the Austro-Hungarian Bank in order to obtain ten new silver crown-pieces destined for Christmas gifts. Absorbed in ambitious fantasies which dealt with the contrast of my meager means to the enormous sums in the banking-house, I turned into the narrow street to the bank. In front of the door I saw an automobile and many people going in and out. I thought to myself: 'The officials will have plenty of time for my new crowns; naturally I shall be quick about it; I shall put down the paper notes to be exchanged, and say, "Please give me gold."' I realized my mistake at once—I was to have asked for silver—and awoke from my fantasies.

"I was now only a few steps front the entrance, and noticed a young man coming toward me who looked familiar, but whom I could not definitely identify on account of my short-sightedness. As he came nearer I recognized him as a classmate of my brother whose name was Gold and from whose brother, a well-known journalist, I had great expectations in the beginning of my literary career. But these expectations had not materialized, and with them had vanished the hoped-for material success with which my fantasies were occupying; themselves on my way to the bank. Thus engrossed I must have unconsciously perceived the approach of Mr. Gold, who impressed himself on my conscience while I was dreaming of material success, and thereby caused me to ask the cashier for gold instead of the inferior silver. But, on the other hand, the paradoxical fact that my unconscious was able to perceive an object long before it was recognized by the eye might in part be explained by the complex readiness (*Komplexbereitschaft*) of Bleuler. For my mind was attuned to the material, and, contrary to my better knowledge, it guided my steps from the very beginning to buildings where gold and paper money were exchanged."

To the category of the wonderful and uncanny we may also add that strange feeling we perceive in certain moments and situations when it seems as if we had already had exactly the same experience, or had previously found ourselves in the same situation. Yet we are never successful in our efforts to recall clearly; those former experiences and situations. I know that I follow only the loose colloquial expression when I designate that which stimulates us in such moments as a "feeling." We undoubtedly deal with a judgment, and, indeed, with a judgment of cognition; but these cases, nevertheless, have a character peculiar to themselves, and besides, we must not ignore the fact that we never recall what we are seeking.

I do not know whether this phenomenon of *Déjà vu* was ever seriously offered as a proof of a former psychic existence of the individual; but it is certain that psychologists have taken an interest in it, and have attempted to solve the riddle in a multitude of speculative ways. None of the proposed tentative explanations seems right to me, because none takes account of anything but the accompanying manifestations and the favoring conditions of the phenomenon. Those psychic processes which, according to my observation, are alone responsible for the explanation of the *Déjà vu*—namely, the unconscious fantasies—are generally neglected by the psychologists even today.

I believe that it is wrong to designate the feeling of having experienced something before as an illusion. On the contrary, in such moments something is really touched that we have already experienced, only we cannot consciously recall the latter because it never was conscious. In short, the feeling *Déjà vu* corresponds to the memory of an unconscious fantasy. There are unconscious fantasies (or day dreams) just as there are similar conscious creations, which everyone knows from personal experience.

I realize that the object is worthy of most minute study, but I will here give the analysis of only one case of *Déjà vu* in which the feeling was characterized by particular intensity and persistence. A woman of thirty-seven years asserted that she most distinctly remembered that at the age of twelve and a half she paid her first visit to some school friends in the country, and as she entered the garden she immediately had the feeling of having been there before. This feeling was repeated as she went through the living-rooms, so that she believed she knew beforehand how big the next room was, what views one could have on looking out of it, etc. But the belief that this feeling of recognition might have its source in a previous visit to the house and garden, perhaps a visit paid in earliest childhood, was absolutely excluded and disproved by statements from her parents. The woman who related this sought no psychological explanation, but saw in the appearance of this feeling a prophetic reference to the importance which these friends later assumed in her emotional life. On taking into consideration, however, the circumstance under which this phenomenon presented itself to her, we found the way to another conception.

When she decided upon this visit she knew that these girls had an only brother, who was seriously ill. In the course of the visit she actually saw him. She found him looking very badly, and thought to herself that he would soon die. But it happened that her own only brother had had a serious attack of diphtheria some months before, and during his illness she had lived for weeks with relatives far from her parental home. She believed that her brother was taking part in this visit to the country, imagined even that this was his first long journey since his illness; still, her memory was remarkably indistinct in regard to these points, whereas all other details, and particularly the dress which she wore that day, remained most clearly before her eyes.

To the initiated it will not be difficult to conclude from these suggestions that the expectation of her brother's death had played a great part in the girl's mind at that time, and that either it never became conscious or it was more energetically repressed after the favorable issue of' the illness. Under other circumstances she would have been compelled to wear another dress—namely, mourning clothes. She found the analogous situation in her friends' home; their only: brother was in danger of an early death, an event that really came to pass a short time after. She might have consciously remembered that she lived through a similar situation a few months previous, but instead of recalling what was inhibited through repression she transferred the memory feeling to the locality, to the garden and the house, and merged it into the *fausse reconnaissance* that she had already seen everything exactly as it was.

From the fact of the repression we may conclude that the former expectation of the death of her brother was not far from evincing the character of a wish-fantasy. She would then have become the only: child. In her later neurosis she suffered in the most intense manner from the fear of losing her parents, behind which the analysis disclosed, as usual, the unconscious wish of the same content.

My own experience of *Déjà vu* I can trace in a similar manner to the emotional constellation of the moment. It may he expressed as follows: "That would be another occasion for awakening certain fantasies (unconscious and unknown) which were formed in me at one time or another as a wish to improve my situation."[13]

V. Recently when I had occasion to recite to a colleague of a philosophical turn of mind some examples of name-forgetting, with their analyses, he hastened to reply: "That is all very well, but with me the forgetting of a name proceeds in a different manner." Evidently one cannot dismiss this question as simply as that; I do not believe that my colleague had ever thought of an analysis for the forgetting of a name, nor could he say how the process differed in him. But his remark, nevertheless, touches upon a problem which many would be inclined to place in the foreground. Does the solution given for faulty and chance actions apply in general or only in particular cases, and if only in the latter, what are the conditions under which it may also be employed in the explanation of the other phenomena?

In answer to this question my experiences leave me in the lurch. I can only urge against considering the demonstrated connections as rare, for as often as I have made the test in myself and with my patients it was always definitely demonstrated exactly as in the examples reported, or there were at least good reasons to assume this. One should not be surprise, however, when one does not succeed every time in finding the concealed meaning of the symptomatic action, as the amount of inner resistances ranging themselves against the solution must be considered a deciding factor. Also, it is not always possible to explain every individual dream of one's self of patients. To substantiate the general validity of the theory, it is enough if one can penetrate only a certain distance into the hidden associations. The dream which proves refractory when the solution is attempted on the following day can often be robbed of its secret a week or a month later, when the psychic factors combating one another have been reduced as a consequence of a real change that has meanwhile taken place. The same applies to the solution of faulty and symptomatic actions. It would therefore be wrong to affirm of all cases which resist analysis that they are caused by another psychic mechanism than that here revealed; such assumption requires more than negative proofs; moreover, the readiness to believe in a difference explanation of faulty and symptomatic actions, which probably exists universally in all normal persons, does not prove anything; it is obviously an expression of the same psychic forces which produced the secret, which therefore strives to protect and struggle against its elucidation.

On the other hand, we must not overlook the fact that the repressed thoughts and feelings are not independent in attaining expression in symptomatic and faulty actions. The technical possibility for such an adjustment of the innervations must be furnished independently of them, and this is then gladly utilized by the intention of the repressed material to come to conscious expression. In the case of linguistic faulty actions an attempt has been made by philosophers and philologists to verify through minute observations what structural and functional relations enter into the service of such intention. If in the determinations of faulty and symptomatic actions we separate the unconscious motive from its co-active physiological and psychophysical relations, the question remains open whether there are still other factors within normal limits which, like the unconscious motive, and in its place can produce faulty and symptomatic actions on the road of the relations. It is not my; task to answer this question.

VI. Since the discussion of speech blunders we have been content to demonstrate that faulty actions have a concealed motive, and through the aid of psychoanalysis we have traced our way to the knowledge of their motivation. The general nature and the peculiarities of the psychic factors brought to expression in these faulty actions we have hitherto left almost without consideration; at any rate, we have not attempted to define them more accurately or to examine into their lawfulness. Nor will we now attempt a thorough elucidation of the subject, as the first steps have already taught us that it is more feasible to enter this structure from another side. Here we can put before ourselves certain questions which I will cite in their order. (1) What is the content and the origin of the thoughts and feelings ;which show; themselves through faulty and chance actions? (2) What are the conditions which force a thought or a feeling to make use of these occurrences as a means of expression and place it in a position to do sol (3) Can constant and definite associations be demonstrated between the manner of the faulty action and the qualities brought to expression through it.

I shall begin by bringing together some material for answering the last question. In the discussion of the examples of speech blunders we found it necessary to go beyond the contents of the intended speech, and we had to seek the cause of the speech disturbance outside the intention. The latter was quite clear in a series of cases, and as known to the consciousness of the speaker. In the example that seemed most simple and transparent it was a similar sounding but different conception of the same thought, which disturbed its expression without anyone being able to say why the one succumbed and the other came to the surface (Meringer and Mayers' *Contaminations*).

In a second group of cases one conception succumbed to a motive which did not, however, prove strong enough to cause complete submersion. The conception which was withheld was clearly presented to consciousness.

Only of the third group can we affirm unreservedly that the disturbing thought differed from the one intended, and it is obvious that it may establish an essential distinction. The disturbing thought is either connected with the disturbed on through a thought association (disturbance through inner contradiction), or it is substantially strange to it, and just the disturbed word is connected with the disturbing thought through a surprising outer association, which is frequently unconscious.

In the examples which I have given from my psychoanalyses it is found that the entire speech is either under the influence of thoughts which have become active simultaneously, or under absolutely unconscious thoughts which betray themselves either through the disturbance itself, or which evince an indirect influence by making it possible for the individual parts of the unconsciously intended speech to disturb one another. The retained unconscious thoughts from which the disturbances in speech emanate are of most varied origin. A general survey does not reveal any definite direction.

Comparative examinations of examples of mistakes in reading and writing lead me to the same conclusions. Isolated cases, as in speech blunders, seem to owe their origin to an unmotivated work of condensation (e.g., the *Apel*). But we should be pleased to know whether special conditions must not be fulfilled in order that such condensation, which is considered regular in the dream-work and faulty in our waking thoughts, should take place. No information concerning this can be obtained from the examples themselves. But I merely refuse from this to draw the conclusion that there are no such conditions, as, for instance, the relaxation of conscious attention; for I have learned elsewhere that automatic actions are especially characterized by correctness and reliability. I would rather emphasize the fact that here, as so frequently in biology, it is the normal relations, or those approaching the normal, that are less favorable objects for investigation than the pathological. What remains obscure in the explanation of these most simple disturbances will, according to my expectation, be made clear through the explanation of more serious disturbances.

Also mistakes in reading and writing do not lack examples in which more remote and more complicated motivation can be recognized.

There is no doubt that the disturbances of the speech functions occur more easily and make less demand on the disturbing forces than other psychic acts.

But one is on different ground when it comes to the examination of forgetting in the literal sense— *i.e.*, the forgetting of past experiences. (To distinguish this forgetting from the others we designate *sensu strictiori* the forgetting of proper names and foreign words, as in Chapters I and II, as "slips"; and the forgetting of resolutions as "omissions.") The principal conditions of the normal process in forgetting are unknown.[14] We are also reminded of the fact that not all is forgotten which we believe to be. Our explanation here deals only with those cases in which the forgetting arouses our astonishment, in so far as it infringes the rule that the unimportant is forgotten, while the important matter is guarded by memory. Analysis of these examples of forgetting - is always an unwillingness to recall something which may evoke painful feelings. We may come to the conjecture that this motive universally strives for expression in psychic life, but is inhibited through other and contrary forces from regularly manifesting itself. The extent and significance of this dislike to recall painful impressions seems worthy of the most painstaking psychological investigation. The question as to what special conditions render possible the universally resistant forgetting in individual cases cannot be solved through this added association.

A different factor steps into the foreground in the forgetting of resolutions; the supposed conflict resulting in the repression of the painful memory becomes tangible, and in the analysis of the examples one regularly recognizes a counter-will which opposes but does not put an end to the resolution. As in previously discussed faulty act, we here also recognize two types of the psychic process: the counter-will either turns directly against the resolution (in intentions of some consequence) or it is substantially foreign to the resolution itself and establishes its connection with it through an outer association (in almost indifferent resolutions).

The same conflict governs the phenomena of erroneously carried-out actions. The impulse which manifests itself in the disturbances of the action is frequently a counter-impulse. Still oftener it is altogether a strange impulse which only utilizes the opportunity to express itself through a disturbance in the execution of the action. The cases in which the disturbance is the result of an inner contradiction are the most significant ones, and also deal with the more important activities.

The inner conflict in the chance or symptomatic actions then merges into the background. Those motor expressions which are least thought of, or are entirely overlooked by consciousness, serve as the expression of numerous unconscious or restrained feelings. For the most part they represent symbolically wishes and phantoms. The first question (as to the origin of the thoughts and emotions which find expression in faulty actions) we can answer by saying that in a series of cases the origin of the disturbing thoughts can be readily traced to repressed emotions of the psychic life. Even in healthy persons egotistic, jealous and hostile feelings and impulses, burdened by the pressure of moral education, often utilize the path of faulty actions to express in some way their undeniably existing force which is not recognized by the higher psychic instances. Allowing these faulty and chance actions to continue corresponds in great part to a comfortable toleration of the unmoral. The manifold sexual currents play no insignificant part m these repressed feelings. That they appear so seldom in the thoughts revealed by the analyses of my examples is simply a matter of coincidence. As I have undertaken the analyses of numerous examples from my own psychic life, the selection was partial from the first, and aimed at the exclusion of sexual matters. At other times it seemed that the disturbing thoughts originated from the most harmless objection and consideration.

We have now reached the answer to the second question—that is, what psychologic conditions are responsible for the fact that a thought must seek expression not in its complete form but, as it were, in parasitic form, as a modification and disturbance of another. From the most striking examples of faulty actions it is quite obvious that this determinant should be sought in a relation to conscious capacity, or in the more or less firmly pronounced character of the "repressed" material. But an examination of this series of examples shows that this character consists of many indistinct elements. The tendency to overlook something because it is wearisome, or because the concerned thought does not really belong to the intended matter—these feelings seem to play the same role as motives for the suppression of a thought (which later depends for expression on the disturbance of another), as the moral condemnation of a rebellious emotional feeling, or as the origin of absolutely unconscious trains of thought. An insight into the general nature of the condition of faulty and chance actions cannot be gained in this way.

However, this investigation gives us one single significant fact; the more harmless the motivation of the faulty act the less obnoxious, and hence less incapable of consciousness, the thought to which it gives expression is; the easier also becomes the solution of the phenomenon after we have turned our attention toward it. The simplest cases of speech blunders are immediately noticed and instantaneously corrected. Where one deals with motivation through actually repressed feelings the solution requires a painstaking analysis, which may sometimes strike against difficulties or turn out unsuccessful.

One is therefore justified in taking the result of this last investigation as an indication of the fact that the satisfactory explanation of the psychologic determinations of faulty and chance actions is to be acquired in another way and from another source. The indulgent reader can therefore see in these discussions the demonstration of the surfaces of fracture in which this theme was quite artificially. evolved from a broader connection.

VII. Just a few words to indicate the direction of this broader connection. The mechanism of the faulty and chance actions, as we have learned to know it through the application of analysis, shows in the most essential points an agreement with the mechanism of dream formation, which I have discussed in the chapter "The Dream Work" of my book on the interpretation of dreams. Here, as there, one finds the condensation and compromise formation ("*contaminations*"); in addition the situation is much the same, since unconscious thoughts find expression as modifications of other thoughts in unusual ways and through outer associations. The incongruities, absurdities, and errors in the dream content by virtue of which the dream is scarcely recognized as a psychic achievement originate in the same way—to be sure, through freer usage of the existing material—as the common error of our everyday life; *here, as there, the appearance of the incorrect function is explained through the peculiar interference of two or more correct actions.*

An important conclusion call be drawn from this combination: the peculiar mode of operation, whose most striking function we recognize in the dream content, should not be adjudged only to the sleeping state of the psychic life when we possess abundant proof of its activity during the waking state in the form of faulty actions. The same connection also forbids us assuming that these psychic processes which impress us as abnormal and strange are determined by deep-seated decay of psychic activity or by morbid state of function.[15]

The correct understanding of this strange psychic work which allows the faulty actions to originate like the dream pictures will only be possible after we have discovered that the psychoneurotic symptoms, particularly the psychic formations of hysteria and compulsion neurosis, repeat in their mechanisms all the essential features of this mode of operation. The continuation of our investigation would therefore have to begin at this point.

There is still another special interest for us in considering the faulty, chance, and symptomatic actions in the light of this last analogy. If we compare them to the function of the psychoneuroses and the neurotic symptoms, two frequently recurring statements gain in sense and support—namely, that the border-line between the nervous, normal, and abnormal states is indistinct, and that we are all slightly nervous. Regardless of all medical experience, one may construe various types of such barely suggested nervousness, the *formes frustes* of the neuroses. There may, ;be cases in which only a few symptoms appear, or they may manifest themselves rarely or in mild forms; the extenuation may be transferred to the number; intensity, or to the temporal outbreak of the morbid manifestation. It may also happen that just this type, which forms the most frequent transition between health and disease, may never be discovered. The transition type, whose morbid manifestations come in the form of faulty and symptomatic actions, is characterized by the fact that the symptoms are transformed to the least important psychic activities, while everything that can lay claim to a higher psychic value remains free from disturbance. When the symptoms are disposed of in a reverse manner—that is, when they appear in the most important individual and social activities in a manner to disturb the functions of nourishment and sexual relations, professional and social life—such disposition is found in the severe cases of neuroses, and is perhaps more characteristic of the latter than the multiformity or vividness of the morbid manifestations.

But the common character of the mildest as well as the severest cases, to which the faulty and chance actions contribute, lies *in the ability to refer the phenomena to unwelcome, repressed, psychic material, which, though pushed away from consciousness, is nevertheless not robbed of all capacity to express itself.*

Footnotes

[1] *Alfred Adler, "Drei Psychoanalysen von Zahlen einfällen und obsedierenden Zahlen," Psych. Neur. Wochenschr., No. 28, 1905.*

[2] *As an explanation of Macbeth, No. 17 of the U. L., I was informed by Dr. Adler that in his seventeenth year this man had joined an anarchistic society whose aim was regicide. Probably this is why he forgot the content of the play Macbeth. The same person invented at that time a secret code in which numbers substituted letters.*

[3] *For the sake of simplicity I have omitted some of the not less suitable thoughts of the patients.*

[4] *Loc. cit., p. 36.*

[5]. *"Ein Beitrag zur Kenntnis des Zahlentraumes," Zentralb. f. Psychoanalyse, i. 12.*

[6] *"Unconscious Manipulation of Numbers" (ibid., ii. 5, 1912).*

[7] *This is another excellent example showing how a conscious intention was powerless to counteract an unconscious resistance.*

[8] These conceptions of strict determinism in seemingly arbitrary actions have already borne rich fruit for psychology—perhaps also for the administration of justice. Bleuler and Jung have in this way made intelligible the reaction in the so-called association experiments, wherein the test person answers to a given word with one occurring to him (stimulus-word reaction), while the time elapsing between the stimulus word and answer is measured (reaction-time). Jung has shown in his Diagnostische Assoziationsstudien, 1906, what fine reagents for psychic occurrences we possess in this association-experiment. Three students of criminology, H. Gross, of Prague, and Wertheimer and Kiein, have developed from these experiments a technique for the diagnosis of facts (Tatbestands-Diagnostik) in criminal cases, the examination of which is now tested by psychologists and jurists.

[9] Proceeding from other points of view, this interpretation of the trivial and accidental by the patient has been designated as "delusions of reference."

[10] For example, the fantasies of the hysterical regarding sexual and cruel abuse which are made conscious by analysis often correspond in every detail with the complaints of persecuted paranoiacs. It is remarkable but not altogether unexpected that we also meet the identical content as reality in the contrivances of perverts for the gratification of their desires.

[11] Which naturally has nothing of the character of perception.

[12] Zenltralb. f. Psychoanalyse, ii. 5.

[13] Thus far this explanation of Déjà vu has been appreciated by only one observer. Dr. Ferenczi, to whom the third edition of this is book is indebted for so many contributions, writes to me concerning this:"I have been convinced, through myself as well as others, that the inexplicable feeling of familiarity can be referred to unconscious fantasies of which we are unconsciously reminded in an actual situation. With one of my patients the process was apparently different but in reality it was quite analogous. This feeling returned to him very often, but showed itself regularly as originating in a forgotten (repressed) portion of a dream of the preceding night. Thus it appears that the Déjà vu can originate not only from day dreams but also from night dreams."

[14] I can perhaps give the following outline concerning the mechanism of actual forgetting. The memory material succumbs in general to two influences, condensation and disfigurement. Disfigurement is the work of the tendencies dominating the psychic life, and directs itself above all against the affective remnants of memory traces which maintain a more resistive attitude towards condensation. The traces which have grown indifferent merge into a process of condensation without opposition; in addition it may be observed that tendencies of disfigurement also feed on the indifferent material, because they have not been gratified where they wished to manifest themselves. As these processes of condensation and disfigurement continue for long periods during which all fresh experiences act upon the transformation of the memory content, it is our belief that it is time that makes memory uncertain and indistinctFrom the repressed memory traces it can be verified that they suffer no changes even in the longest periods. The unconscious, at all events, knows no time limit. The most important as well as the most peculiar character of psychic fixation consists in the fact that all impressions are on the one hand retained in the same form as they were received, and also in the forms that they have assumed in their further development. This state of affairs cannot be elucidated by any comparison from any other sphere. By virtue of this theory every former state of the memory content may thus be restored, even though all original relations have long been replaced by newer ones.

[15] Cf. here The Interpretation of Dreams, p. 483. Macmillan: New York ; and Allen : London.

THE THEORY OF
SEXUALITY

TABLE OF CONTENTS

INTRODUCTION

THE SOMEWHAT FAMOUS "Three Essays," which Dr. Brill is here bringing to the attention of an English-reading public, occupy—brief as they are—an important position among the achievements of their author, a great investigator and pioneer in an important line. It is not claimed that the facts here gathered are altogether new. The subject of the sexual instinct and its aberrations has long been before the scientific world and the names of many effective toilers in this vast field are known to every student. When one passes beyond the strict domains of science and considers what is reported of the sexual life in folkways and art-lore and the history of primitive culture and in romance, the sources of information are immense. Freud has made considerable additions to this stock of knowledge, but he has done also something f far greater consequence than this. He has worked out, with incredible penetration, the part which this instinct plays in every phase of human life and in the development of human character, and has been able to establish on a firm footing the remarkable thesis that psychoneurotic illnesses never occur with a perfectly normal sexual life. Other sorts of emotions contribute to the result, but some aberration of the sexual life is always present, as the cause of especially insistent emotions and repressions.

The instincts with which every child is born furnish desires or cravings which must be dealt with in some fashion. They may be refined ("sublimated"), so far as is necessary and desirable, into energies of other sorts—as happens readily with the play-instinct—or they may remain as the source of perversions and inversions, and of cravings of new sorts substituted for those of the more primitive kinds under the pressure of a conventional civilization. The symptoms of the functional psychoneuroses represent, after a fashion, some of these distorted attempts to find a substitute for the imperative cravings born of the sexual instincts, and their form often depends, in part at least, on the peculiarities of the sexual life in infancy and early childhood. It is Freud's service to have investigated this inadequately chronicled period of existence with extraordinary acumen. In so doing he made it plain that the "perversions" and "inversions," which reappear later under such striking shapes, belong to the normal sexual life of the young child and are seen, in veiled forms, in almost every case of nervous illness.

It cannot too often be repeated that these discoveries represent no fanciful deductions, but are the outcome of rigidly careful observations which anyone who will sufficiently prepare himself can verify. Critics fret over the amount of "sexuality" that Freud finds evidence of in the histories of his patients, and assume that he puts it there. But such criticisms are evidences of misunderstandings and proofs of ignorance.

Freud had learned that the amnesias of hypnosis and of hysteria were not absolute but relative and that in covering the lost memories, much more, of unexpected sort, was often found. Others, too, had gone as far as this, and stopped. But this investigator determined that nothing but the absolute impossibility of going further should make him cease from urging his patients into an inexorable scrutiny of the unconscious regions of their memories and thoughts, such as never had been made before. Every species of forgetfulness, even the forgetfulness of childhood's years, was made to yield its hidden stores of knowledge; dreams, even though apparently absurd, were found to be interpreters of a varied class of thoughts, active, although repressed as out of harmony with the selected life of consciousness; layer after layer, new sets of motives underlying motives were laid bare, and each patient's interest was strongly enlisted in the task of learning to know himself in order more truly and wisely to "sublimate" himself. Gradually other workers joined patiently in this laborious undertaking, which now stands, for those who have taken pains to comprehend it, as by far the most important movement in psychopathology.

It must, however, be recognized that these essays, of which Dr. Brill has given a translation that cannot but be timely, concern a subject which is not only important but unpopular. Few physicians read the works of v. Krafft-Ebing, Magnus Hirschfeld, Moll, and others of like sort. The remarkable volumes of Havelock Ellis were refused publication in his native England. The sentiments which inspired this hostile attitude towards the study of the sexual life are still active, though growing steadily less common. One may easily believe that if the facts which Freud's truth-seeking researches forced him to recognize and to publish had not been of an unpopular sort, his rich and abundant contributions to observational psychology, to the significance of dreams, to the etiology and therapeutics of the psychoneuroses, to the interpretation of mythology, would have won for him, by universal acclaim, the same recognition among all physicians that he has received from a rapidly increasing band of followers and colleagues.

May Dr. Brill's translation help toward this end.

There are two further points on which some comments should be made. The first is this, that those who conscientiously desire to learn all that they can from Freud's remarkable contributions should not be content to read any one of them alone. His various publications, such as "The Selected Papers on Hysteria and Other Psychoneuroses,"[1] "The Interpretation of Dreams,"[2] "The Psychopathology of Everyday Life,"[3] "Wit and its Relation to the Unconscious,"[4] the analysis of the case of the little boy called Hans, the study of Leonardo da Vinci,[4a] and the various short essays in the four Sammlungen kleiner Schriften, not only all hang together, but supplement each other to a remarkable extent. Unless a course of study such as this is undertaken many critics may think various statements and inferences in this volume to be farfetched or find them too obscure for comprehension.

The other point is the following: One frequently hears the psychoanalytic method referred to as if it was customary for those practicing it to exploit the sexual experiences of their patients and nothing more, and the insistence on the details of the sexual life, presented in this book, is likely to emphasize that notion. But the fact is, as every thoughtful inquirer is aware, that the whole progress of civilization, whether in the individual or the race, consists largely in a "sublimation" of infantile instincts, and especially certain portions of the sexual instinct, to other ends than those which they seemed designed to serve. Art and poetry are fed on this fuel and the evolution of character and mental force is largely of the same origin. All the forms which this sublimation, or the abortive attempts at sublimation, may take in any given case, should come out in the course of a thorough psychoanalysis. It is not the sexual life alone, but every interest and every motive, that must be inquired into by the physician who is seeking to obtain all the data about the patient, necessary for his reeducation and his cure. But all the thoughts and emotions and desires and motives which appear in the man or woman of adult years were once crudely represented in the obscure instincts of the infant, and among these instincts those which were concerned directly or indirectly with the sexual emotions, in a wide sense, are certain to be found in every case to have been the most important for the end-result.

JAMES J. PUTNAM.

Note 1: Translated by A.A. Brill, NERVOUS AND MENTAL DISEASE MONOGRAPH SERIES, NO. 4.
Note 2: Translated by A.A. Brill, The Macmillan Co., New York, and Allen & Unwin, London.
Note 3: Translated by A.A. Brill, The Macmillan Co., New York.
Note 4: Translated by A.A. Brill, Moffatt, Yard & Co., New York.
Note 4a: Translated by A.A. Brill, Moffatt, Yard & Co., New York.

AUTHOR'S PREFACE

NOW THAT THE flood-waters of war have subsided, it is satisfactory to be able to record the fact that interest in psycho-analytic research remains unimpaired in the world at large. But the different parts of the theory have not all had the same history. The purely psychological theses and findings of psycho-analysis on the unconscious, repression, conflict as a cause of illness, the advantage accruing from illness, the mechanisms of the formation of symptoms, etc., have come to enjoy increasing recognition and have won notice even from those who are in general opposed to our views. That part of the theory, however, which lies on the frontiers of biology and the foundations of which are contained in this little work is still faced with undiminished contradiction. It has even led some who for a time took a very active interest in psycho-analysis to abandon it and to adopt fresh views which were intended to restrict once more the part played by the factor of sexuality in normal and pathological mental life.

Nevertheless I cannot bring myself *to* accept the idea that this part of psycho-analytic theory can be very much more distant than the rest from the reality which it is its business to discover. My recollections, as well as a constant re-examination of the material, assure me that this part of the theory is based upon equally careful and impartial observation. There is, moreover, no difficulty in finding an explanation of this discrepancy in the general acceptance of my views. In the first place, the beginnings of human sexual life which are here described can only be confirmed by investigators who have enough patience and technical skill to trace back an analysis to the first years of a patient's childhood. And there is often no possibility of doing this, since medical treatment demands that an illness should, at least in appearance, be dealt with more rapidly. None, however, but physicians who practice psycho-analysis can have any access whatever to this sphere of knowledge or any possibility of forming a judgment that is uninfluenced by their own dislikes and prejudices. If mankind had been able to learn from a direct observation of children, these three essays could have remained unwritten.

It must also be remembered, however, that some of what this book contains—its insistence on the importance of sexuality in all human achievements and the attempt that it makes at enlarging the concept of sexuality—has from the first provided the strongest motives for the resistance against psycho-analysis. People have gone so far in their search for high-sounding catchwords as to talk of the 'pan-sexualism' of psycho-analysis and to raise the senseless charge against it of explaining 'everything' by sex. We might be astonished at this, if we ourselves could forget the way in which emotional factors make people confused and forgetful. For it is some time since Arthur Schopenhauer, the philosopher, showed mankind the extent to which their activities are determined by sexual impulses—in the ordinary sense of the word. It should surely have been impossible for a whole world of readers to banish such a startling piece of information so completely from their minds. And as for the 'stretching' of the concept of sexuality which has been necessitated by the analysis of children and what are called perverts, anyone who looks down with contempt upon psycho-analysis from a superior vantage-point should remember how closely the enlarged sexuality of psycho-analysis coincides with the Eros of the divine Plato. (Cf. Nachmansohn, 1915.)

FIRST ESSAY
The Sexual Aberrations[1]

THE FACT OF sexual need in man and animal is expressed in biology by the assumption of a "sexual impulse." This impulse is made analogous to the impulse of taking nourishment, and to hunger. The sexual expression corresponding to hunger not being found colloquilly, science uses the expression "libido."[2]

Popular conception makes definite assumptions concerning the nature and qualities of this sexual impulse. It is supposed to be absent during childhood and to commence about the time of and in connection with the maturing process of puberty; it is supposed that it manifests itself in irresistible attractions exerted by one sex upon the other, and that its aim is sexual union or at least such actions as would lead to union.

But we have every reason to see in these assumptions a very untrustworthy picture of reality. On closer examination they are found to abound in errors, inaccuracies and hasty conclusions.

If we introduce two terms and call the person from whom the sexual attraction emanates the *sexual object*, and the action towards which the impulse strives the *sexual aim*, then the scientifically examined experience shows us many deviations in reference to both sexual object and sexual aim, the relations of which to the accepted standard require thorough investigation.

1. DEVIATION IN REFERENCE TO THE SEXUAL OBJECT

The popular theory of the sexual impulse corresponds closely to the poetic fable of dividing the person into two halves—man and woman—who strive to become reunited through love. It is therefore very surprising to hear that there are men for whom the sexual object is not woman but man, and that there are women for whom it is not man but woman. Such *persons* are called contrary sexuals, or better, inverts; the *condition*, that of inversion. The number of such individuals is considerable though difficult of accurate determination.[3]

A. *Inversion*

The Behavior of Inverts.—The above-mentioned persons behave in many ways quite differently.

(*a*) They are absolutely inverted; *i.e.*, their sexual object must be always of the same sex, while the opposite sex can never be to them an object of sexual longing, but leaves them indifferent or may even evoke sexual repugnance. As men they are unable, on account of this repugnance, to perform the normal sexual act or miss all pleasure in its performance.

(*b*) They are amphigenously inverted (psychosexually hermaphroditic); *i.e.*, their sexual object may belong indifferently to either the same or to the other sex. The inversion lacks the character of exclusiveness.

(*c*) They are occasionally inverted; *i.e.*, under certain external conditions, chief among which are the inaccessibility of the normal sexual object and initiation, they are able to take as the sexual object a person of the same sex and thus find sexual gratification.

The inverted also manifest a manifold behavior in their judgment about the peculiarities of their sexual impulse. Some take the inversion as a matter of course, just as the normal person does regarding his libido, firmly demanding the same rights as the normal. Others, however, strive against the fact of their inversion and perceive in it a morbid compulsion.[4]

Other variations concern the relations of time. The characteristics of the inversion in any individual may date back as far as his memory goes, or they may become manifest to him at a definite period before or after puberty.[5] The character is either retained throughout life, or it occasionally recedes or represents an episode on the road to normal development. A periodical fluctuation between the normal and the inverted sexual object has also been observed. Of special interest are those cases in which the libido changes, taking on the character of inversion after a painful experience with the normal sexual object.

These different categories of variation generally exist independently of one another. In the most extreme cases it can regularly be assumed that the inversion has existed at all times and that the person feels contented with his peculiar state.

Many authors will hesitate to gather into a unit all the cases enumerated here and will prefer to emphasize the differences rather than the common characters of these groups, a view which corresponds with their preferred judgment of inversions. But no matter what divisions may be set up, it cannot be overlooked that all transitions are abundantly met with, so that the formation of a series would seem to impose itself.

Conception of Inversion.—The first attention bestowed upon inversion gave rise to the conception that it was a congenital sign of nervous degeneration. This harmonized with the fact that doctors first met it among the nervous, or among persons giving such an impression. There are two elements which should be considered independently in this conception: the congenitality, and the degeneration.

Degeneration.—This term *degeneration* is open to the objections which may be urged against the promiscuous use of this word in general. It has in fact become customary to designate all morbid manifestations not of traumatic or infectious origin as degenerative. Indeed, Magnan's classification of degenerates makes it possible that the highest general configuration of nervous accomplishment need not exclude the application of the concept of degeneration. Under the circumstances, it is a question what use and what new content the judgment of "degeneration" still possesses. It would seem more appropriate not to speak of degeneration: (1) Where there are not many marked deviations from the normal; (2) where the capacity for working and living do not in general appear markedly impaired.[6]

That the inverted are not degenerates in this qualified sense can be seen from the following facts:

1. The inversion is found among persons who otherwise show no marked deviation from the normal.

2. It is found also among persons whose capabilities are not disturbed, who on the contrary are distinguished by especially high intellectual development and ethical culture.[7]

3. If one disregards the patients of one's own practice and strives to comprehend a wider field of experience, he will in two directions encounter facts which will prevent him from assuming inversions as a degenerative sign.

(*a*) It must be considered that inversion was a frequent manifestation among the ancient nations at the height of their culture. It was an institution endowed with important functions. (*b*) It is found to be unusually prevalent among savages and primitive races, whereas the term degeneration is generally limited to higher civilization (I. Bloch). Even among the most civilized nations of Europe, climate and race have a most powerful influence on the distribution of, and attitude toward, inversion.[8]

Innateness.—Only for the first and most extreme class of inverts, as can be imagined, has innateness been claimed, and this from their own assurance that at no time in their life has their sexual impulse followed a different course. The fact of the existence of two other classes, especially of the third, is difficult to reconcile with the assumption of its being congenital. Hence, the propensity of those holding this view to separate the group of absolute inverts from the others results in the abandonment of the general conception of inversion. Accordingly in a number of cases the inversion would be of a congenital character, while in others it might originate from other causes.

In contradistinction to this conception is that which assumes inversion to be an *acquired* character of the sexual impulse. It is based on the following facts. (1) In many inverts (even absolute ones) an early affective sexual impression can be demonstrated, as a result of which the homosexual inclination developed. (2) In many others outer influences of a promoting and inhibiting nature can be demonstrated, which in earlier or later life led to a fixation of the inversion—among which are exclusive relations with the same sex, companionship in war, detention in prison, dangers of heterosexual intercourse, celibacy, sexual weakness, etc. (3) Hypnotic suggestion may remove the inversion, which would be surprising in that of a congenital character.

In view of all this, the existence of congenital inversion can certainly be questioned. The objection may be made to it that a more accurate examination of those claimed to be congenitally inverted will probably show that the direction of the libido was determined by a definite experience of early childhood, which has not been retained in the conscious memory of the person, but which can be brought back to memory by proper influences (Havelock Ellis). According to that author inversion can be designated only as a frequent variation of the sexual impulse which may be determined by a number of external circumstances of life.

The apparent certainty thus reached is, however, overthrown by the retort that manifestly there are many persons who have experienced even in their early youth those very sexual influences, such as seduction, mutual onanism, without becoming inverts, or without constantly remaining so. Hence, one is forced to assume that the alternatives congenital and acquired are either incomplete or do not cover the circumstances present in inversions.

Explanation of Inversion.—The nature of inversion is explained neither by the assumption that it is congenital nor that it is acquired. In the first case, we need to be told what there is in it of the congenital, unless we are satisfied with the roughest explanation, namely, that a person brings along a congenital sexual impulse connected with a definite sexual object. In the second case it is a question whether the manifold accidental influences suffice to explain the acquisition unless there is something in the individual to meet them half way. The negation of this last factor is inadmissible according to our former conclusions.

The Relation of Bisexuality.—Since the time of Frank Lydston, Kiernan, and Chevalier, a new series of ideas has been introduced for the explanation of the possibility of sexual inversion. This contains a new contradiction to the popular belief which assumes that a human being is either a man or a woman. Science shows cases in which the sexual characteristics appear blurred and thus the sexual distinction is made difficult, especially on an anatomical basis. The genitals of such persons unite the male and female characteristics (hermaphroditism). In rare cases both parts of the sexual apparatus are well developed (true hermaphroditism), but usually both are stunted.[9]

The importance of these abnormalities lies in the fact that they unexpectedly facilitate the understanding of the normal formation. A certain degree of anatomical hermaphroditism really belongs to the normal. In no normally formed male or female are traces of the apparatus of the other sex lacking; these either continue functionless as rudimentary organs, or they are transformed for the purpose of assuming other functions.

The conception which we gather from this long known anatomical fact is the original predisposition to bisexuality, which in the course of development has changed to monosexuality, leaving slight remnants of the stunted sex.

It was natural to transfer this conception to the psychic sphere and to conceive the inversion in its aberrations as an expression of psychic hermaphroditism. In order to bring the question to a decision, it was only necessary to have one other circumstance, viz., a regular concurrence of the inversion with the psychic and somatic signs of hermaphroditism.

But this second expectation was not realized. The relations between the assumed psychical and the demonstrable anatomical androgyny should never be conceived as being so close. There is frequently found in the inverted a diminution of the sexual impulse (H. Ellis) and a slight anatomical stunting of the organs. This, however, is found frequently but by no means regularly or preponderately. Thus we must recognize that inversion and somatic hermaphroditism are totally independent of each other.

Great importance has also been attached to the so-called secondary and tertiary sex characters and their aggregate occurrence in the inverted has been emphasized (H. Ellis). There is much truth in this but it should not be forgotten that the secondary and tertiary sex characteristics very frequently manifest themselves in the other sex, thus indicating androgyny without, however, involving changes in the sexual object in the sense of an inversion.

Psychic hermaphroditism would gain in substantiality if parallel with the inversion of the sexual object there should be at least a change in the other psychic qualities, such as in the impulses and distinguishing traits characteristic of the other sex. But such inversion of character can be expected with some regularity only in inverted women; in men the most perfect psychic manliness may be united with the inversion. If one firmly adheres to the hypothesis of a psychic hermaphroditism, one must add that in certain spheres its manifestations allow the recognition of only a very slight contrary determination. The same also holds true in the somatic androgyny. According to Halban, the appearance of individual stunted organs and secondary sex characters are quite independent of each other.[10]

A spokesman of the masculine inverts stated the bisexual theory in its crudest form in the following words: "It is a female brain in a male body." But we do not know the characteristics of a "female brain." The substitution of the anatomical for the psychological is as frivolous as it is unjustified. The tentative explanation by v. Krafft-Ebing seems to be more precisely formulated than that of Ulrich but does not essentially differ from it. v. Krafft-Ebing thinks that the bisexual predisposition gives to the individual male and female brain centers as well as somatic sexual organs. These centers develop first towards puberty mostly under the influence of the independent sex glands. We can, however, say the same of the male and female "centers" as of the male and female brains; and, moreover, we do not even know whether we can assume for the sexual functions separate brain locations ("centers") such as we may assume for language.

After this discussion, two notions, at all events, persist; first, that a bisexual predisposition is to be presumed for the inversion also, only we do not know of what it consists beyond the anatomical formations; and, second, that we are dealing with disturbances which are experienced by the sexual impulse during its development.[11]

The Sexual Object of Inverts.—The theory of psychic hermaphroditism presupposed that the sexual object of the inverted is the reverse of the normal. The inverted man, like the woman, succumbs to the charms emanating from manly qualities of body and mind; he feels himself like a woman and seeks a man.

But however true this may be for a great number of inverts, it by no means indicates the general character of inversion. There is no doubt that a great part of the male inverted have retained the psychic character of virility, that proportionately they show but little of the secondary characters of the other sex, and that they really look for real feminine psychic features in their sexual object. If that were not so it would be incomprehensible why masculine prostitution, in offering itself to inverts, copies in all its exterior, to-day as in antiquity, the dress and attitudes of woman. This imitation would otherwise be an insult to the ideal of the inverts. Among the Greeks, where the most manly men were found among inverts, it is quite obvious that it was not the masculine character of the boy which kindled the love of man, but it was his physical resemblance to woman as well as his feminine psychic qualities, such as shyness, demureness, and the need of instruction and help. As soon as the boy himself became a man he ceased to be a sexual object for men and in turn became a lover of boys. The sexual object in this case as in many others is therefore not of the like sex, but it unites both sex characters, a compromise between the impulses striving for the man and for the woman, but firmly conditioned by the masculinity of body (the genitals).[12]

The conditions in the woman are more definite; here the active inverts, with special frequency, show the somatic and psychic characters of man and desire femininity in their sexual object; though even here greater variation will be found on more intimate investigation.

The Sexual Aim of Inverts.—The important fact to bear in mind is that no uniformity of the sexual aim can be attributed to inversion. Intercourse per anum in men by no means goes with inversion; masturbation is just as frequently the exclusive aim; and the limitation of the sexual aim to mere effusion of feelings is here even more frequent than in hetero-sexual love. In women, too, the sexual aims of the inverted are manifold, among which contact with the mucous membrane of the mouth seems to be preferred.

Conclusion.—Though from the material on hand we are by no means in a position satisfactorily to explain the origin of inversion, we can say that through this investigation we have obtained an insight which can become of greater significance to us than the solution of the above problem. Our attention is called to the fact that we have assumed a too close connection between the sexual impulse and the sexual object. The experience gained from the so called abnormal cases teaches us that a connection exists between the sexual impulse and the sexual object which we are in danger of overlooking in the uniformity of normal states where the impulse seems to bring with it the object. We are thus instructed to separate this connection between the impulse and the object. The sexual impulse is probably entirely independent of its object and is not originated by the stimuli proceeding from the object.

B. *The Sexually Immature and Animals as Sexual Objects*

Whereas those sexual inverts whose sexual object does not belong to the normally adapted sex, appear to the observer as a collective number of perhaps otherwise normal individuals, the persons who choose for their sexual object the sexually immature (children) are apparently from the first sporadic aberrations. Only exceptionally are children the exclusive sexual objects. They are mostly drawn into this rôle by a faint-hearted and impotent individual who makes use of such substitutes, or when an impulsive urgent desire cannot at the time secure the proper object. Still it throws some light on the nature of the sexual impulse, that it should suffer such great variation and depreciation of its object, a thing which hunger, adhering more energetically to its object, would allow only in the most extreme cases. The same may be said of sexual relations with animals—a thing not at all rare among farmers—where the sexual attraction goes beyond the limits of the species.

For esthetic reasons one would fain attribute this and other excessive aberrations of the sexual impulse to the insane, but this cannot be done. Experience teaches that among the latter no disturbances of the sexual impulse can be found other than those observed among the sane, or among whole races and classes. Thus we find with gruesome frequency sexual abuse of children by teachers and servants merely because they have the best opportunities for it. The insane present the aforesaid aberration only in a somewhat intensified form; or what is of special significance is the fact that the aberration becomes exclusive and takes the place of the normal sexual gratification.

This very remarkable relation of sexual variations ranging from the normal to the insane gives material for reflection. It seems to me that the fact to be explained would show that the impulses of the sexual life belong to those which even normally are most poorly controlled by the higher psychic activities. He who is in any way psychically abnormal, be it in social or ethical conditions, is, according to my experience, regularly so in his sexual life. But many are abnormal in their sexual life who in every other respect correspond to the average; they have followed the human cultural development, but sexuality remained as their weak point.

As a general result of these discussions we come to see that, under numerous conditions and among a surprising number of individuals, the nature and value of the sexual object steps into the background. There is something else in the sexual impulse which is the essential and constant.[13]

2. DEVIATION IN REFERENCE TO THE SEXUAL AIM

The union of the genitals in the characteristic act of copulation is taken as the normal sexual aim. It serves to loosen the sexual tension and temporarily to quench the sexual desire (gratification analogous to satisfaction of hunger). Yet even in the most normal sexual process those additions are distinguishable, the development of which leads to the aberrations described as *perversions*. Thus certain intermediary relations to the sexual object connected with copulation, such as touching and looking, are recognized as preliminary to the sexual aim. These activities are on the one hand themselves connected with pleasure and on the other hand they enhance the excitement which persists until the definite sexual aim is reached. One definite kind of contiguity, consisting of mutual approximation of the mucous membranes of the lips in the form of a kiss, has received among the most civilized nations a sexual value, though the parts of the body concerned do not belong to the sexual apparatus but form the entrance to the digestive tract.

This therefore supplies the factors which allow us to bring the perversions into relation with the normal sexual life, and which are available also for their classification. The perversions are either (*a*) anatomical *transgressions* of the bodily regions destined for sexual union, or (*b*) a *lingering* at the intermediary relations to the sexual object which should normally be rapidly passed on the way to the definite sexual aim.

(A) Anatomical Transgression

Overestimation of the Sexual Object.—The psychic estimation in which the sexual object as a goal of the sexual impulse shares is only in the rarest cases limited to the genitals; generally it embraces the whole body and tends to include all sensations emanating from the sexual object. The same overestimation spreads over the psychic sphere and manifests itself as a logical blinding (diminished judgment) in the face of the psychic attainments and perfections of the sexual object, as well as a blind obedience to the judgments issuing from the latter. The full faith of love thus becomes an important, if not the primordial source of authority.[14]

It is this sexual overvaluation, which so ill agrees with the restriction of the sexual aim to the union of the genitals only, that assists other parts of the body to participate as sexual aims.[15] In the development of this most manifold anatomical overestimation there is an unmistakable desire towards variation, a thing denominated by Hoche as "excitement-hunger" (Reiz-hunger).[16]

Sexual Utilization of the Mucous Membrane of the Lips and Mouth.—The significance of the factor of sexual overestimation can be best studied in the man, in whom alone the sexual life is accessible to investigation, whereas in the woman it is veiled in impenetrable darkness, partly in consequence of cultural stunting and partly on account of the conventional reticence and dishonesty of women.

The employment of the mouth as a sexual organ is considered as a perversion if the lips (tongue) of the one are brought into contact with the genitals of the other, but not when the mucous membrane of the lips of both touch each other. In the latter exception we find the connection with the normal. He who abhors the former as perversions, though these since antiquity have been common practices among mankind, yields to a distinct *feeling of loathing* which protects him from adopting such sexual aims. The limit of such loathing is frequently purely conventional; he who kisses fervently the lips of a pretty girl will perhaps be able to use her tooth brush only with a sense of loathing, though there is no reason to assume that his own oral cavity for which he entertains no loathing is cleaner than that of the girl. Our attention is here called to the factor of loathing which stands in the way of the libidinous overestimation of the sexual aim, but which may in turn be vanquished by the libido. In the loathing we may observe one of the forces which have brought about the restrictions of the sexual aim. As a rule these forces halt at the genitals; there is, however, no doubt that even the genitals of the other sex themselves may be an object of loathing. Such behavior is characteristic of all hysterics, especially women. The force of the sexual impulse prefers to occupy itself with the overcoming of this loathing (see below).

Sexual Utilization of the Anal Opening.—It is even more obvious than in the former case that it is the loathing which stamps as a perversion the use of the anus as a sexual aim. But it should not be interpreted as espousing a cause when I observe that the basis of this loathing—namely, that this part of the body serves for the excretion and comes in contact with the loathsome excrement—is not more plausible than the basis which hysterical girls have for the disgust which they entertain for the male genital because it serves for urination.

The sexual rôle of the mucous membrane of the anus is by no means limited to intercourse between men; its preference has nothing characteristic of the inverted feeling. On the contrary, it seems that the *pedicatio* of the man owes its rôle to the analogy with the act in the woman, whereas among inverts it is mutual masturbation which is the most common sexual aim.

The Significance of Other Parts of the Body.—Sexual infringement on the other parts of the body, in all its variations, offers nothing new; it adds nothing to our knowledge of the sexual impulse which herein only announces its intention to dominate the sexual object in every way. Besides the sexual overvaluation, a second and generally unknown factor may be mentioned among the anatomical transgressions. Certain parts of the body, like the mucous membrane of the mouth and anus, which repeatedly appear in such practices, lay claim as it were to be considered and treated as genitals. We shall hear how this claim is justified by the development of the sexual impulse, and how it is fulfilled in the symptomatology of certain morbid conditions.

Unfit Substitutes for the Sexual Object. Fetichism.—We are especially impressed by those cases in which for the normal sexual object another is substituted which is related to it but which is totally unfit for the normal sexual aim. According to the scheme of the introduction we should have done better to mention this most interesting group of aberrations of the sexual impulse among the deviations in reference to the sexual object, but we have deferred mention of these until we became acquainted with the factor of sexual overestimation, upon which these manifestations, connected with the relinquishing of the sexual aim, depend.

The substitute for the sexual object is generally a part of the body but little adapted for sexual purposes, such as the foot, or hair, or an inanimate object which is in demonstrable relation with the sexual person, and preferably with the sexuality of the same (fragments of clothing, white underwear). This substitution is not unjustly compared with the fetich in which the savage sees the embodiment of his god.

The transition to the cases of fetichism, with a renunciation of a normal or of a perverted sexual aim, is formed by cases in which a fetichistic determination is demanded in the sexual object if the sexual aim is to be attained (definite color of hair, clothing, even physical blemishes). No other variation of the sexual impulse verging on the pathological claims our interest as much as this one, owing to the peculiarity occasioned by its manifestations. A certain diminution in the striving for the normal sexual aim may be presupposed in all these cases (executive weakness of the sexual apparatus).[17] The connection with the normal is occasioned by the psychologically necessary overestimation of the sexual object, which inevitably encroaches upon everything associatively related to it (sexual object). A certain degree of such fetichism therefore regularly belong to the normal, especially during those stages of wooing when the normal sexual aim seems inaccessible or its realization deferred.

"Get me a handkerchief from her bosom—a garter of my love."
—FAUST.

The case becomes pathological only when the striving for the fetich fixes itself beyond such determinations and takes the place of the normal sexual aim; or again, when the fetich disengages itself from the person concerned and itself becomes a sexual object. These are the general determinations for the transition of mere variations of the sexual impulse into pathological aberrations.

The persistent influence of a sexual impress mostly received in early childhood often shows itself in the selection of a fetich, as Binet first asserted, and as was later proven by many illustrations,—a thing which may be placed parallel to the proverbial attachment to a first love in the normal ("On revient toujours à ses premiers amours"). Such a connection is especially seen in cases with only fetichistic determinations of the sexual object. The significance of early sexual impressions will be met again in other places.

In other cases it was mostly a symbolic thought association, unconscious to the person concerned, which led to the replacing of the object by means of a fetich. The paths of these connections cannot always be definitely demonstrated. The foot is a very primitive sexual symbol already found in myths.[18] Fur is used as a fetich probably on account of its association with the hairiness of the mons veneris. Such symbolism seems often to depend on sexual experiences in childhood.[19]

(B) Fixation of Precursory Sexual Aims

The Appearance of New Intentions.—All the outer and inner determinations which impede or hold at a distance the attainment of the normal sexual aim, such as impotence, costliness of the sexual object, and dangers of the sexual act, will conceivably strengthen the inclination to linger at the preparatory acts and to form them into new sexual aims which may take the place of the normal. On closer investigation it is always seen that the ostensibly most peculiar of these new intentions have already been indicated in the normal sexual act.

Touching and Looking.—At least a certain amount of touching is indispensable for a person in order to attain the normal sexual aim. It is also generally known that the touching of the skin of the sexual object causes much pleasure and produces a supply of new excitement. Hence, the lingering at the touching can hardly be considered a perversion if the sexual act is proceeded with.

The same holds true in the end with looking which is analogous to touching. The manner in which the libidinous excitement is frequently awakened is by the optical impression, and selection takes account of this circumstance—if this teleological mode of thinking be permitted—by making the sexual object a thing of beauty. The covering of the body, which keeps abreast with civilization, serves to arouse sexual inquisitiveness, which always strives to restore for itself the sexual object by uncovering the hidden parts. This can be turned into the artistic ("sublimation") if the interest is turned from the genitals to the form of the body.[20] The tendency to linger at this intermediary sexual aim of the sexually accentuated looking is found to a certain degree in most normals; indeed it gives them the possibility of directing a certain amount of their libido to a higher artistic aim. On the other hand, the fondness for looking becomes a perversion (*a*) when it limits itself entirely to the genitals; (*b*) when it becomes connected with the overcoming of loathing (voyeurs and onlookers at the functions of excretion); and (*c*) when instead of preparing for the normal sexual aim it suppresses it. The latter, if I may draw conclusions from a single analysis, is in a most pronounced way true of exhibitionists, who expose their genitals so as in turn to bring to view the genitals of others.

In the perversion which consists in striving to look and be looked at we are confronted with a very remarkable character which will occupy us even more intensively in the following aberration. The sexual aim is here present in twofold formation, in an *active* and a *passive* form.

The force which is opposed to the peeping mania and through which it is eventually abolished is *shame* (like the former loathing).

Sadism and Masochism.—The desire to cause pain to the sexual object and its opposite, the most frequent and most significant of all perversions, was designated in its two forms by v. Krafft-Ebing as sadism or the active form, and masochism or the passive form. Other authors prefer the narrower term algolagnia which emphasizes the pleasure in pain and cruelty, whereas the terms selected by v. Krafft-Ebing place the pleasure secured in all kinds of humility and submission in the foreground.

The roots of active algolagnia, sadism, can be readily demonstrable in the normal. The sexuality of most men shows a taint of *aggression*, it is a propensity to subdue, the biological significance of which lies in the necessity of overcoming the resistance of the sexual object by actions other than mere *courting*. Sadism would then correspond to an aggressive component of the sexual impulse which has become independent and exaggerated and has been brought to the foreground by displacement.

The conception of sadism fluctuates in the usage of language from a mere active or impetuous attitude towards the sexual object to the exclusive attachment of the gratification to the subjection and maltreatment of the object. Strictly speaking only the last extreme case has a claim to the name of perversion.

Similarly, the designation of masochism comprises all passive attitude to the sexual life and to the sexual object; in its most extreme form the gratification is connected with suffering of physical or mental pain at the hands of the sexual object. Masochism as a perversion seems to be still more remote from the normal sexual life by forming a contrast to it; it may be doubted whether it ever appears as a primary form or whether it does not more regularly originate through transformation from sadism. It can often be recognized that the masochism is nothing but a continuation of the sadism turning against one's own person in which the latter at first takes the place of the sexual object. Analysis of extreme cases of masochistic perversions show that there is a coöperation of a large series of factors which exaggerate and fix the original passive sexual attitude (castration complex, conscience).

The pain which is here overcome ranks with the loathing and shame which were the resistances opposed to the libido.

Sadism and masochism occupy a special place among the perversions, for the contrast of activity and passivity lying at their bases belong to the common traits of the sexual life.

That cruelty and sexual impulse are most intimately connected is beyond doubt taught by the history of civilization, but in the explanation of this connection no one has gone beyond the accentuation of the aggressive factors of the libido. The aggression which is mixed with the sexual impulse is according to some authors a remnant of cannibalistic lust, a participation on the part of the domination apparatus (Bemächtigungsapparatus), which served also for the gratification of the great wants of the other, ontogenetically the older impulse.[21] It has also been claimed that every pain contains in itself the possibility of a pleasurable sensation. Let us be satisfied with the impression that the explanation of this perversion is by no means satisfactory and that it is possible that many psychic efforts unite themselves into one effect.

The most striking peculiarity of this perversion lies in the fact that its active and passive forms are regularly encountered together in the same person. He who experiences pleasure by causing pain to others in sexual relations is also able to experience the pain emanating from sexual relations as pleasure. A sadist is simultaneously a masochist, though either the active or the passive side of the perversion may be more strongly developed and thus represent his preponderate sexual activity.[22]

We thus see that certain perverted propensities regularly appear in *contrasting pairs*, a thing which, in view of the material to be produced later, must claim great theoretical value. It is furthermore clear that the existence of the contrast, sadism and masochism, cannot readily be attributed to the mixture of aggression. On the other hand one may be tempted to connect such simultaneously existing contrasts with the united contrast of male and female in bisexuality, the significance of which is reduced in psychoanalysis to the contrast of activity and passivity.

3. GENERAL STATEMENTS APPLICABLE TO ALL PERVERSIONS

Variation and Disease.—The physicians who at first studied the *perversions* in pronounced cases and under peculiar conditions were naturally inclined to attribute to them the character of a morbid or degenerative sign similar to the *inversions*. This view, however, is easier to refute in this than in the former case. Everyday experience has shown that most of these transgressions, at least the milder ones, are seldom wanting as components in the sexual life of normals who look upon them as upon other intimacies. Wherever the conditions are favorable such a perversion may for a long time be substituted by a normal person for the normal sexual aim or it may be placed near it. In no normal person does the normal sexual aim lack some designable perverse element, and this universality suffices in itself to prove the inexpediency of an opprobrious application of the name perversion. In the realm of the sexual life one is sure to meet with exceptional difficulties which are at present really unsolvable, if one wishes to draw a sharp line between the mere variations within physiological limits and morbid symptoms.

Nevertheless, the quality of the new sexual aim in some of these perversions is such as to require special notice. Some of the perversions are in content so distant from the normal that we cannot help calling them "morbid," especially those in which the sexual impulse, in overcoming the resistances (shame, loathing, fear, and pain) has brought about surprising results (licking of feces and violation of cadavers). Yet even in these cases one ought not to feel certain of regularly finding among the perpetrators persons of pronounced abnormalities or insane minds. We cannot lose sight of the fact that persons who otherwise behave normally are recorded as sick in the realm of the sexual life where they are dominated by the most unbridled of all impulses. On the other hand, a manifest abnormality in any other relation in life generally shows an undercurrent of abnormal sexual behavior.

In the majority of cases we are able to find the morbid character of the perversion not in the content of the new sexual aim but in its relation to the normal. It is morbid if the perversion does not appear beside the normal (sexual aim and sexual object), where favorable circumstances promote it and unfavorable impede the normal, or if it has under all circumstances repressed and supplanted the normal; *the exclusiveness* and *fixation* of the perversion justifies us in considering it a morbid symptom.

The Psychic Participation in the Perversions.—Perhaps it is precisely in the most abominable perversions that we must recognize the most prolific psychic participation for the transformation of the sexual impulse. In these cases a piece of psychic work has been accomplished in which, in spite of its gruesome success, the value of an idealization of the impulse cannot be disputed. The omnipotence of love nowhere perhaps shows itself stronger than in this one of her aberrations. The highest and the lowest everywhere in sexuality hang most intimately together. ("From heaven through the world to hell.")

Two Results.—In the study of perversions we have gained an insight into the fact that the sexual impulse has to struggle against certain psychic forces, resistances, among which shame and loathing are most prominent. We may presume that these forces are employed to confine the impulse within the accepted normal limits, and if they have become developed in the individual before the sexual impulse has attained its full strength, it is really they which have directed it in the course of development.[23]

We have furthermore remarked that some of the examined perversions can be comprehended only by assuming the union of many motives. If they are amenable to analysis—disintegration—they must be of a composite nature. This may give us a hint that the sexual impulse itself may not be something simple, that it may on the contrary be composed of many components which detach themselves to form perversions. Our clinical observation thus calls our attention to *fusions* which have lost their expression in the uniform normal behavior.

4. THE SEXUAL IMPULSE IN NEUROTICS

Psychoanalysis.—A proper contribution to the knowledge of the sexual impulse in persons who are at least related to the normal can be gained only from one source, and is accessible only by one definite path. There is only one way to obtain a thorough and unerring solution of problems in the sexual life of so-called psychoneurotics (hysteria, obsessions, the wrongly-named neurasthenia, and surely also dementia præcox, and paranoia), and that is by subjecting them to the psychoanalytic investigations propounded by J. Breuer and myself in 1893, which we called the "cathartic" treatment.

I must repeat what I have said in my published work, that these psychoneuroses, as far as my experience goes, are based on sexual motive powers. I do not mean that the energy of the sexual impulse merely contributes to the forces supporting the morbid manifestations (symptoms), but I wish distinctly to maintain that this supplies the only constant and the most important source of energy in the neurosis, so that the sexual life of such persons manifests itself either exclusively, preponderately, or partially in these symptoms. As I have already stated in different places, the symptoms are the sexual activities of the patient. The proof for this assertion I have obtained from the psychoanalysis of hysterics and other neurotics during a period of twenty years, the results of which I hope to give later in a detailed account.

Psychoanalysis removes the symptoms of hysteria on the supposition that they are the substitutes—the transcriptions as it were—for a series of emotionally accentuated psychic processes, wishes, and desires, to which a passage for their discharge through the conscious psychic activities has been cut off by a special process (repression). These thought formations which are restrained in the state of the unconscious strive for expression, that is, for *discharge*, in conformity to their affective value, and find such in hysteria through a process of *conversion* into somatic phenomena—the hysterical symptoms.

If, *lege artis*, and with the aid of a special technique, retrogressive transformations of the symptoms into the affectful and conscious thoughts can be effected, it then becomes possible to get the most accurate information about the nature and origin of these previously unconscious psychic formations.

Results of Psychoanalysis.—In this manner it has been discovered that the symptoms represent the equivalent for the strivings which received their strength from the source of the sexual impulse. This fully concurs with what we know of the character of hysterics, which we have taken as models for all psycho-neurotics, before they have become diseased, and with what we know concerning the causes of the disease. The hysterical character evinces a part of sexual repression which reaches beyond the normal limits, an exaggeration of the resistances against the sexual impulse which we know as shame and loathing. It is an instinctive flight from intellectual occupation with the sexual problem, the consequence of which in pronounced cases is a complete sexual ignorance, which is preserved till the age of sexual maturity is attained.[24]

This feature, so characteristic of hysteria, is not seldom concealed in crude observation by the existence of the second constitutional factor of hysteria, namely, the enormous development of the sexual craving. But the psychological analysis will always reveal it and solves the very contradictory enigma of hysteria by proving the existence of the contrasting pair, an immense sexual desire and a very exaggerated sexual rejection.

The provocation of the disease in hysterically predisposed persons is brought about if in consequence of their progressive maturity or external conditions of life they are earnestly confronted with the real sexual demand. Between the pressure of the craving and the opposition of the sexual rejection an outlet for the disease results, which does not remove the conflict but seeks to elude it by transforming the libidinous strivings into symptoms. It is an exception only in appearance if a hysterical person, say a man, becomes subject to some banal emotional disturbance, to a conflict in the center of which there is no sexual interest. Psychoanalysis will regularly show that it is the sexual components of the conflict which make the disease possible by withdrawing the psychic processes from normal adjustment.

Neurosis and Perversion.—A great part of the opposition to my assertion is explained by the fact that the sexuality from which I deduce the psychoneurotic symptoms is thought of as coincident with the normal sexual impulse. But psychoanalysis teaches us better than this. It shows that the symptoms do not by any means result at the expense only of the so called normal sexual impulse (at least not exclusively or preponderately), but they represent the converted expression of impulses which in a broader sense might be designated as *perverse* if they could manifest themselves directly in phantasies and acts without deviating from consciousness. The symptoms are therefore partially formed at the cost of abnormal sexuality. *The neurosis is, so to say, the negative of the perversion.*[25]

The sexual impulse of the psychoneurotic shows all the aberrations which we have studied as variations of the normal and as manifestations of morbid sexual life.

(*a*) In all the neurotics without exception we find feelings of inversion in the unconscious psychic life, fixation of libido on persons of the same sex. It is impossible, without a deep and searching discussion, adequately to appreciate the significance of this factor for the formation of the picture of the disease; I can only assert that the unconscious propensity to inversion is never wanting and is particularly of immense service in explaining male hysteria.[26]

(*b*) All the inclinations to anatomical transgression can be demonstrated in psychoneurotics in the unconscious and as symptom-creators. Of special frequency and intensity are those which impart to the mouth and the mucous membrane of the anus the rôle of genitals.

(*c*) The partial desires which usually appear in contrasting pairs play a very prominent rôle among the symptom-creators in the psychoneuroses. We have learned to know them as carriers of new sexual aims, such as peeping mania, exhibitionism, and the actively and passively formed impulses of cruelty. The contribution of the last is indispensable for the understanding of the morbid nature of the symptoms; it almost regularly controls some portion of the social behavior of the patient. The transformation of love into hatred, of tenderness into hostility, which is characteristic of a large number of neurotic cases and apparently of all cases of paranoia, takes place by means of the union of cruelty with the libido.

The interest in these deductions will be more heightened by certain peculiarities of the diagnosis of facts.

α. There is nothing in the unconscious streams of thought of the neuroses which would correspond to an inclination towards fetishism; a circumstance which throws light on the psychological peculiarity of this well understood perversion.

β. Wherever any such impulse is found in the unconscious which can be paired with a contrasting one, it can regularly be demonstrated that the latter, too, is effective. Every active perversion is here accompanied by its passive counterpart. He who in the unconscious is an exhibitionist is at the same time a voyeur, he who suffers from sadistic feelings as a result of repression will also show another reinforcement of the symptoms from the source of masochistic tendencies. The perfect concurrence with the behavior of the corresponding positive perversions is certainly very noteworthy. In the picture of the disease, however, the preponderant rôle is played by either one or the other of the opposing tendencies.

γ. In a pronounced case of psychoneurosis we seldom find the development of one single perverted impulse; usually there are many and regularly there are traces of all perversions. The individual impulse, however, on account of its intensity, is independent of the development of the others, but the study of the positive perversions gives us the accurate counterpart to it.

PARTIAL IMPULSES AND EROGENOUS ZONES

Keeping in mind what we have learned from the examination of the positive and negative perversions, it becomes quite obvious that they can be referred to a number of "partial impulses," which are not, however, primary but are subject to further analysis. By an "impulse" we can understand in the first place nothing but the psychic representative of a continually flowing internal somatic source of excitement, in contradistinction to the "stimulus" which is produced by isolated excitements coming from without. The impulse is thus one of the concepts marking the limits between the psychic and the physical. The simplest and most obvious assumption concerning the nature of the impulses would be that in themselves they possess no quality but are only taken into account as a measure of the demand for effort in the psychic life. What distinguishes the impulses from one another and furnishes them with specific attributes is their relation to their somatic *sources* and to their *aims*. The source of the impulse is an exciting process in an organ, and the immediate aim of the impulse lies in the elimination of this organic stimulus.

Another preliminary assumption in the theory of the impulse which we cannot relinquish, states that the bodily organs furnish two kinds of excitements which are determined by differences of a chemical nature. One of these forms of excitement we designate as the specifically sexual and the concerned organ as the *erogenous zone*, while the sexual element emanating from it is the partial impulse.[27]

In the perversions which claim sexual significance for the oral cavity and the anal opening the part played by the erogenous zone is quite obvious. It behaves in every way like a part of the sexual apparatus. In hysteria these parts of the body, as well as the tracts of mucous membrane proceeding from them, become the seat of new sensations and innervating changes in a manner similar to the real genitals when under the excitement of normal sexual processes.

The significance of the erogenous zones in the psychoneuroses, as additional apparatus and substitutes for the genitals, appears to be most prominent in hysteria though that does not signify that it is of lesser validity in the other morbid forms. It is not so recognizable in compulsion neurosis and paranoia because here the symptom formation takes place in regions of the psychic apparatus which lie at a great distance from the central locations for bodily control. The more remarkable thing in the compulsion neurosis is the significance of the impulses which create new sexual aims and appear independently of the erogenous zones. Nevertheless, the eye corresponds to an erogenous zone in the looking and exhibition mania, while the skin takes on the same part in the pain and cruelty components of the sexual impulse. The skin, which in special parts of the body becomes differentiated as sensory organs and modified by the mucous membrane, is the erogenous zone, κατ εξ ογεν.[28]

EXPLANATION OF THE MANIFEST PREPONDERANCE OF SEXUAL PERVERSIONS IN THE PSYCHONEUROSES

The sexuality of psychoneurotics has perhaps been placed in a false light by the above discussions. It appears that the sexual behavior of the psychoneurotic approaches in predisposition to the pervert and deviates by just so much from the normal. Nevertheless, it is very possible that the constitutional disposition of these patients besides containing an immense amount of sexual repression and a predominant force of sexual impulse also possesses an unusual tendency to perversions in the broadest sense. However, an examination of milder cases shows that the last assumption is not an absolute requisite, or at least that in pronouncing judgment on the morbid effects one ought to discount the effect of one of the factors. In most psychoneurotics the disease first appears after puberty following the demands of the normal sexual life.

Against these the repression above all directs itself. Or the disease comes on later, owing to the fact that the libido is unable to attain normal sexual gratification. In both cases the libido behaves like a stream the principal bed of which is dammed; it fills the collateral roads which until now perhaps have been empty. Thus the manifestly great (though to be sure negative) tendency to perversion in psychoneurotics may be collaterally conditioned; at any rate, it is certainly collaterally increased. The fact of the matter is that the sexual repression has to be added as an inner factor to such external ones as restriction of freedom, inaccessibility to the normal sexual object, dangers of the normal sexual act, etc., which cause the origin of perversions in individuals who might have otherwise remained normal.

In individual cases of neurosis the behavior may be different; now the congenital force of the tendency to perversion may be more decisive and at other times more influence may be exerted by the collateral increase of the same through the deviation of the libido from the normal sexual aim and object. It would be unjust to construe a contrast where a cooperation exists. The greatest results will always be brought about by a neurosis if constitution and experience cooperate in the same direction. A pronounced constitution may perhaps be able to dispense with the assistance of daily impressions, while a profound disturbance in life may perhaps bring on a neurosis even in an average constitution. These views similarly hold true in the etiological significance of the congenital and the accidental experiences in other spheres.

If, however, preference is given to the assumption that an especially formed tendency to perversions is characteristic of the psychoneurotic constitution, there is a prospect of being able to distinguish a multiformity of such constitutions in accordance with the congenital preponderance of this or that erogenous zone, or of this or that partial impulse. Whether there is a special relationship between the predisposition to perversions and the selection of the morbid picture has not, like many other things in this realm, been investigated.

THE INFANTILISM OF SEXUALITY

By demonstrating the perverted feelings as symptomatic formations in psychoneurotics, we have enormously increased the number of persons who can be added to the perverts. This is not only because neurotics represent a very large proportion of humanity, but we must consider also that the neuroses in all their gradations run in an uninterrupted series to the normal state. Moebius was quite justified in saying that we are all somewhat hysterical. Hence, the very wide dissemination of perversions urged us to assume that the predisposition to perversions is no rare peculiarity but must form a part of the normally accepted constitution.

We have heard that it is a question whether perversions should be referred to congenital determinations or whether they originate from accidental experiences, just as Binet showed in fetichisms. Now we are forced to the conclusion that there is indeed something congenital at the basis of perversions, but it is something *which is congenital in all persons*, which as a predisposition may fluctuate in intensity and is brought into prominence by influences of life. We deal here with congenital roots in the constitution of the sexual impulse which in one series of cases develop into real carriers of sexual activity (perverts); while in other cases they undergo an insufficient suppression (repression), so that as morbid symptoms they are enabled to attract to themselves in a round-about way a considerable part of the sexual energy; while again in favorable cases between the two extremes they originate the normal sexual life through effective restrictions and other elaborations.

But we must also remember that the assumed constitution which shows the roots of all perversions will be demonstrable only in the child, though all impulses can be manifested in it only in moderate intensity. If we are led to suppose that neurotics conserve the infantile state of their sexuality or return to it, our interest must then turn to the sexual life of the child, and we will then follow the play of influences which control the processes of development of the infantile sexuality up to its termination in a perversion, a neurosis or a normal sexual life.

Note 1: The facts contained in the first "Contribution" have been gathered from the familiar publications of Krafft-Ebing, Moll, Moebius, Havelock Ellis, Schrenk-Notzing, Löwenfeld, Eulenberg, J. Bloch, and M. Hirschfeld, and from the later works published in the "Jahrbuch für sexuelle Zwischenstufen." As these publications also mention the other literature bearing on this subject I may forbear giving detailed references.

The conclusions reached through the investigation of sexual inverts are all based on the reports of J. Sadger and on my own experience.

Note 2: For general use the word "libido" is best translated by "craving." (Prof. James J. Putnam, Journal of Abnormal Psychology, Vol. IV, 6.)

Note 3: For the difficulties entailed in the attempt to ascertain the proportional number of inverts compare the work of M. Hirschfeld in the Jahrbuch für sexuelle Zwischenstufen, 1904. Cf. also Brill, The Conception of Homosexuality, Journal of the A.M.A., August 2, 1913.

Note 4: Such a striving against the compulsion to inversion favors cures by suggestion of psychoanalysis.

Note 5: Many have justly emphasized the fact that the autobiographic statements of inverts, as to the time of the appearance of their tendency to inversion, are untrustworthy as they may have repressed from memory any evidences of heterosexual feelings.

Psychoanalysis has confirmed this suspicion in all cases of inversion accessible, and has decidedly changed their anamnesis by filling up the infantile amnesias.

Note 6: With what reserve the diagnosis of degeneration should be made and what slight practical significance can be attributed to it can be gathered from the discussions of Moebius (Ueber Entartung; Grenzfragen des Nerven- und Seelenlebens, No. III, 1900). He says: "If we review the wide sphere of degeneration upon which we have here turned some light we can conclude without further ado that it is really of little value to diagnose degeneration."

Note 7: We must agree with the spokesman of "Uranism" that some of the most prominent men known have been inverts and perhaps absolute inverts.

Note 8: In the conception of inversion the pathological features have been Separated from the anthropological. For this credit is due to I. Bloch (Beiträge zur Ätiologie der Psychopathia Sexualis, 2 Teile, 1902-3), who has also brought into prominence the existence of inversion in the old civilized nations.

Note 9: Compare the last detailed discussion of somatic hermaphroditism (Taruffi, Hermaphroditismus und Zeugungsunfähigkeit, German edit. by R. Teuscher, 1903), and the works of Neugebauer in many volumes of the Jahrbuch für sexuelle Zwischenstufen.

Note 10: J. Halban, "Die Entstehung der Geschlechtscharaktere," Arch. für Gynäkologie, Bd. 70, 1903. See also there the literature on the subject.

Note 11: According to a report in Vol. 6 of the Jahrbuch f. sexuelle Zwischenstufen, E. Gley is supposed to have been the first to mention bisexuality as an explanation of inversion. He published a paper (Les Abérrations de l'instinct Sexuel) in the Revue Philosophique as early as January, 1884. It is moreover noteworthy that the majority of authors who trace the inversion to bisexuality assume this factor not only for the inverts but also for those who have developed normally, and justly interpret the inversion as a result of a disturbance in development. Among these authors are Chevalier (Inversion Sexuelle, 1893), and v. Krafft-Ebing ("Zur Erklärung der konträren Sexualempfindung," Jahrbücher f. Psychiatrie u. Nervenheilkunde, XIII), who states that there are a number of observations "from which at least the virtual and continued existence *of this second center (of the underlying sex) results." A Dr. Arduin (Die Frauenfrage und die sexuellen Zwischenstufen, 2d vol. of the Jahrbuch f. sexuelle Zwischenstufen, 1900) states that "in every man there exist male and female elements." See also the same Jahrbuch, Bd. I, 1899 ("Die objektive Diagnose der Homosexualitat," by M. Hirschfeld, pp. 8-9). In the determination of sex, as far as heterosexual persons are concerned, some are disproportionately more strongly developed than others. G. Herman is firm in his belief "that in every woman there are male, and in every man there are female germs and qualities" (Genesis, das Gesetz der Zeugung, 9 Bd., Libido und Manie, 1903). As recently as 1906 W. Fliess (Der Ablauf des Lebens) has claimed ownership of the idea of bisexuality (in the sense of double sex). Psychoanalytic investigation very strongly opposes the attempt to separate homosexuals from other persons as a group of a special nature. By also studying sexual excitations other than the manifestly open ones it discovers that all men are capable of homosexual object selection and actually accomplish this in the unconscious. Indeed the attachments of libidinous feelings to persons of the same sex play no small rôle as factors in normal psychic life, and as causative factors of disease they play a greater rôle than those belonging to the opposite sex. According to psychoanalysis, it rather seems that it is the independence of the object, selection of the sex of the object, the same free disposal over male and female objects, as observed in childhood, in primitive states and in prehistoric times, which forms the origin from which the normal as well as the inversion types developed, following restrictions in this or that direction. In the psychoanalytic sense the exclusive sexual interest of the man for the woman is also a problem requiring an explanation, and is not something that is self-evident and explainable on the basis of chemical attraction. The determination as to the definite sexual behavior does not occur until after puberty and is the result of a series of as yet not observable factors, some of which are of a constitutional, while some are of an accidental nature. Certainly some of these factors can turn out to be so enormous that by their character they influence the result. In general, however, the multiplicity of the determining factors is reflected by the manifoldness of the outcomes in the manifest sexual behavior of the person. In the inversion types it can be ascertained that they are altogether controlled by an archaic constitution and by primitive psychic mechanisms. The importance of the narcissistic object selection and the clinging to the erotic significance of the anal zone seem to be their most essential characteristics. But one gains nothing by separating the most extreme inversion types from the others on the basis of such constitutional peculiarities. What is found in the latter as seemingly an adequate determinant can also be demonstrated only in lesser force in the constitution of transitional types and in manifestly normal persons. The differences in the results may be of a qualitative nature, but analysis shows that the differences in the determinants are only quantitative. As a remarkable factor among the accidental influences of the object selection, we found the sexual rejection or the early sexual intimidation, and our attention was also called to the fact that the existence of both parents plays an important rôle in the child's life. The disappearance of a strong father in childhood not infrequently favors the inversion. Finally, one might demand that the inversion of the sexual object should notionally be strictly separated from the mixing of the sex characteristics in the subject. A certain amount of independence is unmistakable also in this relation.*

Note 12: Although psychoanalysis has not yet given us a full explanation for the origin of inversion, it has revealed the psychic mechanism of its genesis and has essentially enriched the problems in question. In all the cases examined we have ascertained that the later inverts go through in their childhood a phase of very intense but short-lived fixation on the woman (usually on the mother) and after overcoming it they identify themselves with the woman and take themselves as the sexual object; that is, proceeding on a narcissistic basis, they look for young men resembling themselves in persons whom they wish to love as their mother has loved them. We have, moreover, frequently found that alleged inverts are by no means indifferent to the charms of women, but the excitation evoked by the woman is always transferred to a male object. They thus repeat through life the mechanism which gave origin to their inversion. Their obsessive striving for the man proves to be determined by their restless flight from the woman.

Note 13: The most pronounced difference between the sexual life (Liebesleben) of antiquity and ours lies in the fact that the ancients placed the emphasis on the impulse itself, while we put it on its object. The ancients extolled the impulse and were ready to ennoble through it even an inferior object, while we disparage the activity of the impulse as such and only countenance it on account of the merits of the object.

Note 14: I must mention here that the blind obedience evinced by the hypnotized subject to the hypnotist causes me to think that the nature of hypnosis is to be found in the unconscious fixation of the libido on the person of the hypnotizer (by means of the masochistic component of the sexual impulse).

Ferenczi connects this character of suggestibility with the "parent complex" (Jahrbuch für Psychoanalytische und psychopathologische Forschungen, I, 1909).

Note 15: Moreover, it is to be noted that sexual overvaluation does not become pronounced in all mechanisms of object selection, and that we shall later learn to know another and more direct explanation for the sexual rôle of the other parts of the body.

Note 16: Further investigations lead to the conclusion that I. Bloch has overestimated the factor of excitement-hunger (Reizhunger). The various roads upon which the libido moves behave to each other from the very beginning like communicating pipes; the factor of collateral streaming must also be considered.

Note 17: This weakness corresponds to the constitutional predisposition. The early sexual intimidation which pushes the person away from the normal sexual aim and urges him to seek a substitute, has been demonstrated by psychoanalysis, as an accidental determinant.

Note 18: The shoe or slipper is accordingly a symbol for the female genitals.

Note 19: Psychoanalysis has filled up the gap in the understanding of fetichisms by showing that the selection of the fetich depends on a coprophilic smell-desire which has been lost by repression. Feet and hair are strong smelling objects which are raised to fetiches after the renouncing of the now unpleasant sensation of smell. Accordingly, only the filthy and ill-smelling foot is the sexual object in the perversion which corresponds to the foot fetichism. Another contribution to the explanation of the fetichistic preference of the foot is found in the Infantile Sexual Theories (see later). The foot replaces the penis which is so much missed in the woman. In some cases of foot fetishism it could be shown that the desire for looking originally directed to the genitals, which wished to reach its object from below, was stopped on the way by prohibition and repression, and therefore adhered to the foot or shoe as a fetich. In conformity with infantile expectation, the female genital was hereby imagined as a male genital.

Note 20: I have no doubt that the conception of the "beautiful" is rooted in the soil of sexual excitement and originally signified the sexual excitant. The more remarkable, therefore, is the fact that the genitals, the sight of which provokes the greatest sexual excitement, can really never be considered "beautiful."

Note 21: Cf. here the later communication on the pregenital phases of the sexual development, in which this view is confirmed. See below, "Ambivalence."

Note 22: Instead of substantiating this statement by many examples I will merely cite Havelock Ellis (The Sexual Impulse, 1903): "All known cases of sadism and masochism, even those cited by v. Krafft-Ebing, always show (as has already been shown by Colin, Scott, and Féré) traces of both groups of manifestations in the same individual."

Note 23: On the other hand the restricting forces of the sexual evolution—disgust, shame, morality—must also be looked upon as historic precipitates of the outer inhibitions which the sexual impulse experienced in the psychogenesis of humanity. One can observe that they appear in their time during the development of the individual almost spontaneously at the call of education and influence.

Note 24: Studien über Hysterie, 1895, J. Breuer tells of the patient on whom he first practiced the cathartic method: "The sexual factor was surprisingly undeveloped."

Note 25: The well-known fancies of perverts which under favorable conditions are changed into contrivances, the delusional fears of paranoiacs which are in a hostile manner projected on others, and the unconscious fancies of hysterics which are discovered in their symptoms by psychoanalysis, agree as to content in the minutest details.

Note 26: A psychoneurosis very often associates itself with a manifest inversion in which the heterosexual feeling becomes subjected to complete repression.—It is but just to state that the necessity of a general recognition of the tendency to inversion in psychoneurotics was first imparted to me personally by Wilh. Fliess, of Berlin, after I had myself discovered it in some cases.

Note 27: It is not easy to justify here this assumption which was taken from a definite class of neurotic diseases. On the other hand, it would be impossible to assert anything definite concerning the impulses if one did not take the trouble of mentioning these presuppositions.

Note 28: One should here think of Moll's assertion, who divides the sexual impulse into the impulses of contrectation and detumescence. Contrectation signifies a desire to touch the skin.

SECOND ESSAY
The Infantile Sexuality

IT IS A part of popular belief about the sexual impulse that it is absent in childhood and that it first appears in the period of life known as puberty. This, though a common error, is serious in its consequences and is chiefly due to our present ignorance of the fundamental principles of the sexual life. A comprehensive study of the sexual manifestations of childhood would probably reveal to us the existence of the essential features of the sexual impulse, and would make us acquainted with its development and its composition from various sources.

The Neglect of the Infantile.—It is remarkable that those writers who endeavor to explain the qualities and reactions of the adult individual have given so much more attention to the ancestral period than to the period of the individual's own existence—that is, they have attributed more influence to heredity than to childhood. As a matter of fact, it might well be supposed that the influence of the latter period would be easier to understand, and that it would be entitled to more consideration than heredity.[1] To be sure, one occasionally finds in medical literature notes on the premature sexual activities of small children, about erections and masturbation and even actions resembling coitus, but these are referred to merely as exceptional occurrences, as curiosities, or as deterring examples of premature perversity. No author has to my knowledge recognized the normality of the sexual impulse in childhood, and in the numerous writings on the development of the child the chapter on "Sexual Development" is usually passed over.[2]

Infantile Amnesia.—This remarkable negligence is due partly to conventional considerations, which influence the writers on account of their own bringing up, and partly to a psychic phenomenon which has thus far remained unexplained. I refer to the peculiar amnesia which veils from most people (not from all!) the first years of their childhood, usually the first six or eight years. So far it has not occurred to us that this amnesia ought to surprise us, though we have good reasons for surprise. For we are informed that in those years from which we later obtain nothing except a few incomprehensible memory fragments, we have vividly reacted to impressions, that we have manifested pain and pleasure like any human being, that we have evinced love, jealousy, and other passions as they then affected us; indeed we are told that we have uttered remarks which proved to grown-ups that we possessed understanding and a budding power of judgment. Still we know nothing of all this when we become older. Why does our memory lag behind all our other psychic activities? We really have reason to believe that at no time of life are we more capable of impressions and reproductions than during the years of childhood.[3]

On the other hand we must assume, or we may convince ourselves through psychological observations on others, that the very impressions which we have forgotten have nevertheless left the deepest traces in our psychic life, and acted as determinants for our whole future development. We conclude therefore that we do not deal with a real forgetting of infantile impressions but rather with an amnesia similar to that observed in neurotics for later experiences, the nature of which consists in their being detained from consciousness (repression). But what forces bring about this repression of the infantile impressions? He who can solve this riddle will also explain hysterical amnesia.

We shall not, however, hesitate to assert that the existence of the infantile amnesia gives us a new point of comparison between the psychic states of the child and those of the psychoneurotic. We have already encountered another point of comparison when confronted by the fact that the sexuality of the psychoneurotic preserves the infantile character or has returned to it. May there not be an ultimate connection between the infantile and the hysterical amnesias?

The connection between the infantile and the hysterical amnesias is really more than a mere play of wit. The hysterical amnesia which serves the repression can only be explained by the fact that the individual already possesses a sum of recollections which have been withdrawn from conscious disposal and which by associative connection now seize that which is acted upon by the repelling forces of the repression emanating from consciousness.[4] We may say that without infantile amnesia there would be no hysterical amnesia.

I believe that the infantile amnesia which causes the individual to look upon his childhood as if it were a *prehistoric* time and conceals from him the beginning of his own sexual life—that this amnesia is responsible for the fact that one does not usually attribute any value to the infantile period in the development of the sexual life. One single observer cannot fill the gap which has been thus produced in our knowledge. As early as 1896 I had already emphasized the significance of childhood for the origin of certain important phenomena connected with the sexual life, and since then I have not ceased to put into the foreground the importance of the infantile factor for sexuality.

THE SEXUAL LATENCY PERIOD OF CHILDHOOD AND ITS INTERRUPTIONS

The extraordinary frequent discoveries of apparently abnormal and exceptional sexual manifestations in childhood, as well as the discovery of infantile reminiscences in neurotics, which were hitherto unconscious, allow us to sketch the following picture of the sexual behavior of childhood.[5]

It seems certain that the newborn child brings with it the germs of sexual feelings which continue to develop for some time and then succumb to a progressive suppression, which is in turn broken through by the proper advances of the sexual development and which can be checked by individual idiosyncrasies. Nothing is known concerning the laws and periodicity of this oscillating course of development. It seems, however, that the sexual life of the child mostly manifests itself in the third or fourth year in some form accessible to observation.[6]

The Sexual Inhibition.—It is during this period of total or at least partial latency that the psychic forces develop which later act as inhibitions on the sexual life, and narrow its direction like dams. These psychic forces are loathing, shame, and moral and esthetic ideal demands. We may gain the impression that the erection of these dams in the civilized child is the work of education; and surely education contributes much to it. In reality, however, this development is organically determined and can occasionally be produced without the help of education. Indeed education remains properly within its assigned realm only if it strictly follows the path of the organic determinant and impresses it somewhat cleaner and deeper.

Reaction Formation and Sublimation.—What are the means that accomplish these very important constructions so significant for the later personal culture and normality? They are probably brought about at the cost of the infantile sexuality itself, the influx of which has not stopped even in this latency period—the energy of which indeed has been turned away either wholly or partially from sexual utilization and conducted to other aims. The historians of civilization seem to be unanimous in the opinion that such deviation of sexual motive powers from sexual aims to new aims, a process which merits the name of *sublimation*, has furnished powerful components for all cultural accomplishments. We will therefore add that the same process acts in the development of every individual, and that it begins to act in the sexual latency period.[7]

We can also venture an opinion about the mechanisms of such sublimation. The sexual feelings of these infantile years on the one hand could not be utilizable, since the procreating functions are postponed,—this is the chief character of the latency period; on the other hand, they would in themselves be perverse, as they would emanate from erogenous zones and would be born of impulses which in the individual's course of development could only evoke a feeling of displeasure. They therefore awaken contrary forces (feelings of reaction), which in order to suppress such displeasure, build up the above mentioned psychic dams: loathing, shame, and morality.[8]

The Interruptions of the Latency Period.—Without deluding ourselves as to the hypothetical nature and deficient clearness of our understanding regarding the infantile period of latency and delay, we will return to reality and state that such a utilization of the infantile sexuality represents an ideal bringing up from which the development of the individual usually deviates in some measure and often very considerably. A portion of the sexual manifestation which has withdrawn from sublimation occasionally breaks through, or a sexual activity remains throughout the whole duration of the latency period until the reinforced breaking through of the sexual impulse in puberty. In so far as they have paid any attention to infantile sexuality the educators behave as if they shared our views concerning the formation of the moral forces of defence at the cost of sexuality, and as if they knew that sexual activity makes the child uneducable; for the educators consider all sexual manifestations of the child as an "evil" in the face of which little can be accomplished. We have, however, every reason for directing our attention to those phenomena so much feared by the educators, for we expect to find in them the solution of the primitive formation of the sexual impulse.

THE MANIFESTATIONS OF THE INFANTILE SEXUALITY

For reasons which we shall discuss later we will take as a model of the infantile sexual manifestations thumbsucking (pleasure-sucking), to which the Hungarian pediatrist, Lindner, has devoted an excellent essay.[9]

Thumbsucking.—Thumbsucking, which manifests itself in the nursing baby and which may be continued till maturity or throughout life, consists in a rhythmic repetition of sucking contact with the mouth (the lips), wherein the purpose of taking nourishment is excluded. A part of the lip itself, the tongue, which is another preferable skin region within reach, and even the big toe—may be taken as objects for sucking. Simultaneously, there is also a desire to grasp things, which manifests itself in a rhythmical pulling of the ear lobe and which may cause the child to grasp a part of another person (generally the ear) for the same purpose. The pleasure-sucking is connected with an entire exhaustion of attention and leads to sleep or even to a motor reaction in the form of an orgasm.[10] Pleasure-sucking is often combined with a rubbing contact with certain sensitive parts of the body, such as the breast and external genitals. It is by this road that many children go from thumb-sucking to masturbation.

Lindner himself has recognized the sexual nature of this action and openly emphasized it. In the nursery thumbsucking is often treated in the same way as any other sexual "naughtiness" of the child. A very strong objection was raised against this view by many pediatrists and neurologists which in part is certainly due to the confusion of the terms "sexual" and "genital." This contradiction raises the difficult question, which cannot be rejected, namely, in what general traits do we wish to recognize the sexual manifestations of the child. I believe that the association of the manifestations into which we gained an insight through psychoanalytic investigation justify us in claiming thumbsucking as a sexual activity and in studying through it the essential features of the infantile sexual activity.

Autoerotism.—It is our duty here to arrange this state of affairs differently. Let us insist that the most striking character of this sexual activity is that the impulse is not directed against other persons but that it gratifies itself on its own body; to use the happy term invented by Havelock Ellis, we will say that it is autoerotic.[11]

It is, moreover, clear that the action of the thumbsucking child is determined by the fact that it seeks a pleasure which has already been experienced and is now remembered. Through the rhythmic sucking on a portion of the skin or mucous membrane it finds the gratification in the simplest way. It is also easy to conjecture on what occasions the child first experienced this pleasure which it now strives to renew.

The first and most important activity in the child's life, the sucking from the mother's breast (or its substitute), must have acquainted it with this pleasure. We would say that the child's lips behaved like an *erogenous zone,* and that the excitement through the warm stream of milk was really the cause of the pleasurable sensation. To be sure, the gratification of the erogenous zone was at first united with the gratification of taking nourishment. He who sees a satiated child sink back from the mother's breast, and fall asleep with reddened cheeks and blissful smile, will have to admit that this picture remains as typical of the expression of sexual gratification in later life. But the desire for repetition of the sexual gratification is separated from the desire for taking nourishment; a separation which becomes unavoidable with the appearance of the teeth when the nourishment is no longer sucked in but chewed.

The child does not make use of a strange object for sucking but prefers its own skin because it is more convenient, because it thus makes itself independent of the outer world which it cannot yet control, and because in this way it creates for itself, as it were, a second, even if an inferior, erogenous zone. The inferiority of this second region urges it later to seek the same parts, the lips of another person. ("It is a pity that I cannot kiss myself," might be attributed to it.)

Not all children suck their thumbs. It may be assumed that it is found only in children in whom the erogenous significance of the lip-zone is constitutionally reënforced. Children in whom this is retained are habitual kissers as adults and show a tendency to perverse kissing, or as men they have a marked desire for drinking and smoking. But if repression comes into play they experience disgust for eating and evince hysterical vomiting. By virtue of the community of the lip-zone the repression encroaches upon the impulse of nourishment. Many of my female patients showing disturbances in eating, such as hysterical globus, choking sensations, and vomiting, have been energetic thumbsuckers during infancy.

In the thumbsucking or pleasure-sucking we have already been able to observe the three essential characters of an infantile sexual manifestation. The latter has its origin in conjunction with a bodily function which is very important for life, it does not yet know any sexual object, it is *autoerotic* and its sexual aim is under the control of an *erogenous zone*. Let us assume for the present that these characters also hold true for most of the other activities of the infantile sexual impulse.

THE SEXUAL AIM OF THE INFANTILE SEXUALITY

The Characters of the Erogenous Zones.—From the example of thumbsucking we may gather a great many points useful for the distinguishing of an erogenous zone. It is a portion of skin or mucous membrane in which the stimuli produce a feeling of pleasure of definite quality. There is no doubt that the pleasure-producing stimuli are governed by special determinants which we do not know. The rhythmic characters must play some part in them and this strongly suggests an analogy to tickling. It does not, however, appear so certain whether the character of the pleasurable feeling evoked by the stimulus can be designated as "peculiar," and in what part of this peculiarity the sexual factor exists. Psychology is still groping in the dark when it concerns matters of pleasure and pain, and the most cautious assumption is therefore the most advisable. We may perhaps later come upon reasons which seem to support the peculiar quality of the sensation of pleasure.

The erogenous quality may adhere most notably to definite regions of the body. As is shown by the example of thumbsucking, there are predestined erogenous zones. But the same example also shows that any other region of skin or mucous membrane may assume the function of an erogenous zone; it must therefore carry along a certain adaptability. The production of the sensation of pleasure therefore depends more on the quality of the stimulus than on the nature of the bodily region. The thumbsucking child looks around on his body and selects any portion of it for pleasure-sucking, and becoming accustomed to it, he then prefers it. If he accidentally strikes upon a predestined region, such as breast, nipple or genitals, it naturally has the preference. A quite analogous tendency to displacement is again found in the symptomatology of hysteria. In this neurosis the repression mostly concerns the genital zones proper; these in turn transmit their excitation to the other erogenous zones, usually dormant in mature life, which then behave exactly like genitals. But besides this, just as in thumbsucking, any other region of the body may become endowed with the excitation of the genitals and raised to an erogenous zone. Erogenous and hysterogenous zones show the same characters.[12]

The Infantile Sexual Aim.—The sexual aim of the infantile impulse consists in the production of gratification through the proper excitation of this or that selected erogenous zone. In order to leave a desire for its repetition this gratification must have been previously experienced, and we may be sure that nature has devised definite means so as not to leave this occurrence to mere chance. The arrangement which has fulfilled this purpose for the lip-zone we have already discussed; it is the simultaneous connection of this part of the body with the taking of nourishment. We shall also meet other similar mechanisms as sources of sexuality. The state of desire for repetition of gratification can be recognized through a peculiar feeling of tension which in itself is rather of a painful character, and through a centrally-determined feeling of itching or sensitiveness which is projected into the peripheral erogenous zone. The sexual aim may therefore be formulated as follows: the chief object is to substitute for the projected feeling of sensitiveness in the erogenous zone that outer stimulus which removes the feeling of sensitiveness by evoking the feeling of gratification. This external stimulus consists usually in a manipulation which is analogous to sucking.

It is in full accord with our physiological knowledge if the desire happens to be awakened also peripherally through an actual change in the erogenous zone. The action is puzzling only to some extent as one stimulus for its suppression seems to want another applied to the same place.

THE MASTURBATIC SEXUAL MANIFESTATIONS[13]

It is a matter of great satisfaction to know that there is nothing further of greater importance to learn about the sexual activity of the child after the impulse of one erogenous zone has become comprehensible to us. The most pronounced differences are found in the action necessary for the gratification, which consists in sucking for the lip zone and which must be replaced by other muscular actions according to the situation and nature of the other zones.

The Activity of the Anal Zone.—Like the lip zone the anal zone is, through its position, adapted to conduct the sexuality to the other functions of the body. It should be assumed that the erogenous significance of this region of the body was originally very large. Through psychoanalysis one finds, not without surprise, the many transformations that are normally undertaken with the usual excitations emanating from here, and that this zone often retains for life a considerable fragment of genital irritability.[14] The intestinal catarrhs so frequent during infancy produce intensive irritations in this zone, and we often hear it said that intestinal catarrh at this delicate age causes "nervousness." In later neurotic diseases they exert a definite influence on the symptomatic expression of the neurosis, placing at its disposal the whole sum of intestinal disturbances. Considering the erogenous significance of the anal zone which has been retained at least in transformation, one should not laugh at the hemorrhoidal influences to which the old medical literature attached so much weight in the explanation of neurotic states.

Children utilizing the erogenous sensitiveness of the anal zone can be recognized by their holding back of fecal masses until through accumulation there result violent muscular contractions; the passage of these masses through the anus is apt to produce a marked irritation of the mucus membrane. Besides the pain this must produce also a sensation of pleasure. One of the surest premonitions of later eccentricity or nervousness is when an infant obstinately refuses to empty his bowel when placed on the chamber by the nurse and reserves this function at its own pleasure. It does not concern him that he will soil his bed; all he cares for is not to lose the subsidiary pleasure while defecating. The educators have again the right inkling when they designate children who withhold these functions as bad. The content of the bowel which is an exciting object to the sexually sensitive surface of mucous membrane behaves like the precursor of another organ which does not become active until after the phase of childhood. In addition it has other important meanings to the nursling. It is evidently treated as an additional part of the body, it represents the first "donation," the disposal of which expresses the pliability while the retention of it can express the spite of the little being towards its environment. From the idea of "donation" he later gains the meaning of the "babe" which according to one of the infantile sexual theories is acquired through eating and is born through the bowel.

The retention of fecal masses, which is at first intentional in order to utilize them, as it were, for masturbatic excitation of the anal zone, is at least one of the roots of constipation so frequent in neuropaths. The whole significance of the anal zone is mirrored in the fact that there are but few neurotics who have not their special scatologic customs, ceremonies, etc., which they retain with cautious secrecy.

Real masturbatic irritation of the anal zone by means of the fingers, evoked through either centrally or peripherally supported itching, is not at all rare in older children.

The Activity of the Genital Zone.—Among the erogenous zones of the child's body there is one which certainly does not play the main rôle, and which cannot be the carrier of earliest sexual feeling— which, however, is destined for great things in later life. In both male and female it is connected with the voiding of urine (penis, clitoris), and in the former it is enclosed in a sack of mucous membrane, probably in order not to miss the irritations caused by the secretions which may arouse the sexual excitement at an early age. The sexual activities of this erogenous zone, which belongs to the real genitals, are the beginning of the later normal sexual life.

Owing to the anatomical position, the overflowing of secretions, the washing and rubbing of the body, and to certain accidental excitements (the wandering of intestinal worms in the girl), it happens that the pleasurable feeling which these parts of the body are capable of producing makes itself noticeable to the child even during the sucking age, and thus awakens desire for its repetition. When we review all the actual arrangements, and bear in mind that the measures for cleanliness have the same effect as the uncleanliness itself, we can then scarcely mistake nature's intention, which is to establish the future primacy of these erogenous zones for the sexual activity through the infantile onanism from which hardly an individual escapes.

The action of removing the stimulus and setting free the gratification consists in a rubbing contiguity with the hand or in a certain previously-formed pressure reflex effected by the closure of the thighs. The latter procedure seems to be the more primitive and is by far the more common in girls. The preference for the hand in boys already indicates what an important part of the male sexual activity will be accomplished in the future by the impulse to mastery (Bemächtigungstrieb).[15] It can only help towards clearness if I state that the infantile masturbation should be divided into three phases. The first phase belongs to the nursing period, the second to the short flourishing period of sexual activity at about the fourth year, only the third corresponds to the one which is often considered exclusively as onanism of puberty.

The infantile onanism seems to disappear after a brief time, but it may continue uninterruptedly till puberty and thus represent the first marked deviation from the development desirable for civilized man. At some time during childhood after the nursing period, the sexual impulse of the genitals reawakens and continues active for some time until it is again suppressed, or it may continue without interruption. The possible relations are very diverse and can only be elucidated through a more precise analysis of individual cases. The details, however, of this *second* infantile sexual activity leave behind the profoundest (unconscious) impressions in the persons's memory; if the individual remains healthy they determine his character and if he becomes sick after puberty they determine the symptomatology of his neurosis.[16] In the latter case it is found that this sexual period is forgotten and the conscious reminiscences pointing to them are displaced; I have already mentioned that I would like to connect the normal infantile amnesia with this infantile sexual activity. By psychoanalytic investigation it is possible to bring to consciousness the forgotten material, and thereby to remove a compulsion which emanates from the unconscious psychic material.

The Return of the Infantile Masturbation.—The sexual excitation of the nursing period returns during the designated years of childhood as a centrally determined tickling sensation demanding onanistic gratification, or as a pollution-like process which, analogous to the pollution of maturity, may attain gratification without the aid of any action. The latter case is more frequent in girls and in the second half of childhood; its determinants are not well understood, but it often, though not regularly, seems to have as a basis a period of early active onanism. The symptomatology of this sexual manifestation is poor; the genital apparatus is still undeveloped and all signs are therefore displayed by the urinary apparatus which is, so to say, the guardian of the genital apparatus. Most of the so-called bladder disturbances of this period are of a sexual nature; whenever the enuresis nocturna does not represent an epileptic attack it corresponds to a pollution.

The return of the sexual activity is determined by inner and outer causes which can be conjectured from the formation of the symptoms of neurotic diseases and definitely revealed by psychoanalytic investigations. The internal causes will be discussed later, the accidental outer causes attain at this time a great and permanent significance. As the first outer cause we have the influence of seduction which prematurely treats the child as a sexual object; under conditions favoring impressions this teaches the child the gratification of the genital zones, and thus usually forces it to repeat this gratification in onanism. Such influences can come from adults or other children. I cannot admit that I overestimated its frequency or its significance in my contributions to the etiology of hysteria,[17] though I did not know then that normal individuals may have the same experiences in their childhood, and hence placed a higher value on seductions than on the factors found in the sexual constitution and development.[18] It is quite obvious that no seduction is necessary to awaken the sexual life of the child, that such an awakening may come on spontaneously from inner sources.

Polymorphous-perverse Disposition.—It is instructive to know that under the influence of seduction the child may become polymorphous-perverse and may be misled into all sorts of transgressions. This goes to show that it carries along the adaptation for them in its disposition. The formation of such perversions meets but slight resistance because the psychic dams against sexual transgressions, such as shame, loathing and morality—which depend on the age of the child—are not yet erected or are only in the process of formation. In this respect the child perhaps does not behave differently from the average uncultured woman in whom the same polymorphous-perverse disposition exists. Such a woman may remain sexually normal under usual conditions, but under the guidance of a clever seducer she will find pleasure in every perversion and will retain the same as her sexual activity. The same polymorphous or infantile disposition fits the prostitute for her professional activity, and in the enormous number of prostitutes and of women to whom we must attribute an adaptation for prostitution, even if they do not follow this calling, it is absolutely impossible not to recognize in their uniform disposition for all perversions the universal and primitive human.

Partial Impulses.—For the rest, the influence of seduction does not aid us in unravelling the original relations of the sexual impulse, but rather confuses our understanding of the same, inasmuch as it prematurely supplies the child with the sexual object at a time when the infantile sexual impulse does not yet evince any desire for it. We must admit, however, that the infantile sexual life, though mainly under the control of erogenous zones, also shows components in which from the very beginning other persons are regarded as sexual objects. Among these we have the impulses for looking and showing off, and for cruelty, which manifest themselves somewhat independently of the erogenous zones and which only later enter into intimate relationship with the sexual life; but along with the erogenous sexual activity they are noticeable even in the infantile years as separate and independent strivings. The little child is above all shameless, and during its early years it evinces definite pleasure in displaying its body and especially its sexual organs. A counterpart to this desire which is to be considered as perverse, the curiosity to see other persons' genitals, probably appears first in the later years of childhood when the hindrance of the feeling of shame has already reached a certain development.

Under the influence of seduction the looking perversion may attain great importance for the sexual life of the child. Still, from my investigations of the childhood years of normal and neurotic patients, I must conclude that the impulse for looking can appear in the child as a spontaneous sexual manifestation. Small children, whose attention has once been directed to their own genitals—usually by masturbation—are wont to progress in this direction without outside interference, and to develop a vivid interest in the genitals of their playmates. As the occasion for the gratification of such curiosity is generally afforded during the gratification of both excrementitious needs, such children become *voyeurs* and are zealous spectators at the voiding of urine and feces of others, After this tendency has been repressed, the curiosity to see the genitals of others (one's own or those of the other sex) remains as a tormenting desire which in some neurotic cases furnishes the strongest motive power for the formation of symptoms.

The cruelty component of the sexual impulse develops in the child with still greater independence of those sexual activities which are connected with erogenous zones. Cruelty is especially near the childish character, since the inhibition which restrains the impulse to mastery before it causes pain to others—that is, the capacity for sympathy—develops comparatively late. As we know, a thorough psychological analysis of this impulse has not as yet been successfully accomplished; we may assume that the cruel feelings emanate from the impulse to mastery and appear at a period in the sexual life before the genitals have taken on their later rôle. It then dominates a phase of the sexual life, which we shall later describe as the pregenital organization. Children who are distinguished for evincing especial cruelty to animals and playmates may be justly suspected of intensive and premature sexual activity in the erogenous zones; and in a simultaneous prematurity of all sexual impulses, the erogenous sexual activity surely seems to be primary. The absence of the barrier of sympathy carries with it the danger that the connections between cruelty and the erogenous impulses formed in childhood cannot be broken in later life.

An erogenous source of the passive impulse for cruelty (masochism) is found in the painful irritation of the gluteal region which is familiar to all educators since the confessions of J.J. Rousseau. This has justly caused them to demand that physical punishment, which usually concerns this part of the body, should be withheld from all children in whom the libido might be forced into collateral roads by the later demands of cultural education.[19]

THE INFANTILE SEXUAL INVESTIGATION

Inquisitiveness.—At the same time when the sexual life of the child reaches its first bloom, from the age of three to the age of five, it also evinces the beginning of that activity which is ascribed to the impulse for knowledge and investigation. The desire for knowledge can neither be added to the elementary components of the impulses nor can it be altogether subordinated under sexuality. Its activity corresponds on the one hand to a sublimating mode of acquisition and on the other hand it labors with the energy of the desire for looking. Its relations to the sexual life, however, are of particular importance, for we have learned from psychoanalysis that the inquisitiveness of children is attracted to the sexual problems unusually early and in an unexpectedly intensive manner, indeed it perhaps may first be awakened by the sexual problems.

The Riddle of the Sphinx.—It is not theoretical but practical interests which start the work of the investigation activity in the child. The threat to the conditions of his existence through the actual or expected arrival of a new child, the fear of the loss in care and love which is connected with this event, cause the child to become thoughtful and sagacious. Corresponding with the history of this awakening, the first problem with which it occupies itself is not the question as to the difference between the sexes, but the riddle: from where do children come? In a distorted form, which can easily be unraveled, this is the same riddle which was given by the Theban Sphinx. The fact of the two sexes is usually first accepted by the child without struggle and hesitation. It is quite natural for the male child to presuppose in all persons it knows a genital like his own, and to find it impossible to harmonize the lack of it with his conception of others.

The Castration Complex.—This conviction is energetically adhered to by the boy and tenaciously defended against the contradictions which soon result, and are only given up after severe internal struggles (castration complex). The substitutive formations of this lost penis of the woman play a great part in the formation of many perversions.

The assumption of the same (male) genital in all persons is the first of the remarkable and consequential infantile sexual theories. It is of little help to the child when biological science agrees with his preconceptions and recognizes the feminine clitoris as the real substitute for the penis. The little girl does not react with similar refusals when she sees the differently formed genital of the boy. She is immediately prepared to recognize it, and soon becomes envious of the penis; this envy reaches its highest point in the consequentially important wish that she also should be a boy.

Birth Theories.—Many people can remember distinctly how intensely they interested themselves, in the prepubescent period, in the question where children came from. The anatomical solutions at that time read very differently; the children come out of the breast or are cut out of the body, or the navel opens itself to let them out. Outside of analysis one only seldom remembers the investigation corresponding to the early childhood years; it had long merged into repression but its results were thoroughly uniform. One gets children by eating something special (as in the fairy tale) and they are born through the bowel like a passage. These infantile theories recall the structures in the animal kingdom, especially do they recall the cloaca of the types which stand lower than the mammals.

Sadistic Conception of the Sexual Act.—If children of so delicate an age become spectators of the sexual act between grown-ups, for which an occasion is furnished by the conviction of the grown-ups that little children cannot understand anything sexual, they cannot help conceiving the sexual act as a kind of maltreating or overpowering, that is, it impresses them in a sadistic sense. Psychoanalysis also teaches us that such an early childhood impression contributes much to the disposition for a later sadistic displacement of the sexual aim. Besides this children also occupy themselves with the problem of what the sexual act consists in or, as they grasp it, of what marriage consists, and seek the solution of the mystery mostly in an association to which the functions of urination and defecation give occasion.

The Typical Failure of the Infantile Sexual Investigation.—It can be stated in general about the infantile sexual theories that they are reproductions of the child's own sexual constitution, and that despite their grotesque mistakes they evince more understanding of the sexual processes than is credited to their creators. Children also perceive the pregnancy of the mother and know how to interpret it correctly; the stork fable is very often related before auditors who confront it with a deep, but mostly mute suspicion. But as two elements remain unknown to the infantile sexual investigation, namely, the rôle of the propagating semen and the female genital opening—precisely the same points in which the infantile organization is still backward—the effort of the infantile investigator regularly remains fruitless, and ends in a renunciation which not infrequently leaves a lasting injury to the desire for knowledge. The sexual investigation of these early childhood years is always conducted alone, it signifies the first step towards independent orientation in the world, and causes a marked estrangement between the child and the persons of his environment who formerly enjoyed its full confidence.

The Phases of Development of the Sexual Organization.—As characteristics of the infantile sexuality we have hitherto emphasized the fact that it is essentially autoerotic (it finds its object in its own body), and that its individual partial impulses, which on the whole are unconnected and independent of one another, are striving for the acquisition of pleasure. The end of this development forms the so-called normal sexual life of the adult in which the acquisition of pleasure has been put into the service of the function of propagation, and the partial impulses, under the primacy of one single erogenous zone, have formed a firm organization for the attainment of the sexual aim in a strange sexual object.

Pregenital Organizations.—The study, with the help of psychoanalysis, of the inhibitions and disturbances in this course of development now permits us to recognize additions and primary stages of such organization of the partial impulses which likewise furnish a sort of sexual regime. These phases of the sexual organization normally will pass over smoothly and will only be recognizable by slight indications. Only in pathological cases do they become active and discernible to coarse observation.

Organizations of the sexual life in which the genital zones have not yet assumed the dominating rôle we would call the *pregenital* phase. So far we have become acquainted with two of them which recall reversions to early animal states.

One of the first of such pregenital sexual organizations is the *oral*, or if we wish, the cannibalistic. Here the sexual activity is not yet separated from the taking of nourishment, and the contrasts within the same not yet differentiated. The object of the one activity is also that of the other, the sexual aim consists in the *incorporating* into one's own body of the object, it is the prototype of that which later plays such an important psychic rôle as *identification*. As a remnant of this fictitious phase of organization forced on us by pathology we can consider thumbsucking. Here the sexual activity became separated from the nourishment activity and the strange object was given up in favor of one from his own body.

A second pregenital phase is the sadistic-anal organization. Here the contrasts which run through the whole sexual life are already developed, but cannot yet be designated as *masculine* and *feminine*, but must be called *active* and *passive*. The activity is supplied by the musculature of the body through the mastery impulse; the erogenous mucous membrane of the bowel manifests itself above all as an organ with a passive sexual aim, for both strivings there are objects present, which however do not merge together. Besides them there are other partial impulses which are active in an autoerotic manner. The sexual polarity and the strange object can thus already be demonstrated in this phase. The organization and subordination under the function of propagation are still lacking.

Ambivalence.—This form of the sexual organization could be retained throughout life and continue to draw to itself a large part of the sexual activity. The prevalence of sadism and the rôle of the cloaca of the anal zone stamps it with an exquisitely archaic impression. As another characteristic belonging to it we can mention the fact that the contrasting pair of impulses are developed in almost the same manner, a behavior which was designated by Bleuler with the happy name of *ambivalence*.

The assumption of the pregenital organizations of the sexual life is based on the analysis of the neuroses and hardly deserves any consideration without a knowledge of the same. We may expect that continued analytic efforts will furnish us with still more disclosures concerning the structure and development of the normal sexual function.

To complete the picture of the infantile sexual life one must add that frequently or regularly an object selection takes place even in childhood which is as characteristic as the one we have represented for the phase of development of puberty. This object selection proceeds in such a manner that all the sexual strivings proceed in the direction of one person in whom they wish to attain their aim. This is then the nearest approach to the definitive formation of the sexual life after puberty, that is possible in childhood. It differs from the latter only in the fact that the collection of the partial impulses and their subordination to the primacy of the genitals is very imperfectly or not at all accomplished in childhood. The establishment of this primacy in the service of propagation is therefore the last phase through which the sexual organization passes.

The Two Periods of Object Selection.—That the object selection takes place in two periods, or in two shifts, can be spoken of as a typical occurrence. The first shift has its origin between the age of three and five years, and is brought to a stop or to retrogression by the latency period; it is characterized by the infantile nature of its sexual aims. The second shift starts with puberty and determines the definitive formation of the sexual life.

The fact of the double object selection which is essentially due to the effect of the latency period, becomes most significant for the disturbance of this terminal state. The results of the infantile object selection reach into the later period; they are either preserved as such or are even refreshed at the time of puberty. But due to the development of the repression which takes place between the two phases they turn out as unutilizable. The sexual aims have become softened and now represent what we can designate as the *tender* streams of the sexual life. Only psychoanalytic investigation can demonstrate that behind this tenderness, such as honoring and esteeming, there is concealed the old sexual strivings of the infantile partial impulses which have now become useless. The object selection of the pubescent period must renounce the infantile objects and begin anew as a sensuous stream. The fact that the two streams do not meet often enough has as a result that one of the ideals of the sexual life, namely, the union of all desires in one object, cannot be attained.

THE SOURCES OF THE INFANTILE SEXUALITY

In our effort to follow up the origins of the sexual impulse, we have thus far found that the sexual excitement originates (*a*) as an imitation of a gratification which has been experienced in conjunction with other organic processes; (*b*) through the appropriate peripheral stimulation of erogenous zones; (*c*) and as an expression of some "impulse," like the looking and cruelty impulses, the origin of which we do not yet fully understand. The psychoanalytic investigation of later life which leads back to childhood and the contemporary observation of the child itself coöperate to reveal to us still other regularly-flowing sources of the sexual excitement. The observation of childhood has the disadvantage of treating easily misunderstood material, while psychoanalysis is made difficult by the fact that it can reach its objects and conclusions only by great detours; still the united efforts of both methods achieve a sufficient degree of positive understanding.

In investigating the erogenous zones we have already found that these skin regions merely show the special exaggeration of a form of sensitiveness which is to a certain degree found over the whole surface of the skin. It will therefore not surprise us to learn that certain forms of general sensitiveness in the skin can be ascribed to very distinct erogenous action. Among these we will above all mention the temperature sensitiveness; this will perhaps prepare us for the understanding of the therapeutic effects of warm baths.

Mechanical Excitation.—We must, moreover, describe here the production of sexual excitation by means of rhythmic mechanical shaking of the body. There are three kinds of exciting influences: those acting on the sensory apparatus of the vestibular nerves, those acting on the skin, and those acting on the deep parts, such as the muscles and joints. The sexual excitation produced by these influences seems to be of a pleasurable nature—it is worth emphasizing that for some time we shall continue to use indiscriminately the terms "sexual excitement" and "gratification" leaving the search for an explanation of the terms to a later time—and that the pleasure is produced by mechanical stimulation is proved by the fact that children are so fond of play involving passive motion, like swinging or flying in the air, and repeatedly demand its repetition.[20]

As we know, rocking is regularly used in putting restless children to sleep. The shaking sensation experienced in wagons and railroad trains exerts such a fascinating influence on older children, that all boys, at least at one time in their lives, want to become conductors and drivers. They are wont to ascribe to railroad activities an extraordinary and mysterious interest, and during the age of phantastic activity (shortly before puberty) they utilize these as a nucleus for exquisite sexual symbolisms. The desire to connect railroad travelling with sexuality apparently originates from the pleasurable character of the sensation of motion. When the repression later sets in and changes so many of the childish likes into their opposites, these same persons as adolescents and adults then react to the rocking and rolling with nausea and become terribly exhausted by a railroad journey, or they show a tendency to attacks of anxiety during the journey, and by becoming obsessed with railroad phobia they protect themselves against a repetition of the painful experiences.

This also fits in with the not as yet understood fact that the concurrence of fear with mechanical shaking produces the severest hysterical forms of traumatic neurosis. It may at least be assumed that inasmuch as even a slight intensity of these influences becomes a source of sexual excitement, the action of an excessive amount of the same will produce a profound disorder in the sexual mechanism.

Muscular Activity.—It is well known that the child has need for strong muscular activity, from the gratification of which it draws extraordinary pleasure. Whether this pleasure has anything to do with sexuality, whether it includes in itself sexual satisfaction? or can be the occasion of sexual excitement; all this may be refuted by critical consideration, which will probably be directed also to the position taken above that the pleasure in the sensations of passive movement are of sexual character or that they are sexually exciting. The fact remains, however, that a number of persons report that they experienced the first signs of excitement in their genitals during fighting or wrestling with playmates, in which situation, besides the general muscular exertion, there is an intensive contact with the opponent's skin which also becomes effective. The desire for muscular contest with a definite person, like the desire for word contest in later years, is a good sign that the object selection has been directed toward this person. "Was sich liebt, das neckt sich."[21] In the promotion of sexual excitement through muscular activity we might recognize one of the sources of the sadistic impulse. The infantile connection between fighting and sexual excitement acts in many persons as a determinant for the future preferred course of their sexual impulse.[22]

Affective Processes.—The other sources of sexual excitement in the child are open to less doubt. Through contemporary observations, as well as through later investigations, it is easy to ascertain that all more intensive affective processes, even excitements of a terrifying nature, encroach upon sexuality; this can at all events furnish us with a contribution to the understanding of the pathogenic action of such emotions. In the school child, fear of a coming examination or exertion expended in the solution of a difficult task can become significant for the breaking through of sexual manifestations as well as for his relations to the school, inasmuch as under such excitements a sensation often occurs urging him to touch the genitals, or leading to a pollution-like process with all its disagreeable consequences. The behavior of children at school, which is so often mysterious to the teacher, ought surely to be considered in relation with their germinating sexuality. The sexually-exciting influence of some painful affects, such as fear, shuddering, and horror, is felt by a great many people throughout life and readily explains why so many seek opportunities to experience such sensations, provided that certain accessory circumstances (as under imaginary circumstances in reading, or in the theater) suppress the earnestness of the painful feeling.

If we might assume that the same erogenous action also reaches the intensive painful feelings, especially if the pain be toned down or held at a distance by a subsidiary determination, this relation would then contain the main roots of the masochistic-sadistic impulse, into the manifold composition of which we are gaining a gradual insight.

Intellectual Work.—Finally, is is evident that mental application or the concentration of attention on an intellectual accomplishment will result, especially often in youthful persons, but in older persons as well, in a simultaneous sexual excitement, which may be looked upon as the only justified basis for the otherwise so doubtful etiology of nervous disturbances from mental "overwork."

If we now, in conclusion, review the evidences and indications of the sources of the infantile sexual excitement, which have been reported neither completely nor exhaustively, we may lay down the following general laws as suggested or established. It seems to be provided in the most generous manner that the process of sexual excitement—the nature of which certainly remains quite mysterious to us—should be set in motion. The factor making this provision in a more or less direct way is the excitation of the sensible surfaces of the skin and sensory organs, while the most immediate exciting influences are exerted on certain parts which are designated as erogenous zones. The criterion in all these sources of sexual excitement is really the quality of the stimuli, though the factor of intensity (in pain) is not entirely unimportant. But in addition to this there are arrangements in the organism which induce sexual excitement as a subsidiary action in a large number of inner processes as soon as the intensity of these processes has risen above certain quantitative limits. What we have designated as the partial impulses of sexuality are either directly derived from these inner sources of sexual excitation or composed of contributions from such sources and from erogenous zones. It is possible that nothing of any considerable significance occurs in the organism that does not contribute its components to the excitement of the sexual impulse.

It seems to me at present impossible to shed more light and certainty on these general propositions, and for this I hold two factors responsible; first, the novelty of this manner of investigation, and secondly, the fact that the nature of the sexual excitement is entirely unfamiliar to us. Nevertheless, I will not forbear speaking about two points which promise to open wide prospects in the future.

Diverse Sexual Constitutions.—(*a*) We have considered above the possibility of establishing the manifold character of congenital sexual constitutions through the diverse formation of the erogenous zones; we may now attempt to do the same in dealing with the indirect sources of sexual excitement. We may assume that, although these different sources furnish contributions in all individuals, they are not all equally strong in all persons; and that a further contribution to the differentiation of the diverse sexual constitution will be found in the preferred developments of the individual sources of sexual excitement.

The Paths of Opposite Influences.—(*b*) Since we are now dropping the figurative manner of expression hitherto employed, by which we spoke of *sources* of sexual excitement, we may now assume that all the connecting ways leading from other functions to sexuality must also be passable in the reverse direction. For example, if the lip zone, the common possession of both functions, is responsible for the fact that the sexual gratification originates during the taking of nourishment, the same factor offers also an explanation for the disturbances in the taking of nourishment if the erogenous functions of the common zone are disturbed. As soon as we know that concentration of attention may produce sexual excitement, it is quite natural to assume that acting on the same path, but in a contrary direction, the state of sexual excitement will be able to influence the availability of the voluntary attention. A good part of the symptomatology of the neuroses which I trace to disturbance of sexual processes manifests itself in disturbances of the other non-sexual bodily functions, and this hitherto incomprehensible action becomes less mysterious if it only represents the counterpart of the influences controlling the production of the sexual excitement.

However the same paths through which sexual disturbances encroach upon the other functions of the body must in health be supposed to serve another important function. It must be through these paths that the attraction of the sexual motive-powers to other than sexual aims, the sublimation of sexuality, is accomplished. We must conclude with the admission that very little is definitely known concerning the paths beyond the fact that they exist, and that they are probably passable in both directions.

Note 1: For it is really impossible to have a correct knowledge of the part belonging to heredity without first understanding the part belonging to the infantile.

Note 2: This assertion on revision seemed even to myself so bold that I decided to test its correctness by again reviewing the literature. The result of this second review did not warrant any change in my original statement. The scientific elaboration of the physical as well as the psychic phenomena of the infantile sexuality is still in its initial stages. One author (S. Bell, "A Preliminary Study of the Emotions of Love Between the Sexes," American Journal of Psychology, XIII, 1902) says: "I know of no scientist who has given a careful analysis of the emotion as it is seen in the adolescent." The only attention given to somatic sexual manifestations occurring before the age of puberty was in connection with degenerative manifestations, and these were referred to as a sign of degeneration. A chapter on the sexual life of children is not to be found in all the representative psychologies of this age which I have read. Among these works I can mention the following: Preyer; Baldwin (The Development of the Mind in the Child and in the Race, 1898); Pérez (L'enfant de 3-7 ans, 1894); Strümpel (Die pädagogische Pathologie, 1899); Karl Groos (Das Seelenleben des Kindes, 1904); Th. Heller (Grundriss der Heilpädagogic, 1904); Sully (Observations Concerning Childhood, 1897). The best impression of the present situation of this sphere can be obtained from the journal Die Kinderfehler (issued since 1896). On the other hand one gains the impression that the existence of love in childhood is in no need of demonstration. Pérez (l.c.) speaks for it; K. Groos (Die Spiele der Menschen, 1899) states that some children are very early subject to sexual emotions, and show a desire to touch the other sex (p. 336); S. Bell observed the earliest appearance of sex-love in a child during the middle part of its third year. See also Havelock Ellis, The Sexual Impulse, Appendix II.

The above-mentioned judgment concerning the literature of infantile sexuality no longer holds true since the appearance of the great and important work of G. Stanley Hall (Adolescence, Its Psychology and its Relation to Physiology, Anthropology, Sociology, Sex, Crime, Religion, and Education, 2 vols., New York, 1908). The recent book of A. Moll, Das Sexualleben des Kindes, Berlin, 1909, offers no occasion for such a modification. See, on the other hand, Bleuler, Sexuelle abnormitäten der Kinder (Jahrbuch der Schweizerischen Gesellschaft für Schulgesundheitspflege, IX, 1908). A book by Mrs. Dr. H.v. Hug-Hellmuth, Aus dem Seelenleben des Kindes (1913), has taken full account of the neglected sexual factors. [Translated in Monograph Series.]

Note 3: I have attempted to solve the problems presented by the earliest infantile recollections in a paper, "Über Deckerinnerungen" (Monatsschrift für Psychiatrie und Neurologie, VI, 1899). Cf. also The Psychopathology of Everyday Life, The Macmillan Co., New York, and Unwin, London.

Note 4: One cannot understand the mechanism of repression when one takes into consideration only one of the two cooperating processes. As a comparison one may think of the way the tourist is despatched to the top of the great pyramid of Gizeh; he is pushed from one side and pulled from the other.

Note 5: The use of the latter material is justified by the fact that the years of childhood of those who are later neurotics need not necessarily differ from those who are later normal except in intensity and distinctness.

Note 6: An anatomic analogy to the behavior of the infantile sexual function formulated by me is perhaps given by Bayer (Deutsches Archiv für klinische Medizin, Bd. 73) who claims that the internal genitals (uterus) are regularly larger in newborn than in older children. However, Halban's conception, that after birth there is also an involution of the other parts of the sexual apparatus, has not been verified. According to Halban (Zeitschrift für Geburtshilfe u. Gynäkologie, LIII, 1904) this process of involution ends after a few weeks of extra-uterine life.

Note 7: *The expression "sexual latency period" (sexuelle latenz-periode) I have borrowed from W. Fliess.*

Note 8: *In the case here discussed the sublimation of the sexual motive powers proceed on the road of reaction formations. But in general it is necessary to separate from each other sublimation and reaction formation as two diverse processes. Sublimation may also result through other and simpler mechanisms.*

Note 9: *Jahrbuch für Kinderheilkunde, N.F., XIV, 1879.*

Note 10: *This already shows what holds true for the whole life, namely, that sexual gratification is the best hypnotic. Most nervous insomnias are traced to lack of sexual gratification. It is also known that unscrupulous nurses calm crying children to sleep by stroking their genitals.*

Note 11: *Ellis spoils, however, the sense of his invented term by comprising under the phenomena of autoerotism the whole of hysteria and masturbation in its full extent.*

Note 12: *Further reflection and observation lead me to attribute the quality of erogenity to all parts of the body and inner organs. See later on narcism.*

Note 13: *Compare here the very comprehensive but confusing literature on onanism, e.g., Rohleder, Die Masturbation, 1899. Cf. also the pamphlet, "Die Onanie," which contains the discussion of the Vienna Psychoanalytic Society, Wiesbaden, 1912.*

Note 14: *Compare here the essay on "Charakter und Analerotic" in the Sammlung kleiner Schriften zur Neurosenlehre, Zweite Folge, 1909. Cf. also Brill, Psychanalysis, Chap. XIII, Anal Eroticism and Character, W.B. Saunders, Philadelphia.*

Note 15: *Unusual techniques in the performance of onanism seem to point to the influence of a prohibition against onanism which has been overcome.*

Note 16: *Why neurotics, when conscience stricken, regularly connect it with their onanistic activity, as was only recently recognized by Bleuler, is a problem which still awaits an exhaustive analysis.*

Note 17: *Freud, Selected Papers on Hysteria and Other Psychoneuroses, 3d edition, translated by A.A. Brill, N.Y. Nerv. and Ment. Dis. Pub. Co. Nervous and Mental Disease Monograph, Series No. 4.*

Note 18: *Havelock Ellis, in an appendix to his study on the Sexual Impulse, 1903, gives a number of autobiographic reports of normal persons treating their first sexual feelings in childhood and the causes of the same. These reports naturally show the deficiency due to infantile amnesia; they do not cover the prehistoric time in the sexual life and therefore must be supplemented by psychoanalysis of individuals who became neurotic. Notwithstanding this these reports are valuable in more than one respect, and information of a similar nature has urged me to modify my etiological assumption as mentioned in the text.*

Note 19: *The above-mentioned assertions concerning the infantile sexuality were justified in 1905, in the main through the results of psychoanalytic investigations in adults. Direct observation of the child could not at the time be utilized to its full extent and resulted only in individual indications and valuable confirmations. Since then it has become possible through the analysis of some cases of nervous disease in the delicate age of childhood to gain a direct understanding of the infantile psychosexuality (Jahrbuch für psychoanalytische und psychopathologische Forschungen, Bd. 1, 2, 1909). I can point with satisfaction to the fact that direct observation has fully confirmed the conclusion drawn from psychoanalysis, and thus furnishes good evidence for the reliability of the latter method of investigation.*

Moreover, the "Analysis of a Phobia in a Five-year-old Boy" (Jahrbuch, Bd. 1) has taught us something new for which psychoanalysis had not prepared us, to wit, that sexual symbolism, the representation of the sexual by non-sexual objects and relations—reaches back into the years when the child is first learning to master the language. My attention has also been directed to a deficiency in the above-cited statement which for the sake of clearness described any conceivable separation between the two phases of autoerotism and object love as a temporal separation. From the cited analysis (as well as from the above-mentioned work of Bell) we learn that children from three to five are capable of evincing a very strong object-selection which is accompanied by strong affects.

Note 20: Some persons can recall that the contact of the moving air in swinging caused them direct sexual pleasure in the genitals.

Note 21: "Those who love each other tease each other."

Note 22: The analyses of neurotic disturbances of walking and of agoraphobia remove all doubt as to the sexual nature of the pleasure of motion. As everybody knows modern cultural education utilizes sports to a great extent in order to turn away the youth from sexual activity; it would be more proper to say that it replaces the sexual pleasure by motion pleasure, and forces the sexual activity back upon one of its autoerotic components.

THIRD ESSAY
The Transformation of Puberty

WITH THE BEGINNING of puberty the changes set in which transform the infantile sexual life into its definite normal form. Hitherto the sexual impulse has been preponderantly autoerotic; it now finds the sexual object. Thus far it has manifested itself in single impulses and in erogenous zones seeking a certain pleasure as a single sexual aim. A new sexual aim now appears for the production of which all partial impulses coöperate, while the erogenous zones subordinate themselves to the primacy of the genital zone.[1] As the new sexual aim assigns very different functions to the two sexes their sexual developments now part company. The sexual development of the man is more consistent and easier to understand, while in the woman there even appears a form of regression. The normality of the sexual life is guaranteed only by the exact concurrence of the two streams directed to the sexual object and sexual aim. It is like the piercing of a tunnel from opposite sides.

The new sexual aim in the man consists in the discharging of the sexual products; it is not contradictory to the former sexual aim, that of obtaining pleasure; on the contrary, the highest amount of pleasure is connected with this final act in the sexual process. The sexual impulse now enters into the service of the function of propagation; it becomes, so to say, altruistic. If this transformation is to succeed its process must be adjusted to the original dispositions and all the peculiarities of the impulses.

Just as on every other occasion where new connections and compositions are to be formed in complicated mechanisms, here, too, there is a possibility for morbid disturbance if the new order of things does not get itself established. All morbid disturbances of the sexual life may justly be considered as inhibitions of development.

THE PRIMACY OF THE GENITAL ZONES AND THE FORE-PLEASURE

From the course of development as described we can clearly see the issue and the end aim. The intermediary transitions are still quite obscure and many a riddle will have to be solved in them.

The most striking process of puberty has been selected as its most characteristic; it is the manifest growth of the external genitals which have shown a relative inhibition of growth during the latency period of childhood. Simultaneously the inner genitals develop to such an extent as to be able to furnish sexual products or to receive them for the purpose of forming a new living being. A most complicated apparatus is thus formed which waits to be claimed.

This apparatus can be set in motion by stimuli, and observation teaches that the stimuli can affect it in three ways: from the outer world through the familiar erogenous zones; from the inner organic world by ways still to be investigated; and from the psychic life, which merely represents a depository of external impressions and a receptacle of inner excitations. The same result follows in all three cases, namely, a state which can be designated as "sexual excitation" and which manifests itself in psychic and somatic signs. The psychic sign consists in a peculiar feeling of tension of a most urgent character, and among the manifold somatic signs the many changes in the genitals stand first. They have a definite meaning, that of readiness; they constitute a preparation for the sexual act (the erection of the penis and the glandular activity of the vagina).

The Sexual Tension—The character of the tension of sexual excitation is connected with a problem the solution of which is as difficult as it would be important for the conception of the sexual process. Despite all divergence of opinion regarding it in psychology, I must firmly maintain that a feeling of tension must carry with it the character of displeasure. For me it is conclusive that such a feeling carries with it the impulse to alter the psychic situation, and acts incitingly, which is quite contrary to the nature of perceived pleasure. But if we ascribe the tension of the sexual excitation to the feelings of displeasure we encounter the fact that it is undoubtedly pleasurably perceived. The tension produced by sexual excitation is everywhere accompanied by pleasure; even in the preparatory changes of the genitals there is a distinct feeling of satisfaction. What relation is there between this unpleasant tension and this feeling of pleasure?

Everything relating to the problem of pleasure and pain touches one of the weakest spots of present-day psychology. We shall try if possible to learn something from the determinations of the case in question and to avoid encroaching on the problem as a whole. Let us first glance at the manner in which the erogenous zones adjust themselves to the new order of things. An important rôle devolves upon them in the preparation of the sexual excitation. The eye which is very remote from the sexual object is most often in position, during the relations of object wooing, to become attracted by that particular quality of excitation, the motive of which we designate as beauty in the sexual object. The excellencies of the sexual object are therefore also called "attractions." This attraction is on the one hand already connected with pleasure, and on the other hand it either results in an increase of the sexual excitation or in an evocation of the same where it is still wanting. The effect is the same if the excitation of another erogenous zone, *e.g.*, the touching hand, is added to it. There is on the one hand the feeling of pleasure which soon becomes enhanced by the pleasure from the preparatory changes, and on the other hand there is a further increase of the sexual tension which soon changes into a most distinct feeling of displeasure if it cannot proceed to more pleasure. Another case will perhaps be clearer; let us, for example, take the case where an erogenous zone, like a woman's breast, is excited by touching in a person who is not sexually excited at the time. This touching in itself evokes a feeling of pleasure, but it is also best adapted to awaken sexual excitement which demands still more pleasure. How it happens that the perceived pleasure evokes the desire for greater pleasure, that is the real problem.

Fore-pleasure Mechanism.—But the rôle which devolves upon the erogenous zones is clear. What applies to one applies to all. They are all utilized to furnish a certain amount of pleasure through their own proper excitation, which increases the tension, and which is in turn destined to produce the necessary motor energy in order to bring to a conclusion the sexual act. The last part but one of this act is again a suitable excitation of an erogenous zone; *i.e.*, the genital zone proper of the glans penis is excited by the object most fit for it, the mucous membrane of the vagina, and through the pleasure furnished by this excitation it now produces reflexly the motor energy which conveys to the surface the sexual substance. This last pleasure is highest in its intensity, and differs from the earliest ones in its mechanism. It is altogether produced through discharge, it is altogether gratification pleasure and the tension of the libido temporarily dies away with it.

It does not seem to me unjustified to fix by name the distinction in the nature of these pleasures, the one through the excitation of the erogenous zones, and the other through the discharge of the sexual substance. In contradistinction to the end-pleasure, or pleasure of gratification of sexual activity, we can properly designate the first as *fore-pleasure*. The fore-pleasure is then the same as that furnished by the infantile sexual impulse, though on a reduced scale; while the *end-pleasure* is new and is probably connected with determinations which first appear at puberty. The formula for the new function of the erogenous zones reads as follows: they are utilized for the purpose of making possible the production of the greater pleasure of gratification by means of the fore-pleasure which is gained from them as in infantile life.

I have recently been able to elucidate another example from a quite different realm of the psychic life, in which likewise a greater feeling of pleasure is achieved by means of a lesser feeling of pleasure which thereby acts as an alluring premium. We had there also the opportunity of entering more deeply into the nature of pleasure.[2]

Dangers of the Fore-pleasure.—However the connection of fore-pleasure with the infantile life is strengthened by the pathogenic rôle which may devolve upon it. In the mechanism through which the fore-pleasure is expressed there exists an obvious danger to the attainment of the normal sexual aim. This occurs if it happens that there is too much fore-pleasure and too little tension in any part of the preparatory sexual process. The motive power for the further continuation of the sexual process then escapes, the whole road becomes shortened, and the preparatory action in question takes the place of the normal sexual aim. Experience shows that such a hurtful condition is determined by the fact that the erogenous zone concerned or the corresponding partial impulse has already contributed an unusual amount of pleasure in infantile life. If other factors favoring fixation are added a compulsion readily results for the later life which prevents the fore-pleasure from arranging itself into a new combination. Indeed, the mechanism of many perversions is of such a nature; they merely represent a lingering at a preparatory act of the sexual process.

The failure of the function of the sexual mechanism through the fault of the fore-pleasure is generally avoided if the primacy of the genital zones has also already been sketched out in infantile life. The preparations of the second half of childhood (from the eighth year to puberty) really seem to favor this. During these years the genital zones behave almost as at the age of maturity; they are the seat of exciting sensations and of preparatory changes if any kind of pleasure is experienced through the gratification of other erogenous zones; although this effect remains aimless, *i.e.*, it contributes nothing towards the continuation of the sexual process. Besides the pleasure of gratification a certain amount of sexual tension appears even in infancy, though it is less constant and less abundant. We can now understand also why in the discussion of the sources of sexuality we had a perfectly good reason for saying that the process in question acts as sexual gratification as well as sexual excitement. We note that on our way towards the truth we have at first enormously exaggerated the distinctions between the infantile and the mature sexual life, and we therefore supplement what has been said with a correction. The infantile manifestations of sexuality determine not only the deviations from the normal sexual life but also the normal formations of the same.

THE PROBLEM OF SEXUAL EXCITEMENT

It remains entirely unexplained whence the sexual tension comes which originates simultaneously with the gratification of erogenous zones and what is its nature. The obvious supposition that this tension originates in some way from the pleasure itself is not only improbable in itself but untenable, inasmuch as during the greatest pleasure which is connected with the voiding of sexual substance there is no production of tension but rather a removal of all tension. Hence, pleasure and sexual tension can be only indirectly connected.

The Role of the Sexual Substance.—Aside from the fact that only the discharge of the sexual substance can normally put an end to the sexual excitement, there are other essential facts which bring the sexual tension into relation with the sexual products. In a life of continence the sexual activity is wont to discharge the sexual substance at night during pleasurable dream hallucinations of a sexual act, this discharge coming at changing but not at entirely capricious intervals; and the following interpretation of this process—the nocturnal pollution—can hardly be rejected, viz., that the sexual tension which brings about a substitute for the sexual act by the short hallucinatory road is a function of the accumulated semen in the reservoirs for the sexual products. Experiences with the exhaustibility of the sexual mechanism speak for the same thing. Where there is no stock of semen it is not only impossible to accomplish the sexual act, but there is also a lack of excitability in the erogenous zones, the suitable excitation of which can evoke no pleasure. We thus discover incidentally that a certain amount of sexual tension is itself necessary for the excitability of the erogenous zones.

One would thus be forced to the assumption, which if I am not mistaken is quite generally adopted, that the accumulation of sexual substance produces and maintains the sexual tension. The pressure of these products on the walls of their receptacles acts as an excitant on the spinal center, the state of which is then perceived by the higher centers which then produce in consciousness the familiar feeling of tension. If the excitation of erogenous zones increases the sexual tension, it can only be due to the fact that the erogenous zones are connected with these centers by previously formed anatomical connections. They increase there the tone of the excitation, and with sufficient sexual tension they set in motion the sexual act, and with insufficient tension they merely stimulate a production of the sexual substance.

The weakness of the theory which one finds adopted, *e.g.*, in v. Krafft-Ebing's description of the sexual process, lies in the fact that it has been formed for the sexual activity of the mature man and pays too little heed to three kinds of relations which should also have been elucidated. We refer to the relations as found in the child, in the woman, and in the castrated male. In none of the three cases can we speak of an accumulation of sexual products in the same sense as in the man, which naturally renders difficult the general application of this scheme; still it may be admitted without any further ado that ways can be found to justify the subordination of even these cases. Nevertheless one should be cautious about burdening the factor of accumulation of sexual products with actions which it seems incapable of supporting.

Overestimation of the Internal Genitals.—That sexual excitement can be independent to a considerable extent of the production of sexual substance seems to be shown by observations on castrated males, in whom the libido sometimes escapes the injury caused by the operation, although the opposite behavior, which is really the motive for the operation, is usually the rule. It is therefore not at all surprising, as C. Rieger puts it, that the loss of the male germ glands in maturer age should exert no new influence on the psychic life of the individual. The germ glands are really not the sexuality, and the experience with castrated males only verifies what we had long before learned from the removal of the ovaries, namely that it is impossible to do away with the sexual character by removing the germ glands. To be sure, castration performed at a tender age, before puberty, comes nearer to this aim, but it would seem in this case that besides the loss of the sexual glands we must also consider the inhibition of development and other factors which are connected with that loss.

Chemical Theories.—The truth remains, however, that we are unable to give any information about the nature of the sexual excitement for the reason that we do not know with what organ or organs sexuality is connected, since we have seen that the sexual glands have been overestimated in this significance. Since surprising discoveries have taught us the important rôle of the thyroid gland in sexuality, we may assume that the knowledge of the essential factors of sexuality are still withheld from us. One who feels the need of filling up the large gap in our knowledge with a preliminary assumption may formulate for himself the following theory based on the active substances found in the thyroid. Through the appropriate excitement of erogenous zones, as well as through other conditions under which sexual excitement originates, a material which is universally distributed in the organism becomes disintegrated, the decomposing products of which supply a specific stimulus to the organs of reproduction or to the spinal center connected with them. Such a transformation of a toxic stimulus in a particular organic stimulus we are already familiar with from other toxic products introduced into the body from without. To treat, if only hypothetically, the complexities of the pure toxic and the physiologic stimulations which result in the sexual processes is not now our appropriate task. To be sure, I attach no value to this special assumption and I shall be quite ready to give it up in favor of another, provided its original character, the emphasis on the sexual chemism, were preserved. For this apparently arbitrary statement is supported by a fact which, though little heeded, is most noteworthy. The neuroses which can be traced only to disturbances of the sexual life show the greatest clinical resemblance to the phenomena of intoxication and abstinence which result from the habitual introduction of pleasure-producing poisonous substances (alkaloids.)

THE THEORY OF THE LIBIDO

These assumptions concerning the chemical basis of the sexual excitement are in full accord with the auxiliary conception which we formed for the purpose of mastering the psychic manifestations of the sexual life. We have determined the concept of *libido* as that of a force of variable quantity which has the capacity of measuring processes and transformations in the spheres of sexual excitement. This libido we distinguished from the energy which is to be generally adjudged to the psychic processes with reference to its special origin and thus we attribute to it also a qualitative character. In separating libidinous from other psychic energy we give expression to the assumption that the sexual processes of the organism are differentiated from the nutritional processes through a special chemism. The analyses of perversions and psychoneuroses have taught us that this sexual excitement is furnished not only from the so-called sexual parts alone but from all organs of the body. We thus formulate for ourselves the concept of a libido-quantum whose psychic representative we designate as the ego-libido; the production, increase, distribution and displacement of this ego-libido will offer the possible explanation for the observed psycho-sexual phenomena.

But this ego-libido becomes conveniently accessible to psychoanalytic study only when the psychic energy is employed on sexual objects, that is when it becomes object libido. Then we see it as it concentrates and fixes itself on objects, or as it leaves those objects and passes over to others from which positions it directs the individual's sexual activity, that is, it leads to partial and temporary extinction of the libido. Psychoanalysis of the so-called transference neuroses (hysteria and compulsion neurosis) offers us here a reliable insight.

Concerning the fates of the object libido we also state that it is withdrawn from the object, that it is preserved floating in special states of tension and is finally taken back into the ego, so that it again becomes ego-libido. In contradistinction to the object-libido we also call the ego-libido narcissistic libido. From psychoanalysis we look over the boundary which we are not permitted to pass into the activity of the narcissistic libido and thus form an idea of the relations between the two. The narcissistic or ego-libido appears to us as the great reservoir from which the energy for the investment of the object is sent out and into which it is drawn back again, while the narcissistic libido investment of the ego appears to us as the realized primitive state in the first childhood, which only becomes hidden by the later emissions of the libido, and is retained at the bottom behind them.

The task of a theory of libido of neurotic and psychotic disturbances would have for its object to express in terms of the libido-economy all observed phenomena and disclosed processes. It is easy to divine that the greater significance would attach thereby to the destinies of the ego-libido, especially where it would be the question of explaining the deeper psychotic disturbances. The difficulty then lies in the fact that the means of our investigation, psychoanalysis, at present gives us definite information only concerning the transformation of the object-libido, but cannot distinguish without further study the ego-libido from the other effective energies in the ego.[3]

DIFFERENTIATION BETWEEN MAN AND WOMAN

It is known that the sharp differentiation of the male and female character originates at puberty, and it is the resulting difference which, more than any other factor, decisively influences the later development of personality. To be sure, the male and female dispositions are easily recognizable even in infantile life; thus the development of sexual inhibitions (shame, loathing, sympathy, etc.) ensues earlier and with less resistance in the little girl than in the little boy. The tendency to sexual repression certainly seems much greater, and where partial impulses of sexuality are noticed they show a preference for the passive form. But, the autoerotic activity of the erogenous zones is the same in both sexes, and it is this agreement that removes the possibility of a sex differentiation in childhood as it appears after puberty. In respect to the autoerotic and masturbatic sexual manifestations, it may be asserted that the sexuality of the little girl has entirely a male character. Indeed, if one could give a more definite content to the terms "masculine and feminine," one might advance the opinion that *the libido is regularly and lawfully of a masculine nature, whether in the man or in the woman; and if we consider its object, this may be either the man or the woman.*[4]

Since becoming acquainted with the aspect of bisexuality I hold this factor as here decisive, and I believe that without taking into account the factor of bisexuality it will hardly be possible to understand the actually observed sexual manifestations in man and woman.

The Leading Zones in Man and Woman.—Further than this I can only add the following. The chief erogenous zone in the female child is the clitoris, which is homologous to the male penis. All I have been able to discover concerning masturbation in little girls concerned the clitoris and not those other external genitals which are so important for the later sexual functions. With few exceptions I myself doubt whether the female child can be seduced to anything but clitoris masturbation. The frequent spontaneous discharges of sexual excitement in little girls manifest themselves in a twitching of the clitoris, and its frequent erections enable the girl to understand correctly even without any instruction the sexual manifestations of the other sex; they simply transfer to the boys the sensations of their own sexual processes.

If one wishes to understand how the little girl becomes a woman, he must follow up the further destinies of this clitoris excitation. Puberty, which brings to the boy a great advance of libido, distinguishes itself in the girl by a new wave of repression which especially concerns the clitoris sexuality. It is a part of the male sexual life that sinks into repression. The reinforcement of the sexual inhibitions produced in the woman by the repression of puberty causes a stimulus in the libido of the man and forces it to increase its capacity; with the height of the libido there is a rise in the overestimation of the sexual, which can be present in its full force only when the woman refuses and denies her sexuality. If the sexual act is finally submitted to and the clitoris becomes excited its rôle is then to conduct the excitement to the adjacent female parts, and in this it acts like a chip of pine wood which is utilized to set fire to the harder wood. It often takes some time for this transference to be accomplished; during which the young wife remains anesthetic. This anesthesia may become permanent if the clitoris zone refuses to give up its excitability; a condition brought on by abundant activities in infantile life. It is known that anesthesia in women is often only apparent and local. They are anesthetic at the vaginal entrance but not at all unexcitable through the clitoris or even through other zones. Besides these erogenous causes of anesthesia there are also psychic causes likewise determined by the repression.

If the transference of the erogenous excitability from the clitoris to the vagina has succeeded, the woman has thus changed her leading zone for the future sexual activity; the man on the other hand retains his from childhood. The main determinants for the woman's preference for the neuroses, especially for hysteria, lie in this change of the leading zone as well as in the repression of puberty. These determinants are therefore most intimately connected with the nature of femininity.

THE OBJECT-FINDING

While the primacy of the genital zones is being established through the processes of puberty, and the erected penis in the man imperiously points towards the new sexual aim, *i.e.*, towards the penetration of a cavity which excites the genital zone, the object-finding, for which also preparations have been made since early childhood, becomes consummated on the psychic side. While the very incipient sexual gratifications are still connected with the taking of nourishment, the sexual impulse has a sexual object outside its own body in his mother's breast. This object it loses later, perhaps at the very time when it becomes possible for the child to form a general picture of the person to whom the organ granting him the gratification belongs. The sexual impulse later regularly becomes autoerotic, and only after overcoming the latency period is there a resumption of the original relation. It is not without good reason that the suckling of the child at its mother's breast has become a model for every amour. The object-finding is really a re-finding.[5]

The Sexual Object of the Nursing Period.—However, even after the separation of the sexual activity from the taking of nourishment, there still remains from this first and most important of all sexual relations an important share, which prepares the object selection and assists in reestablishing the lost happiness. Throughout the latency period the child learns to love other persons who assist it in its helplessness and gratify its wants; all this follows the model and is a continuation of the child's infantile relations to his wet nurse. One may perhaps hesitate to identify the tender feelings and esteem of the child for his foster-parents with sexual love; I believe, however, that a more thorough psychological investigation will establish this identity beyond any doubt. The intercourse between the child and its foster-parents is for the former an inexhaustible source of sexual excitation and gratification of erogenous zones, especially since the parents—or as a rule the mother—supplies the child with feelings which originate from her own sexual life; she pats it, kisses it, and rocks it, plainly taking it as a substitute for a full-valued sexual object.[6]

The mother would probably be terrified if it were explained to her that all her tenderness awakens the sexual impulse of her child and prepares its future intensity. She considers her actions as asexually "pure" love, for she carefully avoids causing more irritation to the genitals of the child than is indispensable in caring for the body. But as we know the sexual impulse is not awakened by the excitation of genital zones alone. What we call tenderness will someday surely manifest its influence on the genital zones also. If the mother better understood the high significance of the sexual impulse for the whole psychic life and for all ethical and psychic activities, the enlightenment would spare her all reproaches. By teaching the child to love she only fulfills her function; for the child should become a fit man with energetic sexual needs, and accomplish in life all that the impulse urges the man to do. Of course, too much parental tenderness becomes harmful because it accelerates the sexual maturity, and also because it "spoils" the child and makes it unfit to temporarily renounce love or be satisfied with a smaller amount of love in later life. One of the surest premonitions of later nervousness is the fact that the child shows itself insatiable in its demands for parental tenderness; on the other hand, neuropathic parents, who usually display a boundless tenderness, often with their caressing awaken in the child a disposition for neurotic diseases. This example at least shows that neuropathic parents have nearer ways than inheritance by which they can transfer their disturbances to their children.

Infantile Fear.—The children themselves behave from their early childhood as if their attachment to their foster-parents were of the nature of sexual love. The fear of children is originally nothing but an expression for the fact that they miss the beloved person. They therefore meet every stranger with fear, they are afraid of the dark because they cannot see the beloved person, and are calmed if they can grasp that person's hand. The effect of childish fears and of the terrifying stories told by nurses is overestimated if one blames the latter for producing the fear in children. Children who are predisposed to fear absorb these stories, which make no impression whatever upon others; and only such children are predisposed to fear whose sexual impulse is excessive or prematurely developed, or has become exigent through pampering. The child behaves here like the adult, that is, it changes its libido into fear when it cannot bring it to gratification, and the grown-up who becomes neurotic on account of ungratified libido behaves in his anxiety like a child; he fears when he is alone, *i.e.*, without a person of whose love he believes himself sure, and who can calm his fears by means of the most childish measures.[7]

Incest Barriers.—If the tenderness of the parents for the child has luckily failed to awaken the sexual impulse of the child prematurely, *i.e.*, before the physical determinations for puberty appear, and if that awakening has not gone so far as to cause an unmistakable breaking through of the psychic excitement into the genital system, it can then fulfill its task and direct the child at the age of maturity in the selection of the sexual object. It would, of course, be most natural for the child to select as the sexual object that person whom it has loved since childhood with, so to speak, a suppressed libido.[8] But owing to the delay of sexual maturity time has been gained for the erection beside the sexual inhibitions of the incest barrier, that moral prescription which explicitly excludes from the object selection the beloved person of infancy or blood relation. The observance of this barrier is above all a demand of cultural society which must guard against the absorption by the family of those interests which it needs for the production of higher social units. Society, therefore, uses every means to loosen those family ties in every individual, especially in the boy, which are authoritative in childhood only.[9]

The object selection, however, is first accomplished in the imagination, and the sexual life of the maturing youth has hardly any escape except indulgence in phantasies or ideas which are not destined to be brought to execution. In the phantasies of all persons the infantile inclinations, now reënforced by somatic emphasis, reappear, and among them one finds in regular frequency and in the first place the sexual feeling of the child for the parents. This has usually already been differentiated by the sexual attraction, the attraction of the son for the mother and of the daughter for the father.[10] Simultaneously with the overcoming and rejection of these distinctly incestuous phantasies there occurs one of the most important as well as one of the most painful psychic accomplishments of puberty; it is the breaking away from the parental authority, through which alone is formed that opposition between the new and old generations which is so important for cultural progress.

Many persons are detained at each of the stations in the course of development through which the individual must pass; and accordingly there are persons who never overcome the parental authority and never, or very imperfectly, withdraw their affection from their parents. They are mostly girls, who, to the delight of their parents, retain their full infantile love far beyond puberty, and it is instructive to find that in their married life these girls are incapable of fulfilling their duties to their husbands. They make cold wives and remain sexually anesthetic. This shows that the apparently non-sexual love for the parents and the sexual love are nourished from the same source, *i.e.*, that the first merely corresponds to an infantile fixation of the libido.

The nearer we come to the deeper disturbances of the psychosexual development the more easily we can recognize the evident significance of the incestuous object-selection. As a result of sexual rejection there remains in the unconscious of the psychoneurotic a great part or the whole of the psychosexual activity for object finding. Girls with an excessive need for affection and an equal horror for the real demands of the sexual life experience an uncontrollable temptation on the one hand to realize in life the ideal of the asexual love and on the other hand to conceal their libido under an affection which they may manifest without self reproach; this they do by clinging for life to the infantile attraction for their parents or brothers or sisters which has been repressed in puberty. With the help of the symptoms and other morbid manifestations, psychoanalysis can trace their unconscious thoughts and translate them into the conscious, and thus easily show to such persons that they are in love with their consanguineous relations in the popular meaning of the term. Likewise when a once healthy person falls sick after an unhappy love affair, the mechanism of the disease can distinctly be explained as a return of his libido to the persons preferred in his infancy.

The After Effects of the Infantile Object Selection.—Even those who have happily eluded the incestuous fixation of their libido have not completely escaped its influence. It is a distinct echo of this phase of development that the first serious love of the young man is often for a mature woman and that of the girl for an older man equipped with authority—*i.e.*, for persons who can revive in them the picture of the mother and father. Generally speaking object selection unquestionably takes place by following more freely these prototypes. The man seeks above all the memory picture of his mother as it has dominated him since the beginning of childhood; this is quite consistent with the fact that the mother, if still living, strives against this, her renewal, and meets it with hostility. In view of this significance of the infantile relation to the parents for the later selection of the sexual object, it is easy to understand that every disturbance of this infantile relation brings to a head the most serious results for the sexual life after puberty. Jealousy of the lover, too, never lacks the infantile sources or at least the infantile reinforcement. Quarrels between parents and unhappy marital relations between the same determine the severest predispositions for disturbed sexual development or neurotic diseases in the children.

The infantile desire for the parents is, to be sure, the most important, but not the only trace revived in puberty which points the way to the object selection. Other dispositions of the same origin permit the man, still supported by his infancy, to develop more than one single sexual series and to form different determinations for the object selection.[11]

Prevention of Inversion.—One of the tasks imposed in the object selection consists in not missing the opposite sex. This, as we know, is not solved without some difficulty. The first feelings after puberty often enough go astray, though not with any permanent injury. Dessoir has called attention to the normality of the enthusiastic friendships formed by boys and girls with their own sex. The greatest force which guards against a permanent inversion of the sexual object is surely the attraction exerted by the opposite sex characters on each other. For this we can give no explanation in connection with this discussion. This factor, however, does not in itself suffice to exclude the inversion; besides this there are surely many other supporting factors. Above all, there is the authoritative inhibition of society; experience shows that where the inversion is not considered a crime it fully corresponds to the sexual inclinations of many persons. Moreover, it may be assumed that in the man the infantile memories of the mother's tenderness, as well as that of other females who cared for him as a child, energetically assist in directing his selection to the woman, while the early sexual intimidation experienced through the father and the attitude of rivalry existing between them deflects the boy from the same sex.

Both factors also hold true in the case of the girl whose sexual activity is under the special care of the mother. This results in a hostile relation to the same sex which decisively influences the object selection in the normal sense. The bringing up of boys by male persons (slaves in the ancient times) seems to favor homosexuality; the frequency of inversion in the present day nobility is probably explained by their employment of male servants, and by the scant care that mothers of that class give to their children. It happens in some hysterics that one of the parents has disappeared (through death, divorce, or estrangement), thus permitting the remaining parent to absorb all the love of the child, and in this way establishing the determinations for the sex of the person to be selected later as the sexual object; thus a permanent inversion is made possible.

SUMMARY

It is now time to attempt a summing-up. We have started from the aberrations of the sexual impulse in reference to its object and aim and have encountered the question whether these originate from a congenital predisposition, or whether they are acquired in consequence of influences from life. The answer to this question was reached through an examination of the relations of the sexual life of psychoneurotics, a numerous group not very remote from the normal. This examination has been made through psychoanalytic investigations. We have thus found that a tendency to all perversions might be demonstrated in these persons in the form of unconscious forces revealing themselves as symptom creators and we could say that the neurosis is, as it were, the negative of the perversion. In view of the now recognized great diffusion of tendencies to perversion the idea forced itself upon us that the disposition to perversions is the primitive and universal disposition of the human sexual impulse, from which the normal sexual behavior develops in consequence of organic changes and psychic inhibitions in the course of maturity.

We hoped to be able to demonstrate the original disposition in the infantile life; among the forces restraining the direction of the sexual impulse we have mentioned shame, loathing and sympathy, and the social constructions of morality and authority. We have thus been forced to perceive in every fixed aberration from the normal sexual life a fragment of inhibited development and infantilism. The significance of the variations of the original dispositions had to be put into the foreground, but between them and the influences of life we had to assume a relation of coöperation and not of opposition. On the other hand, as the original disposition must have been a complex one, the sexual impulse itself appeared to us as something composed of many factors, which in the perversions becomes separated, as it were, into its components. The perversions, thus prove themselves to be on the one hand inhibitions, and on the other dissociations from the normal development. Both conceptions became united in the assumption that the sexual impulse of the adult due to the composition of the diverse feelings of the infantile life became formed into one unit, one striving, with one single aim.

We also added an explanation for the preponderance of perversive tendencies in the psychoneurotics by recognizing in these tendencies collateral fillings of side branches caused by the shifting of the main river bed through repression, and we then turned our examination to the sexual life of the infantile period.[12] We found it regrettable that the existence of a sexual life in infancy has been disputed, and that the sexual manifestations which have been often observed in children have been described as abnormal occurrences. It rather seemed to us that the child brings along into the world germs of sexual activity and that even while taking nourishment it at the same time also enjoys a sexual gratification which it then seeks again to procure for itself through the familiar activity of "thumbsucking."

The sexual activity of the child, however, does not develop in the same measure as its other functions, but merges first into the so-called latency period from the age of three to the age of five years. The production of sexual excitation by no means ceases at this period but continues and furnishes a stock of energy, the greater part of which is utilized for aims other than sexual; namely, on the one hand for the delivery of sexual components for social feelings, and on the other hand (by means of repression and reaction formation) for the erection of the future sexual barriers. Accordingly, the forces which are destined to hold the sexual impulse in certain tracks are built up in infancy at the expense of the greater part of the perverse sexual feelings and with the assistance of education.

Another part of the infantile sexual manifestations escapes this utilization and may manifest itself as sexual activity. It can then be discovered that the sexual excitation of the child flows from diverse sources. Above all gratifications originate through the adapted sensible excitation of so-called erogenous zones. For these probably any skin region or sensory organ may serve; but there are certain distinguished erogenous zones the excitation of which by certain organic mechanisms is assured from the beginning. Moreover, sexual excitation originates in the organism, as it were, as a by-product in a great number of processes, as soon as they attain a certain intensity; this especially takes place in all strong emotional excitements even if they be of a painful nature. The excitations from all these sources do not yet unite, but they pursue their aim individually—this aim consisting merely in the gaining of a certain pleasure. The sexual impulse of childhood is therefore objectless or *autoerotic*.

Still during infancy the erogenous zone of the genitals begins to make itself noticeable, either by the fact that like any other erogenous zone it furnishes gratification through a suitable sensible stimulus, or because in some incomprehensible way the gratification from other sources causes at the same time the sexual excitement which has a special connection with the genital zone. We found cause to regret that a sufficient explanation of the relations between sexual gratification and sexual excitement, as well as between the activity of the genital zone and the remaining sources of sexuality, was not to be attained.

We were unable to state what amount of sexual activity in childhood might be designated as normal to the extent of being incapable of further development. The character of the sexual manifestation showed itself to be preponderantly masturbatic. We, moreover, verified from experience the belief that the external influences of seduction, might produce premature breaches in the latency period leading as far as the suppression of the same, and that the sexual impulse of the child really shows itself to be polymorphous-perverse; furthermore, that every such premature sexual activity impairs the educability of the child.

Despite the incompleteness of our examinations of the infantile sexual life we were subsequently forced to attempt to study the serious changes produced by the appearance of puberty. We selected two of the same as criteria, namely, the subordination of all other sources of the sexual feeling to the primacy of the genital zones, and the process of object finding. Both of them are already developed in childhood. The first is accomplished through the mechanism of utilizing the fore-pleasure, whereby all other independent sexual acts which are connected with pleasure and excitement become preparatory acts for the new sexual aim, the voiding of the sexual products, the attainment of which under enormous pleasure puts an end to the sexual feeling.

 At the same time we had to consider the differentiation of the sexual nature of man and woman, and we found that in order to become a woman a new repression is required which abolishes a piece of infantile masculinity, and prepares the woman for the change of the leading genital zones. Lastly, we found the object selection, tracing it through infancy to its revival in puberty; we also found indications of sexual inclinations on the part of the child for the parents and foster-parents, which, however, were turned away from these persons to others resembling them by the incest barriers which had been erected in the meantime. Let us finally add that during the transition period of puberty the somatic and psychic processes of development proceed side by side, but separately, until with the breaking through of an intense psychic love-stimulus for the innervation of the genitals, the normally demanded unification of the erotic function is established.

The Factors Disturbing the Development.—As we have already shown by different examples, every step on this long road of development may become a point of fixation and every joint in this complicated structure may afford opportunity for a dissociation of the sexual impulse. It still remains for us to review the various inner and outer factors which disturb the development, and to mention the part of the mechanism affected by the disturbance emanating from them. The factors which we mention here in a series cannot, of course, all be in themselves of equal validity and we must expect to meet with difficulties in the assigning to the individual factors their due importance.

Constitution and Heredity.—In the first place, we must mention here the congenital *variation of the sexual constitution*, upon which the greatest weight probably falls, but the existence of which, as may be easily understood, can be established only through its later manifestations and even then not always with great certainty. We understand by it a preponderance of one or another of the manifold sources of the sexual excitement, and we believe that such a difference of disposition must always come to expression in the final result, even if it should remain within normal limits. Of course, we can also imagine certain variations of the original disposition that even without further aid must necessarily lead to the formation of an abnormal sexual life. One can call these "degenerative" and consider them as an expression of hereditary deterioration.

In this connection I have to report a remarkable fact. In more than half of the severe cases of hysteria, compulsion neuroses, etc., which I have treated by psychotherapy, I have succeeded in positively demonstrating that their fathers have gone through an attack of syphilis before marriage; they have either suffered from tabes or general paresis, or there was a definite history of lues. I expressly add that the children who were later neurotic showed absolutely no signs of hereditary lues, so that the abnormal sexual constitution was to be considered as the last off-shoot of the luetic heredity. As far as it is now from my thoughts to put down a descent from syphilitic parents as a regular and indispensable etiological determination of the neuropathic constitution, I nevertheless maintain that the coincidence observed by me is not accidental and not without significance.

The hereditary relations of the positive perverts are not so well known because they know how to avoid inquiry. Still there is reason to believe that the same holds true in the perversions as in the neuroses. We often find perversions and psychoneuroses in the different sexes of the same family, so distributed that the male members, or one of them, is a positive pervert, while the females, following the repressive tendencies of their sex, are negative perverts or hysterics. This is a good example of the substantial relations between the two disturbances which I have discovered.

Further Elaboration.—It cannot, however, be maintained that the structure of the sexual life is rendered finally complete by the addition of the diverse components of the sexual constitution. On the contrary, qualifications continue to appear and new possibilities result, depending upon the fate experienced by the sexual streams originating from the individual sources. This *further elaboration* is evidently the final and decisive one while the constitution described as uniform may lead to three final issues. If all the dispositions assumed to be abnormal retain their relative proportion, and are strengthened with maturity, the ultimate result can only be a perverse sexual life. The analysis of such abnormally constituted dispositions has not yet been thoroughly undertaken, but we already know cases that can be readily explained in the light of these theories. Authors believe, for example, that a whole series of fixation perversions must necessarily have had as their basis a congenital weakness of the sexual impulse. The statement seems to me untenable in this form, but it becomes ingenious if it refers to a constitutional weakness of one factor in the sexual impulse, namely, the genital zone, which later in the interests of propagation accepts as a function the sum of the individual sexual activities. In this case the summation which is demanded in puberty must fail and the strongest of the other sexual components continues its activity as a perversion.[13]

Repression.—Another issue results if in the course of development certain powerful components experience a *repression*—which we must carefully note is not a suspension. The excitations in question are produced as usual but are prevented from attaining their aim by psychic hindrances, and are driven off into many other paths until they express themselves in a symptom. The result can be an almost normal sexual life—usually a limited one—but supplemented by psychoneurotic disease. It is these cases that become so familiar to us through the psychoanalytic investigation of neurotics. The sexual life of such persons begins like that of perverts, a considerable part of their childhood is filled up with perverse sexual activity which occasionally extends far beyond the period of maturity, but owing to inner reasons a repressive change then results—usually before puberty, but now and then even much later—and from this point on without any extinction of the old feelings there appears a neurosis instead of a perversion. One may recall here the saying, "Junge Hure, alte Betschwester,"—only here youth has turned out to be much too short. The relieving of the perversion by the neurosis in the life of the same person, as well as the above mentioned distribution of perversion and hysteria in different persons of the same family, must be placed side by side with the fact that the neurosis is the negative of the perversion.

Sublimation.—The third issue in abnormal constitutional dispositions is made possible by the process of "sublimation," through which the powerful excitations from individual sources of sexuality are discharged and utilized in other spheres, so that a considerable increase of psychic capacity results from an, in itself dangerous, predisposition. This forms one the sources of artistic activity, and, according as such sublimation is complete or incomplete, the analysis of the character of highly gifted, especially of artistically disposed persons, will show any proportionate, blending between productive ability, perversion, and neurosis. A sub-species of sublimation is the suppression through *reaction-formation*, which, as we have found, begins even in the latency period of infancy, only to continue throughout life in favorable cases. What we call the *character* of a person is built up to a great extent from the material of sexual excitations; it is composed of impulses fixed since infancy and won through sublimation, and of such constructions as are destined to suppress effectually those perverse feelings which are recognized as useless. The general perverse sexual disposition of childhood can therefore be esteemed as a source of a number of our virtues, insofar as it incites their creation through the formation of reactions.[14]

Accidental Experiences.—All other influences lose in significance when compared with the sexual discharges, shifts of repressions, and sublimations; the inner determinations for the last two processes are totally unknown to us. He who includes repressions and sublimations among constitutional predispositions, and considers them as the living manifestations of the same, has surely the right to maintain that the final structure of the sexual life is above all the result of the congenital constitution. No intelligent person, however, will dispute that in such a coöperation of factors there is also room for the modifying influences of occasional factors derived from experience in childhood and later on.

It is not easy to estimate the effectiveness of the constitutional and of the occasional factors in their relation to each other. Theory is always inclined to overestimate the first while therapeutic practice renders prominent the significance of the latter. By no means should it be forgotten that between the two there exists a relation of coöperation and not of exclusion. The constitutional factor must wait for experiences which bring it to the surface, while the occasional needs the support of the constitutional factor in order to become effective. For the majority of cases one can imagine a so-called "etiological group" in which the declining intensities of one factor become balanced by the rise in the others, but there is no reason to deny the existence of extremes at the ends of the group.

It would be still more in harmony with psychoanalytic investigation if the experiences of early childhood would get a place of preference among the occasional factors. The one etiological group then becomes split up into two which may be designated as the dispositional and the definitive groups. Constitution and occasional infantile experiences are just as coöperative in the first as disposition and later traumatic experiences in the second group. All the factors which injure the sexual development show their effect in that they produce a *regression*, or a return to a former phase of development.

We may now continue with our task of enumerating the factors which have become known to us as influential for the sexual development, whether they be active forces or merely manifestations of the same.

Prematurity.—Such a factor is the spontaneous sexual *prematurity* which can be definitely demonstrated at least in the etiology of the neuroses, though in itself it is as little adequate for causation as the other factors. It manifests itself in a breaking through, shortening, or suspending of the infantile latency period and becomes a cause of disturbances inasmuch as it provokes sexual manifestations which, either on account of the unready state of the sexual inhibitions or because of the undeveloped state of the genital system, can only carry along the character of perversions. These tendencies to perversion may either remain as such, or after the repression sets in they may become motive powers for neurotic symptoms; at all events, the sexual prematurity renders difficult the desirable later control of the sexual impulse by the higher psychic influences, and enhances the compulsive-like character which even without this prematurity would be claimed by the psychic representatives of the impulse. Sexual prematurity often runs parallel with premature intellectual development; it is found as such in the infantile history of the most distinguished and most productive individuals, and in such connection it does not seem to act as pathogenically as when appearing isolated.

Temporal Factors.—Just like prematurity, other factors, which under the designation of *temporal* can be added to prematurity, also demand consideration. It seems to be phylogenetically established in what sequence the individual impulsive feelings become active, and how long they can manifest themselves before they succumb to the influence of a newly appearing active impulse or to a typical repression. But both in this temporal succession as well as in the duration of the same, variations seem to occur, which must exercise a definite influence on the experience. It cannot be a matter of indifference whether a certain stream appears earlier or later than its counterstream, for the effect of a repression cannot be made retrogressive; a temporal deviation in the composition of the components regularly produces a change in the result. On the other hand impulsive feelings which appear with special intensity often come to a surprisingly rapid end, as in the case of the heterosexual attachment of the later manifest homosexuals.

The strivings of childhood which manifest themselves most impetuously do not justify the fear that they will lastingly dominate the character of the grown-up; one has as much right to expect that they will disappear in order to make room for their counterparts. (Harsh masters do not rule long.) To what one may attribute such temporal confusions of the processes of development we are hardly able to suggest. A view is opened here to a deeper phalanx of biological, and perhaps also historical problems, which we have not yet approached within fighting distance.

Adhesion.—The significance of all premature sexual manifestations is enhanced by a psychic factor of unknown origin which at present can be put down only as a psychological preliminary. I believe that it is the *heightened adhesion* or *fixedness* of these impressions of the sexual life which in later neurotics, as well as in perverts, must be added for the completion of the other facts; for the same premature sexual manifestations in other persons cannot impress themselves deeply enough to repeat themselves compulsively and to succeed in prescribing the way for the sexual impulse throughout later life.

Perhaps a part of the explanation for this adhesion lies in another psychic factor which we cannot miss in the causation of the neuroses, namely, in the preponderance which in the psychic life falls to the share of memory traces as compared with recent impressions. This factor is apparently dependent on the intellectual development and grows with the growth of personal culture. In contrast to this the savage has been characterized as "the unfortunate child of the moment."[15] Owing to the oppositional relation existing between culture and the free development of sexuality, the results of which may be traced far into the formation of our life, the problem how the sexual life of the child evolves is of very little importance for the later life in the lower stages of culture and civilization, and of very great importance in the higher.

Fixation.—The influence of the psychic factors just mentioned favored the development of the accidentally experienced impulses of the infantile sexuality. The latter (especially in the form of seductions through other children or through adults) produce the material which, with the help of the former, may become fixed as a permanent disturbance. A considerable number of the deviations from the normal sexual life observed later have been thus established in neurotics and perverts from the beginning through the impressions received during the alleged sexually free period of childhood. The causation is produced by the responsiveness of the constitution, the prematurity, the quality of heightened adhesion, and the accidental excitement of the sexual impulse through outside influence.

The unsatisfactory conclusions which have resulted from this investigation of the disturbances of the sexual life is due to the fact that we as yet know too little concerning the biological processes in which the nature of sexuality consists to form from our isolated examinations a satisfactory theory for the explanation of either the normal or the pathological.

Note 1: The differences will be emphasized in the schematic representation given in the text. To what extent the infantile sexuality approaches the definitive sexual organization through its object selection has been discussed before (p. 60).

Note 2: See my work, Wit and its Relation to the Unconscious, translated by A.A. Brill, Moffat Yard Pub. Co., New York: "The fore-pleasure gained by the technique of wit is utilized for the purpose of setting free a greater pleasure by the removal of inner inhibitions."

Note 3: Cf. Zur Einführung des Narzismus, Jahrbuch der Psychoanalyse, VI, 1913.

Note 4: It is necessary to make clear that the conceptions "masculine" and "feminine," whose content seems so unequivocal to the ordinary meaning, belong to the most confused terms in science and can be cut up into at least three paths. One uses masculine and feminine at times in the sense of activity and passivity, again, in the biological sense, and then also in the sociological sense. The first of these three meanings is the essential one and the only one utilizable in psychoanalysis. It agrees with the masculine designation of the libido in the text above, for the libido is always active even when it is directed to a passive aim. The second, the biological significance of masculine and feminine, is the one which permits the clearest determination. Masculine and feminine are here characterized by the presence of semen or ovum and through the functions emanating from them. The activity and its secondary manifestations, like stronger developed muscles, aggression, a greater intensity of libido, are as a rule soldered to the biological masculinity but not necessarily connected with it, for there are species of animals in whom these qualities are attributed to the female. The third, the sociological meaning, receives its content through the observation of the actual existing male and female individuals. The result of this in man is that there is no pure masculinity or feminity either in the biological or psychological sense. On the contrary every individual person shows a mixture of his own biological sex characteristics with the biological traits of the other sex and a union of activity and passivity; this is the case whether these psychological characteristic features depend on the biological or whether they are independent of it.

Note 5: Psychoanalysis teaches that there are two paths of object-finding; the first is the one discussed in the text which is guided by the early infantile prototypes. The second is the narcissistic which seeks its own ego and finds it in the other. The latter is of particularly great significance for the pathological outcomes, but does not fit into the connection treated here.

Note 6: Those to whom this conception appears "wicked" may read Havelock Ellis's treatise on the relations between mother and child which expresses almost the same ideas.

Note 7: For the explanation of the origin of the infantile fear I am indebted to a three-year-old boy whom I once heard calling from a dark room: "Aunt, talk to me, I am afraid because it is dark." "How will that help you," answered the aunt; "you cannot see anyhow." "That's nothing," answered the child; "if someone talks then it becomes light."—He was, as we see, not afraid of the darkness but he was afraid because he missed the person he loved, and he could promise to calm down as soon as he was assured of her presence.

Note 8: Cf. here what was said on page 83 concerning the object selection of the child; the "tender stream."

Note 9: The incest barrier probably belongs to the historical acquisitions of humanity and like other moral taboos it must be fixed in many individuals through organic heredity. (Cf. my work, Totem and Taboo, 1913.) Psychoanalytic studies show, however, how intensively the individual struggles with the incest temptations during his development and how frequently he puts them into phantasies and even into reality.

Note 10: Compare the description concerning the inevitable relation in the Oedipus legend (The Interpretation of Dreams, p. 222, translated by A.A. Brill, The Macmillan Co., New York, and Allen & Unwin, London).

Note 11: Innumerable peculiarities of the human love-life as well as the compulsiveness of being in love itself can surely only be understood through a reference to childhood or as an effective remnant of the same.

Note 12: This was true not only of the "negative" tendencies to perversion appearing in the neurosis, but also of the so-called positive perversions. The latter are not only to be attributed to the fixation of the infantile tendencies, but also to regression to these tendencies owing to the misplacement of other paths of the sexual stream. Hence the positive perversions are also accessible to psychoanalytic therapy. (Cf. the works of Sadger, Ferenczi, and Brill.)

Note 13: Here one often sees that at first a normal sexual stream begins at the age of puberty, but owing to its inner weakness it breaks down at the first outer hindrance and then changes from regression, to perverse fixation.

Note 14: That keen observer of human nature, E. Zola, describes a girl in his book, La Joie de vivre, who in cheerful self renunciation offers all she has in possession or expectation, her fortune and her life's hopes to those she loves without thought of return. The childhood of this girl was dominated by an insatiable desire for love which whenever she was depreciated caused her to merge into a fit of cruelty.

Note 15: It is possible that the heightened adhesion is only the result of a special intensive somatic sexual manifestation of former years.

BEYOND THE PLEASURE
PRINCIPLE

CONTENTS

CHAPTER ONE

IN THE THEORY of psychoanalysis, we have no hesitation in assuming that the course taken by mental events is automatically regulated by the pleasure principle. We believe, that is to say, that the course of those events is invariably set in motion by an unpleasurable tension; and that it takes a direction such that its final outcome coincides with a lowering of that tension—that is, with an avoidance of unpleasure or a production of pleasure.

In taking that course into account, in our consideration of the mental processes that are the subject of our study, we are introducing an economic point of view into our work. If, in describing those processes, we try to estimate this economic factor in addition to the topographical and dynamic ones, we shall, I think, be giving the most complete description of them we can presently conceive, and one that deserves to be distinguished by the term meta-psychological.

It is of no concern to us, in this connection, to enquire how far—with this hypothesis of the pleasure principle—we have approached or adopted any particular, historically established, philosophical system. We have arrived at these speculative assumptions in an attempt to describe and to account for the facts of daily observation in our field of study.

Priority and originality are not among the aims that psycho-analytic work sets itself; and the impressions that underlie the hypothesis of the pleasure principle are so obvious that they can scarcely be overlooked. On the other hand, we would readily express our gratitude to any philosophical or psychological theory that was able to inform us of the meaning of the feelings of pleasure and unpleasure, which act so imperatively upon us.

However, on this point we are, alas, offered nothing to our purpose. This is the most obscure and inaccessible region of the mind, and, because we cannot avoid contact with it, the least rigid hypothesis, it seems to me, will be the best.

We have decided to relate pleasure and unpleasure to the quantity of excitation that is present in the mind but is not in any way bound; and to relate them in such a manner that unpleasure corresponds to an *increase* in the quantity of excitation and pleasure to a *diminution*.

What we are implying is not a simple relation between the strength of the feelings of pleasure and unpleasure, and the corresponding modifications in the quantity of excitation; least of all—in view of all we have been taught by psychophysiology—are we suggesting any directly proportional ratio. The factor that determines the feeling is probably the amount of increase or diminution in the quantity of excitation *in a given period of time*.

Experiment might possibly play a part here; but it is not advisable for analysts to go into the problem further, so long as our way is not pointed by quite definite observations.

We cannot, however, remain indifferent to the discovery that an investigator of such penetration as G. T. Fechner held a view upon the subject of pleasure and unpleasure that coincides in all essentials with the one that has been forced upon us by psycho-analytic work.

Fechner's statement is to be found contained in a small work, *Einige Ideen zur Schöpfungs*, and reads as follows:

"In so far as conscious impulses always have some relation to pleasure or unpleasure, pleasure and unpleasure, too, can be regarded as having a psycho-physical relation to conditions of stability and instability. This provides a basis for a hypothesis into which I propose to enter in greater detail elsewhere. According to this hypothesis, every psycho-physical movement crossing the threshold of consciousness is attended by pleasure in proportion as, beyond a certain limit, it approximates to complete stability, and is attended by unpleasure in proportion as, beyond a certain limit, it deviates from complete stability. While between the two limits, which may be described as qualitative thresholds of pleasure and unpleasure, there is a certain margin of aesthetic indifference..."

The facts that have caused us to believe in the dominance of the pleasure principle in mental life also find expression in the hypothesis that the mental apparatus endeavors to keep the quantity of excitation present in it as low as possible, or at least to keep it constant.

This latter hypothesis is only another way of stating the pleasure principle. For if the work of the mental apparatus is directed toward keeping the quantity of excitation low, then anything calculated to increase that quantity is bound to be felt as adverse to the functioning of the apparatus, that is, as unpleasurable.

The pleasure principle follows from the constancy principle. Moreover, a more detailed discussion will show that the tendency, which we thus attribute to the mental apparatus, is subsumed as a special case under Fechner's principle of the *tendency towards stability*, to which he has brought the feelings of pleasure and unpleasure into relation.

It must be pointed out, however, that strictly speaking it is incorrect to talk of the dominance of the pleasure principle over the course of mental processes. If such a dominance existed, the immense majority of our mental processes would have to be accompanied by pleasure or to lead to pleasure, whereas universal experience completely contradicts any such conclusion. The most that can be said, therefore, is that there exists, in the mind, a strong *tendency* toward the pleasure principle, but that tendency is opposed by certain other forces or circumstances, so that the final outcome cannot always be in harmony with the tendency toward pleasure.

We may compare what Fechner remarks on a similar point: "Because tendency toward an aim does not imply that the aim is attained, and because, in general, the aim is attainable only by approximations..."

If we turn now to the question of what circumstances are able to prevent the pleasure principle from being carried into effect, we find ourselves once more on secure and well-trodden ground. In framing our answer, we have at our disposal a rich fund of analytic experience.

The first example of the pleasure principle being inhibited in this way is a familiar one, which occurs with regularity. We know that the pleasure principle is proper to a *primary* method of working on the part of the mental apparatus, but that, from the point of view of the self-preservation of the organism among the difficulties of the external world, it is from the very outset inefficient and even highly dangerous.

Under the influence of the ego's instincts of self-preservation, the pleasure principle is replaced by the *reality principle*. This latter principle does not abandon the intention of ultimately obtaining pleasure, but it nevertheless demands and carries into effect the postponement of satisfaction, the abandonment of a number of possibilities of gaining satisfaction, and the temporary toleration of unpleasure, as a step on the long indirect road to pleasure.

The pleasure principle long persists, however, as the method of working, employed by the sexual instincts, which are so hard to educate, and, starting out from those instincts, or in the ego itself, it often succeeds in overcoming the reality principle, to the detriment of the organism as a whole.

There can be no doubt, however, that the replacement of the pleasure principle by the reality principle can only be made responsible for a small number, and by no means the most intense of unpleasurable experiences. Another occasion of the release of unpleasure, which occurs with no less regularity, is to be found in the conflicts and dissensions that take place in the mental apparatus while the ego is passing through its development into more highly composite organizations.

Almost all the energy, with which the apparatus is filled, arises from its innate instinctual impulses. These are not all allowed to reach the same phases of development. In the course of development, it happens again and again that individual instincts or parts of instincts turn out to be incompatible in their aims or demands with the remaining ones, which are able to combine into the inclusive unity of the ego.

The former are then split off from this unity by the process of repression, held back at lower levels of psychical development and cut off, to begin with, from the possibility of satisfaction. If they succeed subsequently, as can so easily happen with repressed sexual instincts, in struggling through, by roundabout paths, to a direct or to a substitutive satisfaction, that event, which would in other cases have been an opportunity for pleasure, is felt by the ego as unpleasure.

Consequently, of the old conflict which ended in repression, a new breach has occurred in the pleasure principle at the very time when certain instincts were endeavoring, in accordance with the principle, to obtain fresh pleasure.

The details of the process by which repression turns a possibility of pleasure into a source of unpleasure are not yet clearly understood or cannot be clearly represented. However, there is no doubt that all neurotic unpleasure is of that kind—pleasure that cannot be felt as such.

The two sources of unpleasure, which I have just indicated, are very far from covering the majority of our unpleasurable experiences. As regards the remainder, it can be asserted, with some show of justification, that their presence does not contradict the dominance of the pleasure principle. Most of the unpleasure that we experience is *perceptual* unpleasure. It is either perception of pressure by unsatisfied instincts, or external perception that is either distressing in itself, or that which excites unpleasurable expectations in the mental apparatus, that is, which is recognized by it as a danger.

The reaction to these instinctual demands and threats of danger, a reaction that constitutes the proper activity of the mental apparatus, can then be directed in a correct manner by the pleasure principle or the modified reality principle. This does not seem to necessitate any far-reaching limitation of the pleasure principle.

Nevertheless, the investigation of the mental reaction to external danger is precisely a subject that may produce new material and raise fresh questions bearing upon our present problem.

CHAPTER TWO

A CONDITION HAS long been known and described which occurs after severe mechanical concussions, railway disasters, and other accidents involving a risk to life. It has been given the name, traumatic neurosis. The terrible war, which has just ended, gave rise to a great number of illnesses of this kind, but it at least put an end to the temptation to attribute the cause of the disorder to organic lesions of the nervous system, brought about by mechanical force.

The symptomatic picture presented by traumatic neurosis approaches that of hysteria in the wealth of its similar motor symptoms, but surpasses it, as a rule, in its strongly marked signs of subjective ailment (in which it resembles hypochondria or melancholia), as well as in the evidence it gives of a far more comprehensive general enfeeblement and disturbance of the mental capacities.

No complete explanation has yet been reached either of war neuroses or of the traumatic neuroses of peace. In the case of the war neuroses, the fact that the same symptoms sometimes came about without the intervention of any gross mechanical violence, seemed at once enlightening and bewildering.

In the case of the ordinary traumatic neuroses, two characteristics emerge prominently. First, that the chief weight in their causation seems to rest upon the factor of surprise, of fright; and secondly, that a wound or injury inflicted simultaneously works, as a rule, *against* the development of a neurosis.

Fright, fear, and anxiety are improperly used as synonymous expressions; they are, in fact, capable of clear distinction in their relation to danger. Anxiety describes a particular state of expecting the danger or preparing for it, even though it may be an unknown one. Fear requires a definite object of which to be afraid. Fright, however, is the name we give to the state a person gets into when he has run into danger without being prepared for it. It emphasizes the factor of surprise.

I do not believe anxiety can produce a traumatic neurosis. There is something about anxiety that protects its subject against fright and so against fright-neuroses. We shall return to this point later.

The study of dreams may be considered the most trustworthy method of investigating deep mental processes. Now, dreams occurring in traumatic neuroses have the characteristic of repeatedly bringing the patient back into the situation of his accident, a situation from which he wakes up in another fright. This astonishes people far too little. They think the fact that the traumatic experience is constantly forcing itself upon the patient even in his sleep is a proof of the strength of that experience. The patient is, as one might say, fixated to his trauma.

Fixations to the experience that started the illness have long been familiar to us in hysteria. Hysterics are, to a great extent, suffering from reminiscences. In the war neuroses, too, observers like

Ferenczi and Simmel have been able to explain certain motor symptoms by fixation to the moment at which the trauma occurred.

I am not aware, however, that patients suffering from traumatic neurosis are much occupied in their waking lives with memories of their accident. Perhaps, they are more concerned with not thinking of it. Anyone who accepts it as something self-evident that their dreams should put them back at night into the situation that caused them to fall ill has misunderstood the nature of dreams.

It would be more in harmony with their nature to show the patient pictures from his healthy past, or of the cure for which he hopes. If we are not to be shaken in our belief in the wish-fulfilling tenor of dreams by the dreams of traumatic neurotics, we still have one resource open to us: we may argue that the function of dreaming, like so much else, is upset in this condition and diverted from its purposes, or we may be driven to reflect on the mysterious masochistic trends of the ego.

At this point, I propose to leave the dark and dismal subject of the traumatic neurosis and pass on to examine the method of working employed by

the mental apparatus in one of its earliest *normal* activities—I mean in children's play.

The different theories of children's play have only recently been summarized and discussed from the psycho-analytic point of view by Pfeifer (1919), to whose paper I would refer my readers. These theories attempt to discover the motives that lead children to play, but they fail to bring into the foreground the *economic* motive—the consideration of the yield of pleasure involved.

Without wishing to include the whole field covered by these phenomena, I have been able, through a chance opportunity that presented itself, to throw some light upon the first game played by a little boy of one and a half and invented by himself.

It was more than a mere fleeting observation, for I lived under the same roof as the child and his parents for some weeks, and it was some time before I discovered the meaning of the puzzling activity, which he constantly repeated.

The child was not at all precocious in his intellectual development. At the age of one and a half, he could say only a few comprehensible words. He could also make use of a number of sounds, which expressed a meaning intelligible to those around him. He was, however, on good terms with his parents and their one servant-girl, and tributes were paid to his being a good boy.

He did not disturb his parents at night; he conscientiously obeyed orders not to touch certain things or go into certain rooms, and above all he never cried when his mother left him for a few hours. At the same time, he was greatly attached to his mother, who had not only fed him herself but had also looked after him without any outside help.

This good little boy, however, had an occasional disturbing habit of taking any small objects he could get hold of and throwing them away from himself, into a corner, under the bed, and so on, so that hunting for his toys and picking them up was often quite a business. As he did this, he gave vent to a loud, long-drawn-out "o-o-o-o," accompanied by an expression of interest and satisfaction.

His mother, and the writer of the present account, were agreed in thinking that this was not a mere interjection but represented the German word for "gone". I eventually realized that it was a game and that the only use he made of any of his toys was to play *gone* with them.

One day, I made an observation that confirmed my view. The child had a wooden reel with a piece of string tied around it. It never occurred to him to pull it along the floor behind him, for instance, and play at its being a carriage. What he did was to hold the reel by the string and, very skillfully, throw it over the edge of his curtained cot, so that it disappeared into it, at the same time uttering his expressive "o-o-o-o."

He then pulled the reel out of the cot again by the string and hailed its reappearance with a joyful "da" ("there"). This, then, was the complete game—disappearance and return. As a rule, one only witnessed its first act, which was repeated untiringly as a game in itself, though there is no doubt that greater pleasure was attached to the second act.

The interpretation of the game then became obvious. It was related to the child's great cultural achievement—the instinctual renunciation (that is, the renunciation of instinctual satisfaction) which he had made in allowing his mother to go away without protesting. He compensated himself for this, as it were, by himself staging the disappearance and return of the objects within his reach.

It is, of course, a matter of indifference from the point of view of judging the affective nature of the game, whether the child invented it himself or took it over on some outside suggestion. Our interest is directed to another point. The child cannot possibly have felt his mother's departure as something agreeable or even indifferent. How then does his repetition of this distressing experience as a game fit in with the pleasure principle?

It may, perhaps, be said in reply that her departure had to be enacted as a necessary preliminary to her joyful return, and that it was in the latter that lay the true purpose of the game. But against this must be counted the observed fact that the first act, that of the departure, was staged as a game, in itself, and far more frequently than the episode in its entirety with its pleasurable ending.

A further observation subsequently confirmed this interpretation fully. One day, the child's mother had been away for several hours and on her return was met with the words, "Baby, o-o-o-o!" which was at first incomprehensible. It soon turned out, however, that during this long period of solitude, the child had found a method of making *himself* disappear. He had discovered his reflection in a full-length mirror, which did not quite reach to the ground, so that by crouching down he could make his mirror-image "gone."

No certain decision can be reached from the analysis of a single case like this. On an unprejudiced view, one gets an impression that the child turned his experience into a game from another motive. At the outset, he was in a *passive* situation. He was overpowered by the experience; but, by repeating it, unpleasurable though it was, as a game, he took on an *active* part.

These efforts might be put down to an instinct for mastery, acting independently of whether the repeated memory was, in itself, pleasurable or not. But still, another interpretation may be attempted. Throwing away the object so that it was "gone," might satisfy an impulse of the child's, which was suppressed in his actual life, to revenge himself on his mother for going away from him.

In that case, it would have a defiant meaning: "All right, then, go away! I don't need you. I'm sending you away myself."

A year later, the same boy, whom I had observed at his first game, used to take a toy if he was angry with it, and throw it on the floor, exclaiming: "Go to the fwont!" He had heard, at that time, that his absent father was "at the front," and was far from regretting his absence. On the contrary, he made it quite clear that he had no desire to be disturbed in his sole possession of his mother.

We know of other children who like to express similar hostile impulses by throwing away objects instead of persons. We are, therefore, left in doubt as to whether the impulse to work over in the mind some overpowering experience, so as to make oneself master of it can find expression as a primary event, and independently of the pleasure principle.

For, in the case we have been discussing, the child may, after all, only have been able to repeat his unpleasant experience in play because the repetition carried, along with it, a yield of pleasure of another sort, but none the less a direct one.

Nor shall we be helped in our hesitation between these two views by further considering children's play. It is clear that in their play, children repeat everything that has made a great impression on them in real life, and that in so doing they abreact the strength of the impression and, as one might put it, make themselves master of the situation.

But on the other hand, it is obvious that all their play is influenced by a wish that dominates them the whole time—the wish to be grown-up and to be able to do what grown-up people do. It can also be observed that the unpleasurable nature of an experience does not always un-suit it for play. If the doctor looks down a child's throat, or carries out some small operation on him, we may be quite sure that these frightening experiences will be the subject of the next game; but we must not, in that connection, overlook the fact that there is a yield of pleasure from another source.

As the child passes over from the passivity of the experience to the activity of the game, he hands on the disagreeable experience to one of his playmates, and in this way revenges himself on a substitute.

Nevertheless, it emerges from this discussion that there is no need to assume the existence of a special imitative instinct in order to provide a motive for play. Finally, a reminder may be added that the artistic play and artistic imitation carried out by adults, which, unlike children's, are aimed at an audience, do not spare the spectators (in tragedy, for instance) the most painful experiences, and can yet, be felt by them as highly enjoyable.

This is convincing proof that, even under the dominance of the pleasure principle, there are ways and means enough of making what is in itself unpleasurable into a subject to be recollected and worked over in the mind.

The consideration of these cases and situations, which have a yield of pleasure as their final outcome, should be undertaken by some system of aesthetics with an economic approach to its subject-matter. They are of no use for our purposes, because they presuppose the existence and dominance of the pleasure principle. They give no evidence of the operation of tendencies *beyond* the pleasure principle, that is, of tendencies more primitive than it and independent of it.

CHAPTER THREE

TWENTY-FIVE YEARS of intense work have had, as their result, that the immediate aims of psychoanalytic technique are quite other today than they were at the outset. At first, the analyzing physician could do no more than discover the unconscious material that was concealed from the patient, put it together, and, at the right moment, communicate it to him.

Psychoanalysis was then, first and foremost, an art of interpreting. Because this did not solve the therapeutic problem, a further aim quickly came in view: to oblige the patient to confirm the analyst's construction from his own memory. In that endeavor, the chief emphasis lay upon the patient's resistances: the art consisted now in uncovering these as quickly as possible, in pointing them out to the patient, and in inducing him by human influence. This was where suggestion, operating as transference, played its part to abandon his resistances.

But it became ever clearer that the aim which had been set up—namely, that what was unconscious should become conscious—is not completely attainable by that method. The patient cannot remember the whole of what is repressed in him, and what he cannot remember may be precisely the essential part of it. Thus, he acquires no sense of conviction of the correctness of the construction that has been communicated to him.

He is obliged to *repeat* the repressed material as a contemporary experience instead of, as the physician would prefer to see, *remembering* it as something belonging to the past. These reproductions, which emerge with such unwished-for exactitude, always have, as their subject, some portion of infantile sexual life—of the Oedipus complex, that is, and its derivatives.

They are invariably played out in the sphere of the transference, of the patient's relation to the physician. When things have reached this stage, it may be said that the earlier neurosis has now been replaced by a fresh, transference neurosis. It has been the physician's endeavor to keep this transference neurosis within the narrowest limits: to force as much as possible into the channel of memory and to allow as little as possible to emerge as repetition.

The ratio between what is remembered and what is reproduced varies from case to case. The physician cannot, as a rule, spare his patient this phase of the treatment. He must get him to re-experience some portion of his forgotten life, but must see to it, on the other hand, that the patient retains some degree of aloofness, which will enable him, in spite of everything, to recognize that what appears to be reality is, in fact, only a reflection of a forgotten past.

If this can be successfully achieved, the patient's sense of conviction is won, together with the therapeutic success that is dependent on it.

In order to make it easier to understand this compulsion to repeat, which emerges during the psycho-analytic treatment of neurotics, we must above all get rid of the mistaken notion that what we are dealing with, in our struggle against resistances, is resistance on the part of the unconscious.

The unconscious—that is to say, the repressed—offers no resistance whatever to the efforts of the treatment. Indeed, it itself has no other endeavor than to break through the pressure weighing down on it and force its way either into consciousness or to discharge through some real action.

Resistance during treatment arises from the same higher strata and systems of the mind, which originally carried out repression. But the fact that, as we know from experience, the motives of the resistances, and indeed the resistances themselves, are unconscious at first during the treatment, is a hint to us that we should correct a shortcoming in our terminology. We shall avoid a lack of clarity if we make our contrast, not between the conscious and the unconscious, but between the coherent ego and the repressed.

It is certain that much of the ego is itself unconscious, and notably, what we may describe as its nucleus. Only a small part of it is covered by the term preconscious. Having replaced a purely descriptive terminology by one that is systematic or dynamic, we can say that the patient's resistance arises from his ego, and we then, at once, perceive that the compulsion to repeat must be ascribed to the unconscious repressed. It seems probable that that compulsion can only express itself after the work of treatment has gone half-way to meet it, and has loosened the repression.

There is no doubt that the resistance of the conscious and unconscious ego operates under the sway of the pleasure principle. It seeks to avoid the unpleasure, which would be produced by the liberation of the repressed. Our efforts, on the other hand, are directed toward procuring the toleration of that unpleasure by an appeal to the reality principle. But how is the compulsion to repeat—the manifestation of the power of the repressed—related to the pleasure principle?

It is clear that the greater part of what is re-experienced under the compulsion to repeat must cause the ego unpleasure, because it brings to light activities of repressed instinctual impulses. That, however, is unpleasure of a kind we have already considered and does not contradict the pleasure principle: unpleasure for one system and simultaneously satisfaction for the other.

But we come, now, to a new and remarkable fact, namely that the compulsion to repeat also recalls from the past experiences, which include no possibility of pleasure, and which can never, even long ago, have brought satisfaction even to instinctual impulses that have since been repressed.

The early efflorescence of infantile sexual life is doomed to come to an end because its wishes are incompatible with reality and with the inadequate stage of development that the child has reached. That efflorescence perishes in the most distressing circumstances and to the accompaniment of the most painful feelings. Loss of love and failure leave behind them a permanent injury to self-assurance in the form of a narcissistic scar, which in my opinion, as well as in Marcinowski's (1918), contributes more than anything to the sense of inferiority that is so common in neurotics.

Sexual researches, on which limits are imposed by a child's physical development, lead to no satisfactory conclusion; hence such later complaints as "I can't accomplish anything; I can't succeed in anything."

The tie of affection, which binds the child as a rule to the parent of the opposite sex, succumbs to disappointment, to a vain expectation of satisfaction, or to jealousy over the birth of a new baby—

unmistakable proof of the infidelity of the object of the child's affections. His own attempt to make a baby himself, carried out with tragic seriousness, fails shamefully. The lessening amount of affection he receives, the increasing demands of education, hard words, and an occasional punishment—these show him at last the full extent to which he has been scorned. These are a few typical and constantly recurring instances of the ways in which the love characteristic of the age of childhood is brought to an end.

Patients repeat all of these unwanted situations

and painful emotions in the transference, and revive them with the greatest ingenuity. They seek to bring about the interruption of the treatment while it is still incomplete; they contrive once more to feel themselves scorned, to oblige the physician to speak severely to them, and treat them coldly.

They discover appropriate objects for their jealousy; instead of the passionately desired baby of their childhood, they produce a plan or a promise of some grand present—which turns out, as a rule, to be no less unreal.

None of these things can have produced pleasure in the past; and it might be supposed that they would cause less unpleasure today if they emerged as memories or dreams rather than taking the form of fresh experiences. They are, of course, the activities of instincts intended to lead to satisfaction; but no lesson has been learned from the old experience of these activities, having led instead only to unpleasure. In spite of that, they are repeated, under pressure of a compulsion.

What psychoanalysis reveals in the transference phenomena of neurotics can also be observed in the lives of some normal people. The impression they give is of being pursued by a malignant fate or possessed by some extraneous power; but psychoanalysis has always taken the view that their fate is, for the most part, arranged by themselves and determined by early infantile influences. The compulsion, which is here in evidence, differs in no way from the compulsion to repeat—which we have found in neurotics, even though the people we are now considering have never shown any signs of dealing with a neurotic conflict by producing symptoms.

Thus we have come across people all of whose human relationships have the same outcome: such as the benefactor who is abandoned in anger after a time by each of his *protégés*, however much they may otherwise differ from one another, and who thus seems doomed to taste all the bitterness of ingratitude; or the man whose friendships all end in betrayal by his friend; or the man who, time after time, in the course of his life raises someone else into a position of great private or public authority and then, after a certain interval, himself upsets that authority and replaces him by a new one; or, again, the lover each of whose love affairs with a woman passes through the same phases and reaches the same conclusion.

This *ewige Wiederkehr des Gleichen* causes us no astonishment when it relates to active behavior on the part of the person concerned, and when we can discern in him an essential character-trait, which always remains the same, and which is compelled to find expression in a repetition of the same experiences.

We are much more impressed by cases where the subject appears to have a passive experience, over which he has no influence, but in which he meets with a repetition of the same fatality. There is the case, for instance, of the woman who married three successive husbands, each of whom fell ill soon afterwards and had to be nursed by her on their death-beds.

The most moving poetic picture of a fate such as this is given by Tasso in his romantic epic *Gerusalemme Liberata*. Its hero, Tancred, unwittingly kills his beloved Clorinda in a duel while she is disguised in the armor of an enemy knight. After her burial, he makes his way into a strange magic forest which strikes the Crusaders' army with terror. He slashes with his sword at a tall tree; but blood streams from the cut and the voice of *Clorinda*, whose soul is imprisoned in the tree, is heard complaining that he has wounded his beloved once again.

If we take into account observations such as these, based upon behavior in the transference, and upon the life-histories of men and women, we shall find courage to assume that there really does exist, in the mind, a compulsion to repeat that overrides the pleasure principle. Now, too, we shall be inclined to relate to this compulsion the dreams that occur in traumatic neuroses and the impulse that leads children to play.

It is to be noted, however, that only in rare instances can we observe the pure effects of the compulsion to repeat, unsupported by other motives. In the case of children's play, we have already laid stress on the other ways in which the emergence of the compulsion may be interpreted; the compulsion to repeat and instinctual satisfaction that is immediately pleasurable, seem to converge here into an intimate partnership.

The phenomena of transference are obviously exploited by the resistance, which the ego maintains in its pertinacious insistence upon repression; the compulsion to repeat, which the treatment tries to bring into its service, is enticed over to its side, as it were, by the ego, clinging as it does to the pleasure principle.

A great deal of what might be described as the compulsion of destiny seems intelligible on a rational basis; so that we are under no necessity to call in a new and mysterious motive to explain it. The least dubious instance (of the presence of such a motive) is perhaps that of traumatic dreams. However, on mature reflection, we shall be forced to admit that even in the other instances, the whole ground is not covered by the operation of the familiar motives. Enough is left unexplained to justify the hypothesis of a compulsion to repeat something that seems more primitive, more elementary, more instinctual than the pleasure principle, which it sets aside.

But if a compulsion to repeat does operate in the mind, we should be glad to know something about it, to learn what function it corresponds to, under what conditions it can emerge, and what its relation is to the pleasure principle—to which, after all, we have hitherto ascribed dominance over the course of the processes of excitation in mental life.

CHAPTER FOUR

WHAT FOLLOWS IS speculation, often far-fetched speculation, which the reader will consider or dismiss according to his individual predilection. It is further an attempt to follow out an idea consistently, out of curiosity to see where it will lead.

Psycho-analytic speculation takes, as its point of departure, the impression, derived from examining unconscious processes, that consciousness may be, not the most universal attribute of mental processes, but only a particular function of them. Speaking in meta-psychological terms, it asserts that consciousness is a function of a particular system which it describes as Cs.

What consciousness yields, consists essentially of perceptions of excitations coming from the external world, and of feelings of pleasure and unpleasure, which can only arise from within the mental apparatus. It is, therefore, possible to assign to the system Pcpt.-Cs. a position in space. It must lie on the borderline between outside and inside; it must be turned towards the external world and must envelop the other psychical systems.

It will be seen that there is nothing daringly new in these assumptions; we have merely adopted the views on localization held by cerebral anatomy, which locates the seat of consciousness in the cerebral cortex—the outermost, enveloping layer of the central organ.

Cerebral anatomy has no need to consider why, speaking anatomically, consciousness should be lodged on the surface of the brain, instead of being safely housed somewhere in its inmost interior. Perhaps *we* shall be more successful in accounting for this situation in the case of our system Pcpt.-Cs.

Consciousness is not the only distinctive character that we ascribe to the processes in that system. Based on impressions derived from our psychoanalytic experience, we assume that all excitatory processes that occur in the *other* systems leave permanent traces behind in them, which form the foundation of memory. Such memory traces, then, have nothing to do with the fact of becoming conscious; indeed they are often most powerful and most enduring when the process which left them behind was one that never entered consciousness.

We find it hard to believe, however, that permanent traces of excitation, such as these, are also left in the system Pcpt.-Cs. If they remained constantly conscious, they would very soon set limits to the system's aptitude for receiving fresh excitations.

If, on the other hand, they were unconscious, we should be faced with the problem of explaining the existence of unconscious processes in a system whose functioning was otherwise accompanied by the phenomenon of consciousness. We should, so to say, have altered nothing and gained nothing by our hypothesis relegating the process of becoming conscious to a special system. Though this consideration is not absolutely conclusive, it nevertheless leads us to suspect that becoming conscious and leaving behind a memory trace are processes incompatible with each other, within one and the same system.

Thus we should be able to say that the excitatory process becomes conscious in the system Cs. but leaves no permanent trace behind there; but that the excitation is transmitted to the systems lying next within, and that it is in *them* that its traces are left. I followed these same lines in the schematic picture, which I included in the speculative section of my *Interpretation of Dreams*.

It must be borne in mind that little enough is known from other sources of the origin of consciousness. When, therefore, we lay down the proposition that consciousness arises instead of a memory trace, the assertion deserves consideration, at all events on the ground of its being framed in fairly precise terms.

If this is so, the system Cs. is characterized by the peculiarity that in it (in contrast to what happens in the other psychical systems), excitatory processes do not leave behind any permanent change in its elements, but expire, as it were, in the phenomenon of becoming conscious.

An exception of this sort, to the general rule, requires to be explained by some factor that applies exclusively to that one system. Such a factor, which is absent in the other systems Cs. might well be the exposed situation of the system Cs., immediately abutting, as it does, on the external world.

Let us picture a living organism in its most simplified possible form as an undifferentiated vesicle of a substance that is susceptible to stimulation. Then, the surface turned toward the external world will, from its very situation, be differentiated and will serve as an organ for receiving stimuli. Indeed embryology, in its capacity as a recapitulation of developmental history, actually shows us that the central nervous system originates from the ectoderm. The grey matter of the cortex remains a derivative of the primitive superficial layer of the organism and may have inherited some of its essential properties.

It would be easy to suppose, then, that as a result of the ceaseless impact of external stimuli on the surface of the vesicle, its substance to a certain depth may have become permanently modified, so that excitatory processes run a different course in it from what they run in the deeper layers. A crust would thus be formed which would, at last, have been so thoroughly baked through, by stimulation, that it would present the most favorable possible conditions for the reception of stimuli, and become incapable of any further modification.

In terms of the system Cs., this would mean that its elements could undergo no further permanent modification from the passage of excitation, because they had already been modified in the respect in question to the greatest possible extent. Now, however, they would have become capable of giving rise to consciousness.

Various ideas may be formed that cannot, at present, be verified as to the nature of this modification of the substance and of the excitatory process. It may be supposed that, in passing from one element to another, an excitation has to overcome a resistance, and that the diminution of resistance thus effected is what lays down a permanent trace of the excitation, that is, a pathway.

In the system Cs., then, resistance, of this kind, to passage from one element to another, would no longer exist. This picture can be brought into relation with Breuer's distinction between quiescent (or bound) and mobile cathectic energy in the elements of the psychical systems. The elements of the system Cs. would carry no bound energy but only energy capable of free discharge. It seems best, however, to express oneself as cautiously as possible on these points. None the less, this speculation will have enabled us to bring the origin of consciousness into some sort of connection with the situation of the system Cs. and with the peculiarities that must be ascribed to the excitatory processes taking place in it.

But we have more to say of the living vesicle with its receptive cortical layer. This little fragment of living substance is suspended in the middle of an external world charged, with the most powerful energies. It would be killed by the stimulation emanating from these if it were not provided with a protective shield against stimuli.

It acquires the shield in this way: its outermost surface ceases to have the structure proper to living matter, becomes to some degree inorganic, and thenceforward functions as a special envelope or membrane resistant to stimuli. In consequence, the energies of the external world are able to pass into the next underlying layers, which have remained living, with only a fragment of their original intensity.

These layers can devote themselves, behind the protective shield, to the reception of the amounts of stimulus which have been allowed through it. By its death, the outer layer has saved all the deeper ones from a similar fate—unless, that is to say, stimuli reach it, which are so strong that they break through the protective shield.

Protection against stimuli is an almost more important function for the living organism than *reception* of stimuli. The protective shield is supplied with its own store of energy and must, above all, endeavor to preserve the special forms of conversion of energy operating in it, against the effects threatened by the enormous energies at work in the external world—effects which tend toward an equalization of potential and hence toward destruction.

The main purpose of the *reception* of stimuli is to discover the direction and nature of the external stimuli; and for that it is enough to take small specimens of the external world, to sample it in small quantities. In highly developed organisms, the receptive cortical layer of the former vesicle has long been withdrawn into the depths of the interior of the body, though portions of it have been left behind on the surface immediately beneath the general shield against stimuli.

These are the sense organs, which consist essentially of apparatus for the reception of certain specific effects of stimulation, but which also include special arrangements for further protection against excessive amounts of stimulation and for excluding unsuitable kinds of stimuli. It is characteristic of them that they deal only with very small quantities of external stimulation and only take in samples of the external world. They may, perhaps, be compared with feelers that are, all the time, making tentative advances towards the external world and then drawing back from it.

At this point, I shall venture to touch for a moment upon a subject which would merit the most exhaustive treatment. As a result of certain psycho-analytic discoveries, we are today in a position to embark on a discussion of the Kantian theorem that time and space are necessary forms of thought. We have learned that unconscious mental processes are in themselves timeless. This means, in the first place, that they are not ordered in time, that time does not change them in any way, and that the idea of time cannot be applied to them.

These are negative characteristics that can only be clearly understood if a comparison is made with *conscious* mental processes. On the other hand, our abstract idea of time seems to be wholly derived from the method of working of the system Pcpt.-Cs. and to correspond to a perception on its own part of that method of working. This mode of functioning may, perhaps, constitute another way of providing a shield against stimuli. I know that these remarks must sound very obscure, but I must limit myself to these hints.

We have pointed out how the living vesicle is provided with a shield against stimuli from the external world; and we had previously shown that the cortical layer next to that shield must be differentiated as an organ for receiving stimuli from without. This sensitive cortex, however, which is later to become the system Cs., also receives excitations from *within*. The situation of the system between the outside and the inside, and the difference between the conditions governing the reception of excitations in the two cases, have a decisive effect on the functioning of the system and of the whole mental apparatus.

Toward the outside, it is shielded against stimuli, and the amounts of excitation impinging on it have only a reduced effect. Toward the inside, there can be no such shield; the excitations in the deeper layers extend into the system directly and in undiminished amount, in so far as certain of their characteristics give rise to feelings in the pleasure-unpleasure series.

The excitations coming from within are, however, in their intensity and in other qualitative respects—in their amplitude, perhaps—more commensurate with the system's method of working than the stimuli that stream in from the external world.

This state of things produces two definite results. First, the feelings of pleasure and unpleasure (which are an index to what is happening in the interior of the apparatus) predominate over all external stimuli. And secondly, a particular way is adopted of dealing with any internal excitations that produce too great an increase of unpleasure: there is a tendency to treat them as though they were acting, not from the inside, but from the outside, so that it may be possible to bring the shield against stimuli into operation as a means of defense against them. This is the origin of *projection*, which is destined to play such a large part in the causation of pathological processes.

I have an impression that these last considerations have brought us to a better understanding of the dominance of the pleasure principle; but no light has yet been thrown on the cases that contradict that dominance. Let us therefore go a step further. We describe as traumatic, any excitations from outside powerful enough to break through the protective shield. It seems to me that the concept of trauma necessarily implies a connection of this kind with a breach in an otherwise efficacious barrier against stimuli.

Such an event as an external trauma is bound to provoke a disturbance on a large scale in the functioning of the organism's energy and to set in motion every possible defensive measure.

At the same time, the pleasure principle is for the moment put out of action. There is no longer any possibility of preventing the mental apparatus from being flooded with large amounts of stimulus, and another problem arises instead—the problem of mastering the amounts of stimulus that have broken in and of binding them, in the psychical sense, so that they can subsequently be discharged.

The specific unpleasure of physical pain is probably the result of the protective shield having been broken through in a limited area. There is, then, a continuous stream of excitations from the part of the periphery concerned to the central apparatus of the mind, such as could normally arise only from *within* the apparatus.

And how shall we expect the mind to react to this invasion? Cathectic energy is summoned from all sides to provide sufficiently high cathexes of energy in the environs of the breach. An anticathexis, on a grand scale, is set up for whose benefit all the other psychical systems are impoverished, so that the remaining psychical functions are extensively paralyzed or reduced.

We must endeavor to draw a lesson from examples such as this and use them as a basis for our metapsychological speculations. From the present case, then, we infer that a system, which is itself highly cathected, is capable of taking up an additional stream of fresh inflowing energy and of converting it into quiescent cathexis—that is of binding it psychically.

The higher the system's own quiescent cathexis, the greater seems to be its binding force. Conversely, therefore, the lower its cathexis, the less capacity it will have for taking up inflowing energy, and the more violent must be the consequences of such a breach in the protective shield against stimuli. To this view, it cannot be justly objected that the increase of cathexis, around the breach, can be explained far more simply as the direct result of the inflowing masses of excitation.

If that were so, the mental apparatus would merely receive an increase in its cathexes of energy, and the paralyzing character of pain and the impoverishment of all the other systems would remain unexplained. Nor do the very violent phenomena of discharge, to which pain gives rise, affect our explanation, for they occur in a reflex manner. That is, they follow without the intervention of the mental apparatus.

The indefiniteness of all our discussions on what we describe as meta-psychology is, of course, due to the fact that we know nothing of the nature of the excitatory process that takes place in the elements of the psychical systems, and that we do not feel justified in framing any hypothesis on the subject. We are, consequently, operating all the time with a large unknown quantity, which we are obliged to carry over into every new formula.

It may be reasonably supposed that this excitatory process can be carried out with energies that vary *quantitatively*; it may also seem probable that it has more than one *quality* (in the nature of amplitude, for instance). As a new factor, we have taken into consideration Breuer's hypothesis that charges of energy occur in two forms; so that we have to distinguish between two kinds of cathexis of the psychical systems or their elements—a freely flowing cathexis that presses on toward discharge, and a quiescent cathexis. We may suspect that the binding of the energy that streams into the mental apparatus consists, in its conversion, from a freely flowing into a quiescent state.

We may, I think, tentatively venture to regard the common traumatic neurosis as a consequence of an extensive breach being made in the protective shield against stimuli. This would seem to reinstate the old, naive theory of shock, in apparent contrast to the later and psychologically more pretentious theory, which attributes etiological importance not to the effects of mechanical violence, but to fright and the threat to life.

These opposing views are not, however, irreconcilable; nor is the psychoanalytic view of the traumatic neurosis identical with the shock theory in its crudest form. The latter regards the essence of the shock as being the direct damage to the molecular structure or even to the histological structure of the elements of the nervous system; whereas what *we* seek to understand are the effects produced on the organ of the mind by the breach in the shield against stimuli and by the problems that follow in its train.

But we too attribute importance to the element of fright. It is caused by the absence of any preparedness for anxiety, including a hypercathexis of the systems that would be the first to receive the stimulus. Owing to their low cathexis, those systems are not in a good position for binding the inflowing amounts of excitation, and the consequences of the breach in the protective shield follow all the more easily. It will be seen, then, that preparedness for anxiety and the hypercathexis of the receptive systems constitute the last line of defense of the shield against stimuli.

In the case of quite a number of traumas, the difference between systems that are unprepared and systems that are well prepared, through being hypercathected, may be a decisive factor in determining the outcome. Though where the strength of a trauma exceeds a certain limit, this factor will no doubt cease to carry weight.

The fulfillment of wishes is, as we know, brought about in a hallucinatory manner by dreams, and under the dominance of the pleasure principle, this has become their function. But it is not in the service of that principle that the dreams of patients suffering from traumatic neuroses lead them back with such regularity to the situation in which the trauma occurred. We may assume, rather, that dreams are, here, helping to carry out another task, which must be accomplished before the dominance of the pleasure principle can even begin.

These dreams are endeavoring to master the stimulus retrospectively, by developing the anxiety whose omission was the cause of the traumatic neurosis. They thus afford us a view of a function of the mental apparatus, which, though it does not contradict the pleasure principle, is nevertheless independent of it and seems to be more primitive than the purpose of gaining pleasure and avoiding unpleasure.

This would seem to be the place, then, at which to admit, for the first time, an exception to the proposition that dreams are fulfillments of wishes. Anxiety dreams, as I have shown repeatedly and in detail, offer no such exception. Nor do punishment dreams, for they merely replace the forbidden wish fulfillment with the appropriate punishment for it. That is to say, they fulfill the wish of the sense of guilt, which is the reaction to the repudiated impulse.

But it is impossible to classify as wish-fulfillments the dreams we have been discussing that occur in traumatic neuroses, or the dreams during psychoanalyses, which bring to memory the psychical traumas of childhood. They arise, rather, in obedience to the compulsion to repeat, though it is true that, in analysis, that compulsion is supported by the wish (which is encouraged by suggestion) to conjure up what has been forgotten and repressed.

Thus, it would seem that the function of dreams, which consists in setting aside any motives that might interrupt sleep, by fulfilling the wishes of the disturbing impulses, is not their *original* function. It would not be possible for them to perform that function until the whole of mental life had accepted the dominance of the pleasure principle.

If there is a *beyond the pleasure principle,* it is only consistent to grant that there was also a time before the purpose of dreams was the fulfillment of wishes. This would imply no denial of their later function. But, if once, this general rule has been broken, a further question arises. May not dreams which, with a view to the psychical binding of traumatic impressions, obey the compulsion to repeat— may not such dreams occur *outside* analysis as well? And the reply can only be a decided affirmative.

I have argued, elsewhere, that the war neuroses (in so far as that term implies something more than a reference to the circumstances of the illness's onset) may very well be traumatic neuroses thathave been facilitated by a conflict in the ego.

The fact to which I have referred, that a gross physical injury caused simultaneously by the trauma, diminishes the chances that a neurosis will develop, becomes intelligible if one bears in mind two facts, which have been stressed by psychoanalytic research. Firstly, that mechanical agitation must be recognized as one of the sources of sexual excitation, and secondly, that painful and feverish illnesses exercise a powerful effect, so long as they last, on the distribution of libido.

Thus, on the one hand, the mechanical violence of the trauma would liberate a quantity of sexual excitation which, owing to the lack of preparation for anxiety, would have a traumatic effect. On the other hand, the simultaneous physical injury, by calling for a narcissistic hypercathexis of the injured organ, would bind the excess of excitation.

It is also well known, though the libido theory has not yet made sufficient use of the fact, that such severe disorders in the distribution of libido as melancholia are temporarily brought to an end by intercurrent organic illness, and indeed that even a fully developed condition of dementia praecox is capable of a temporary remission in these same circumstances.

CHAPTER FIVE

THE FACT THAT the cortical layer, which receives stimuli, is without any protective shield against excitations from within must have, as its result, that these latter transmissions of stimulus have a preponderance in economic importance and often occasion economic disturbances comparable with traumatic neuroses. The most abundant sources of this internal excitation are what are described as the organism's instincts—the representatives of all the forces originating in the interior of the body and transmitted to the mental apparatus—at once the most important and the most obscure element of psychological research.

It will, perhaps, not be thought too rash to suppose that the impulses arising from the instincts do not belong to the type of *bound* nervous processes but to the type of *mobile* processes that press towards discharge. The best part of what we know of these processes is derived from our study of the dream activity. We there discovered that the processes in the unconscious systems were fundamentally different from those in the preconscious (or conscious) systems. In the unconscious, cathexes can easily be completely transferred, displaced, and condensed.

Such treatment, however, could only produce invalid results if it were applied to preconscious material. This accounts for the familiar peculiarities exhibited by manifest dreams after the preconscious residues of the preceding day have been worked over in accordance with the laws operating in the unconscious. I described the type of process found in the unconscious as the primary psychical process, in contra-distinction to the secondary process, which is the one obtaining in our normal waking life.

Because all instinctual impulses have the unconscious systems as their point of impact, it is hardly an innovation to say that they obey the primary process. Again, it is not difficult to identify the primary psychical process with Breuer's mobile cathexis and the secondary process with changes in his bound or tonic cathexis. If so, it would be the task of the higher strata of the mental apparatus to bind the instinctual excitation reaching the primary process.

A failure to effect this binding would provoke a disturbance analogous to a traumatic neurosis; and only after the binding has been accomplished would it be possible for the dominance of the pleasure principle (and of its modification, the reality principle) to proceed unhindered. Until then, the other task of the mental apparatus, the task of mastering or binding excitations, would have precedence—not, indeed, in *opposition* to the pleasure principle, but independently of it and to some extent in disregard of it.

The manifestations of a compulsion to repeat (which we have described as occurring in the early activities of infantile mental life, as well as among the events of psycho-analytic treatment) exhibit, to a high degree, an instinctual character. When they act in opposition to the pleasure principle, they give the appearance of some extraneous force at work.

In the case of children's play, we seemed to see that children repeat unpleasurable experiences for the additional reason that they can master a powerful impression, far more thoroughly, by being active than they could by merely experiencing it passively. Each fresh repetition seems to strengthen the mastery they are in search of.

Nor can children have their pleasurable experiences repeated often enough, and they are inexorable in their insistence that the repetition shall be an identical one. This character trait disappears later on. If a joke is heard for a second time, it produces almost no effect; a theatrical production never creates so great an impression the second time as the first. Indeed, it is hardly possible to persuade an adult who has very much enjoyed reading a book to re-read it immediately.

Novelty is always the condition of enjoyment. But children will never tire of asking an adult to repeat a game that he has shown them or played with them, until he is too exhausted to go on. And if a child has been told a nice story, he will insist on hearing it over and over again, rather than a new one. He will remorselessly stipulate that the repetition shall be an identical one, and will correct any alterations of which the narrator may be guilty—though they may actually have been made in the hope of gaining fresh approval.

None of this contradicts the pleasure principle. Repetition, the re-experiencing of something identical, is clearly in itself a source of pleasure. In the case of a person in analysis, on the contrary, the compulsion to repeat the events of his childhood in the transference evidently disregards the pleasure principle in every way. The patient behaves in a purely infantile fashion and, thus, shows us that the repressed memory-traces of his primeval experiences are not present in him in a bound state, and are indeed, in a sense, incapable of obeying the secondary process.

It is to this fact of not being bound, moreover, that they owe their capacity for forming, in conjunction with the residues of the previous day, a wishful fantasy that emerges in a dream. This same compulsion to repeat frequently meets us as an obstacle to our treatment, when, at the end of an analysis, we try to induce the patient to detach himself completely from his physician. It may be presumed, too, that when people unfamiliar with analysis feel an obscure fear—a dread of rousing something that, so they feel, is better left sleeping—what they are afraid of, at bottom, is the emergence of this compulsion with its hint of possession by some extraneous power.

But how is the predicate of being instinctual related to the compulsion to repeat? At this point, we cannot escape a suspicion that we may have come upon the track of a universal attribute of the instincts and perhaps of organic life, in general, which has not hitherto been clearly recognized or, at least, not explicitly stressed. It seems, then, that an instinct is a compulsion inherent in organic life to restore an earlier state of things, which the living entity has been obliged to abandon under the pressure of external disturbing forces. That is, it is a kind of organic elasticity, or, to put it another way, the expression of the inertia inherent in organic life.

This view of instincts strikes us as strange because we have become used to see, in them, a factor impelling toward change and development, whereas we are now asked to recognize, in them, the precise contrary—an expression of the *conservative* nature of living substance. On the other hand, we soon call to mind examples from animal life that seem to confirm the view that instincts are historically determined.

Certain fish, for instance, undertake laborious migrations at spawning-time, in order to deposit their spawn in particular waters far removed from their customary haunts. In the opinion of many biologists, what they are doing is merely to seek out the localities in which their species formerly resided but which, in the course of time, they have exchanged for others.

The same explanation is believed to apply to the migratory flights of birds of passage. We are quickly relieved of the necessity for seeking for further examples by the reflection that the most impressive proofs of there being an organic compulsion to repeat, lie in the phenomena of heredity and the facts of embryology.

We see how the germ of a living animal is obliged, in the course of its development, to recapitulate (even if only in a transient and abbreviated fashion) the structures of all the forms from which it is sprung, instead of proceeding quickly by the shortest path to its final shape. This behavior is only to a very slight degree attributable to mechanical causes. The historical explanation cannot accordingly be neglected. So, too, the power of regenerating a lost organ by growing afresh a precisely similar one, extends far up into the animal kingdom.

We shall be met by the plausible objection that it may very well be that, in addition to the conservative instincts that impel toward repetition, there may be others that push forward toward progress and the production of new forms. This argument must certainly not be overlooked, and it will be taken into account at a later stage. But for the moment, it is tempting to pursue the hypothesis that all instincts tend toward the restoration of an earlier state of things to its logical conclusion.

The outcome may give an impression of mysticism or of sham profundity; but we can feel quite innocent of having had any such purpose in view. We seek only for the sober results of research or of reflection based on it; and we have no wish to find, in those results, any quality other than certainty.

Let us suppose, then, that all the organic instincts are conservative, are acquired historically, and tend toward the restoration of an earlier state of things. It follows that the phenomena of organic development must be attributed to external disturbing and diverting influences. The elementary living entity would, from its very beginning, have had no wish to change; if conditions remained the same, it would do no more than constantly repeat the same course of life. (The reader should not overlook the fact that what follows is the development of an extreme line of thought. Later on, when account is taken of the sexual instincts, it will be found that the necessary limitations and corrections are applied to it.)

In the last resort, what has left its mark on the development of organisms, must be the history of the earth we live in and of its relation to the sun. Every modification, that is thus imposed upon the course of the organism's life, is accepted by the conservative organic instincts and stored up for further repetition. Those instincts are, therefore, bound to give a deceptive appearance of being forces tending toward change and progress, while, in fact, they are merely seeking to reach an ancient goal by paths alike old and new.

Moreover, it is possible to specify this final goal of all organic striving. It would be in contradiction to the conservative nature of the instincts if the goal of life were a state of things that had never yet been attained. On the contrary, it must be an *old* state of things, an initial state from which the living entity has, at one time or other, departed, and to which it is striving to return by the circuitous paths along which its development leads.

If we are to take it as a truth that knows no exception that everything living dies for *internal* reasons—becomes inorganic once again—then we shall be compelled to say that "the goal of all life is death" and, looking backward, that what was inanimate existed before what is living.

The attributes of life were, at some time, evoked in inanimate matter by the action of a force of whose nature we can form no conception. It may, perhaps, have been a process similar in type to that which later caused the development of consciousness in a particular stratum of living matter. The tension, which then arose in what had previously been an inanimate substance, endeavored to equalize its potential.

In this way, the first instinct came into being: the instinct to return to the inanimate state. It was still an easy matter, at that time, for a living substance to die. The course of its life was probably only a brief one, whose direction was determined by the chemical structure of the young life. For a long time, perhaps, living substance was thus being constantly created afresh and easily dying, until decisive external influences altered in such a way as to oblige the still surviving substance to diverge ever more widely from its original course of life and to make ever more complicated detours before reaching its goal in death.

These circuitous paths to death, faithfully kept to by the conservative instincts, would present us today with the picture of the phenomena of life. If we firmly maintain the exclusively conservative nature of instincts, we cannot arrive at any other notions as to the origin and goal of life.

The implications, concerning the great groups of instincts, which, as we believe, lie behind the phenomena of life in organisms, must appear no less bewildering. The hypothesis of self-preservative instincts, such as we attribute to all living beings, stands in marked opposition to the idea that instinctual life, as a whole, serves to bring about death.

Seen in this light, the theoretical importance of the instincts of self-preservation, of self-assertion, and of mastery greatly diminishes. They are component instincts whose function it is to assure that the organism shall follow its own path to death, and to ward off any possible ways of returning to inorganic existence, other than those that are immanent in the organism itself.

We have no longer to reckon with the organism's puzzling determination (so hard to fit into any context) to maintain its own existence in the face of every obstacle. What we are left with is the fact that the organism wishes to die only in its own fashion. Thus, these guardians of life, too, were originally the myrmidons of death. Hence arises the paradoxical situation that the living organism struggles most energetically against events (dangers, in fact) that might help it to attain its life's goal rapidly—by a kind of short-circuit. Such behavior is, however, precisely what characterizes instinctual as contrasted with intelligent efforts.

But let us pause for a moment and reflect. It cannot be so. The sexual instincts, to which the theory of the neuroses gives a quite special place, appear under a very different aspect.

The external pressure, which provokes a constantly increasing extent of development, has not imposed itself upon *every* organism. Many have succeeded in remaining, up to the present time, at their lowly level. Many, if not all, of such creatures, which are living today, must resemble the earliest stages of the higher animals and plants.

In the same way, the whole path of development to natural death is not trodden by *all* the elementary entities that compose the complicated body of one of the higher organisms. Some of them, the germ-cells, probably retain the original structure of living matter and, after a certain time, with their full complement of inherited and freshly acquired instinctual dispositions, separate themselves from the organism as a whole.

These two characteristics may be precisely what enable them to have an independent existence. Under favorable conditions, they begin to develop—that is, to repeat the performance to which they owe their existence. In the end, once again, one portion of their substance pursues its development to a finish, while another portion harks back, once again, as a fresh residual germ to the beginning of the process of development.

These germ-cells, therefore, work against the death of the living substance and succeed in winning, for it, what we can only regard as potential immortality, though that may mean no more than a lengthening of the road to death. We must regard, as in the highest degree significant, the fact that this function of the germ-cell is reinforced, or only made possible, if it coalesces with another cell similar to itself and yet differing from it.

The instincts that watch over the destinies of these elementary organisms that survive the whole individual, which provide them with a safe shelter while they are defenseless against the stimuli of the external world, which bring about their meeting with other germ-cells, and so on—these constitute the group of the sexual instincts. They are conservative in the same sense as the other instincts in that they bring back earlier states of living substance; but they are conservative to a higher degree, in that they are peculiarly resistant to external influences.

They are conservative, too, in another sense, in that they preserve life itself for a comparatively long period. Yet it is to them, alone, that we can attribute an internal impulse toward progress and toward higher development! They are the true life instincts. They operate against the purpose of the other instincts, which leads, by reason, of their function to death; and this fact indicates that there is an opposition between them and the other instincts, an opposition whose importance was long ago recognized by the theory of the neuroses.

It is as though the life of the organism moved with a vacillating rhythm. One group of instincts rushes forward, to reach the final goal of life as swiftly as possible; but when a particular stage in the advance has been reached, the other group jerks back to a certain point to make a fresh start and so prolong the journey. Even though it is certain that sexuality and the distinction between the sexes did not exist when life began, the possibility remains that the instincts, which were later to be described as sexual, may have been in operation from the very start. It may not be true that it was only at a later time that they started upon their work of opposing the activities of the ego instincts.

Let us now hark back, for a moment, ourselves, and consider whether there is any basis at all for these speculations. Is it really the case that, apart from the sexual instincts, there are no instincts that do not seek to restore an earlier state of things? That there are none that aim at a state of things which has never yet been attained?

I know of no certain example, from the organic world, that would contradict the characterization I have thus proposed. There is, unquestionably, no universal instinct toward higher development observable in the animal or plant world, even though it is undeniable that development does, in fact, occur in that direction. But, on the one hand, it is often merely a matter of opinion when we declare that, one stage of development, is higher than another; and on the other hand, biology teaches us that higher development, in one respect, is very frequently balanced or outweighed by involution in another.

Moreover, there are plenty of animal forms, from whose early stages we can infer, that their development has, on the contrary, assumed a retrograde character. Both higher development and involution might well be the consequences of adaptation to the pressure of external forces; and in both cases the part played by instincts might be limited to the retention (in the form of an internal source of pleasure) of an obligatory modification.

It may be difficult, too, for many of us, to abandon the belief that there is an instinct toward perfection at work in human beings, which has brought them to their present high level of intellectual achievement and ethical sublimation, and which may be expected to watch over their development into supermen.

I have no faith, however, in the existence of any such internal instinct, and I cannot see how this benevolent illusion is to be preserved. The present development of human beings requires, as it seems to me, no different explanation from that of animals. What appears in a minority of human individuals as an untiring impulsion toward further perfection, can easily be understood as a result of the instinctual repression upon, which is based, all that is most precious in human civilization.

The repressed instinct never ceases to strive for complete satisfaction, which would consist in the repetition of a primary experience of satisfaction. No substitutive or reactive formations and no sublimations will suffice to remove the repressed instinct's persisting tension. It is the difference in amount between the gratificatory pleasure, which is demanded, and that which is actually achieved, that provides the driving factor that will permit of no halting, at any established position.

The backward path that leads to complete satisfaction is, as a rule, obstructed by the resistances that maintain the repressions. So there is no alternative but to advance in the direction in which growth is still free—though with no prospect of bringing the process to a conclusion or of being able to reach the goal.

The processes involved in the formation of a neurotic phobia, which is nothing else than an attempt at flight from the satisfaction of an instinct, present us with a model of the manner of origin of this supposititious instinct towards perfection—an instinct which cannot possibly be attributed to *every* human being. The *dynamic* conditions for its development are, indeed, universally present; but it is only in rare cases that the *economic* situation appears to favor the production of the phenomenon.

I will add only a word to suggest that the efforts of Eros, to combine organic substances into ever larger unities, probably provide a substitute for this instinct towards perfection, whose existence we cannot admit. The phenomena that are attributed to it seem capable of explanation by these efforts of Eros, taken in conjunction with the results of repression.

CHAPTER SIX

THE UPSHOT OF our enquiry, so far, has been the drawing of a sharp distinction between the ego instincts and the sexual instincts, and the view that the former exercise a thrust toward death, and the latter towards a prolongation of life. But this conclusion is bound to be unsatisfactory in many respects, even to ourselves. Moreover, it is actually only of the former group of instincts, that we can predicate a conservative, or rather retrograde, character corresponding to a compulsion to repeat.

For on our hypothesis the ego instincts arise from the coming to life of inanimate matter, and they seek to restore the inanimate state. Whereas as regards the sexual instincts, though it is true that they reproduce primitive states of the organism, what they are clearly aiming at, by every possible means, is the coalescence of two germ-cells that are differentiated in a particular way.

If this union is not effected, the germ-cell dies along with all the other elements of the multi-cellular organism. It is only on this condition that the sexual function can prolong the cell's life and lend it the appearance of immortality. But what is the important event in the development of living substance that is being repeated in sexual reproduction, or in its fore-runner, the conjugation of two protista?

We cannot say, and we should, consequently, feel relieved if the whole structure of our argument turned out to be mistaken. The opposition between the ego or death instincts and the sexual, or life instincts, would then cease to hold, and the compulsion to repeat would no longer possess the importance we have ascribed to it.

Let us turn back, then, to one of the assumptions that we have already made, with the expectation that we shall be able to give it a categorical denial. We have drawn far-reaching conclusions from the hypothesis that all living substance is bound to die from internal causes.

We made this assumption thus carelessly, because it does not seem to us to *be* an assumption. We are accustomed to think that such is the fact, and we are strengthened in our thought by the writings of our poets. Perhaps we have adopted the belief because there is some comfort in it. If we are to die ourselves, and first to lose in death those who are dearest to us, it is easier to submit to a remorseless law of nature, to the sublime than to a chance that might have been escaped.

It may be, however, that this belief in the internal necessity of dying is only another of those illusions we have created, *to bear the burden of existence*. It is certainly not a primeval belief. The notion of natural death is quite foreign to primitive races; they attribute every death that occurs, among them, to the influence of an enemy or of an evil spirit.

We must, therefore, turn to biology in order to test the validity of the belief. If we do so, we may be astonished to find how little agreement there is among biologists on the subject of natural death and, in fact, that the whole concept of death melts away under their hands. The fact that there is a fixed average duration of life, at least among the higher animals, naturally argues in favor of there being such a thing as death from natural causes.

But this impression is countered when we consider that certain large animals and certain gigantic arboreal growths reach a very advanced age, and one that cannot, at present, be computed. According to the grandiose conception of Wilhelm Fliess (1906), all the vital phenomena exhibited by organisms—including, no doubt, their death—are linked with the completion of fixed periods, which express the dependence of two kinds of living substance (one male and the other female) upon the solar year.

When we see, however, how easily and how extensively the influence of external forces is able to modify the date of the appearance of vital phenomena (especially in the plant world), to precipitate them or hold them back—doubts must be cast upon the rigidity of Fliess's formulas, or at least, upon whether the laws laid down by him are the sole determining factors.

The greatest interest attaches from our point of view to the treatment given to the subject of the duration of life and the death of organisms in the writings of Weismann (1882, 1884, 1892, etc.) It was he who introduced the division of living substance into mortal and immortal parts.

The mortal part is the body in the narrower sense—the soma, which alone is subject to natural death. The germ cells, on the other hand, are potentially immortal, in so far as they are able, under certain favorable conditions, to develop into a new individual, or, in other words, to surround themselves with a new soma (Weismann, 1884).

What strikes us, in this, is the unexpected analogy with our own view, which was arrived at along such a different path. Weismann, regarding living substance morphologically, sees in it one portion that is destined to die—the soma, the body apart from the substance concerned with sex and inheritance and an immortal portion—the germ-plasm, which is concerned with the survival of the species, with reproduction.

We, on the other hand, dealing not with the living substance, but with the forces operating in it, have been led to distinguish two kinds of instincts: those which seek to lead what is living to death, and others, the sexual instincts, which are perpetually attempting and achieving a renewal of life. This sounds like a dynamic corollary to Weismann's morphological theory.

But the appearance of a significant correspondence is dissipated as soon as we discover Weismann's views on the problem of death. For he only relates the distinction between the mortal soma and the immortal germ-plasm to *multicellular* organisms. In unicellular organisms the individual and the reproductive cell are still one and the same (Weismann, 1882).

Thus, he considers that unicellular organisms are potentially immortal, and that death only makes its appearance with the multicellular metazoa. It is true that this death of the higher organisms is a natural one, a death from internal causes; but it is not founded upon any primal characteristic of living substance (Weismann, 1884), and cannot be regarded as an absolute necessity with its basis in the very nature of life (Weismann, 1882).

Death is, rather, a matter of expediency, a manifestation of adaptation to the external conditions of life. For, when once the cells of the body have been divided into soma and germ-plasm, an unlimited duration of individual life would become a quite pointless luxury. When this differentiation had been made in the multicellular organisms, death became possible and expedient.

Because, then, the soma of the higher organisms has died at fixed periods for internal reasons, while the protista have remained immortal. It is not the case, on the other hand, that reproduction was only introduced at the same time as death. On the contrary, it is a primal characteristic of living matter, like growth (from which it originated), and life has been continuous from its first beginning upon earth (Weismann, 1884).

It will be seen, at once, that to concede in this way that higher organisms have a natural death, is of very little help to us. If death is a late acquisition of organisms, then there can be no question of there having been death instincts from the very beginning of life on this earth.

Multi-cellular organisms may die for internal reasons, owing to defective differentiation or to imperfections in their metabolism, but the matter is of no interest from the point of view of our problem. An account of the origin of death, such as this, is, moreover, far less at variance with our habitual modes of thought than the strange assumption of death instincts.

The discussion, which followed upon Weismann's suggestions, led, so far as I can see, to no conclusive results in any direction. Some writers returned to the views of Goette (1883), who regarded death as a direct result of reproduction. Hartmann (1906) does not regard the appearance of a dead body a dead portion of the living substance—as the criterion of death, but defines death as "the termination of individual development."

In this sense, protozoa too are mortal. In their case, death always coincides with reproduction, but is to some extent obscured by it, since the whole substance of the parent animal may be transmitted directly into the young offspring.

Soon afterward, research was directed to the experimental testing upon unicellular organisms of the alleged immortality of living substance. An American biologist, Woodruff, experimenting with a ciliate infusorian, the "slipper-animalcule," which reproduces by fission into two individuals, persisted until the 3029th generation (at which point he broke off the experiment), isolating one of the part products on each occasion and placing it in fresh water.

This remote descendent of the first slipper-animalcule was just as lively as its ancestor was, and showed no signs of ageing or degeneration. Thus, in so far as figures of this kind prove anything, the immortality of the protista seemed to be experimentally demonstrable.

Other experimenters arrived at different results. Maupas, Calkins, and others, in contrast to Woodruff, found that after a certain number of divisions, these infusoria become weaker, diminish in size, suffer the loss of some part of their organization, and eventually die—unless certain recuperative measures are applied to them.

If this is so, protozoa would appear to die after a phase of senescence exactly like the higher animals—thus completely contradicting the assertion that death is a late acquisition of living organisms.

From the aggregate of these experiments, two facts emerge that seem to offer us a firm footing. First: If two of the animalculae, at the moment before they show signs of senescence, are able to coalesce with each other, that is to conjugate, (soon after which they once more separate), they are saved from growing old and become rejuvenated.

Conjugation is no doubt the fore-runner of the sexual reproduction of higher creatures; it is as yet unconnected with propagation and is limited to the mixing of the substances of the two individuals. The recuperative effects of conjugation can, however, be replaced by certain stimulating agents, by alterations in the composition of the fluid that provides their nourishment, by raising their temperature or by shaking them.

We are reminded of the celebrated experiment made by J. Loeb, in which, by means of certain chemical stimuli, he induced segmentation in sea-urchins' eggs—a process which can normally occur only after fertilization.

Second: It is probable, nevertheless, that infusoria die a natural death as a result of their own vital processes. For the contradiction between Woodruff's findings, and the others, is due to his having provided each generation with fresh nutrient fluid.

If he omitted to do so, he observed the same signs of senescence as the other experimenters. He concluded that the animalculae were injured by the products of metabolism, which they extruded into the surrounding fluid. He was then able to prove, conclusively, that it was only the products of its *own* metabolism that had fatal results for a particular generation.

For the same animalculae, which inevitably perished if they were crowded together in their own nutrient fluid, flourished in a solution that was over-saturated with the waste products of a distantly related species. An infusorian, therefore, if it is left to itself, dies a natural death owing to its incomplete voidance of the products of its own metabolism. It may be, however, that the same incapacity is the ultimate cause of the death of all higher animals as well.

At this point, the question may well arise in our minds whether any object, what-so-ever, is served by trying to solve the problem of natural death from a study of the protozoa. The primitive organization of these creatures may conceal, from our eyes, important conditions which, though in fact present in them too, only become *visible* in higher animals where they are able to find morphological expression. If we abandon the morphological point of view and adopt the dynamic one, it becomes a matter of complete indifference to us whether natural death can be shown to occur in protozoa or not.

The substance, which is later recognized as being immortal, has not yet become separated in them from the mortal one. The instinctual forces, which seek to conduct life into death, may also be operating in protozoa from the first, and yet their effects may be so completely concealed by the life-preserving forces, that it may be very hard to find any direct evidence of their presence.

We have seen, moreover, that the observations made by biologists allow us to assume that internal processes, of this kind, leading to death, do occur also in protista. But, even if protista turned out to be immortal in Weismann's sense, his assertion that death is a late acquisition would apply only to its *manifest* phenomena and would not make impossible the assumption of processes *tending* toward it.

Thus, our expectation that biology would flatly contradict the recognition of death instincts has not been fulfilled. We are at liberty to continue concerning ourselves with their possibility, if we have other reasons for doing so. The striking similarity between Weismann's distinction of soma and germ-plasm, and our separation of the death instincts from the life instincts, persists and retains its significance.

Let us pause, for a moment, over this pre-eminently dualistic view of instinctual life. According to E. Hering's theory, two kinds of processes are constantly at work in living substance, operating in contrary directions, one constructive or assimilatory, and the other destructive or dissimilatory.

May we venture to recognize, in these two directions taken by the vital processes, the activity of our two instinctual impulses, the life instincts and the death instincts? There is something else, at any rate, that we cannot remain blind to. We have unwittingly steered our course into the harbor of Schopenhauer's philosophy. For him, death is the "true result and to that extent the purpose of life," while the sexual instinct is the embodiment of the will to live.

Let us make a bold attempt at another step forward. It is generally considered that the union of a number of cells into a vital association—the multi-cellular character of organisms—has become a means of prolonging their life. One cell helps to preserve the life of another, and the community of cells can survive, even if individual cells have to die.

We have already heard that conjugation, too, the temporary coalescence of two unicellular organisms, has a life-preserving and rejuvenating effect on both of them. Accordingly, we might attempt to apply the libido theory, which has been arrived at in psychoanalysis, to the mutual relationship of cells.

We might suppose that the life instincts, or sexual instincts that are active in each cell, take the other cells as their object, that they partly neutralize the death instincts (the processes set up by them) in those other cells and, thus, preserve their life; while the other cells do the same for *them*, and still others sacrifice themselves in the performance of this libidinal function.

The germ-cells, themselves, would behave in a completely narcissistic fashion—to use the phrase that we are accustomed to use in the theory of the neuroses to describe a whole individual who retains his libido in his ego and pays none of it out in object-cathexes.

The germ-cells require their libido, the activity of their life instincts, for themselves, as a reserve against their later momentous constructive activity. The cells of the malignant neoplasms, which destroy the organism, should also be described as narcissistic in this same sense: pathology is prepared to regard their germs as innate and to ascribe embryonic attributes to them. In this way, the libido of our sexual instincts would coincide with the Eros of the poets and philosophers that binds all living things together.

Here, then, is an opportunity for looking back over the slow development of our libido theory. In the first instance, the analysis of the transference neuroses, forced upon our notice, the opposition between the sexual instincts, which are directed toward an object, and certain other instincts, with which we were very insufficiently acquainted, and which we described, provisionally, as the ego instincts.

A foremost place among these was necessarily given to the instincts serving the self-preservation of the individual. It was impossible to say what other distinctions were to be drawn among them. No knowledge would have been more valuable, as a foundation for true psychological knowledge, than an approximate grasp of the common characteristics and possible distinctive features of the instincts. But in no region of psychology were we groping more in the dark.

Everyone assumed the existence of as many instincts or, basic instincts, as he chose, and juggled with them like the ancient Greek natural philosophers with their four elements—earth, air, fire, and water. Psychoanalysis, which could not escape making *some* assumption about the instincts, kept, at first, to the popular division of instincts typified in the phrase "hunger and love." At least, there was nothing arbitrary in this; and by its help, the analysis of the psycho-neuroses was carried forward quite a distance.

The concept of sexuality, and, at the same time, of the sexual instinct, had, it is true, to be extended to cover many things that could not be classed under the reproductive function; and this caused no little hubbub in an austere, respectable, or merely hypocritical world.

The next step was taken when psychoanalysis felt its way closer toward the ego of psychology, which it had first come to know only as a repressive, censoring agency, capable of erecting protective structures and reactive formations.

Critical and far-seeing minds had, it is true, long since objected to the concept of libido being restricted to the energy of the sexual instincts directed towards an object. But they failed to explain how they had arrived at their better knowledge, or, to derive from it, anything of which analysis could make use.

Advancing more cautiously, psychoanalysis observed the regularity with which libido is withdrawn from the object and directed on to the ego (the process of introversion); and, by studying the libidinal development of children in its earliest phases, came to the conclusion that the ego is the true and original reservoir of libido, and that it is only from that reservoir that libido is extended on to objects.

The ego found its way among the child's sexual objects and was, at once given, the foremost place among them. Libido, which was in this way lodged in the ego, was described as narcissistic.

This narcissistic libido was, of course, also a manifestation of the force of the sexual instinct in the analytical sense of those words, and it had, necessarily, to be identified with the self-preservative instincts, whose existence had been recognized from the first.

Thus, the original opposition between the ego instincts and the sexual instincts proved to be inadequate. A portion of the ego instincts was seen to be libidinal; sexual instincts—probably alongside others—operated in the ego. Nevertheless, we are justified in saying that the old formula, which lays it down that psycho-neuroses are based on a conflict between ego instincts and sexual instincts, contains nothing that we need reject today. It is merely that the distinction between the two kinds of instinct, which was originally regarded as in some sort of way *qualitative*, must now be characterized differently, namely as being *topographical*. And in particular, it is still true that the transference neuroses, the essential subject of psycho-analytic study, are the result of a conflict between the ego and the libidinal cathexis of objects.

But it is all the more necessary for us to lay stress upon the libidinal character of the self-preservative instincts, now that we are venturing upon the further step of recognizing the sexual instinct as Eros, the preserver of all things, and of deriving the narcissistic libido of the ego, from the stores of libido—by means, of which, the cells of the soma are attached to one another.

But we now find ourselves suddenly faced by another question. If the self-preservative instincts, too, are of a libidinal nature, are there perhaps no other instincts whatever but the libidinal ones? At all events, there are none other visible. But, in that case, we shall, after all, be driven to agree with the critics who suspected, from the first, that psychoanalysis explains *everything* by sexuality, or with innovators like Jung, who, making a hasty judgment, have used the word libido to mean instinctual force in general. Must not this be so?

It was not our *intention,* at all events, to produce such a result. Our argument had, as its point of departure, a sharp distinction between ego instincts (which we equated with death instincts), and sexual instincts (which we equated with life instincts). We were prepared, at one stage, to include the, so-called, self-preservative instincts of the ego among the death instincts; but we subsequently corrected ourselves on this point and withdrew it.

Our views have, from the very first, been *dualistic,* and today they are even more definitely dualistic than before—now that we describe the opposition as being, not between ego instincts and sexual instincts, but between life instincts and death instincts.

Jung's libido theory is, on the contrary, *monistic*; the fact that he has called his one instinctual force "libido," is bound to cause confusion, but need not affect us otherwise. We suspect that instincts, other than those of self-preservation, operate in the ego, and it ought to be possible for us to point to them. Unfortunately, however, the analysis of the ego has made so little headway that it is very difficult for us to do so. It is possible, indeed, that the libidinal instincts in the ego may be linked in a peculiar manner with the other ego instincts that are still strange to us.

Even before we had any clear understanding of narcissism, psycho-analysts had a suspicion that the ego instincts had libidinal components attached to them. But these are very uncertain possibilities, to which our opponents will pay very little attention. The difficulty remains that psychoanalysis has not enabled us, until now, to point to any instincts other than the libidinal ones. That, however, is no reason for our falling in with the conclusion that no others, in fact, exist.

In the obscurity that reigns, at present, in the theory of the instincts, it would be unwise to reject any idea that promises to throw light on it. We started out, from the great opposition, between the life and death instincts. Now, object-love itself presents us with a second example of a similar polarity—that between love (or affection) and hate (or aggressiveness).

If only we could succeed in relating these two polarities to each other and in deriving one from the other! From the very first, we recognized the presence of a sadistic component in the sexual instinct. As we know, it can make itself independent and can, in the form of a perversion, dominate an individual's entire sexual activity.

It also emerges as a predominant component instinct in one of the pre-genital organizations, as I have named them. But how can the sadistic instinct, whose aim it is to injure the object, be derived from Eros, the preserver of life? Is it not plausible to suppose that this sadism is, in fact, a death instinct which, under the influence of the narcissistic libido, has been forced out of the ego and has consequently emerged in relation to the object? It now enters the service of the sexual function.

During the oral stage of organization of the libido, the act of obtaining erotic possession of an object coincides with that object's destruction; later, the sadistic instinct separates off, and finally, at the stage of genital primacy, it takes on, for the purposes of reproduction, the function of overpowering the sexual object to the extent necessary for carrying out the sexual act.

It might, indeed, be said that the sadism, which has been forced out of the ego, has pointed the way for the libidinal components of the sexual instinct, and that these follow after it to the object. Wherever the original sadism has undergone no mitigation or intermixture, we find the familiar ambivalence of love and hate in erotic life.

If such an assumption as this is permissible, then we have met the demand that we should produce an example of a death instinct—though it is true that our example is a displaced one. But, this way of looking at things is very far from being easy to grasp and creates a positively mystical impression. It looks, suspiciously, as though we were trying to find a way out of a highly embarrassing situation at any price.

We may recall, however, that there is nothing new in an assumption of this kind. We put one forward on an earlier occasion, before there was any question of an embarrassing situation. Clinical observations led us, at that time, to the view that masochism, the component instinct that is complementary to sadism, must be regarded as sadism that has been turned around upon the subject's own ego.

But, there is no difference in principle between an instinct turning from an object to the ego and its turning from the ego to an object—which is the novelty now under discussion. Masochism, the turning around of the instinct upon the object's own ego, would appear, in fact, to be a return to an earlier phase of the instinct's history, a regression. The account that was then given of masochism would need to be emended for being too sweeping: there *might* be such a thing as primary masochism—a possibility that I contested at that time.

Let us, however, return to the self-preservative sexual instincts. The experiments upon protista have already shown us that conjugation—that is, the coalescence of two individuals that separate soon afterward, without any subsequent cell-division occurring—has a strengthening and rejuvenating effect upon both of them.

In later generations, they show no signs of degenerating and seem able to put up a longer resistance to the injurious effects of their own metabolism. This single observation may, I think, be taken as typical of the effect produced by sexual union as well. But how is it that the coalescence of two only slightly different cells can bring about this renewal of life?

The experiment, which replaces the conjugation of protozoa by the application of chemical or even of mechanical stimuli (Lipschütz, 1914), enables us to give what is, no doubt, a conclusive reply to this question. The result is brought about by the influx of fresh amounts of stimulus. This tallies well with the hypothesis that the vital process of the individual leads, for internal reasons, to an equalization of chemical tensions—that is to say, to death, whereas union with the living substance of a different individual increases those tensions, introducing what may be described as fresh, vital differences of potential, which must then be lived down.

As regards these differences, there must of course be one or more optima. The dominating tendency of mental life, and perhaps of nervous life in general, is the effort to reduce, to keep constant or to remove internal tension due to stimuli—the Nirvana principle, to borrow a term from Barbara Low—a tendency, which finds expression in the pleasure principle; and our recognition of that fact is one of our strongest reasons for believing in the existence of death instincts.

But, we still feel our line of thought appreciably hampered by the fact that we cannot ascribe to the sexual instinct, the characteristic of a compulsion to repeat, which first put us on the track of the death instincts. The sphere of embryonic developmental processes is, no doubt, extremely rich in such phenomena of repetition. The two germ-cells that are involved in sexual reproduction, and their life history, are, themselves, only repetitions of the beginnings of organic life. But the essence of the processes, to which sexual life is directed, is the coalescence of two cell bodies. That, alone, is what guarantees the immortality of the living substance in the higher organisms.

In other words, we need more information on the origin of sexual reproduction and of the sexual instincts, in general. This is a problem, which is calculated to daunt an outsider, and which the specialists, themselves, have not yet been able to solve. We shall, therefore, give only the briefest summary of whatever seems relevant to our line of thought, from among the many discordant assertions and opinions.

One of these views deprives the problem of reproduction of its mysterious fascination by representing it as a part manifestation of growth. The origin of reproduction by sexually differentiated germ-cells might be pictured along sober Darwinian lines, by supposing that the advantage of amphimixis, arrived at, on some occasion, by the chance conjugation of two protista, was retained and further exploited in later development.

On this view, sex would not be anything very ancient; and the extraordinarily violent instincts, whose aim it is to bring about sexual union, would be repeating something that had once occurred by chance and had, since, become established as being advantageous.

The question arises here, as in the case of death, whether we are only justified in ascribing to the protista those characteristics they actually exhibit, and whether it is right to assume that forces and processes that only become visible in the higher organisms, first originated in those organisms.

The view of sexuality we have just mentioned is of little help for our purposes. The objection may be raised against it that it postulates the existence of life instincts already operating in the simplest organisms; for otherwise conjugation, which works counter to the course of life and makes the task of ceasing to live more difficult, would not be retained and elaborated, but would be avoided.

If, therefore, we are not to abandon the hypothesis of death instincts, we must suppose them to be associated from the very first with life instincts. But, it must be admitted that, in that case, we shall be working upon an equation with two unknown quantities.

Apart from this, science has so little to tell us about the origin of sexuality that we can liken the problem to a darkness, into which, not so much as a ray of an hypothesis has penetrated. In quite a different region, it is true, we *do* meet with such an hypothesis; but it is of so fantastic a kind—a myth rather than a scientific explanation—that I should not venture to produce it here, were it not that it fulfills precisely the one condition whose fulfillment we desire. For it traces the origin of an instinct to a need to restore an earlier state of things.

What I have in mind is, of course, the theory that Plato put into the mouth of Aristophanes in the *Symposium*, and which deals not only with the origin of the sexual instinct, but also with the most important of its variations in relation to its object:

"The original human nature was not like the present, but different. In the first place, the sexes were originally three in number, not two as they are now; there was man, woman, and the union of the two..."

Everything about these primeval men was double: they had four hands and four feet, two faces, two privy parts, and so on. Eventually, Zeus decided to cut these men in two, "like a sorb-apple which is halved for pickling."

After the division had been made, "the two parts of man, each desiring his other half, came together, and threw their arms about one another eager to grow into one."

Shall we follow the hint given us by the poet philosopher, and venture upon the hypothesis that living substance, at the time of its coming to life, was torn apart into small particles, which have ever since endeavored to reunite through the sexual instincts? that these instincts, in which the chemical affinity of inanimate matter persisted, gradually succeeded, as they developed through the kingdom of the protista, in overcoming the difficulties put in the way of that endeavor, by an environment charged with dangerous stimuli—stimuli which compelled them to form a protective cortical layer? that these splintered fragments of living substance, in this way, attained a multi-cellular condition and finally transferred the instinct for reuniting, in the most highly concentrated form, to the germ-cells?

But here, I think, the moment has come for breaking off. Not, however, without the addition of a few words of critical reflection. It may be asked whether, and how far, I am, myself, convinced of the truth of the hypotheses that have been set out in these pages. My answer would be that I am not convinced, myself, and that I do not seek to persuade other people to believe in them.

Or, more precisely, that I do not know how far I believe in them. There is no reason, as it seems to me, why the emotional factor of conviction should enter into this question at all. It is surely possible to throw oneself into a line of thought and to follow it wherever it leads, out of simple scientific curiosity, or, if the reader prefers, as an *advocatus diaboli*, who is not on that account himself sold to the devil.

I do not dispute the fact that the third step in the theory of the instincts, which I have taken here, cannot lay claim to the same degree of certainty as the two earlier ones—the extension of the concept of sexuality and the hypothesis of narcissism. These two innovations were a direct translation of observation into theory and were no more open to sources of error than is inevitable in all such cases.

It is true that my assertion of the regressive character of instincts also rests upon observed material—namely on the facts of the compulsion to repeat. It may be, however, that I have overestimated their significance, and, in any case, it is impossible to pursue an idea of this kind except by repeatedly combining factual material with what is purely speculative, and, thus, diverging widely from observation.

The more frequently this is done in the course of constructing a theory, the more untrustworthy, as we know, must be the final result. But, the degree of uncertainty is not assignable. One may have made a lucky hit or one may have gone shamefully astray. I do not attach much importance to the part played by what is called intuition in work of this kind.

What I have seen of it, seems to me, rather, to be the result of a kind of intellectual impartiality. Unfortunately, however, people are seldom impartial where ultimate things, the great problems of science and life, are concerned. Each of us is governed, in such cases, by deep-rooted internal prejudices, into whose hands our speculation unwittingly plays. Because we have such good grounds for being distrustful, our attitude toward the results of our own deliberations cannot well be other than one of cool benevolence.

I hasten to add, however, that self-criticism such as this is far from binding one to any special tolerance toward dissentient opinions. It is perfectly legitimate to reject, remorselessly, theories that are contradicted by the very first steps in the analysis of observed facts, while yet being aware, at the same time, that the validity of one's own theory is only a provisional one.

We need not feel greatly disturbed in judging our speculation upon the life and death instincts by the fact that so many bewildering and obscure processes occur in it—such as one instinct being driven out by another or an instinct turning from the ego to an object, and so on. This is merely due to our being obliged to operate with scientific terms, that is to say with the figurative language peculiar to psychology (or, more precisely, to depth psychology).

We could not otherwise describe the processes in question at all, and indeed, we could not have become aware of them. The deficiencies in our description would probably vanish if we were already in a position to replace the psychological terms by physiological or chemical ones. It is true that they, too, are only part of a figurative language; but it is one with which we have long been familiar, and which is, perhaps, a simpler one as well.

On the other hand, it should be made quite clear that the uncertainty of our speculation has been greatly increased by the necessity for borrowing from the science of biology. Biology is truly a land of unlimited possibilities. We may expect it to give us the most surprising information, and we cannot guess what answers it will return in a few dozen years to the questions we have put to it.

They may be of a kind that will blow away the whole of our artificial structure of hypotheses. If so, it may be asked, why I have embarked upon such a line of thought as the present one, and in particular, why I have decided to make it public. Well—I cannot deny that some of the analogies, correlations, and connections that it contains seemed to me to deserve consideration.

I will add a few words to clarify our terminology, which has undergone some development in the course of the present work. We came to know what the sexual instincts were, from their relation to the sexes and to the reproductive function. We retained this name after we had been obliged by the findings of psychoanalysis, to connect them less closely with reproduction. With the hypothesis of narcissistic libido, and the extension of the concept of libido to the individual cells, the sexual instinct was transformed for us into Eros, which seeks to force together and hold together the portions of living substance.

What are commonly called the sexual instincts are looked upon, by us, as the part of Eros that is directed towards objects. Our speculations have suggested that Eros operates from the beginning of life and appears as a life instinct, in opposition to the death instinct, which was brought into being by the coming to life of inorganic substance.

These speculations seek to solve the riddle of life by supposing that these two instincts were struggling with each other from the very first. It is not so easy, perhaps, to follow the transformations through which the concept of the ego instincts has passed. To begin with, we applied that name to all the instinctual trends (of which we had no closer knowledge), which could be distinguished from the sexual instincts directed towards an object. We opposed the ego instincts to the sexual instincts of which the libido is the manifestation.

Subsequently, we came to closer grips with the analysis of the ego and recognized that a portion of the ego instincts is also of a libidinal character and has taken the subject's own ego as its object. These narcissistic self-preservative instincts had thenceforward to be counted among the libidinal sexual instincts.

The opposition between the ego instincts and the sexual instincts was transformed into one, between the ego instincts and the object instincts, both of a libidinal nature. But, in its place, a fresh opposition appeared between the libidinal (ego and object) instincts and others, which must be presumed to be present in the ego and which may actually be observed in the destructive instincts.

Our speculations have transformed this opposition into one between the life instincts (Eros) and the death instincts.

CHAPTER SEVEN

IF IT IS really the case, that seeking to restore an earlier state of things is such a universal characteristic of instincts, we need not be surprised that so many processes take place in mental life independently of the pleasure principle. This characteristic would be shared by all the component instincts, and, in their case, would aim at returning once more to a particular stage in the course of development.

These are matters over which the pleasure principle has, as yet, no control; but it does not follow that any of them are necessarily opposed to it, and we have still to solve the problem of the relation of the instinctual processes of repetition to the dominance of the pleasure principle.

We have found that one of the earliest and most important functions of the mental apparatus is to bind the instinctual impulses which impinge on it, to replace the primary process prevailing in them, by the secondary process and to convert their mobile cathectic energy into a predominantly quiescent (tonic) cathexis.

While this transformation is taking place, no attention can be paid to the development of unpleasure; but this does not imply the suspension of the pleasure principle. On the contrary, the transformation occurs in the service of the pleasure principle; the binding is a preparatory act that introduces and assures the dominance of the pleasure principle.

Let us make a sharper distinction than we have so far made between function and tendency. The pleasure principle, then, is a tendency operating in the service of a function, whose business it is to free the mental apparatus entirely from excitation, or to keep the amount of excitation in it constant, or to keep it as low as possible.

We cannot yet decide with certainty in favor of any of these ways of putting it; but it is clear that the function thus described would be concerned with the most universal endeavor of all living substance—namely, to return to the quiescence of the inorganic world. We have all experienced how the greatest pleasure attainable, that of the sexual act, is associated with a momentary extinction of a highly intensified excitation.

The binding of an instinctual impulse would be a preliminary function designed to prepare the excitation for its final elimination in the pleasure of discharge.

This raises the question of whether feelings of pleasure and unpleasure can be produced equally from bound and from unbound excitational processes. And, there seems to be no doubt, what-so-ever, that the unbound or primary processes give rise to far more intense feelings, in both directions, than the bound or secondary ones. Moreover, the primary processes are the earlier in time; at the beginning of mental life, there are no others, and we may infer that if the pleasure principle had not already been operative in *them*, it could never have been established for the later ones.

We thus reach what is at bottom, no very simple conclusion, namely that at the beginning of mental life, the struggle for pleasure was far more intense than later, but not so unrestricted. It had to submit to frequent interruptions. In later times, the dominance of the pleasure principle is very much more secure, but it, itself, has no more escaped the process of taming than the other instincts in general. In any case, whatever it is that causes the appearance of feelings of pleasure and unpleasure, in processes of excitation, must be present in the secondary process, just as it is in the primary one.

Here might be the starting-point for fresh investigations. Our consciousness communicates to us feelings from within, not only of pleasure and unpleasure, but also of a peculiar tension, which, in its turn, can be either pleasurable or unpleasurable. Should the difference between these feelings enable us to distinguish between bound and unbound processes of energy? or is the feeling of tension to be related to the absolute magnitude, or perhaps to the level, of the cathexis, while the pleasure and unpleasure series indicates a change in the magnitude of the cathexis *within a given unit of time?*

Another striking fact is that the life instincts have so much more contact with our internal perception—emerging as breakers of the peace and constantly producing tensions, whose release is felt as pleasure—while the death instincts seem to do their work unobtrusively. The pleasure principle seems actually to serve the death instincts.

It is true that it keeps watch upon stimuli from without, which are regarded as dangers by both kinds of instincts. It is more especially on guard against increases of stimulation from within, which would make the task of living more difficult.

This, in turn, raises a host of other questions to which we can, at present, find no answer. We must be patient and await fresh methods and occasions of research. We must be ready, too, to abandon a path that we have followed for a time, if it seems to be leading to no good end.

Only believers, who demand that science shall be a substitute for the catechism they have given up, will blame an investigator for developing or even transforming his views. We may take comfort, too, for the slow advances of our scientific knowledge in the words of the poet:

Was man nicht erfliegen kann, muss man erhinken. (What we cannot reach flying, we must reach limping.)

THE EGO AND THE ID

CONTENTS

INTRODUCTION

IN MY ESSAY, *Beyond the Pleasure Principle,* published in 1920, I began the discussion of a train of thought; my personal attitude towards which, as I mentioned there, might be described as a sort of benevolent curiosity. In the following pages, this train of thought is developed further.

I have taken up those ideas and brought them into connection with various facts observed in psychoanalysis and have endeavored to draw fresh conclusions from the combination.

In the present work, however, no further contributions are levied from biology, and it consequently stands in a closer relation to psycho-analysis than does *Beyond the Pleasure Principle.* The thoughts contained in it are synthetic rather than speculative in character, and their aim appears to be an ambitious one.

I am aware, however, that they do not go beyond the baldest outlines, and I am perfectly content to recognize their limitations in this respect.

At the same time, the train of thought touches upon things not, until now, dealt with in the work psychoanalysis has done. It cannot avoid concerning itself with a number of theories propounded by non-analysts or by former analysts on their retreat from analysis. I am, as a rule, always ready to acknowledge my debts to other workers, but on this occasion I feel myself under no such obligation.

If there are certain things to which, until now, psychoanalysis has not given adequate consideration, that is not because it has overlooked their effects or wished to deny their significance, but because it pursues a particular path, which had not yet carried it so far. Moreover, now that these things have at last been overtaken, they appear to psychoanalysis in a different shape from that in which they appear to the other people.

CHAPTER ONE

Consciousness and the Unconscious

IN THIS PRELIMINARY chapter, there is nothing new to be said and it will not be possible to avoid repeating what has often been said before.

The division of mental life into what is conscious and what is unconscious is the fundamental premise on which psychoanalysis is based; and this division alone makes it possible for it to understand pathological mental processes, which are as common as they are important, and to co-ordinate them scientifically.

Stated once more in a different way: psychoanalysis cannot accept the view that consciousness is the essence of mental life, but is obliged to regard consciousness as one property of mental life, which may co-exist along with its other properties or may be absent.

If I were to allow myself to suppose that every one interested in psychology would read this book, I should still be prepared to find that some of them would stop short, even at this point, and go no further. For here we have the first shibboleth of psychoanalysis.

To most people who have had a philosophical education, the idea of anything mental that is not also conscious is so inconceivable that it seems to them absurd and refutable simply by logic. I believe this is only because they have never studied the mental phenomena of hypnosis and dreams, which—quite apart from pathological manifestations—necessitate this conclusion. Thus their psychology of consciousness is incapable of solving the problems of dreams and hypnosis.

The term conscious is, to start with, a purely descriptive one, resting on a perception of the most direct and certain character. Experience shows, next, that a mental element (for instance, an idea) is not, as a rule, permanently conscious.

On the contrary, a state of consciousness is characteristically very transitory; an idea that is conscious now is no longer so a moment later, although it can become so again under certain conditions that are easily brought about. What the idea was in the interval we do not know. We can say that it was *latent,* and by this we mean that it was *capable of becoming conscious* at any time. Or, if we say that it was *unconscious,* we are giving an equally correct description.

Thus, unconscious in this sense of the word coincides with *latent and capable of becoming conscious.* The philosophers would no doubt object:

"No, the term unconscious does not apply here; so long as the idea was in a state of latency, it was not a mental element at all".

To contradict them at this point would lead to nothing more profitable than a war of words.

But we have arrived at the term or concept of *unconscious* along another path, by taking account of certain experiences in which mental dynamics play a part. We have found, that is, we have been obliged to assume, that very powerful mental processes or ideas exist—here a quantitative or *economic* factor comes into question for the first time—which can produce, in the mind all, the effects that ordinary ideas do (including effects that can in their turn become conscious as ideas) without themselves becoming conscious.

It is unnecessary, here, to repeat in detail what has been explained so often before. We need only say that this is the point at which psycho-analytic theory steps in—with the assertion that such ideas cannot become conscious because a certain force is opposed to them; that otherwise they could become conscious, and that then one would see how little they differ from other elements that are admittedly mental.

The fact that in the technique of psychoanalysis, a means has been found which can remove the opposing force, and the ideas in question, made conscious, renders this theory irrefutable. The state in which the ideas existed before being made conscious is called *repression.* And we assert that the force that instituted the repression and maintains it is perceived as *resistance* during the work of analysis.

We obtain our concept of the unconscious, therefore, from the theory of repression. The repressed serves us as a prototype of the unconscious. We see, however, that we have two kinds of unconscious: that which is latent but capable of becoming conscious, and that which is repressed and not capable of becoming conscious in the ordinary way.

This piece of insight into mental dynamics cannot fail to affect terminology and description. That which is latent, and only unconscious in the descriptive and not in the dynamic sense, we call *preconscious.* The term unconscious, we reserve for the dynamically unconscious repressed, so that we now have three terms: conscious (Cs), preconscious (Pcs), and unconscious (Ucs), which are no longer purely descriptive in sense.

The Pcs is presumably a great deal closer to the Cs than is the Ucs, and because we have called the Ucs mental, we shall with even less hesitation call the latent Pcs mental. But why do we not choose, instead of this, to remain in agreement with the philosophers and, in a consistent way, to distinguish the Pcs as well as the Ucs from what is conscious in the mind?

The philosophers would propose that both the Pcs and the Ucs should be described as two varieties or levels of psychoid, and harmony would be established. But endless difficulties in exposition would follow. The one important fact, that the two kinds of psychoid (as thus defined) coincide in almost every other respect with what is admittedly mental, would be forced into the background in the interests of a prejudice, dating from a period in which they, or the most important part of them, were still unknown.

We can now set to work comfortably with our three terms, Cs, Pcs, and Ucs, so long as we do not forget that, while in the descriptive sense, there are two kinds of unconscious. In the dynamic sense there is only one. For purposes of exposition, this distinction can in many cases be ignored, but in others it is indispensable.

At the same time, we have become more or less accustomed to these two meanings of the term unconscious and have managed pretty well with them. As far as I can see, it is impossible to avoid this ambiguity; the distinction between conscious and unconscious is, in the last resort, a question of a perception that must be either affirmed or denied.

The act of perception itself tells us nothing of the reason why a thing is or is not perceived. No one has a right to complain because the actual phenomenon expresses the underlying dynamic factors ambiguously.

A new turn, taken by criticisms of the unconscious, deserves consideration at this point. Many investigators, who do not refuse to recognize the facts of psychoanalysis but who are unwilling to accept the unconscious, find a way out of the difficulty in the fact, which no one contests, that in consciousness (regarded as a phenomenon), it is possible to distinguish a great variety of gradations in intensity or clarity.

Just as there are ideas that are very vividly, keenly, and definitely conscious, so we also entertain others that are but faintly, hardly even noticeably conscious. Those that are most faintly conscious are, it is argued, the ones to which psychoanalysis wishes to apply the unsuitable name unconscious. These, however (the argument proceeds), are also conscious or 'in consciousness' just as much as the others, and can be made fully and intensely conscious if sufficient attention is paid to them.

In so far as it is possible to influence by arguments, the decision of a question of this kind that is based either on a convention or on emotional factors, we may make the following comments. The reference to gradations of clarity in consciousness is in no way conclusive and has no more evidential value than such analogous statements as:

"There are so many gradations in illumination—from the brightest and most dazzling light to the dimmest glimmer—that we may conclude that there is no such thing as darkness at all"; or, "There are varying degrees in the further course of psycho-analytic work."

However, even these distinctions have proved to be inadequate and, for practical purposes, insufficient. This has become clear in more ways than one; but the decisive instance is as follows. We have formulated the idea that in every individual there is a coherent organization of mental processes, which we call his ego. This ego includes consciousness and it controls the approaches to motility, i.e. to the discharge of excitations into the external world; it is this institution in the mind that regulates all its own constituent processes, and which goes to sleep at night, though even then it continues to exercise a censorship upon dreams.

From this ego proceed the repressions, too, by means of which an attempt is made to cut off certain trends in the mind, not merely from consciousness, but also from their other forms of manifestation and activity. In analysis, these trends which have been shut out stand in opposition to the ego and the analysis is faced with the task of removing the resistances that the ego displays against concerning itself with the repressed.

Now we find that during analysis, when we put certain tasks before the patient, he gets into difficulties; his associations fail when they ought to be getting near to the repressed. We then tell him that he is dominated by a resistance; but he is quite unaware of the fact, and, even if he guesses from his feelings of discomfort that a resistance is now at work in him, he does not know what it is nor how to describe it.

Because, however, there can be no question but that this resistance emanates from his ego and belongs to it, we find ourselves in an unforeseen situation. We have come upon something in the ego itself which is also unconscious, which behaves exactly like the repressed, that is, which produces powerful effects without itself being conscious, and which requires special work before it can be made conscious.

From the point of view of analytic practice, the consequence of this piece of observation is that we land in endless confusion and difficulty if we cling to our former way of expressing ourselves and try, for instance, to derive neuroses from a conflict between the conscious and the unconscious.

We shall have to substitute for this antithesis another, taken from our understanding of the structural conditions of the mind, namely, the antithesis between the organized ego and what is repressed and dissociated from it.

For our conception of the unconscious, however, the consequences of our new observation are even more important. Dynamic considerations caused us to make our first correction; our knowledge of the structure of the mind leads to the second. We recognize that the Ucs does not coincide with what is repressed; it is still true that all that is repressed is Ucs, but not that the whole Ucs is repressed.

A part of the ego, too—and we know how important a part—may be Ucs, undoubtedly is Ucs. And this Ucs, belonging to the ego, is not latent like the Pcs; for if it were, it could not be activated without becoming Cs, and the process of making it conscious would not encounter such great difficulties.

When we find ourselves thus confronted by the necessity of postulating a third Ucs, which is not repressed, we must admit that the property of being unconscious begins to lose significance for us. It becomes a quality that can have many implications, so that we are unable to make it, as we should have hoped to do, the basis of far-reaching and inevitable conclusions. Nevertheless, we must beware of ignoring this property, for in the last resort, the quality of being conscious or not is the single ray of light that penetrates the obscurity of depth-psychology.

CHAPTER TWO

The Ego and the Id

PATHOLOGICAL RESEARCH HAS centered our interest, too exclusively, on the repressed. We wish to know more about the ego, now that we know that it, too, can be unconscious in the proper sense of the word. Until now, the only guide we have had, while pursuing our investigations, has been the distinguishing mark of being conscious or unconscious; and in the end, we have come to see that this quality itself is ambiguous.

Now all our knowledge is invariably bound up with consciousness. Even knowledge of the Ucs can only be obtained by making it conscious. But stop, how is that possible? What does it mean when we say "making it conscious?" How can that come about?

We already know the point from which we have to start in this connection. We have said that consciousness is the *outer appearance* of the mental apparatus; that is, we have allocated it as a function to the system that is situated nearest to the external world. Incidentally, on this occasion, the topographical terminology does not merely serve to describe the nature of the function, but actually corresponds to the anatomical facts. Our investigations, too, must take this surface organ of perception as a starting-point.

All perceptions received from without (sense-perceptions) and from within—what we call sensations and feelings—are Cs from the start. But how is it with those internal processes that we may—vaguely and inexactly—sum up under the name of thought-processes?

They represent displacements of mental energy that are affected somewhere in the interior of the apparatus as this energy proceeds on its way towards action. Do they advance towards the superficies, which then allows of the development of consciousness? Or does consciousness make its way towards them?

This is clearly one of the difficulties that spring up when one begins to take the spatial or topographical conception of mental life seriously. Both these possibilities are equally unimaginable; there must be a third contingency to meet the case.

I have already, in another place, suggested that the real difference between a Ucs and a Pcs idea (thought) consists in this: that the former is worked out upon some sort of material that remains unrecognized, whereas the latter (the Pcs) has in addition been brought into connection with verbal images.

This is the first attempt to find a distinguishing mark for the two systems, the Pcs and the Ucs, other than their relation to consciousness. It would seem, then, that the question, "How does a thing become conscious?" could be put more advantageously thus: "How does a thing become preconscious?"

The answer would be, "By coming into connection with the verbal images that correspond to it."

These verbal images are memory-residues. They were at one time perceptions, and like all memory residues they can become conscious again. Before we concern ourselves further with their nature, it dawns upon us, like a new discovery that only something which has once been a Cs perception can become conscious, and that anything arising from within (apart from feelings) that seeks to become conscious must try to transform itself into external perceptions. This can be done by way of memory-traces.

We conceive of memory-residues as contained in systems that are directly adjacent to the system Pcpt-Cs, so that the investment of emotional significance pertaining to the memory-residues can readily extend outward on to the elements of the latter system.

We are immediately reminded of hallucinations here, and of the fact that the most vivid memory is always distinguishable both from a hallucination and from an external perception. It will also occur to us that when a memory is revived, the emotional investment in the memory-system will remain in force, whereas a hallucination, which is not distinguishable from a perception, can arise when the cathexis does not merely extend over from the memory-trace to the Pcpt-element, but passes over to it entirely.

Verbal residues are derived primarily from auditory perceptions, so that the system Pcs has, as it were, a special sensory source. The visual components of verbal images are secondary, acquired through reading, and may, to begin with, be left on one side. So may the sensory-motor images of words, which, except with deaf-mutes, play an auxiliary part. The essence of a word is, after all, the memory-trace of a word that has been heard.

We must not be led away, in the interests of simplification perhaps, into forgetting the importance of optical memory-residues—those of *things* (as opposed to *words*)—or to deny that it is possible for thought-processes to become conscious through a reversion to visual residues, and that in many people this seems to be a favorite method.

The study of dreams and of preconscious fantasies on the lines of J. Varendonck's observations gives us an idea of the special character of this visual thinking. We learn that what becomes conscious is, as a rule, only the concrete subject-matter of the thought, and that the relations between the various elements of this subject-matter, which is what specially characterizes thought, cannot be given visual expression.

Thinking in pictures is, therefore, only a very incomplete form of becoming conscious. In some way, too, it approximates more closely to unconscious processes than does thinking in words, and it is unquestionably older than the latter both ontogenetically and phylogenetically.

To return to our argument: if, therefore, this is the way in which something that is in itself unconscious becomes preconscious, the question how something that is repressed can be made (pre)conscious would be answered as follows. It is done by supplying through the work of the analysis Pcs connecting-links of the kind we have been discussing. Consciousness remains where it is, therefore; but, on the other hand, the Ucs does not rise up into the Cs.

Whereas the relation between external perceptions and the ego is quite perspicuous, that between internal perceptions and the ego requires special investigation. It gives rise once more to a doubt whether we are really justified in referring the whole of consciousness to the single superficial system Pcpt-Cs.

Internal perceptions yield sensations of processes arising in the most diverse and certainly also in the deepest strata of the mental apparatus. Very little is known about these sensations and feelings; the best examples we have of them are still those belonging to the pleasure-pain series. They are more fundamental, more elementary, than perceptions arising externally and they can come into being even when consciousness is clouded.

I have elsewhere expressed my views about their great economic significance and its meta-psychological foundation. These sensations have many small compartments, like external perceptions. They may come from different places simultaneously and may thus have different or even opposite qualities.

Sensations of a pleasurable nature are not characterized by any inherently impelling quality, whereas 'painful' ones possess this quality in a high degree. The latter impel towards change, towards discharge, and that is why we interpret pain as implying a heightening and pleasure a lowering of energetic emotional investment.

Suppose we describe what becomes conscious in the shape of pleasure, and pain as an undetermined quantitative and qualitative element in the mind. The question then, is whether that element can become conscious where it actually is, or whether it must first be transmitted into the system Pcpt.

Clinical experience decides for the latter. It shows us that this undetermined element behaves like a repressed impulse. It can exert driving force without the ego noticing the compulsion. Not until there is resistance to the compulsion, and blocking of the discharge reaction, does the undetermined element instantly become conscious as 'pain'.

In the same way that tensions arising from physical need can remain unconscious, so also can physical pain—a thing intermediate between external and internal perception, which acts like an internal perception even when its source is in the external world.

It remains true again, therefore, that sensations and feelings only become conscious through reaching the system Pcpt; if the way forward is barred, they do not come into being as sensations, although the undetermined element corresponding to them is the same as if they did.

We then come to speak, in a condensed and not entirely correct manner, of unconscious feelings, keeping up an analogy with unconscious ideas, which is not altogether justifiable. Actually, the difference is that, with Ucs *ideas,* connecting-links must be forged before they can be brought into the Cs. With *feelings*, that are themselves transmitted directly, there is no necessity for this.

In other words: the distinction between Cs and Pcs has no meaning where feelings are concerned. The Pcs here falls out of account, and feelings are either conscious or unconscious. Even when they are connected with verbal images, their becoming conscious is not due to that circumstance, but they become so directly.

The part played by verbal images now becomes perfectly clear. By their interposition, internal thought-processes are made into perceptions. It is like a demonstration of the theorem that all knowledge has its origin in external perception. It may sometimes happen that a hyper-cathexis of the process of thinking takes place, in which case thoughts are *perceived* in the literal sense of the word—as if they came from without—and are consequently held to be true.

After this clarifying of the relations between external and internal perception and the superficial system Pcpt-Cs, we can go on to work out our conception of the ego. It clearly starts out from its nucleus, the system Pcpt, and begins by embracing the Pcs, which is adjacent to the memory residues. But the ego, as we have learned, is also unconscious.

Now I think we shall gain a great deal by following the suggestion of a writer who, from personal motives, vainly insists that he has nothing to do with the rigours of pure science. I am speaking of Georg Groddeck, who is never tired of pointing out that the conduct through life of what we call our ego is essentially passive, and that, as he expresses it, we are "lived" by unknown and uncontrollable forces. We have all had impressions of the same kind, even though they may not have overwhelmed us to the exclusion of all others, and we need feel no hesitation in finding a place for Groddeck's discovery in the fabric of science.

I propose to take it into account by calling the entity which starts out from the system Pcpt and begins by being Pcs the ego, and by following Groddeck in giving to the other part of the mind, into which this entity extends and which behaves as though it were Ucs, the name of Id (Es).

We shall soon see whether this conception affords us any gain in understanding or any advantage for purposes of description. We shall now look upon the mind of an individual as an unknown and unconscious id, upon whose surface rests the ego, developed from its nucleus the Pcpt-system.

If we make an effort to conceive of this pictorially, we may add that the ego does not envelop the whole of the id, but only does so to the extent to which the system Pcpt forms its surface, more or less as the germinal layer rests upon the ovum. The ego is not sharply separated from the id; its lower portion merges into it.

But the repressed merges into the id as well, and is simply a part of it. The repressed is only cut off sharply from the ego by the resistances of repression; it can communicate with the ego through the id. We at once realize that almost all the delimitations we have been led into, outlining by our study of pathology, relate only to the superficial levels of the mental apparatus—the only ones known to us.

We might add, perhaps, that the ego wears an auditory lobe—on one side only, as we learn from cerebral anatomy. It wears it crooked, as one might say.

It is easy to see that the ego is that part of the id that has been modified by the direct influence of the external world acting through the Pcpt-Cs. In a sense it is an extension of the surface-differentiation. Moreover, the ego has the task of bringing the influence of the external world to bear upon the id and its tendencies, and endeavors to substitute the reality-principle for the pleasure principle, which reigns supreme in the id.

In the ego, perception plays the part which, in the id, devolves upon instinct. The ego represents what we call reason and sanity, in contrast to the id, which contains the passions. All this falls into line with popular distinctions that we are all familiar with; at the same time, however, it is only to be regarded as holding good in an average or ideal case.

The functional importance of the ego is manifested in the fact that normally, control over the approaches to motility devolves upon it. Thus, in its relation to the id, it is like a man on horseback, who has to hold in check the superior strength of the horse. With this difference, that the rider seeks to do so with his own strength, while the ego uses borrowed forces.

The illustration may be carried further. Often a rider, if he is not to be parted from his horse, is obliged to guide it where it wants to go; so in the same way the ego constantly carries into action the wishes of the id as if they were its own.

It seems that another factor, besides the influence of the system Pcpt, has been at work in bringing about the formation of the ego and its differentiation from the id. The body itself, and above all its surface, is a place from which both external and internal perceptions may spring. It is seen in the same way as any other object, but to the touch, it yields two kinds of sensations, one of which is equivalent to an internal perception.

Psychophysiology has fully discussed the manner in which the body attains its special position among other objects in the world of perception. Pain seems also to play a part in the process, and the way in which we gain new knowledge of our organs during painful illnesses is perhaps a prototype of the way by which, in general, we arrive at the idea of our own body.

The ego is primarily a body-ego; it is not merely a surface entity, but it is itself the projection of a surface. If we wish to find an anatomical analogy for it, we can easily identify it with the cortical homunculus of the anatomists, which stands on its head in the cortex, sticks its heels into the air, faces backwards and, as we know, has its speech-area on the left-hand side.

The relation of the ego to consciousness has been gone into repeatedly; yet there are still some important facts in this connection that remain to be described. Accustomed as we are to taking our social or ethical standard of values along with us wherever we go, we feel no surprise at hearing that the scene of the activities of the lower passions is in the unconscious; we expect, moreover, that the higher any mental function ranks in our scale of values, the more easily it will find access to consciousness assured to it.

Here, however, psychoanalytic experience disappoints us. On the one hand, we have evidence that even subtle and intricate intellectual operations that ordinarily require strenuous concentration can equally be carried out pre-consciously and without coming into consciousness. Instances of this are quite incontestable; they may occur, for instance, during sleep, as is shown when someone finds, immediately after waking, that he knows the solution of a difficult mathematical or other problem with which he had been wrestling in vain the day before.

There is another phenomenon, however, which is far stranger. In our analyses, we discover that there are people in whom the faculties of self-criticism and conscience—mental activities, that is, that rank as exceptionally high ones—are unconscious and unconsciously produce effects of the greatest importance. The example of resistances remaining unconscious during analysis is therefore by no means unique.

But this new discovery, which compels us, in spite of our critical faculties, to speak of an "unconscious sense of guilt", bewilders us far more than the other and sets us fresh problems, especially when we gradually come to see that in a great number of neuroses, this unconscious sense of guilt plays a decisive economic part and puts the most powerful obstacles in the way of recovery.

If we come back once more to our scale of values, we shall have to say that not only what is lowest but also what is highest in the ego can be unconscious. It is as if we were thus supplied with a proof of what we have just asserted of the conscious ego: that it is first and foremost a body-ego.

CHAPTER THREE

The Ego and the Super Ego

IF THE EGO were merely the part of the id that is modified by the influence of the perceptual system, the representative in the mind of the real external world, we should have a simple state of things to deal with. But there is a further complication.

The considerations that led us to assume the existence of a differentiating grade within the ego, which may be called the ego-ideal or super-ego, have been set forth elsewhere. They still hold good. The new proposition which must now be gone into is that this part of the ego is less closely connected with consciousness than the rest.

At this point, we must widen our range a little. We succeeded in explaining the painful disorder of melancholia by supposing that, in those suffering from it, an object that was lost has been reinstated within the ego; that is, that an object cathexis has been replaced by an identification.

When this explanation was first proposed, however, we did not appreciate the full significance of the process and did not know how common and how typical it is. Since then, we have come to understand that this kind of substitution has a great share in determining the form taken on by the ego and that it contributes materially towards building up what is called its character.

At the very beginning, in the primitive oral phase of the individual's existence, object-cathexis and identification are hardly to be distinguished from each other. We can only suppose that later on object-cathexes proceed from the id, in which erotic trends are felt as needs. The ego, which at its inception is still far from robust, becomes aware of the object-cathexes, and either acquiesces in them or tries to defend itself against them by the process of repression.

When it happens that a person has to give up a sexual object, there quite often ensues a modification in his ego which can only be described as a reinstatement of the object within the ego, as it occurs in melancholia; the exact nature of this substitution is as yet unknown to us. It may be that, by undertaking this introjection, which is a kind of regression to the mechanism of the oral phase, the ego makes it easier for an object to be given up or renders that process possible.

It may even be that this identification is the sole condition under which the id can give up its objects. At any rate, the process, especially in the early phases of development, is a very frequent one and it points to the conclusion that the character of the ego is a precipitate of abandoned object-cathexes, and that it contains a record of past object-choices.

It must, of course, be admitted from the outset that there are varying degrees of capacity for resistance, as shown by the extent to which the character of any particular person accepts or resists the influences of the erotic object-choices through which he has lived. In women who have had many love-affairs, there seems to be no difficulty in finding vestiges of their object-cathexes in the traits of their character.

We must also take into consideration the case of simultaneous object-cathexis and identification, *i.e.* in which the alteration in character occurs before the object has been given up. In such a case, the alteration in character would be able to survive the object-relation and in a certain sense to conserve it.

From another point of view it may be said that this transformation of an erotic object-choice into a modification of the ego is also a method by which the ego can obtain control over the id and deepen its relations with it—at the cost, it is true, of acquiescing, to a large extent, in the id's experiences.

When the ego assumes the features of the object, it forces itself, so to speak, upon the id as a love-object and tries to make good the loss of that object by saying, "Look, I am so like the object, you can as well love me."

The transformation of object-libido into narcissistic libido which thus takes place obviously implies an abandonment of sexual aims, a process of desexualization. It is consequently a kind of sublimation.

Indeed, the question arises, and deserves careful consideration, whether this is not always the path taken in sublimation, whether all sublimation does not take place through the agency of the ego, which begins by changing sexual object-libido into narcissistic libido and then, perhaps, goes on to give it another aim.

We shall later on have to consider whether other instinctual vicissitudes may not also result from this transformation, whether, for instance, it may not bring about a defusion of the instincts that are fused together.

Although it is a digression from our theme, we cannot avoid giving our attention, for a moment longer, to the ego's object-identifications. If they obtain the upper hand and become too numerous, unduly intense and incompatible with one another, a pathological outcome will not be far off. It may come to a disruption of the ego in consequence of the individual identifications becoming cut off from one another by resistances; perhaps the secret of the cases of so-called multiple personality is that the various identifications seize possession of consciousness in turn.

Even when things do not go so far as this, there remains the question of conflicts between the different identifications into which the ego is split up, conflicts which cannot, after all, be described as purely pathological.

But, whatever the character's capacity for resisting the influences of abandoned object-cathexes may turn out to be in after years, the effects of the first identifications in earliest childhood will be profound and lasting. This leads us back to the origin of the ego-ideal; for behind the latter there lies hidden the first and most important identification of all, the identification with the father, which takes place in the prehistory of every person.

This is apparently not in the first instance the consequence or outcome of an object-cathexis; it is a direct and immediate identification and takes place earlier than any object-cathexis. But the object-choices belonging to the earliest sexual period and relating to the father and mother seem normally to find their outcome in an identification of the kind discussed, which would thus reinforce the primary one.

The whole subject, however, is so complicated that it will be necessary to go into it more minutely. The intricacy of the problem is due to two factors: the triangular character of the Oedipus situation and the constitutional bisexuality of each individual.

In its simplified form, the case of the male child may be described as follows. At a very early age, the little boy develops an object-cathexis of his *mother*, which originally related to the mother's breast and is the earliest instance of an object-choice on the anaclitic model. His *father,* the boy deals with by identifying himself with him.

For a time these two relationships exist side by side, until the sexual wishes in regard to the mother become more intense, and the father is perceived as an obstacle to them. This gives rise to the Oedipus complex. The identification with the father then takes on a hostile coloring and changes into a wish to get rid of the father in order to take his place with the mother.

Henceforward, the relation to the father is ambivalent; it seems as if the ambivalence inherent in the identification from the beginning had become manifest. An ambivalent attitude to the father and an object-relation of a purely affectionate kind to the mother make up the content of the simple positive Oedipus complex in the boy.

Along with the dissolution of the Oedipus complex, the object-cathexis of the mother must be given up. Its place may be filled by one of two things: either an identification with the mother or an intensified identification with the father. We are accustomed to regard the latter outcome as the more normal; it permits the affectionate relation to the mother to be in a measure retained. In this way, the passing of the Oedipus complex would consolidate the masculinity in the boy's character.

In a precisely analogous way, the outcome of the Oedipus attitude in the little girl may be an intensification of the identification with her mother (or such an identification may thus be set up for the first time), a result which will stamp the child's character in the feminine mould.

These identifications are not what our previous statements would have led us to expect, because they do not involve the absorption of the abandoned object into the ego. But this alternative outcome may also occur; it is more readily observed in girls than in boys. Analysis very often shows that a little girl, after she has had to relinquish her father as a love-object, will bring her masculinity into prominence and identify herself with her father, that is, with the object that has been lost, instead of with her mother. This will clearly depend on whether the masculinity in her disposition—whatever that may consist of—is strong enough.

It would appear, therefore, that in both sexes the relative strength of the masculine and feminine sexual dispositions is what determines whether the outcome of the Oedipus situation shall be an identification with the father or with the mother. This is one of the ways in which bisexuality takes a hand in the subsequent vicissitudes of the Oedipus complex.

The other way is even more important. For one gets the impression that the simple Oedipus complex is by no means its commonest form, but rather represents a simplification or schematization which, to be sure, is often enough adequate for practical purposes. Closer study usually discloses the more complete Oedipus complex, which is twofold, positive and negative, and is due to the bisexuality originally present in children: that is to say, a boy has not merely an ambivalent attitude towards his father and an affectionate object-relation towards his mother, but at the same time he also behaves like a girl and displays an affectionate feminine attitude to his father and a corresponding hostility and jealousy towards his mother.

It is this complicating element, introduced by bisexuality, that makes it so difficult to obtain a clear view of the facts, in connection with the earliest object-choices and identifications, and still more difficult to describe them intelligibly. It may even be that the ambivalence displayed in the relations to the parents should be attributed entirely to bisexuality and that it is not, as I stated just now, developed out of an identification in consequence of rivalry.

In my opinion, it is advisable in general, and quite especially where neurotics are concerned, to assume the existence of the complete Oedipus complex. Analytic experience then shows that in a number of cases, one or the other of its constituents disappears, except for barely distinguishable traces, so that a series can be formed with the normal positive Oedipus complex—at one end and the inverted negative one at the other—while its intermediate members will exhibit the complete type with one or other of its two constituents preponderating.

As the Oedipus complex dissolves, the four trends of which it consists will group themselves in such a way as to produce a father-identification and a mother-identification. The father-identification will preserve the object-relation to the mother, which belonged to the positive complex and will, at the same time, take the place of the object-relation to the father, which belonged to the inverted complex.

The same will be true, *mutatis mutandis*, of the mother-identification. The relative intensity of the two identifications in any individual will reflect the preponderance in him of one or other of the two sexual dispositions.

The broad general outcome of the sexual Phase governed by the Oedipus complex may, therefore, be taken to be the forming of a precipitate in the ego, consisting of these two identifications in some way combined together. This modification of the ego retains its special position; it stands in contrast to the other constituents of the ego in the form of an ego-ideal or super-ego.

The super-ego is, however, not merely a deposit left by the earliest object-choices of the id; it also represents an energetic reaction-formation against those choices. Its relation to the ego is not exhausted by the precept, "You *ought to be* such and such (like your father)."

It also comprises the prohibition, "You *must not* be such and such (like your father); that is, you may not do all that he does; many things are his prerogative." This double aspect of the ego-ideal derives from the fact that the ego-ideal had the task of effecting the repression of the Oedipus complex, indeed, it is to that revolutionary event that it owes its existence.

Clearly, the repression of the Oedipus complex was no easy task. The parents, and especially the father, were perceived as the obstacle to realization of the Oedipus wishes; so the child's ego brought in a reinforcement to help in carrying out the repression by erecting this same obstacle within itself.

The strength to do this was, so to speak, borrowed from the father, and this loan was an extraordinarily momentous act. The superego retains the character of the father, while the more intense the Oedipus complex was and the more rapidly it succumbed to repression (under the influence of discipline, religious teaching, schooling and reading), the more exacting later on is the domination of the super-ego over the ego—in the form of conscience or perhaps of an unconscious sense of guilt.

I shall, later on, bring forward a suggestion about the source of the power it employs to dominate in this way, the source, that is, of its compulsive character that manifests itself in the form of a categorical imperative.

If we consider, once more, the origin of the super-ego as we have described it, we shall perceive it to be the outcome of two highly important factors: one of them biological and the other historical. Namely, the lengthy duration in man of the helplessness and dependence belonging to childhood, and the fact of his Oedipus complex, the repression of which we have shown to be connected with the interruption of libidinal development by the latency period, and so with the twofold onset of activity characteristic of man's sexual life.

According to the view of one psychoanalyst, the last-mentioned phenomenon, which seems to be peculiar to man, is a heritage of the cultural development necessitated by the glacial epoch.

We see, then, that the differentiation of the super-ego from the ego is no matter of chance. It stands as the representative of the most important events in the development both of the individual and of the race; indeed, by giving permanent expression to the influence of the parents, it perpetuates the existence of the factors to which it owes its origin.

Psycho-analysis has been reproached time after time with ignoring the higher, moral, spiritual side of human nature. The reproach is doubly unjust, both historically and methodologically. For, in the first place, we have from the very beginning, attributed the function of instigating repression to the moral and aesthetic tendencies in the ego.

Secondly, there has been a general refusal to recognize that psycho-analytic research could not produce a complete and finished body of doctrine, like a philosophical system, ready-made, but had to find its way, step by step, along the path towards understanding the intricacies of the mind by making an analytic dissection of both normal and abnormal phenomena.

So long as the study of the repressed part of the mind was our task, there was no need for us to feel any agitated apprehensions about the existence of the higher side of mental life. But now that we have embarked upon the analysis of the ego, we can give an answer to all those whose moral sense has been shocked and who have complained that there must surely be a higher nature in man.

"Very true," we can say, "and here we have that higher nature, in this ego-ideal or super-ego, the representative of our relation to our parents. When we were little children, we knew these higher natures. We admired them and feared them, and later we took them into ourselves."

The ego-ideal, therefore, is the heir of the Oedipus complex and thus it is also the expression of the most powerful impulses and most important vicissitudes experienced by the libido in the id. By setting up this ego-ideal, the ego masters its Oedipus complex and at the same time places itself in subjection to the id.

Whereas the ego is essentially the representative of the external world, of reality, the super-ego stands in contrast to it as the representative of the internal world, of the id.

Conflicts between the ego and the ideal will, as we are now prepared to find, ultimately reflect the contrast between what is real and what is mental, between the external world and the internal world.

Through the forming of the ideal, all the traces left behind in the id, by biological developments and by the vicissitudes gone through by the human race, are taken over by the ego and lived through again by it in each individual. Owing to the way in which it is formed, the ego-ideal has a great many points of contact with the phylogenetic endowment of each individual—his archaic heritage.

And thus, it is that what belongs to the lowest depths in the minds of each one of us, is changed—through this formation of the ideal—into what we value as the highest in the human soul. It would be vain, however, to attempt to localize the ego-ideal, even in the sense in which we have localized the ego, or to work it into any of those analogies with the help of which we have tried to picture the relation between the ego and the id.

It is easy to show that the ego-ideal answers in every way to what is expected of the higher nature of man. In so far as it is a substitute for the longing for a father, it contains the germ from which all religions have evolved. The self-judgment, which declares that the ego falls short of its ideal, produces the sense of worthlessness with which the religious believer attests his longing.

As a child grows up, the office of father is carried on by masters and by others in authority; the power of their injunctions and prohibitions remains vested in the ego-ideal and continues, in the form of conscience, to exercise the censorship of morals. The tension between the demands of conscience and the actual attainments of the ego is experienced as a sense of guilt. Social feelings rest on the foundation of identifications with others, on the basis of an ego-ideal in common with them.

Religion, morality, and a social sense—the chief elements of what is highest in man—were originally one and the same thing. According to the hypothesis which I have put forward in *Totem and Taboo*, they were acquired phylogenetically out of the father-complex: religion and moral restraint by the actual process of mastering the Oedipus complex itself, and social feeling from the necessity for overcoming the rivalry that then remained between the members of the younger generation.

It seems that the male sex has taken the lead in developing all of these moral acquisitions; and that they have then been transmitted to women by cross-inheritance. Even today, the social feelings arise in the individual as a superstructure founded upon impulses of jealousy and rivalry against his brothers and sisters. Because the enmity cannot be gratified, there develops an identification with the former rival. The study of mild cases of homosexuality confirms the suspicion that in this instance, too, the identification is a substitute for an affectionate object-choice which has succeeded the hostile, aggressive attitude.

With the mention of phylogenesis, however, fresh problems arise, from which one is tempted to shrink back dismayed. But there is no help for it; the attempt must be made, in spite of a fear that it will lay bare the inadequacy of the whole structure that we have so arduously built up.

The question is: which was it, the ego of primitive man or his id, that acquired religion and morality in those early days out of the father-complex?

If it was his ego, why do we not speak simply of these things being inherited by the ego? If it was the id, how does that agree with the character of the id? Or, are we wrong in carrying the differentiation between ego, super-ego, and id back into such early times? Or, should we not honestly confess that our whole conception of the processes within the ego is of no help in understanding phylogenesis and cannot be applied to it?

Let us answer first what is easiest to answer. The differentiation between ego and id must be attributed not only to primitive man but even to much simpler forms of life, for it is the inevitable expression of the influence of the external world. The super-ego, according to our hypothesis, actually originated from the experiences that led to totemism. The question whether it was the ego or the id that experienced and acquired these things soon ceases to have any meaning.

Reflection, at once, shows us that no external vicissitudes can be experienced or undergone by the id, except by way of the ego, which is the representative of the outer world to the id. Nevertheless it is not possible to speak of direct inheritance by the ego.

It is here that the gulf between the actual individual and the conception of the species becomes evident. Moreover, one must not take the difference between ego and id in too hard-and-fast a sense, nor forget that the ego is a part of the id that has been specially modified.

The experiences undergone by the ego seem at first to be lost to posterity; but, when they have been repeated often enough and with sufficient intensity in the successive individuals of many generations, they transform themselves, so to say, into experiences of the id—the impress of which is preserved by inheritance.

Thus in the id, which is capable of being inherited, are stored up vestiges of the existences led by countless former egos; and, when the ego forms its super-ego out of the id, it may perhaps only be reviving images of egos that have passed away and be securing them a resurrection.

The way in which the super-ego came into being explains how it is that the earlier conflicts of the ego with the object-cathexes of the id can be carried on and continued in conflicts with their successor, the super-ego. If the ego has not succeeded in mastering the Oedipus complex satisfactorily, the energic cathexis of the latter, springing from the id, will find an outlet in the reaction- formations of the ego-ideal.

The very free communication possible between the ideal and these Ucs instinctual trends explains how it is that the ideal itself can be, to a great extent, unconscious and inaccessible to the ego. The struggle, which once raged in the deepest strata of the mind, and was not brought to an end by rapid sublimation and identification, is now carried on in a higher region, like the Battle of the Huns, which, in Kaulbach's painting, is being fought out in the sky.

CHAPTER FOUR

The Two Classes of Instincts

WE HAVE ALREADY said that, if the differentiation we have made of the mind into an id, an ego, and a superego represents any advance in our knowledge, it ought to enable us to understand, more thoroughly, the dynamic relations within the mind, and to describe them more clearly. We have also already reached the conclusion that the ego is especially affected by perception, and that, speaking broadly, perceptions may be said to have the same significance for the ego as instincts have for the id. At the same time, the ego is subject to the influence of the instincts, too, like the id, of which it is, in fact, only a specially modified part.

I have lately developed a view of the instincts, which I shall here hold to and take as the basis of further discussions. According to this view, we have to distinguish two classes of instincts—one of which, Eros or the sexual instincts, is by far the more conspicuous and accessible to study. It comprises not merely the uninhibited sexual instinct proper and the impulses of a sublimated or aim-inhibited nature derived from it, but also the self-preservative instinct, which must be assigned to the ego and which, at the beginning of our analytic work, we had good reason for setting in opposition to the sexual object-instincts.

The second class of instincts was not so easy to define; in the end we came to recognize sadism as its representative. As a result of theoretical considerations, supported by biology, we assumed the existence of a death-instinct. The task of which is to lead organic matter back into the inorganic state.

On the other hand, we supposed that Eros aims at complicating life by bringing about a more and more far-reaching coalescence of the particles into which living matter has been dispersed, thus, of course, aiming at the maintenance of life. Acting in this way, both the instincts would be conservative in the strictest sense of the word, since both would be endeavoring to re-establish a state of things that was disturbed by the emergence of life.

The appearance of life would thus be regarded as the cause of the continuance of life and also as the cause of the striving towards death. Life itself would be a conflict and compromise between these two trends. The problem of the origin of life would remain a cosmological one; and the problem of the purpose and goal of life would be answered dualistically.

On this view, a special physiological process (of anabolism or katabolism) would be associated with each of the two classes of instincts; both instincts would be active in every particle of living substance—although in unequal proportions—so that some one substance might be the principal representative of Eros.

This hypothesis throws no light whatever upon the manner in which the two classes of instincts are fused, blended, and mingled with each other. But that this takes place regularly and very extensively is an assumption indispensable to our conception. It appears that, as a result of the combination of unicellular organisms into multicellular forms of life, the death-instinct of the single cell can successfully be neutralized and the destructive impulses be diverted towards the external world through the instrumentality of a special organ.

This special organ would seem to be the musculature; and the death-instinct would thus seem to express itself , though probably only in part, as an instinct of destruction directed against the external world and other living organisms.

Once we have admitted the conception of a fusion of the two classes of instincts with each other, the possibility of a more or less complete defusion of them forces itself upon us. The sadistic component of the sexual instinct would be a classical example of instinctual fusion serving a useful purpose. The perversion in which sadism has made itself independent, would be typical of defusion, though not of absolutely complete defusion.

From this point, we obtain a new view of a great array of facts that have not before been considered in this light. We perceive that for purposes of discharge, the instinct of destruction is habitually enlisted in the service of Eros. We suspect that the epileptic fit is a product and sign of instinctual defusion. We come to understand that defusion and the marked emergence of the death-instinct are among the most noteworthy effects of many severe neuroses, *e.g.* the obsessional neuroses.

Making a swift generalization, we might conjecture that the essence of a regression of libido, *e.g.* from the genital to the sadistic-anal level, would lie in a defusion of instincts. Just as, conversely, the advance from an earlier to the definitive genital phase would be conditioned by an accession of erotic components.

The question also arises whether ordinary ambivalence, which is so often unusually strong in the constitutional disposition to neurosis, should not be regarded as the product of a defusion. Ambivalence, however, is such a fundamental phenomenon that it more probably represents a state of incomplete fusion.

It is natural that we should now turn, with interest, to inquire whether there may not be instructive connections to be traced between the formations we have assumed to exist in the mind: the ego, the super-ego, and the id; the two classes of instincts. And, further, whether the pleasure-principle, which dominates mental processes, can be shown to have any constant relation, both to the two classes of instincts and to these differentiations we have drawn within the mind.

But before we discuss this, we must clear away a doubt that arises concerning the terms of the problem itself. There can be no doubt about the pleasure-principle. The differentiations within the ego have good clinical justification, but the distinction between the two classes of instincts does not seem sufficiently assured. It is possible that facts of clinical analysis may be found to conflict with it.

One such fact appears to exist. Instead of the opposition between the two classes of instincts, let us consider the Polarity of love and hate. (There is no difficulty in finding a representative of Eros; but we must be grateful that we can find a representative of the elusive death-instinct in the instinct of destruction, for which hate points the way.)

Now, clinical observation shows not only that love is with unexpected regularity accompanied by hate (ambivalence), and not only that in human relationships hate is frequently a forerunner of love, but also that in many circumstances, hate changes into love and love into hate. If this change is anything more than a mere succession in time, then clearly the ground is cut away from under a distinction so fundamental as that between erotic instincts and death-instincts. One which presupposes the existence of physiological processes running counter to each other.

Now the case in which someone first loves and then hates the same person (or the reverse), because that person has given him cause for doing so, has obviously nothing to do with our problem. Nor has the other case in which feelings of love that have not yet become manifest express themselves to begin with by enmity and aggressive tendencies. For it may be that here the destructive components in the object-cathexis have outstripped the erotic and are only later on joined by the latter.

But we know of several instances in the psychology of the neuroses in which there are better grounds for assuming that a transformation does take place. In persecutory paranoia, the sufferer takes a particular way of defending himself against an unduly strong homosexual attachment to a given person, with the result that the person he once loved most is changed into a persecutor and then becomes the object of aggressive and often dangerous impulses on the part of the patient.

Here we have grounds for interposing an intermediate phase in which the love is transformed into hate. Analytic investigation has only lately revealed that the sources of homosexuality and of desexualized social feelings include very intense feelings of rivalry, giving rise to aggressive desires, which, after they have been surmounted, are succeeded by love for the object that was formerly hated or by an identification with it.

The question arises whether in these instances we are to assume a direct transformation of hate into love. It is clear that here the changes are purely internal, and an alteration in the behavior of the object plays no part in them.

There is another possible mechanism, however, which we have come to know of by analytic investigation of the processes concerned in the change in paranoia. An ambivalent attitude is present from the outset, and the transformation is effected by means of a reactive shifting of cathexis, by which energy is withdrawn from the erotic impulses and used to supplement the hostile energy.

Not quite the same thing, but something like it, happens when a hostile attitude of rivalry is overcome and leads to homosexuality. The hostile attitude has no prospect of gratification; consequently—as an economic measure—it is replaced by a loving attitude for which there is more hope of satisfaction, that is, possibility of discharge. So, we see that we are not obliged in either of these cases to assume a direct transformation of hate into love that would be incompatible with a qualitative distinction between the two classes of instincts.

It appears, however, that by including in our calculations this other mechanism, by means of which love can be changed into hate, we have tacitly made another assumption that deserves to be formulated explicitly. We have reckoned as though there existed in the mind, whether in the ego or in the id, a displaceable energy, which is in itself neutral, but is able to join forces either with an erotic or with a destructive impulse, differing qualitatively as they do, and augment its total cathexis. Without assuming the existence of a displaceable energy of this kind, we can make no headway. The only questions are where it comes from, what it belongs to, and what it signifies.

The problem of the quality of instinctual impulses and of its persistence throughout their vicissitudes is still very obscure and has hardly been attacked up to the present. In the sexual component-instincts, which are especially accessible to observation, it is possible to perceive the working of processes that are in the same category as what we are discussing.

We see that some degree of communication exists between the component instincts; that an instinct deriving from one particular eroto-genic source can make over its intensity to reinforce another component-instinct, originating in another source; that gratification of one instinct can take the place of gratification of another, and many more facts of the same nature. All of which must encourage us to venture upon certain assumptions.

In the present discussion, moreover, I am putting forward nothing but a supposition; I have no proof to offer. It seems a plausible view that this neutral displaceable energy, which is probably active alike in the ego and in the id, proceeds from the narcissistic reservoir of libido that it is desexualized Eros. (The erotic instincts appear to be altogether more plastic, more readily diverted and displaced than the destructive instincts.)

From this, we can easily go on to assume that this displaceable libido is employed in the service of the pleasure-principle to obviate accumulations and to facilitate discharge. It is clear, incidentally, that there is a certain indifference about the path along which the discharge takes place, so long as it takes place somehow. We know this trait; it is characteristic of the cathectic processes in the id. It is found in erotic cathexes, where a peculiar indifference, in regard to the object displays itself; and it is especially evident in the transferences arising in analysis, which develop inevitably no matter who the analyst may be.

Rank has recently published some good examples of the way in which neurotic acts of revenge can be directed against the wrong people. Such behavior, on the part of the unconscious, reminds one of the comic story of the three village tailors, one of whom had to be hanged because the only village blacksmith had committed a capital offense. The penalty must be exacted, even if it does not fall upon the guilty.

It was in studying dream-work that we first came upon this kind of looseness in the displacements brought about by the primary process. In that case, it was the objects that were thus relegated to a position of no more than secondary importance, just as in the case we are now discussing; it is the paths of discharge. It would seem to be characteristic of the ego to be more particular both about the choice of an object and about the path of discharge.

If this displaceable energy is desexualized libido, it might also be described as sublimated energy; for it would still retain the main purpose of Eros (that of uniting and binding) in so far as it helped towards establishing that unity, or tendency to unity, which is particularly characteristic of the ego. If the intellectual processes, in the wider sense, are to be classed among these displacements, then the energy for the work of thought, itself, must be supplied from sublimated erotic sources.

Here we arrive again at the possibility, which has already been discussed, that sublimation may take place regularly through the mediation of the ego. The other case will be recollected, in which the ego deals with the first object-cathexes of the id (and certainly with later ones too), by taking over the libido from them, into itself and binding it to the ego-modification produced by means of identification.

The transformation of erotic libido into ego-libido, of course, involves an abandonment of sexual aims, a desexualization. In any case, this throws light upon an important function of the ego in its relation to Eros. By thus obtaining possession of the libido from the object-cathexes, setting itself up as sole love-object, and desexualizing or sublimating the libido of the id, the ego is working in opposition to the purposes of Eros and placing itself at the service of the opposing instinctual trends. It has to acquiesce in some of the other object-cathexes of the id; it has to go hand in hand with them, so to speak. We shall come back later to another possible consequence of this activity of the ego.

This would seem to imply an important amplification of the theory of narcissism. At the very beginning, all the libido is accumulated in the id, while the ego is still in process of formation, or far from robust. Part of this libido is sent out by the id into erotic object-cathexes, whereupon the ego, now growing stronger, attempts to obtain possession of this object-libido and to force itself upon the id as a love-object. The narcissism of the ego is thus seen to be secondary, acquired by the withdrawal of the libido from objects.

Over and over again we find, on tracing instinctual impulses back, that they disclose themselves as derivatives of Eros. If it were not for the considerations put forward in *Beyond the Pleasure Principle,* and ultimately for the sadistic constituents, which have attached themselves to Eros, we should have difficulty in holding to our fundamental dualistic point of view. But since we cannot escape that view, we are driven to conclude that the death-instincts are, by their nature, mute and that the clamor of life proceeds for the most part from Eros. (In fact, according to our view it is through the agency of Eros that the destructive instincts that are directed towards the external world have been diverted from the self.)

And from the struggle against Eros! It can hardly be doubted that the pleasure-principle serves the id as a compass in its struggle against the libido—the force that introduces such disturbances into the process of life. If it is true that life is governed by Fechner's principle of constant equilibrium, it consists of a continuous descent towards death; but the falling of the level is delayed and fresh tensions are introduced by the claims of Eros, of the sexual instincts, as expressed in instinctual needs.

The id, guided by the pleasure-principle, that is, by the perception of pain, guards itself against these tensions in various ways. It does so, in the first place, by complying as swiftly as possible with the demands of the non-desexualized libido (by striving for the gratification of the directly sexual trends). But it does so further, and in a far more comprehensive fashion, in relation to one particular form of gratification that subsumes all component claims. That is, by discharge of the sexual substances, which are saturated conductors, so to speak, of the erotic tensions.

The ejection of sexual substances in the sexual act, corresponds in a certain degree with the separation of soma and germ-plasm. This accounts for the likeness between dying and the condition that follows complete sexual satisfaction, and for the fact that death coincides with the act of copulation in some of the lower animals. These creatures die in the act of reproduction, because after Eros has been eliminated through the process of gratification, the death-instinct has a free hand for accomplishing its purposes.

Finally, as we have seen, the ego, by sublimating some of the libido for itself and its purposes, assists the id in its work of mastering the tensions.

CHAPTER FIVE

The Subordinate Relationships of the Ego

THE COMPLEXITY OF our subject-matter must be an excuse for the fact that none of the chapter-headings of this book correspond entirely to their contents, and that in turning to new aspects of the problem, we constantly hark back to matters that have already been dealt with.

As has been said repeatedly, the ego is formed to a great extent out of identifications taking the place of cathexes, on the part of the id which have been abandoned. The earliest of these identifications always fulfill a special office in the ego and stand apart from the rest of the ego in the form of a super-ego. While later on, as it grows stronger, the ego may become more able to withstand the effects of identifications.

The super-ego owes its special position in the ego, or in regard to the ego, to a factor which must be considered from two sides. On the one hand, it was the first identification and one that took place while the ego was still feeble; and on the other hand, it was the heir to the Oedipus complex and thus incorporated into the ego objects of far greater significance than any others.

The super-ego's relation to the subsequent modifications effected in the ego, is roughly that of the primary sexual period in childhood to full-grown sexual activity after puberty. Although it is amenable to every later influence, it preserves, throughout life, the character given to it by its derivation from the father-complex. Namely, the capacity to stand apart from the ego and to rule it.

It is a memorial of the former weakness and dependence of the ego that the mature ego remains subject to its domination. As the child was once compelled to obey its parents, so the ego submits to the categorical imperative pronounced by its super-ego.

The descent of the super-ego, from the first object-cathexes of the id from the Oedipus complex, however, signifies even more for it. This descent, as we have already described, connects it with the phylogenetic acquisitions of the id and makes it a reincarnation of former ego-structures that have left their precipitates behind in the id. Thus, the super-ego is always in close touch with the id and can act as its representative, in relation to the ego. It reaches deep down into the id and is, for that reason, farther from consciousness than the ego.

We can best appreciate these relations by turning our attention to certain clinical facts, which have long since lost their novelty, but that still await theoretical discussion.

There are certain people who behave in a quite peculiar fashion during the work of analysis. When one speaks hopefully to them or expresses satisfaction with the progress of the treatment, they show signs of discontent and their condition invariably becomes worse. One begins by regarding this as defiance and as an attempt to prove their superiority to the physician, but later one comes to take a deeper and truer view.

One becomes convinced, not only that such people cannot endure any praise or appreciation, but that they react inversely to the progress of the treatment. Every partial solution that ought to result (and in other people does result) in an improvement or a temporary suspension of symptoms produces, in them, for the time being, an exacerbation of their illness. They get worse during treatment instead of getting better. They exhibit the so called negative therapeutic reaction.

There is no doubt that something in these people sets itself against their recovery and dreads its approach, as though it were a danger. We are accustomed to say that the need for illness has got the upper hand in them, over the desire for health. If we analyze this resistance in the usual way, then, even after we have subtracted from it the defiant attitude towards the physician and the fixation on the various kinds of advantage that the patient derives from the illness, the greater part of it still remains.

This reveals itself as the most powerful of all obstacles to recovery, more powerful even than such familiar ones as narcissistic inaccessibility, the assumption of a negative attitude towards the physician, or a clinging to the advantages of the illness.

In the end, we come to see that we are dealing with what may be called a moral factor—a sense of guilt that is finding atonement in the illness and is refusing to give up the penalty of suffering. We are justified in regarding this rather disheartening explanation as conclusive. But as far as the patient is concerned, this sense of guilt is dumb; it does not tell him he is guilty; he does not feel guilty. He simply feels ill.

This sense of guilt   expresses itself only as a resistance to recovery, which is extremely difficult to overcome. It is also particularly difficult to convince the patient that this motive lies behind his continuing to be ill; he holds fast to the more obvious explanation—that treatment by analysis is not the right remedy for his case.

The battle with the obstacle of an unconscious sense of guilt is not made easy for the analyst. Nothing can be done against it directly, and nothing indirectly —only the slow procedure of unmasking its unconscious repressed roots, and gradually changing it into a conscious sense of guilt. One has a special opportunity for influencing it when this Ucs sense of guilt is a 'borrowed' one (when it is the product of an identification with some other person who was once the object of an erotic cathexis).

When the sense of guilt has been adopted in this way, it is often the sole remaining trace of the abandoned love-relation and not at all easy to recognize as such. (The likeness between this process and what happens in melancholia is unmistakable.)

If one can unmask this former object-cathexis behind the Ucs sense of guilt, the therapeutic success is often brilliant. Otherwise, the outcome of one's efforts is by no means certain. It depends principally on the intensity of the sense of guilt; there is often no counteracting force of similar strength that the treatment can put in motion against it.

Perhaps it may depend, too, on whether the personality of the analyst allows of the patient's putting him in the place of his ego-ideal; and this involves a temptation for the analyst to play the part of prophet, savior, and redeemer to the patient. Because the rules of analysis are diametrically opposed to the physician's making use of his personality in any such manner, it must be honestly confessed that here we have another limitation to the effectiveness of analysis. After all, analysis does not set out to abolish the possibility of morbid reactions, but to give the patient's ego freedom to choose one way or the other.

The description we have given applies to the most extreme instances of this state of affairs. In a lesser measure, this factor has to be reckoned with in very many cases, perhaps in all severe cases of neurosis. In fact, it may be precisely this element in the situation—the attitude of the ego-ideal—that determines the severity of a neurotic illness. We shall not hesitate, therefore, to discuss rather more fully the way in which the sense of guilt expresses itself under different conditions.

An explanation of the normal conscious sense of guilt (conscience) presents no difficulties. It is due to tension between the ego and the ego-ideal and is the expression of a condemnation of the ego pronounced by its criticizing function. The feelings of inferiority so well known in neurotics are presumably closely related to it. In two very familiar maladies, the sense of guilt is over-strongly conscious. In them, the ego-ideal displays particular severity and often rages against the ego with the utmost cruelty. The attitude of the ego-ideal in these two diseases (obsessional neurosis and melancholia), presents, alongside of this similarity, differences that are no less significant.

In certain forms of obsessional neurosis, the sense of guilt expresses itself loudly but cannot justify itself to the ego. Consequently, the patient's ego rebels against this imputation of guilt and seeks the physician's support in repudiating it. It would be folly to acquiesce in this, for to do so would have no effect. Analysis shows that the super-ego is being influenced by processes that have remained hidden from the ego.

It is possible to discover the repressed impulses that really occasion the sense of guilt. The super-ego is thus proved to have known more than the ego about the unconscious id.

In melancholia, the impression that the superego has obtained a hold upon consciousness is even stronger. But, in this case the ego ventures no objection. It admits the guilt and submits to the punishment. The explanation of this difference is plain. In the obsessional neurosis, the reprehensible impulses that are being criticized by the super-ego have never formed part of the ego; while, in melancholia, the object of the super-ego's wrath has become part of the ego through identification.

It is certainly not clear why the sense of guilt reaches such an extraordinary intensity in these two neurotic disorders. And indeed, the main problem presented in this state of affairs lies in another direction. We shall postpone discussion of it until we have dealt with the other cases in which the sense of guilt remains unconscious.

It is essentially in hysteria and in states of a hysterical type that this condition is found. The mechanism by which the sense of guilt is kept unconscious is easy to discover. The hysterical type of ego defends itself from the painful perception that the criticisms of its super-ego threaten to produce in it)by the same means that it uses to defend itself from an unendurable object-cathexis -by an act of repression).

It is the ego, therefore, that is responsible for the sense of guilt remaining unconscious. We know that, as a rule, the ego carries out repressions in the service and at the behest of its super-ego. In this case, it has turned the same weapon against its harsh taskmaster.

In the obsessional neurosis, as we know, the phenomena of reaction-formation predominate. Here, the ego contents itself with keeping at a distance the material to which the sense of guilt refers.

One may go further and venture the hypothesis that a great part of the sense of guilt must normally remain unconscious, because the origin of conscience is closely connected with the Oedipus complex, which belongs to the unconscious.

If anyone were inclined to put forward the paradoxical proposition that the normal man is not only far more immoral than he believes, but also far more moral than he has any idea of, psychoanalysis, which is responsible for the first half of the assertion, would have no objection to raise against the second half. (This proposition is only apparently a paradox; it simply states that human nature has a far greater capacity, both for good and for evil, than it thinks it has, i.e. than it is aware of through the conscious perceptions of the ego.)

It was a surprise to find that exacerbation of this Ucs sense of guilt could turn people into criminals. However, it is undoubtedly a fact. In many criminals, especially youthful ones, it is possible to detect a very powerful sense of guilt that existed before the crime, and is, therefore, its result rather than its motive. As if it had been a relief to be able to fasten this unconscious sense of guilt on to something real and immediate.

In all these situations, the super-ego displays its independence of the conscious ego and the closeness of its relations with the unconscious id. And now, having regard to the importance we ascribed to preconscious verbal residues in the ego, the question arises whether the super-ego, if it is in part unconscious, can consist in such verbal images; or, if not, in what it does consist.

Our answer, though it does not carry us very far, will be that it cannot possibly be disputed that the super-ego, no less than the ego, is derived from auditory impressions. It is part of the ego and remains, to a great extent, accessible to consciousness by way of these verbal images (concepts, abstractions). However, the cathectic energy of these elements of the superego does not originate from the auditory perceptions, instruction, reading, etc., but from sources in the id.

The question we postponed answering runs thus: How is it that the super-ego manifests itself essentially as a sense of guilt (or rather, as criticism, for the sense of guilt is the perception in the ego which corresponds to the criticism) and at the same time develops such extraordinary harshness and severity towards the ego?

If we turn to melancholia first, we find that the excessively strong super-ego, which has obtained a hold upon consciousness, rages against the ego with merciless fury, as if it had taken possession of the whole of the sadism available in the person concerned. Following our view of sadism, we should say that the destructive component had entrenched itself in the super-ego and turned against the ego.

What is now holding sway in the super-ego is a pure culture of the death-instinct. In fact, it often enough succeeds in driving the ego into death, if the latter does not protect itself from the tyrant in time by a revulsion into mania.

The reproaches of conscience in certain forms of obsessional neurosis are just as painful and tormenting, but here the situation is less perspicuous. It is remarkable that the obsessional neurotic, in contrast to the melancholiac, never takes the step of self-destruction. He is as if immune against the danger of suicide, and is far better protected from it than the hysteric.

We can see that what guarantees the safety of the ego is the fact that the object has been retained. In the obsessional neurosis, it has become possible, through a regression to the pre-genital organization, for the love-impulses to transform themselves into impulses of aggression against the object. Here again the instinct of destruction has been set free and it aims at destroying the object, or at least it appears to have this aim.

These tendencies have not been adopted by the ego. It struggles against them with reaction-formations and precautionary measures, and they remain in the id. The super-ego, however, behaves as if the ego were responsible for them and shows, by its zeal in chastising these destructive intentions, that they are no mere semblance evoked by regression, but an actual substitution of hate for love.

Helpless in either direction, the ego defends itself vainly, alike against the instigations of the murderous id and against the reproaches of the punishing conscience. It succeeds in holding in check, at least, the most brutal actions of both sides. The first outcome is interminable self-torment, and eventually there follows a systematic torturing of the object, in so far as it is within reach.

The activity of the dangerous death-instincts within the individual organism is dealt with in various ways. In part, they are rendered harmless by being fused with erotic components. In part, they are diverted towards the external world in the form of aggression, while, for the most part, they undoubtedly continue their inner work unhindered.

How is it then that in melancholia, the super-ego can become a kind of gathering-place for the death-instincts?

From the point of view of morality, the control and restriction of instinct, it may be said of the id that it is totally non-moral; of the ego that it strives to be moral; and of the super-ego that it can be hyper-moral and then becomes as ruthless as only the id can be.

It is remarkable that the more a man checks his aggressive tendencies towards others, the more tyrannical, that is aggressive, he becomes in his ego-ideal. The ordinary view sees the situation the other way round: the standard set up by the ego-ideal seems to be the motive for the suppression of aggressiveness.

The fact remains, however, as we have stated it— the more a man controls his aggressiveness, the more intense become the aggressive tendencies of his ego-ideal against his ego. It is like a displacement, a turning around upon the self. But even ordinary, normal morality has a harshly restraining, cruelly prohibiting quality. It is from this, indeed, that the conception arises of an inexorable higher being who metes out punishment.

I cannot go further in my consideration of these questions without introducing a fresh assumption. The super-ego arises, as we know, from identification with the father, regarded as a model. Every such identification is in the nature of a desexualization or even a sublimation.

It now seems as though when a transformation of this kind takes place, there occurs, at the same time, an instinctual defusion. After sublimation, the erotic component no longer has the power to bind the whole of the destructive elements that were previously combined with it. Instead, these are released in the form of inclinations to aggression and destruction. This defusion would be the source of the general character of harshness and cruelty exhibited by the ideal. Its dictatorial: "Thou shalt."

Let us again consider the obsessional neurosis for a moment. The state of affairs is different here. The defusion of love into aggressiveness has not been effected by the agency of the ego, but is the result of a regression that has come about in the id. This process has extended beyond the id to the super-ego, which now increases its tyranny over the innocent ego.

It would seem, however, that in this case no less than in that of melancholia, the ego, having gained possession of the libido by means of identification, is punished for doing so by the super-ego through the instrumentality of the aggressiveness, which had before been mixed with the libido.

Our ideas about the ego are beginning to clear, and its various relationships are gaining distinctness. We now see the ego in its strength and in its weaknesses. It is entrusted with important functions. By virtue of its relation to the perceptual system, it arranges the processes of the mind in a temporal order and tests their correspondence with reality. By interposing the process of thinking, it secures a postponement of motor discharges and controls the avenues to motility. This last office is, to be sure, a question more of form than of fact.

In the matter of action, the ego's position is like that of a constitutional monarch, without whose sanction no law can be passed, but who hesitates long before imposing a veto on any measure put forward by Parliament.

All the experiences of life that originate from without enrich the ego. The id, however, is another outer world to it, which it strives to bring into subjection to itself. It withdraws libido from the id and transforms the object-cathexes of the id into ego-constructions. With the aid of the super-ego, though in a manner that is still obscure to us, it draws upon the experiences of past ages stored in the id.

There are two paths by which the contents of the id can penetrate into the ego. The one is direct, the other leads by way of the ego-ideal; which of these two paths they take may, for many mental activities, be of decisive importance. The ego develops from perceiving instincts to controlling them, from obeying instincts to curbing them.

In this achievement, a large share is taken by the ego-ideal, which is partly a reaction formation against the instinctual processes in the id. Psychoanalysis is an instrument to enable the ego to push its conquest of the id further still.

From the other point of view, however, we see this same ego as a poor creature owing service to three masters and consequently menaced by three dangers: from the external world, from the libido of the id, and from the severity of the super-ego. Three kinds of anxiety correspond to these three dangers, because anxiety is the expression of a recoil from danger.

Like the dweller in a borderland that it is, the ego tries to mediate between the world and the id, to make the id comply with the world's demands and, by means of muscular activity, to accommodate the world to the id's desires.

In point of fact, it behaves like the physician during treatment by analysis. It offers itself to the id as a libidinal object, in view of its power of adaptation to the real world, and aims at attaching the id's libido to itself. It is not only the ally of the id; it is also a submissive slave who courts the love of his master.

Whenever possible, it tries to remain on good terms with the id. It draws the veil of its Pcs rationalizations over the id's Ucs demands; it pretends that the id is showing obedience to the mandates of reality, even when in fact it is remaining obdurate and immovable; it throws a disguise over the id's conflicts with reality and, if possible, over its conflicts with the super-ego too. Its position midway between the id and reality tempts it only too often to become sycophantic, opportunist, and false—like a politician who sees the truth but wants to keep his place in popular favor.

Toward the two classes of instincts, the ego's attitude is not impartial. Its work of identification and sublimation gives the death-instincts in the id assistance in mastering the libido. In so doing, it incurs the risk of itself becoming the object of the death-instincts and of perishing. In order to be able to help in this way, it has to become flooded with libido itself; it thus becomes the representative of Eros and thenceforward desires to live and to be loved.

But since the ego's work of sublimation results in a defusion of the instincts and a liberation of the aggressive instincts in the super-ego, its struggle against the libido exposes it to the danger of maltreatment and death. In suffering under the attacks of the super-ego, or perhaps even succumbing to them, the ego is meeting with a fate like that of protozoa that are destroyed by the products of disintegration that they themselves have created. From the economic point of view, the morality that functions in the super-ego seems to be a similar product of disintegration.

Among the subordinate relationships in which the ego stands, that to the super-ego is perhaps the most interesting.

The ego is the true abode of anxiety. Threatened by dangers from three directions, it develops the flight-reflex by withdrawing its own cathexis from the menacing perception or from the equally dreaded process in the id, discharging it as anxiety. This primitive reaction is later replaced by the introduction of protective cathexes (the mechanism of the phobias). What it is that the ego fears, either from an external or from a libidinal danger, cannot be specified. We know that it is in the nature of an overthrow or of extinction, but it is not determined by analysis. The ego is simply obeying the warning of the pleasure-principle.

On the other hand, we can tell what lies hidden behind the ego's dread of the super-ego, its fear of conscience. The higher being that later became the ego-ideal, once threatened the ego with castration, and this dread of castration is probably the kernel round which the subsequent fear of conscience has gathered; it is this dread that persists as the fear of conscience.

The phrase, "Every fear is ultimately the fear of death," has hardly any meaning; at any rate it cannot be justified. It seems to me, on the contrary, perfectly correct to distinguish the fear of death from dread of an external object (objective anxiety) and from neurotic libidinal anxiety. It presents a difficult problem to psychoanalysis, for death is an abstract concept, with a negative content, for which no unconscious correlative can be found.

It would seem that the mechanism of the fear of death can only be that the ego relinquishes its narcissistic libidinal cathexis in a very large measure. In other words, it gives up itself, just as it gives up some *external* object in other cases in which it feels anxiety. I believe that the fear of death concerns an interplay between the ego and the super-ego.

We know that the fear of death makes its appearance under two conditions (which, moreover, are entirely analogous to the other situations in which anxiety develops), namely, as a reaction to an external danger and as an internal process, as for instance in melancholia. Once again, a neurotic manifestation may help us to understand a normal one.

The fear of death in melancholia only admits of one explanation: that the ego gives itself up because it feels itself hated and persecuted by the super-ego, instead of loved. To the ego, therefore, living means the same as being loved—being loved by the super-ego, which here again appears as the representative of the id.

The super-ego fulfils the same function of protecting and saving that which was fulfilled in earlier days by the father and later by Providence or destiny. But, when the ego finds itself in overwhelming danger of a real order, which it believes itself unable to overcome by its own strength, it is bound to draw the same conclusion.

It sees itself deserted by all the forces of protection and lets itself die. Here, moreover, is once again the same situation as that which underlay the first great anxiety-state of birth and the infantile anxiety of longing for an absent person—the anxiety of separation from the protecting mother.

These considerations enable us to conceive of the fear of death, like the fear of conscience, as a development of the fear of castration. The great significance the sense of guilt has in the neuroses makes it conceivable that ordinary neurotic anxiety is reinforced, in severe cases, by a development of anxiety between the ego and the super-ego (fear of castration, of conscience, of death).

The id, to which we finally come back, has no means of showing the ego either love or hate. It cannot say what it wants; it has achieved no unity of will. Eros and the death-instinct struggle within it. We have seen with what weapons the one group of instincts defends itself against the other. It would be possible to picture the id as under the domination of the mute but powerful death-instincts, which desire to be at peace and (as the pleasure-principle demands) to put Eros, the intruder, to rest; but that would be to run the risk of valuing too cheaply the part played by Eros.

THE FUTURE OF AN
ILLUSION

CONTENTS

PREFACE

Illusions commend themselves to us because they save us pain and allow us to enjoy pleasure instead. We must therefore accept it without complaint when they sometimes collide with a bit of reality, against which they are dashed to pieces. Sigmund Freud

THE FUTURE OF AN ILLUSION

WHEN ONE HAS lived for quite a long time in a particular civilization and has often tried to discover what its origins were and along what path it has developed, one sometimes also feels tempted to take a glance in the other direction and to ask what further fate lies before it and what transformations it is destined to undergo. But one soon finds that the value of such an enquiry is diminished from the outset by several factors. Above all, because there are only a few people who can survey human activity in its full compass. Most people have been obliged to restrict themselves to a single, or a few, fields of it.

But the less a man knows about the past and the present, the more insecure must prove to be his judgment of the future. And there is the further difficulty that precisely in a judgment of this kind, the subjective expectations of the individual play a part which it is difficult to assess; and these turn out to be dependent on purely personal factors in his own experience, on the greater or lesser optimism of his attitude to life, as it has been dictated for him by his temperament or by his success or failure.

Finally, the curious fact makes itself felt that in general people experience their present naïvely, as it were, without being able to form an estimate of its contents; they have first to put themselves at a distance from it--the present, that is to say, must have become the past--before it can yield points of vantage from which to judge the future.

Thus, anyone who gives way to the temptation to deliver an opinion on the probable future of our civilization will do well to remind himself of the difficulties I have just pointed out, as well as of the uncertainty that attaches quite generally to any prophecy. It follows from this, so far as I am concerned, that I shall make a hasty retreat before a task that is too great, and shall promptly seek out the small tract of territory which has claimed my attention hitherto, as soon as I have deter- mined its position in the general scheme of things.

Human civilization, by which I mean all those respects in which human life has raised itself above its animal status and differs from the life of beasts—and I scorn to distinguish between culture and civilization—presents, as we know, two aspects to the observer. It includes, on the one hand, all the knowledge and capacity that men have acquired in order to control the forces of nature and extract its wealth for the satisfaction of human needs, and, on the other hand, all the regulations necessary in order to adjust the relations of men to one another and especially the distribution of the available wealth.

The two trends of civilization are not independent of each other: firstly, because the mutual relations of men are profoundly influenced by the amount of instinctual satisfaction which the existing wealth makes possible; secondly, because an individual man can himself come to function as wealth in relation to another one, in so far as the other person makes use of his capacity for work, or chooses him as a sexual object; and thirdly, moreover, because every individual is virtually an enemy of civilization, though civilization is supposed to be an object of universal human interest.

It is remarkable that, little as men are able to exist in isolation, they should nevertheless feel as a heavy burden the sacrifices which civilization expects of them in order to make a communal life possible. Thus, civilization has to be defended against the individual—and its regulations, institutions, and commands are directed to that task. They aim not only at effecting a certain distribution of wealth but at maintaining that distribution; indeed, they have to protect everything that contributes to the conquest of nature and the production of wealth against men's hostile impulses.

Human creations are easily destroyed, and science and technology, which have built them up, can also be used for their annihilation.

One thus gets an impression that civilization is something which was imposed on a resisting majority by a minority which understood how to obtain possession of the means to power and coercion. It is, of course, natural to assume that these difficulties are not inherent in the nature of civilization itself, but are determined by the imperfections of the cultural forms which have so far been developed. And in fact it is not difficult to
indicate those defects.

While mankind has made continual advances in its control over nature, and may expect to make still greater ones, it is not possible to establish with certainty that a similar advance has been made in the management of human affairs; and probably at all periods, just as now once again, many people have asked themselves whether what little civilization has thus acquired is indeed worth defending at all.

One would think that a re-ordering of human relations should be possible, which would remove the sources of dissatisfaction with civilization by renouncing coercion and the suppression of the instincts, so that, undisturbed by internal discord, men might devote themselves to the acquisition of wealth and its enjoyment. That would be the golden age, but it is questionable if such a state of affairs can be realized.

It seems rather that every civilization must be built up on coercion and renunciation of instinct; it does not even seem certain that if coercion were to cease, the majority of human beings would be prepared to perform the work necessary for acquiring new wealth. One has, I think, to reckon with the fact that there are present in all men destructive, and therefore anti-social and anti-cultural, trends and that in a great number of people these are strong enough to determine their behavior in human society.

This psychological fact has a decisive importance for our judgment of human civilization. Whereas we might, at first, think that its essence lies in controlling nature for the purpose of acquiring wealth and that the dangers which threaten it could be eliminated through a suitable distribution of that wealth among men, it now seems that the emphasis has moved over from the material to the mental.

The decisive question is whether and to what extent it is possible to lessen the burden of the instinctual sacrifices imposed on men, to reconcile men to those which must necessarily remain and to provide a compensation for them. It is just as impossible to do without control of the mass by a minority as it is to dispense with coercion in the work of civilization. For masses are lazy and unintelligent; they have no love for instinctual renunciation, and they are not to be convinced by argument of its inevitability; and the individuals composing them support one another in giving free rein to their indiscipline. It is only through the influence of individuals who can set an example and whom masses recognize as their leaders that they can be induced to perform the work and undergo the renunciations on which the existence of civilization depends.

All is well if these leaders are persons who possess superior insight into the necessities of life and who have risen to the height of mastering their own instinctual wishes. But there is a danger that in order not to lose their influence they may give way to the mass more than it gives way to them; and it therefore seems necessary that they shall be independent of the mass by having means to power at their disposal. To put it briefly, there are two widespread human characteristics responsible for the fact that the regulations of civilization can only be maintained by a certain degree of coercion—namely, that men are not spontaneously fond of work and that arguments are of no avail against their passions.

I know the objections that will be raised against these assertions. It will be said that the characteristic of human masses depicted here, which is supposed to prove that coercion cannot be dispensed with in the work of civilization, is itself only the result of defects in the cultural regulations, owing to which men have become embittered, revengeful, and inaccessible.

New generations, who have been brought up in kindness and taught to have a high opinion of reason, and who have experienced the benefits of civilization at an early age, will have a different attitude to it. They will feel it as a possession of their very own and will be ready for its sake to make the sacrifices as regards work and instinctual satisfaction that are necessary for its preservation. They will be able to do without coercion and will differ little from their leaders. If no culture has so far produced human masses of such a quality, it is because no culture has yet devised regulations that will influence men in this way; in particular from childhood onwards.

It may be doubted whether it is possible at all, or at any rate as yet, at the present stage of our control over nature, to set up cultural regulations of this kind. It may be asked where the number of superior, unswerving, and disinterested leaders are to come from who are to act as educators of the future generations; and it may be alarming to think of the enormous amount of coercion that will inevitably be required before these intentions can be carried out.

The grandeur of the plan and its importance for the future of human civilization cannot be disputed. It is securely based on the psychological discovery that man is equipped with the most varied instinctual dispositions, whose ultimate course is determined by the experiences of early childhood, but for the same reason the limitations of man's capacity for education set bounds to the effectiveness of such a transformation in his culture.

One may question whether, and in what degree, it would be possible for a different cultural environment to do away with the two characteristics of human masses which make the guidance of human affairs so difficult. The experiment has not yet been made. Probably a certain percentage of mankind (owing to a pathological disposition or an excess of instinctual strength) will always remain asocial; but if it were feasible merely to reduce the majority that is hostile towards civilization today into a minority, a great deal would have been accomplished—perhaps all that can be accomplished.

I should not like to give the impression that I have strayed a long way from the line laid down for my enquiry. Let me therefore give an express assurance that I have not the least intention of making judgments on the great experiment in civilization that is now in progress in the vast country that stretches between Europe and Asia. I have neither the special knowledge nor the capacity to decide on its practicability, to test the expediency of the methods employed or to measure the width of the inevitable gap between intention and execution. What is in preparation there is unfinished and therefore eludes an investigation for which our own long-consolidated civilization affords us material.

We have slipped unawares out of the economic field into the field of psychology. At first we were tempted to look for the assets of civilization in the available wealth and in the regulations for its distribution. But with the recognition that every civilization rests on a compulsion to work and a renunciation of instinct and, therefore, inevitably provokes opposition from those affected by these demands, it has become clear that civilization cannot consist principally or solely in wealth itself and the means of acquiring it and the arrangements for its distribution; for these things are threatened by the rebelliousness and destructive mania of the participants in civilization. Alongside of wealth we now come upon the means by which civilization can be defended—measures of coercion and other measures that are intended to reconcile men to it and to recompense them for their sacrifices. These latter may be described as the mental assets of civilization.

For the sake of a uniform terminology, we will describe the fact that an instinct cannot be satisfied as a *frustration*, the regulation by which this frustration is established as a *prohibition*, and the condition which is produced by the prohibition as a *privation*. The first step is to distinguish between privations that affect everyone and privations that do not affect everyone but only groups, classes, or even single individuals. The former are the earliest; with the prohibitions that established them, civilization—who knows how many thousands of years ago—began to detach man from his primordial animal condition.

We have found, to our surprise, that these privations are still operative and still form the kernel of hostility to civilization. The instinctual wishes that suffer under them are born afresh with every child; there is a class of people, the neurotics, who already react to these frustrations with asocial behavior.

Among these instinctual wishes are those of incest, cannibalism, and lust for killing. It sounds strange to place alongside one another wishes that everyone seems united in repudiating and others about which there is so much lively dispute in our civilization as to whether they shall be permitted or frustrated; but psychologically it is justifiable to do so. Nor is the attitude of civilization to these oldest instinctual wishes by any means uniform.

Cannibalism alone seems to be universally proscribed and—to the non-psycho-analytic view—to have been completely surmounted. The strength of the incestuous wishes can still be detected behind the prohibition against them; and under certain conditions killing is still practiced, and indeed commanded, by our civilization. It is possible that cultural developments lie ahead of us in which the satisfaction of yet other wishes, which are entirely permissible today, will appear just as unacceptable as cannibalism does now.

These earliest instinctual renunciations already involve a psychological factor that remains important for all further instinctual renunciations, as well. It is not true that the human mind has undergone no development since the earliest times and that, in contrast to the advances of science and technology, it is the same today as it was at the beginning of history. We can point out one of these mental advances at once. It is in keeping with the course of human development that external coercion gradually becomes internalized; for a special mental agency, man's super-ego, takes it over and includes it among its commandments. Every child presents this process of transformation to us; only by that means does it become a moral and social being.

Such a strengthening of the super-ego is a most precious cultural asset in the psychological field. Those in whom it has taken place are turned from being opponents of civilization into being its vehicles. The greater their number in a cultural unit, the more secure is its culture and the more it can dispense with external measures of coercion.

Now, the degree of this internalization differs greatly between the various instinctual prohibitions. As regards the earliest cultural demands, which I have mentioned, the internalization seems to have been very extensively achieved if we leave out of account the unwelcome exception of the neurotics. But the case is altered when we turn to the other instinctual claims. Here we observe with surprise and concern that a majority of people obey the cultural prohibitions on these points only under the pressure of external coercion—that is, only where that coercion can make itself effective and so long as it is to be feared.

This is also true of what are known as the moral demands of civilization, which likewise apply to everyone. Most of one's experiences of man's moral untrustworthiness fall into this category. There are countless civilized people who would shrink from murder or incest but who do not deny themselves the satisfaction of their avarice, their aggressive urges or their sexual lusts, and who do not hesitate to injure other people by lies, fraud, and calumny, so long as they can remain unpunished for it; and this, no doubt, has always been so through many ages of civilization.

If we turn to those restrictions that apply only to certain classes of society, we meet with a state of things which is flagrant and which has always been recognized. It is to be expected that these underprivileged classes will envy the favored ones their privileges and will do all they can to free themselves from their own surplus of privation. Where this is not possible, a permanent measure of discontent will persist within the culture concerned and this can lead to dangerous revolts.

If, however, a culture has not gone beyond a point at which the satisfaction of one portion of its participants depends upon the suppression of another, and perhaps larger portion—and this is the case in all present day cultures—it is understandable that the suppressed people should develop an intense hostility towards a culture whose existence they make possible by their work, but in whose wealth they have too small a share.

In such conditions, an internalization of the cultural prohibitions among the suppressed people is not to be expected. On the contrary, they are not prepared to acknowledge the prohibitions; they are intent on destroying the culture itself, and possibly even on doing away with the postulates on which it is based.

The hostility of these classes to civilization is so obvious that it has caused the more latent hostility of the social strata that are better provided for, to be overlooked. It goes without saying that a civilization which leaves so large a number of its participants unsatisfied and drives them into revolt, neither has nor deserves the prospect of a lasting existence.

The extent to which a civilization's precepts have been internalized—to express it popularly and unpsychologically: the moral level of its participants—comes into consideration in estimating a civilization's value. There are in addition its assets in the shape of ideals and artistic creations—that is, the satisfactions that can be derived from those sources.

People will be only too readily inclined to include among the psychical assets of a culture its ideals—its estimates of what achievements are the highest and the most to be striven after. It will seem at first as though these ideals would determine the achievements of the cultural unit; but the actual course of events would appear to be that the ideals are based on the first achievements, which have been made possible by a combination of the culture's internal gifts and external circumstances; and that these first achievements are then held by the ideal as something to be carried further.

The satisfaction that the ideal offers to the participants in the culture is thus of a narcissistic nature. It rests on their pride in what has already been successfully achieved. To make this satisfaction complete calls for a comparison with other cultures which have aimed at different achievements and have developed different ideals.

On the strength of these differences, every culture claims the right to look down on the rest. In this way, cultural ideals become a source of discord and enmity between different cultural units, as can be seen most clearly in the case of nations.

The narcissistic satisfaction provided by the cultural ideal is also among the forces that are successful in combating the hostility to culture, within the cultural unit. This satisfaction can be shared in, not only by the favored classes that enjoy the benefits of the culture, but also by the suppressed ones, since the right to despise the people outside it compensates them for the wrongs they suffer within their own unit. No doubt one is a wretched plebeian, harassed by debts and military service; but, to make up for it, one is a Roman citizen, one has one's share in the task of ruling other nations and dictating their laws.

This identification of the suppressed classes with the class who rules and exploits them is, however, only part of a larger whole. For, on the other hand, the suppressed classes can be emotionally attached to their masters; in spite of their hostility to them they may see in them their ideals; unless such relations of a fundamentally satisfying kind subsisted, it would be impossible to understand how a number of civilizations have survived so long in spite of the justifiable hostility of large human masses.

A different kind of satisfaction is afforded by art to the participants in a cultural unit, though as a rule it remains inaccessible to the masses, who are engaged in exhausting work and have not enjoyed any personal education. As we discovered long since, art offers substitutive satisfactions for the oldest and still most deeply felt cultural renunciations; and for that reason, it serves as nothing else does to reconcile a man to the sacrifices he has made on behalf of civilization.

On the other hand, the creations of art heighten his feelings of identification, of which every cultural unit stands in so much need, by providing an occasion for sharing highly valued emotional experiences. And when those creations picture the achievements of his particular culture and bring to his mind its ideals in an impressive manner, they also minister to his narcissistic satisfaction.

No mention has yet been made of what is perhaps the most important item in the psychical inventory of a civilization. This consists in its religious ideas in the widest sense—in other words (which will be justified later) in its illusions.

In what does the peculiar value of religious ideas lie?

We have spoken of the hostility to civilization that is produced by the pressure that civilization exercises, the renunciations of instinct which it demands. If one imagines its prohibitions lifted—if, then, one may take any woman one pleases as a sexual object; if one may without hesitation kill one's rival for her love or anyone else who stands in one's way; if, too, one can carry off any of the other man's belongings without asking—how splendid, what a string of satisfactions one's life would be!

True, one soon comes across the first difficulty: everyone else has exactly the same wishes as I have and will treat me with no more consideration than I treat him. And so in reality, only one person could be made unrestrictedly happy by such a removal of the restrictions of civilization, and he would be a tyrant, a dictator, who had seized all the means to power. And even he would have every reason to wish that the others would observe at least one cultural commandment: 'thou shall not kill.'

But how ungrateful, how short-sighted after all, to strive for the abolition of civilization! What would then remain would be a state of nature, and that would be far harder to bear. It is true that nature would not demand any restrictions of instinct from us, she would let us do as we liked; but she has her own particularly effective method of restricting us. She destroys us—coldly, cruelly, relentlessly, as it seems to us, and possibly through the very things that occasioned our satisfaction. It was precisely because of these dangers with which nature threatens us that we came together and created civilization, which is also, among other things, intended to make our communal life possible.

For the principal task of civilization, its actual raison d'être, is to defend us against nature. We all know that in many ways, civilization does this fairly well already, and clearly as time goes on it will do it much better. But no one is under the illusion that nature has already been vanquished; and few dare hope that she will ever be entirely subjected to man. There are the elements, which seem to mock at all human control: the earth, which quakes and is torn apart and buries all human life and its works; water, which deluges and drowns everything in a turmoil; storms, which blow everything before them. There are diseases, which we have only recently recognized as attacks by other organisms; and finally there is the painful riddle of death, against which no medicine has yet been found, nor probably will be.

With these forces, nature rises up against us, majestic, cruel, and inexorable; she brings to our mind once more our weakness and helplessness, which we thought to escape through the work of civilization. One of the few gratifying and exalting impressions mankind can offer is when, in the face of an elemental catastrophe, it forgets the discordances of its civilization and all its internal difficulties and animosities, and recalls the great common task of preserving itself against the superior power of nature.

For the individual, too, life is hard to bear, just as it is for mankind in general. The civilization in which he participates imposes some amount of privation on him, and other men bring him a measure of suffering, either in spite of the precepts of his civilization or because of its imperfections. To this are added the injuries which untamed nature—he calls it Fate—inflicts on him.

One might suppose that this condition of things would result in a permanent state of anxious expectation in him and a severe injury to his natural narcissism. We know already how the individual reacts to the injuries that civilization and other men inflict on him: he develops a corresponding degree of resistance to the regulations of civilization and of hostility to it. But how does he defend himself against the superior powers of nature, of Fate, which threaten him as they threaten all the rest?

Civilization relieves him of this task; it performs it in the same way for all alike; and it is noteworthy that in this, almost all civilizations act alike. Civilization does not call a halt in the task of defending man against nature. It merely pursues it by other means. The task is a manifold one. Man's self-regard, seriously menaced, calls for consolation; life and the universe must be robbed of their terrors; moreover his curiosity, moved, it is true, by the strongest practical interest, demands an answer.

A great deal is already gained with the first step: the humanization of nature. Impersonal forces and destinies cannot be approached; they remain eternally remote. But if the elements have passions that rage as they do in our own soul;, if death itself is not something spontaneous but the violent act of an evil Will; if everywhere in nature there are beings around us of a kind that we know in our own society, then we can breathe freely, can feel at home in the uncanny, and can deal by psychical means with our senseless anxiety. We are still defenseless, perhaps, but we are no longer helplessly paralyzed; we can at least react.

Perhaps, indeed, we are not even defenseless. We can apply the same methods against these violent supermen outside that we employ in our own society; we can try to adjure them, to appease them, to bribe them, and, by so influencing them, we may rob them of a part of their power. A replacement like this of natural science by psychology not only provides immediate relief, but also points the way to a further mastering of the situation. For this situation is nothing new. It has an infantile prototype, of which it is in fact only the continuation.

For once before one has found oneself in a similar state of helplessness: as a small child, in relation to one's parents. One had reason to fear them, and especially one's father; and yet one was sure of his protection against the dangers one knew. Thus it was natural to assimilate the two situations. Here, too, wishing played its part, as it does in dream-life. The sleeper may be seized with a presentiment of death, which threatens to place him in the grave. But the dream-work knows how to select a condition that will turn even that dreaded event into a wish-fulfillment: the dreamer sees himself in an ancient Etruscan grave which he has climbed down into, happy to find his archaeological interests satisfied.

In the same way, a man makes the forces of nature not simply into persons with whom he can associate as he would with his equals—that would not do justice to the overpowering impression those forces make on him—but he gives them the character of a father. He turns them into gods, following in this, as I have tried to show, not only an infantile prototype, but a phylogenetic one.

In the course of time, the first observations were made of regularity and conformity to law in natural phenomena, and with this the forces of nature lost their human traits. But man's helplessness remains and along with it his longing for his father, and the gods.

The gods retain their threefold task: they must exorcize the terrors of nature, they must reconcile men to the cruelty of Fate, particularly as it is shown in death, and they must compensate them for the sufferings and privations which a civilized life in common has imposed on them. But within these functions there is a gradual displacement of accent. It was observed that the phenomena of nature developed automatically according to internal necessities. Without doubt, the gods were the lords of nature; they had arranged it to be as it was and now they could leave it to itself. Only occasionally, in what are known as miracles, did they intervene in its course, as though to make it plain that they had relinquished nothing of their original sphere of power.

As regards the apportioning of destinies, an unpleasant suspicion persisted that the perplexity and helplessness of the human race could not be remedied. It was here that the gods were most apt to fail. If they themselves created Fate, then their counsels must be deemed inscrutable. The notion dawned on the most gifted people of antiquity that Moira (Fate) stood above the gods and that the gods themselves had their own destinies. And the more autonomous nature became and the more the gods withdrew from it, the more earnestly were all expectations directed to the third function of the gods—the more did morality become their true domain.

It now became the task of the gods to even out the defects and evils of civilization, to attend to the sufferings which men inflict on one another in their life together and to watch over the fulfillment of the precepts of civilization, which men obey so imperfectly. Those precepts themselves were credited with a divine origin; they were elevated beyond human society and were extended to nature and the universe.

And thus a store of ideas is created, born from man's need to make his helplessness tolerable and built up from the material of memories of the helplessness of his own childhood and the childhood of the human race. It can clearly be seen that the possession of these ideas protects him in two directions—against the dangers of nature and Fate, and against the injuries that threaten him from human society itself.

Here is the gist of the matter. Life in this world serves a higher purpose; no doubt it is not easy to guess what that purpose is, but it certainly signifies a perfecting of man's nature. It is probably the spiritual part of man, the soul, which in the course of time has so slowly and unwillingly detached itself from the body that is the object of this elevation and exaltation.

Everything that happens in this world is an expression of the intentions of an intelligence superior to us, which in the end, though its ways and byways are difficult to follow, orders everything for the best—that is, to make it enjoyable for us.

Over each one of us, there watches a benevolent Providence which is only seemingly stern and which will not suffer us to become a plaything of the over mighty and pitiless forces of nature. Death itself is not extinction, is not a return to inorganic lifelessness, but the beginning of a new kind of existence, which lies on the path of development to something higher.

And, looking in the other direction, this view announces that the same moral laws which our civilizations have set up, govern the whole universe as well, except that they are maintained by a supreme court of justice with incomparably more power and consistency. In the end, all good is rewarded and all evil punished, if not actually in this form of life then in the later existences that begin after death. In this way all the terrors, the sufferings, and the hardships of life are destined to be obliterated.

Life after death, which continues life on earth just as the invisible part of the spectrum joins on to the visible part, brings us all the perfection that we may perhaps have missed here. And the superior wisdom which directs this course of things; the infinite goodness that expresses itself in it; the justice that achieves its aim in it—these are the attributes of the divine beings who also created us and the world as a whole, or rather, of the one divine being into which, in our civilization, all the gods of antiquity have been condensed.

The people who first succeeded in concentrating the divine attributes were not a little proud of the advance. It had laid open to view the father who had all along been hidden behind every divine figure as its nucleus. Fundamentally, this was a return to the historical beginnings of the idea of God. Now that God was a single person, man's relations to him could recover the intimacy and intensity of the child's relation to his father. But if one had done so much for one's father, one wanted to have a reward, or at least to be his only beloved child, his Chosen People.

Very much later, pious America laid claim to being 'God's own Country'; and, as regards one of the shapes in which men worship the deity, the claim is undoubtedly valid.

The religious ideas that have been summarized above have of course passed through a long process of development and have been adhered to in various phases by various civilizations. I have singled out one such phase, which roughly corresponds to the final form taken by our present-day white Christian civilization. It is easy to see that not all the parts of this picture tally equally well with one another, that not all the questions that press for an answer receive one, and that it is difficult to dismiss the contradiction of daily experience.

Nevertheless, such as they are, those ideas—ideas which are religious in the widest sense—are prized as the most precious possession of civilization, as the most precious thing it has to offer its participants. It is far more highly prized than all the devices for winning treasures from the earth or providing men with sustenance or preventing their illnesses, and so forth. People feel that life would not be tolerable if they did not attach to these ideas the value that is claimed for them. And now the question arises: what are these ideas in the light of psychology? Whence do they derive the esteem in which they are held? And, to take a further timid step, what is their real worth?

An enquiry that proceeds like a monologue, without interruption, is not altogether free from danger. One is too easily tempted into pushing aside thoughts that threaten to break into it, and in exchange, one is left with a feeling of uncertainty that in the end one tries to keep down by over-decisiveness. I shall therefore imagine that I have an opponent who follows my arguments with mistrust, and here and there I shall allow him to interject some remarks. I hear him say:

"You have repeatedly used the expressions 'civilization creates these religious ideas', 'civilization places them at the disposal of its participants'. There is something about this that sounds strange to me. I cannot myself say why, but it does not sound so natural as it does to say that civilization has made rules about distributing the products of labor or about rights concerning women and children."

I think, all the same, that I am justified in expressing myself in this way. I have tried to show that religious ideas have arisen from the same need as have all the other achievements of civilization: from the necessity of defending oneself against the crushingly superior force of nature.

To this a second motive was added—the urge to rectify the shortcomings of civilization which made themselves painfully felt. Moreover, it is especially apposite to say that civilization gives the individual these ideas, for he finds them there already; they are presented to him ready-made, and he would not be able to discover them for himself.

What he is entering into is the heritage of many generations, and he takes it over as he does the multiplication table, geometry, and similar things. There is indeed a difference in this, but that difference lies elsewhere and I cannot examine it yet.

The feeling of strangeness that you mention may be partly due to the fact that this body of religious ideas is usually put forward as a divine revelation. But this presentation of it is itself a part of the religious system, and it entirely ignores the known historical development of these ideas and their differences in different epochs and civilizations.

"Here is another point, which seems to me to be more important. You argue that the humanization of nature is derived from the need to put an end to man's perplexity and helplessness in the face of its dreaded forces, to get into a relation with them and finally to influence them. But a motive of this kind seems superfluous. Primitive man has no choice; he has no other way of thinking.

"It is natural to him, something innate, as it were, to project his existence outwards into the world and to regard every event which he observes as the manifestation of beings who, at bottom, are like himself. It is his only method of comprehension. And it is by no means self-evident. On the contrary, it is a remarkable coincidence, if by thus indulging his natural disposition he succeeds in satisfying one of his greatest needs."

I do not find that so striking. Do you suppose that human thought has no practical motives, that it is simply the expression of a disinterested curiosity? That is surely very improbable. I believe rather that when man personifies the forces of nature, he is again following an infantile model. He has learned from the persons in his earliest environment that the way to influence them is to establish a relation with them; and so, later on, with the same end in view, he treats everything else that he comes across in the same way as he treated those persons.

Thus I do not contradict your descriptive observation; it is in fact natural to man to personify everything that he wants to understand in order later to control it (psychical mastering as a preparation for physical mastering); but I provide, in addition, a motive and a genesis for this peculiarity of human thinking.

"And now here is yet a third point. You have dealt with the origin of religion once before, in the book *Totem and Taboo*. But there it appeared in a different light. Everything was the son-father relationship. God was the exalted father, and the longing for the father was the root of the need for religion. Since then, it seems, you have discovered the factor of human weakness and helplessness, to which indeed the chief role in the formation of religion is generally assigned, and now you transpose everything that was once the father complex into terms of helplessness. May I ask you to explain this transformation?"

With pleasure. I was only waiting for this invitation. But is it really a transformation? In *Totem and Taboo* it was not my purpose to explain the origin of religions but only of totemism. Can you, from any of the views known to you, explain the fact that the first shape in which the protecting deity revealed itself to men should have been that of an animal; that there was a prohibition against killing and eating this animal and that nevertheless the solemn custom was to kill and eat it communally once a year? This is precisely what happens in totemism. And it is hardly to the purpose to argue about whether totemism ought to be called a religion.

It has intimate connections with the later god-religions. The totem animals become the sacred animals of the gods; and the earliest, but most fundamental moral restrictions—the prohibitions against murder and incest originate in totemism. Whether or not you accept the conclusions of *Totem and Taboo*, I hope you will admit that a number of very remarkable, disconnected facts are brought together in it into a consistent whole.

The question of why in the long run the animal god did not suffice, and was replaced by a human one, was hardly touched on in *Totem and Taboo*, and other problems concerning the formation of religion were not mentioned in the book at all. Do you regard a limitation of that kind as the same thing as a denial? My work is a good example of the strict isolation of the particular contribution which psycho-analytic discussion can make to the solution of the problem of religion.

If I am now trying to add the other, less deeply concealed part, you should not accuse me of contradicting myself, just as before you accused me of being one-sided. It is, of course, my duty to point out the connecting links between what I said earlier and what I put forward now, between the deeper and the manifest motives, between the father-complex and man's helplessness and need for protection.

These connections are not hard to find. They consist in the relation of the child's helplessness to the helplessness of the adult, which continues it. So that, as was to be expected, the motives for the formation of religion which psychoanalysis revealed now turn out to be the same as the infantile contribution to the manifest motives. Let us transport ourselves into the mental life of a child.

You remember the choice of object according to the anaclitic type, which psychoanalysis talks of? The libido there follows the paths of narcissistic needs and attaches itself to the objects that ensure the satisfaction of those needs. In this way, the mother, who satisfies the child's hunger, becomes its first love-object and certainly also its first protection against all the undefined dangers that threaten it in the external world—its first protection against anxiety, we may say.

In this function (of protection) the mother is soon replaced by the stronger father, who retains that position for the rest of childhood. But the child's attitude to its father is colored by a peculiar ambivalence. The father himself constitutes a danger for the child, perhaps because of its earlier relation to its mother. Thus it fears him no less than it longs for him and admires him. The indications of this ambivalence in the attitude to the father are deeply imprinted in every religion, as was shown in *Totem and Taboo*.

When the growing individual finds that he is destined to remain a child forever, that he can never do without protection against strange superior powers, he lends those powers the features belonging to the figure of his father; he creates for himself the gods whom he dreads, whom he seeks to propitiate, and whom he nevertheless entrusts with his own protection. Thus his longing for a father is a motive identical with his need for protection against the consequences of his human weakness.

The defense against childish helplessness is what lends its characteristic features to the adult's reaction to the helplessness that he has to acknowledge—a reaction which is precisely the formation of religion. But it is not my intention to enquire any further into the development of the idea of God; what we are concerned with here is the finished body of religious ideas as it is transmitted by civilization to the individual.

Let us now take up the thread of our enquiry. What, then, is the psychological significance of religious ideas and under what heading are we to classify them? The question is not at all easy to answer immediately. After rejecting a number of formulations, we will take our stand on the following one. Religious ideas are teachings and assertions about facts and conditions of external (or internal) reality which tell one something one has not discovered for oneself and which lay claim to one's belief. Since they give us information about what is most important and interesting to us in life, they are particularly highly prized. Anyone who knows nothing of them is very ignorant; and anyone who has added them to his knowledge may consider himself much the richer.

There are, of course, many such teachings about the most various things in the world. Every school lesson is full of them. Let us take geography. We are told that the town of Constance lies on the Bodensee. A student song adds, *if you don't believe it, go and see.*

I happen to have been there and can confirm the fact that that lovely town lies on the shore of a wide stretch of water which all those who live round it call the Bodensee; and I am now completely convinced of the correctness of this geographical assertion. In this connection I am reminded of another, very remarkable, experience. I was already a man of mature years when I stood for the first time on the hill of the Acropolis in Athens, between the temple ruins, looking out over the blue sea. A feeling of astonishment mingled with my joy.

It seemed to say, "So it really is true, just as we learned at school!" How shallow and weak must have been the belief I then acquired in the real truth of what I heard, if I could be so astonished now! But I will not lay too much stress on the significance of this experience; for my astonishment could have had another explanation, which did not occur to me at the time and which is of a wholly subjective nature and has to do with the special character of the place.

All teachings like these, then, demand belief in their contents, but not without producing grounds for their claim. They are put forward as the epitomized result of a longer process of thought based on observation and certainly also on inferences. If anyone wants to go through this process himself instead of accepting its result, they show him how to set about it. Moreover, we are always, in addition, given the source of the knowledge conveyed by them, where that source is not self-evident, as it is in the case of geographical assertions.

For instance, the earth is shaped like a sphere; the proofs adduced for this are Foucault's pendulum experiment, the behavior of the horizon and the possibility of circumnavigating the earth. Since it is impracticable, as everyone concerned realizes, to send every schoolchild on a voyage round the world, we are satisfied with letting what is taught at school be taken on trust; but we know that the path to acquiring a personal conviction remains open.

Let us try to apply the same test to the teachings of religion. When we ask on what their claim to be believed is founded, we are met with three answers, which harmonize remarkably badly with one another. Firstly, these teachings deserve to be believed because they were already believed by our primal ancestors; secondly, we possess proofs which have been handed down to us from those same primeval times; and thirdly, it is forbidden to raise the question of their authentication at all.

In former days, anything so presumptuous was visited with the severest penalties, and even today, society looks askance at any attempt to raise the question again.

This third point is bound to rouse our strongest suspicions. After all, a prohibition like this can only be for one reason—that society is very well aware of the insecurity of the claim it makes on behalf of its religious doctrines. Otherwise, it would certainly be very ready to put the necessary data at the disposal of anyone who wanted to arrive at conviction. This being so, it is with a feeling of mistrust that we pass on to an examination of the other two grounds of proof.

We ought to believe because our forefathers believed. But these ancestors of ours were far more ignorant than we are. They believed in things we could not possibly accept today; and the possibility occurs to us that the doctrines of religion may belong to that class too.

The proofs they have left us are set down in writings, which themselves bear every mark of untrustworthiness. They are full of contradictions, revisions, and falsifications; and where they speak of factual confirmations, they are themselves unconfirmed. It does not help much to have it asserted that their wording, or even their content, originates from divine revelation; for this assertion is itself one of the doctrines whose authenticity is under examination, and no proposition can be a proof of itself.

Thus we arrive at the singular conclusion that of all the information provided by our cultural assets, it is precisely the elements which might be of the greatest importance to us and which have the task of solving the riddles of the universe and of reconciling us to the sufferings of life—it is precisely those elements that are the least well authenticated of any. We should not be able to bring ourselves to accept anything of so little concern to us as the fact that whales bear young instead of laying eggs, if it were not capable of better proof than this.

This state of affairs is in itself a very remarkable psychological problem. And let no one suppose that what I have said about the impossibility of proving the truth of religious doctrines contains anything new. It has been felt at all times—undoubtedly, too, by the ancestors who bequeathed us this legacy. Many of them probably nourished the same doubts as ours, but the pressure imposed on them was too strong for them to have dared to utter them. And since then, countless people have been tormented by similar doubts, and have striven to suppress them because they thought it was their duty to believe. Many brilliant intellects have broken down over this conflict, and many characters have been impaired by the compromises with which they have tried to find a way out of it.

If all the evidence put forward for the authenticity of religious teachings originates in the past, it is natural to look around and see whether the present, about which it is easier to form judgments, may not also be able to furnish evidence of the sort. If by this means we could succeed in clearing even a single portion of the religious system from doubt, the whole of it would gain enormously in credibility.

The proceedings of the spiritualists meet us at this point; they are convinced of the survival of the individual soul and they seek to demonstrate to us, beyond doubt, the truth of this one religious doctrine. Unfortunately, they cannot succeed in refuting the fact that the appearance and utterances of their spirits are merely the products of their own mental activity. They have called up the spirits of the greatest men and of the most eminent thinkers, but all the pronouncements and information which they have received from them have been so foolish and so wretchedly meaningless that one can find nothing credible in them but the capacity of the spirits to adapt themselves to the circle of people who have conjured them up.

I must now mention two attempts that have been made—both of which convey the impression of being desperate efforts to evade the problem. One, of a violent nature, is ancient; the other is subtle and modern. The first is the 'Credo quia absurdum' of the early Father of the Church. ('I believe because it is absurd.') This is attributed to Tertullian. It maintains that religious doctrines are outside the jurisdiction of reason—are above reason. Their truth must be felt inwardly, and they need not be comprehended.

But this Credo is only of interest as a self-confession. As an authoritative statement it has no binding force. Am I to be obliged to believe every absurdity? And if not, why this one in particular? There is no appeal to a court above that of reason. If the truth of religious doctrines is dependent on an inner experience that bears witness to that truth, what is one to do about the many people who do not have this rare experience?

One may require every man to use the gift of reason which he possesses, but one cannot erect, on the basis of a motive that exists only for a very few, an obligation that shall apply to everyone. If one man has gained an unshakable conviction of the true reality of religious doctrines from a state of ecstasy which has deeply moved him, of what significance is that to others?

The second attempt is the one made by the philosophy of 'As if'. This asserts that our thought-activity includes a great number of hypotheses whose groundlessness and even absurdity we fully realize. They are called 'fictions', but for a variety of practical reasons we have to behave 'as if' we believed in these fictions. This is the case with religious doctrines because of their incomparable importance for the maintenance of human society.

This line of argument is not far removed from the *Credo quia absurdum*. But I think the demand made by the 'As if' argument is one that only a philosopher could put forward.

A man whose thinking is not influenced by the artifices of philosophy will never be able to accept it; in such a man's view, the admission that something is absurd or contrary to reason leaves no more to be said. It cannot be expected of him that precisely in treating his most important interests, he shall forgo the guarantees he requires for all his ordinary activities.

I am reminded of one of my children who was distinguished at an early age by a peculiarly marked matter-of-factness. When the children were being told a fairy story and were listening to it with rapt attention, he would come up and ask, "Is that a true story?"

When he was told it was not, he would turn away with a look of disdain. We may expect that people will soon behave in the same way towards the fairy tales of religion, in spite of the advocacy of 'As if'.

But at present they still behave quite differently; and in past times religious ideas, in spite of their incontrovertible lack of authentication, have exercised the strongest possible influence on mankind. This is a fresh psychological problem. We must ask where the inner force of those doctrines lies and to what it is that they owe their efficacy, independent as it is of recognition by reason.

I think we have prepared the way sufficiently for an answer to both these questions. It will be found if we turn our attention to the psychical origin of religious ideas. These, which are given out as teachings, are not precipitates of experience or end results of thinking; they are illusions, fulfillments of the oldest, strongest, and most urgent wishes of mankind.

The secret of their strength lies in the strength of those wishes. As we already know, the terrifying impression of helplessness in childhood aroused the need for protection—for protection through love—which was provided by the father; and the recognition that this helplessness lasts throughout life made it necessary to cling to the existence of a father, but this time a more powerful one.

Thus the benevolent rule of a divine Providence allays our fear of the dangers of life; the establishment of a moral world-order ensures the fulfillment of the demands of justice, which have so often remained unfulfilled in human civilization; and the prolongation of earthly existence in a future life provides the local and temporal framework in which these wish-fulfillments shall take place.

Answers to the riddles that tempt the curiosity of man, such as how the universe began or what the relation is between body and mind, are developed in conformity with the underlying assumptions of this system.

It is an enormous relief to the individual psyche if the conflicts of its childhood arising from the father-complex—conflicts which it has never wholly overcome—are removed from it and brought to a solution which is universally accepted.

When I say that these things are all illusions, I must define the meaning of the word. An illusion is not the same thing as an error; nor is it necessarily an error. Aristotle's belief that vermin are developed out of dung (a belief to which ignorant people still cling) was an error; so was the belief of a former generation of doctors that *tabes dorsalis* is the result of sexual excess. It would be incorrect to call these errors illusions.

On the other hand, it was an illusion of Columbus's that he had discovered a new sea-route to the Indies. The part played by his wish in this error is very clear. One may describe, as an illusion, the assertion made by certain nationalists that the Indo-Germanic race is the only one capable of civilization; or the belief, which was only destroyed by psychoanalysis, that children are creatures without sexuality.

What is characteristic of illusions is that they are derived from human wishes. In this respect, they come near to psychiatric delusions. But they differ from them, too, apart from the more complicated structure of delusions. In the case of delusions, we emphasize, as essential, their being in contradiction with reality. Illusions need not necessarily be false—that is to say, unrealizable or in contradiction to reality. For instance, a middle-class girl may have the illusion that a prince will come and marry her. This is possible; and a few such cases have occurred. That the Messiah will come and found a golden age is much less likely.

Whether one classifies this belief as an illusion or as something analogous to a delusion will depend on one's personal attitude. Examples of illusions that have proved true are not easy to find, but the illusion of the alchemists that all metals can be turned into gold might be one of them.

The wish to have a great deal of gold, as much gold as possible, has, it is true, been a good deal damped by our present-day knowledge of the determinants of wealth, but chemistry no longer regards the transmutation of metals into gold as impossible. Thus we call a belief an illusion when a wish-fulfillment is a prominent factor in its motivation, and in doing so we disregard its relations to reality, just as the illusion itself sets no store by verification.

Having thus taken our bearings, let us return once more to the question of religious doctrines. We can now repeat that all of them are illusions and insusceptible of proof. No one can be compelled to think them true, to believe in them. Some of them are so improbable, so incompatible with everything we have laboriously discovered about the reality of the world, that we may compare them—if we pay proper regard to the psychological differences—to delusions. Of the reality value of most of them we cannot judge; just as they cannot be proved, so they cannot be refuted. We still know too little to make a critical approach to them.

The riddles of the universe reveal themselves only slowly to our investigation; there are many questions to which science today can give no answer. But scientific work is the only road which can lead us to a knowledge of reality outside ourselves. It is once again merely an illusion to expect anything from intuition and introspection; they can give us nothing but particulars about our own mental life, which are hard to interpret, never any information about the questions which religious doctrine finds it so easy to answer.

It would be insolent to let one's own arbitrary will step into the breach and, according to one's personal estimate, declare this or that part of the religious system to be less or more acceptable. Such questions are too momentous for that; they might be called too sacred.

At this point one must expect to meet with an objection:

"Well then, if even obdurate skeptics admit that the assertions of religion cannot be refuted by reason, why should I not believe in them, since they have so much on their side—tradition, the agreement of mankind, and all the consolations they offer?"

Why not, indeed? Just as no one can be forced to believe, so no one can be forced to disbelieve. But do not let us be satisfied with deceiving ourselves that arguments like these take us along the road of correct thinking. If ever there was a case of a lame excuse we have it here.

Ignorance is ignorance; no right to believe anything can be derived from it. In other matters no sensible person will behave so irresponsibly or rest content with such feeble grounds for his opinions and for the line he takes. It is only in the highest and most sacred things that he allows himself to do so.

 In reality, these are only attempts at pretending to oneself or to other people that one is still firmly attached to religion, when one has long since cut oneself loose from it. Where questions of religion are concerned, people are guilty of every possible sort of dishonesty and intellectual misdemeanor.

Philosophers stretch the meaning of words until they retain scarcely anything of their original sense. They give the name God to some vague abstraction they have created for themselves. Having done so, they can pose before the world as deists, as believers in God, and they can even boast that they have recognized a higher, purer concept of God—notwithstanding that their God is now nothing more than an insubstantial shadow and no longer the mighty personality of religious doctrines.

Critics persist in describing as *deeply religious* anyone who admits to a sense of man's insignificance or impotence in the face of the universe. Although what constitutes the essence of the religious attitude is not this feeling but only the next step after it: the reaction to it that seeks a remedy for it.

The man who goes no further, but humbly acquiesces in the small part which human beings play in the great world—such a man is, on the contrary, irreligious in the truest sense of the word.

To assess the truth-value of religious doctrines does not lie within the scope of the present enquiry. It is enough for us that we have recognized them as being, in their psychological nature, illusions. But we do not have to conceal the fact that this discovery also strongly influences our attitude to the question that must appear to many to be the most important of all. We know approximately at what periods and by what kind of men religious doctrines were created.

If, in addition, we discover the motives that led to this, our attitude to the problem of religion will undergo a marked displacement. We shall tell ourselves that it would be very nice if there were a God who created the world and was a benevolent Providence, and if there were a moral order in the universe and an after-life; but it is a very striking fact that all this is exactly as we are bound to wish it to be. And it would be more remarkable still if our wretched, ignorant and downtrodden ancestors had succeeded in solving all these difficult riddles of the universe.

Having recognized religious doctrines as illusions, we are at once faced by a further question: may not other cultural assets of which we hold a high opinion and by which we let our lives be ruled be of a similar nature? Must not the assumptions that determine our political regulations be called illusions as well? And is it not the case that in our civilization, the relations between the sexes are disturbed by an erotic illusion or a number of such illusions? And once our suspicion has been aroused, we shall not shrink from asking too whether our conviction that we can learn something about external reality through the use of observation and reasoning in scientific work—whether this conviction has any better foundation.

Nothing ought to keep us from directing our observation to our own selves or from applying our thought to criticism of itself. In this field, a number of investigations open out before us, whose results could not but be decisive for the construction of a worldview.

We surmise, moreover, that such an effort would not be wasted and that it would at least, in part, justify our suspicion. But the author does not dispose of the means for undertaking so comprehensive a task; his needs must confine his work to following out only one of these illusions—that, namely, of religion.

But now, the loud voice of our opponent brings us to a halt. We are called to account for our wrong-doing:

"Archaeological interests are no doubt most praiseworthy, but no one undertakes an excavation if by doing so he is going to undermine the habitations of the living so that they collapse and bury people under their ruins. The doctrines of religion are not a subject one can quibble about like any other. Our civilization is built upon them, and the maintenance of human society is based on believing in the truth of those doctrines.

"If men are taught that there is no almighty and all-just God, no divine world-order and no future life, they will feel exempt from all obligation to obey the precepts of civilization. Everyone will, without inhibition or fear, follow his asocial, egoistic instincts and seek to exercise his power. Chaos, which we have banished through many thousands of years of the work of civilization, will come again.

"Even if we knew, and could prove, that religion was not in possession of the truth, we ought to conceal the fact and behave in the way prescribed by the philosophy of As if—and this in the interest of the preservation of us all. And apart from the danger of the undertaking, it would be a purposeless cruelty. Countless people find their one consolation in religious doctrines, and can only bear life with their help. You would rob them of their support, without having anything better to give them in exchange.

"It is admitted that so far science has not achieved much, but even if it had advanced much further it would not suffice for man. Man has imperative needs of another sort, which can never be satisfied by cold science; and it is very strange—indeed, it is the height of inconsistency—that a psychologist who has always insisted on what a minor part is played in human affairs by the intelligence as compared with the life of the instincts—that such a psychologist should now try to rob mankind of a precious wish-fulfillment and should propose to compensate them for it with intellectual nourishment."

What a lot of accusations all at once! Nevertheless I am ready with rebuttals for them all; and, what is more, I shall assert the view that civilization runs a greater risk if we maintain our present attitude to religion than if we give it up.

But I hardly know where to begin my reply. Perhaps with the assurance that I myself regard my undertaking as completely harmless and free of risk. It is not I who am overvaluing the intellect this time. If people are as my opponents describe them—and I should not like to contradict them—then there is no danger of a devout believer's being overcome by my arguments and deprived of his faith. Besides, I have said nothing which other and better men have not said before me in a much more complete, forcible, and impressive manner.

Their names are well known, and I shall not cite them, for I should not like to give an impression that I am seeking to rank myself as one of them. All I have done—and this is the only thing that is new in my exposition—is to add some psychological foundation to the criticisms of my great predecessors. It is hardly to be expected that precisely this addition will produce the effect that was denied to those earlier efforts. No doubt I might be asked here, what is the point of writing these things if I am certain that they will be ineffective. But I shall come back to that later.

The one person this publication may injure is myself. I shall have to listen to the most disagreeable reproaches for my shallowness, narrow-mindedness, and lack of idealism or of understanding for the highest interests of mankind. But on the one hand, such remonstrances are not new to me; and on the other, if a man has already learned in his youth to rise superior to the disapproval of his contemporaries, what can it matter to him in his old age when he is certain soon to be beyond the reach of all favor or disfavor?

In former times it was different. Then utterances such as mine brought with them a sure curtailment of one's earthly existence and an effective speeding-up of the opportunity for gaining a personal experience of the afterlife.

But, I repeat, those times are past, and today writings such as this bring no more danger to their author than to their readers. The most that can happen is that the translation and distribution of his book will be forbidden in one country or another—and precisely, of course, in a country that is convinced of the high standard of its culture. But if one puts in any plea at all for the renunciation of wishes and for acquiescence in Fate, one must be able to tolerate this kind of injury too.

The further question occurred to me whether the publication of this work might not after all do harm. Not to a person, however, but to a cause—the cause of psychoanalysis. For it cannot be denied that psychoanalysis is my creation, and it has met with plenty of mistrust and ill-will. If I now come forward with such displeasing pronouncements, people will be only too ready to make a displacement from my person to psychoanalysis.

"Now we see," they will say, "where psychoanalysis leads to. The mask has fallen; it leads to a denial of God and of a moral ideal, as we always suspected. To keep us from this discovery we have been deluded into thinking that psychoanalysis has no worldview and can never construct one."

An outcry of this kind will really be disagreeable to me on account of my many fellow-workers, some of whom do not by any means share my attitude to the problems of religion. But psychoanalysis has already weathered many storms and now it must brave this fresh one. In point of fact, psychoanalysis is a method of research, an impartial instrument, like the infinitesimal calculus, as it were. If a physicist were to discover with the latter's help that after a certain time the earth would be destroyed, we would nevertheless hesitate to attribute destructive tendencies to the calculus itself and therefore to proscribe it.

Nothing that I have said here against the truth-value of religions needed the support of psychoanalysis; it had been said by others long before analysis came into existence. If the application of the psycho-analytic method makes it possible to find a new argument against the truths of religion, too bad for religion; but defenders of religion will by the same right make use of psychoanalysis in order to give full value to the affective significance of religious doctrines.

And now to proceed with our defense. Religion has clearly performed great services for human civilization. It has contributed much toward the taming of the asocial instincts. But not enough. It has ruled human society for many thousands of years and has had time to show what it can achieve. If it had succeeded in making the majority of mankind happy, in comforting them, in reconciling them to life and in making them into vehicles of civilization, no one would dream of attempting to alter the existing conditions.

But what do we see instead? We see that an appallingly large number of people are dissatisfied with civilization and unhappy in it, and feel it as a yoke which must be shaken off; and that these people either do everything in their power to change that civilization, or else go so far in their hostility to it that they will have nothing to do with civilization or with a restriction of instinct.

At this point, it will be objected against us that this state of affairs is due to the very fact that religion has lost a part of its influence over human masses, precisely because of the deplorable effect of the advances of science. We will note this admission and the reason given for it, and we shall make use of it later for our own purposes; but the objection itself has no force.

It is doubtful whether men were, in general, happier at a time when religious doctrines held unrestricted sway; more moral they certainly were not. They have always known how to externalize the precepts of religion and thus to nullify their intentions. The priests, whose duty it was to ensure obedience to religion, met them half-way in this. God's kindness must lay a restraining hand on His justice. One sinned, and then one made a sacrifice or did penance and then one was free to sin once more.

Russian introspectiveness has reached the pitch of concluding that sin is indispensable for the enjoyment of all the blessings of divine grace, so that, at bottom, sin is pleasing to God. It is no secret that the priests could only keep the masses submissive to religion by making such large concessions as these to the instinctual nature of man.

Thus it was agreed: God alone is strong and good, man is weak and sinful. In every age, immorality has found no less support in religion than morality has. If the achievements of religion in respect to man's happiness, susceptibility to culture, and moral control are no better than this, the question cannot but arise whether we are not overrating its necessity for mankind, and whether we do wisely in basing our cultural demands upon it.

Let us consider the unmistakable situation as it is today. We have heard the admission that religion no longer has the same influence on people that it used to. (We are here concerned with European Christian civilization.) And this is not because its promises have grown less but because people find them less credible. Let us admit that the reason—though perhaps not the only reason—for this change is the increase of the scientific spirit in the higher strata of human society.

Criticism has whittled away the evidential value of religious documents. Natural science has shown up the errors in them, and comparative research has been struck by the fatal resemblance between the religious ideas we revere and the mental products of primitive peoples and times.

The scientific spirit brings about a particular attitude towards worldly matters; before religious matters it pauses for a little, hesitates, and finally there too crosses the threshold. In this process there is no stopping; the greater the number of men to whom the treasures of knowledge become accessible, the more widespread is the falling-away from religious belief—at first only from its obsolete and objectionable trappings, but later from its fundamental postulates as well.

The Americans who instituted the 'monkey trial' at Dayton (a small town in Tennessee where, in 1925, a science teacher was prosecuted for breach of a State law by teaching that man is descended from the lower animals) have alone shown themselves consistent. Elsewhere the inevitable transition is accomplished by way of half-measures and insincerities.

Civilization has little to fear from educated people and brainworkers. In them, the replacement of religious motives for civilized behavior by secular motives would proceed unobtrusively; moreover, such people are, to a large extent, themselves vehicles of civilization. But it is another matter with the great mass of the uneducated and oppressed, who have every reason for being enemies of civilization.

So long as they do not discover that people no longer believe in God, all is well. But they will discover it, infallibly, even if this piece of writing of mine is not published. And they are ready to accept the results of scientific thinking, but without the change having taken place in them which scientific thinking brings about in people. Is there not a danger here that the hostility of these masses, to civilization, will throw itself against the weak spot that they have found in their task-mistress?

If the sole reason why you must not kill your neighbor is because God has forbidden it and will severely punish you for it in this or the next life—then, when you learn that there is no God and that you need not fear His punishment, you will certainly kill your neighbor without hesitation, and you can only be prevented from doing so by mundane force.

Thus either these dangerous masses must be held down most severely and kept most carefully away from any chance of intellectual awakening, or else the relationship between civilization and religion must undergo a fundamental revision.

One might think that there would be no special difficulties in the way of carrying out this latter proposal. It is true that it would involve a certain amount of renunciation, but more would perhaps be gained than lost, and a great danger would be avoided.

Everyone is frightened of it, however, as though it would expose civilization to a still greater danger. When St. Boniface (the eighth-century, Devonshire-born, Apostle of Germany) cut down the tree that was venerated as sacred by the Saxons, the bystanders expected some fearful event to follow upon the sacrilege. But nothing happened, and the Saxons accepted baptism.

When civilization laid down the commandment that a man shall not kill the neighbor whom he hates, or who is in his way, or whose property he covets, this was clearly done in the interest of man's communal existence, which would not otherwise be practicable. For the murderer would draw down on himself the vengeance of the murdered man's kinsmen and the secret envy of others, who within themselves, feel as much inclined as he does for such acts of violence.

Thus he would not enjoy his revenge or his robbery for long, but would have every prospect of soon being killed himself. Even if he protected himself against his single foes by extraordinary strength and caution, he would be bound to succumb to a combination of weaker men.

If a combination of this sort did not take place, the murdering would continue endlessly and the final outcome would be that men would exterminate one another. We should arrive at the same state of affairs between individuals as still persists in Corsica between families, though elsewhere only between nations. Insecurity of life, which is an equal danger for everyone, now unites men into a society that prohibits the individual from killing and reserves to itself the right to communal killing of anyone who violates the prohibition. Here, then, we have justice and punishment.

But we do not publish this rational explanation of the prohibition against murder. We assert that the prohibition has been issued by God. Thus we take it upon ourselves to guess His intentions, and we find that He, too, is unwilling for men to exterminate one another. In behaving in this way, we are investing the cultural prohibition with a quite special solemnity, but at the same time we risk making its observance dependent on belief in God.

If we retrace this step—if we no longer attribute to God what is our own will, and if we content ourselves with giving the social reason—then, it is true, we have renounced the transfiguration of the cultural prohibition, but we have also avoided the risk to it.

But we gain something else as well. Through some kind of diffusion or infection, the character of sanctity and inviolability—of belonging to another world, one might say—has spread from a few major prohibitions on to every other cultural regulation, law, and ordinance. But, on these the halo often looks far from becoming: not only do they invalidate one another by giving contrary decisions at different times and places, but apart from this they show every sign of human inadequacy.

It is easy to recognize in them things that can only be the product of shortsighted apprehensiveness, or an expression of selfishly narrow interests, or a conclusion based on insufficient premises. The criticism which we cannot fail to level at them also diminishes, to an unwelcome extent, our respect for other, more justifiable cultural demands.

Since it is an awkward task to separate what God Himself has demanded from what can be traced to the authority of an all-powerful parliament or a high judiciary, it would be an undoubted advantage if we were to leave God out altogether and honestly admit the purely human origin of all the regulations and precepts of civilization.

Along with their pretended sanctity, these commandments and laws would lose their rigidity and unchangeableness as well. People could understand that they are made, not so much to rule them as, on the contrary, to serve their interests; and they would adopt a more friendly attitude to them, and instead of aiming at their abolition, would aim only at their improvement. This would be an important advance along the road that leads to becoming reconciled to the burden of civilization.

But, here our plea for ascribing purely rational reasons to the precepts of civilization—that is to say, for deriving them from social necessity—is interrupted by a sudden doubt.

We have chosen, as our example, the origin of the prohibition against murder. But does our account of it tally with historical truth? We fear not; it appears to be nothing but a rationalistic construction. With the help of psychoanalysis, we have made a study of precisely this piece of the cultural history of mankind, and, basing ourselves on it, we are bound to say that in reality things happened otherwise.

Even in present-day man, purely reasonable motives have little effect against passionate impulses. How much weaker must they have been in the human animal of primeval times! Perhaps his descendants would even now kill one another without inhibition, if it were not that among those murderous acts there was one—the killing of the primitive father—which evoked an irresistible emotional reaction with momentous consequences.

From it arose the commandment: Thou shall not kill. Under totemism, this commandment was restricted to the father-substitute; but it was later extended to other people, though even today it is not universally obeyed.

But, as was shown by arguments that I need not repeat here, the primal father was the original image of God, the model on which later generations have shaped the figure of God. Hence, the religious explanation is right. God actually played a part in the genesis of that prohibition; it was His influence, not any insight into social necessity, which created it. And the displacement of man's will on to God is fully justified. For men knew that they had disposed of their father by violence, and in their reaction to that impious deed, they determined to respect his will thenceforward. Thus religious doctrine tells us the historical truth—though subject, it is true, to some modification and disguise—whereas our rational account disavows it.

We now observe that the store of religious ideas includes not only wish fulfillments but also important historical recollections. This concurrent influence of past and present must give religion a truly incomparable wealth of power. But perhaps with the help of an analogy, yet another discovery may begin to dawn on us. Though it is not a good plan to transplant ideas far from the soil in which they grew up, here is a conformity we cannot avoid pointing out.

We know that a human child cannot successfully complete its development to the civilized stage without passing through a phase of neurosis sometimes of greater and sometimes of less distinctness. These is because so many instinctual demands, which will later be unserviceable, cannot be suppressed by the rational operation of the child's intellect, but have to be tamed by acts of repression, behind which, as a rule, lies the motive of anxiety.

Most of these infantile neuroses are overcome spontaneously in the course of growing up, and this is especially true of the obsessional neuroses of childhood. The remainder can be cleared up later still by psycho-analytic treatment.

In just the same way, one might assume humanity as a whole, in its development through the ages, fell into states analogous to the neuroses, and for the same reasons. Namely because in the times of its ignorance and intellectual weakness, the instinctual renunciations, indispensable for man's communal existence, had only been achieved by means of purely affective forces. The precipitates of these processes resembling repression, which took place in prehistoric times, still remained attached to civilization for long periods.

Religion would thus be the universal obsessional neurosis of humanity; like the obsessional neurosis of children, it arose out of the Oedipus complex, out of the relation to the father. If this view is right, it is to be supposed that a turning-away from religion is bound to occur with the fatal inevitability of a process of growth, and that we find ourselves, at this very juncture, in the middle of that phase of development.

Our behavior should, therefore, be modeled on that of a sensible teacher who does not oppose an impending new development, but seeks to ease its path and mitigate the violence of its irruption. Our analogy does not, to be sure, exhaust the essential nature of religion.

If, on the one hand, religion brings with it obsessional restrictions, exactly as an individual obsessional neurosis does, on the other hand it comprises a system of wishful illusions, together with a disavowal of reality—such as we find in an isolated form nowhere else but in a state of blissful hallucinatory confusion. But these are only analogies, by the help of which we endeavor to understand a social phenomenon; the pathology of the individual does not supply us with a fully valid counterpart.

It has been repeatedly pointed out (by myself and in particular by Theodor Reik) in how great detail the analogy between religion and obsessional neurosis can be followed out, and how many of the peculiarities and vicissitudes in the formation of religion can be understood in that light. And it tallies well with this that devout believers are safeguarded in a high degree against the risk of certain neurotic illnesses; their acceptance of the universal neurosis spares them the task of constructing a personal one.

Our knowledge of the historical worth of certain religious doctrines increases our respect for them, but does not invalidate our proposal that they should cease to be put forward as the reasons for the precepts of civilization.

On the contrary! Those historical residues have helped us to view religious teachings, as it were, as neurotic relics, and we may now argue that the time has probably come, as it does in an analytic treatment, for replacing the effects of repression by the results of the rational operation of the intellect.

We may foresee, but hardly regret, that such a process of remolding will not stop at renouncing the solemn transfiguration of cultural precepts, but that a general revision of them will result in many of them being done away with. In this way, our appointed task of reconciling men to civilization will largely be achieved.

We need not deplore the renunciation of historical truth when we put forward rational grounds for the precepts of civilization. The truths contained in religious doctrines are, after all, so distorted and systematically disguised that the mass of humanity cannot recognize them as truth. The case is similar to what happens when we tell a child that babies are brought by the stork. Here, too, we are telling the truth in symbolic clothing, for we know what the large bird signifies.

But the child does not know it. He hears only the distorted part of what we say, and feels that he has been deceived; and we know how often his distrust of the grown-ups and his refractoriness actually take their start from this impression. We have become convinced that it is better to avoid such symbolic disguising of the truth in what we tell children and not to withhold from them a knowledge of the true state of affairs commensurate with their intellectual level.

"You permit yourself contradictions which are hard to reconcile with one another. You begin by saying that a piece of writing like yours is quite harmless: no one will let himself be robbed of his faith by considerations of the sort put forward in it. But since it is nevertheless your intention, as becomes evident later on, to upset that faith, we may ask why in fact you are publishing your work?

"In another passage, moreover, you admit that it may be dangerous, indeed very dangerous, for someone to discover that people no longer believe in God. Hitherto he has been docile, but now he throws off his obedience to the precepts of civilization. Yet your whole contention, that basing the commandments of civilization on religious grounds constitutes a danger for civilization, rests on the assumption that the believer can be turned into an unbeliever. Surely that is a complete contradiction.

"And here is another. On the one hand, you admit that men cannot be guided through their intelligence; they are ruled by their passions and their instinctual demands. But on the other hand, you propose to replace the affective basis of their obedience to civilization by a rational one. Let who can understand this. To me it seems that it must be either one thing or the other.

"Besides, have you learned nothing from history? Once before, an attempt of this kind was made to substitute reason for religion, officially and in the grand manner. Surely, you remember the French Revolution and Robespierre? And you must also remember how short-lived and miserably ineffectual the experiment was? The same experiment is being repeated in Russia at the present time, and we need not feel curious as to its outcome. Do you not think we may take it for granted that men cannot do without religion?

"You have said yourself that religion is more than an obsessional neurosis. But you have not dealt with this other side of it. You are content to work out the analogy with a neurosis. Men, you say, must be freed from a neurosis. What else may be lost in the process is of no concern to you."

The appearance of contradiction has probably come about because I have dealt with complicated matters too hurriedly. We can remedy this to some extent. I still maintain that what I have written is quite harmless in one respect. No believer will let himself be led astray from his faith by these or any similar arguments. A believer is bound to the teachings of religion by certain ties of affection.

But there are undoubtedly countless other people who are not in the same sense believers. They obey the precepts of civilization because they let themselves be intimidated by the threats of religion, and they are afraid of religion so long as they have to consider it as a part of the reality that hems them in. They are the people who break away as soon, as they are allowed to give up their belief in the reality-value of religion.

But they too are unaffected by arguments. They cease to fear religion when they observe that others do not fear it; and it was of them that I asserted, they would get to know about the decline of religious influence, even if I did not publish my work.

But I think you, yourself, attach more weight to the other contradiction you charge me with. Since men are so little accessible to reasonable arguments and are so entirely governed by their instinctual wishes, why should one set out to deprive them of an instinctual satisfaction and replace it by reasonable arguments?

It is true that men are like this; but have you asked yourself whether they must be like this, whether their innermost nature necessitates it? Can an anthropologist give the cranial index of a people whose custom it is to deform their children's heads by bandaging them round from their earliest years?

Think of the depressing contrast between the radiant intelligence of a healthy child and the feeble intellectual powers of the average adult. Can we be quite certain that it is not precisely religious education that bears a large share of the blame for this relative atrophy?

I think it would be a very long time before a child, who was not influenced, began to trouble himself about God and things in another world. Perhaps his thoughts on these matters would then take the same paths as they did with his forefathers.

But we do not wait for such a development; we introduce him to the doctrines of religion at an age when he is neither interested in them, nor capable of grasping their import. Is it not true that the two main points in the program for the education of children are retardation of sexual development and premature religious influence? Thus by the time, the child's intellect awakens, the doctrines of religion have already become unassailable.

But are you of opinion that it is very conducive to the strengthening of the intellectual function that so important a field should be closed against it by the threat of Hell-fire? When a man has once brought himself to accept, uncritically, all the absurdities that religious doctrines put before him and even to overlook the contradictions between them, we need not be greatly surprised at the weakness of his intellect.

But we have no other means of controlling our instinctual nature but our intelligence. How can we expect people who are under the dominance of prohibitions of thought, to attain the psychological ideal, the primacy of the intelligence?

You know, too, that women in general are said to suffer from physiological feeble-mindedness—that is, from a lesser intelligence than men. The fact itself is disputable and its interpretation doubtful, but one argument in favor of this intellectual atrophy, being of a secondary nature, is that women labor under the harshness of an early prohibition against turning their thoughts to what would most have interested them—namely, the problems of sexual life.

So long as a person's early years are influenced not only by a sexual inhibition of thought, but also by a religious inhibition and by a loyal inhibition derived from this, we cannot really tell what in fact he is like. I will moderate my zeal and admit the possibility that I, too, am chasing an illusion. Perhaps the effect of the religious prohibition of thought may not be so bad as I suppose; perhaps it will turn out that human nature remains the same even if education is not abused in order to subject people to religion. I do not know and you cannot know either.

It is not only the great problems of this life that seem insoluble at the present time; many lesser questions too are difficult to answer.

But you must admit that here we are justified in having a hope for the future—that perhaps there is a treasure to be dug up, capable of enriching civilization, and that it is worth making the experiment of an irreligious education.

Should the experiment prove unsatisfactory, I am ready to give up the reform and to return to my earlier, purely descriptive judgment that man is a creature of weak intelligence who is ruled by his instinctual wishes.

On another point, I agree with you unreservedly. It is certainly senseless to begin by trying to do away with religion by force and at a single blow. Above all, because it would be hopeless. The believer will not let his belief be torn from him, either by arguments or by prohibitions. And even if this did succeed, with some it would be cruelty.

A man who has been taking sleeping draughts for tens of years is naturally unable to sleep if his sleeping draught is taken away from him. That the effect of religious consolations may be likened to that of a narcotic is well illustrated by what is happening in America. There they are now trying—obviously under the influence of petticoat government—to deprive people of all stimulants, intoxicants, and other pleasure-producing substances, and instead, by way of compensation, are surfeiting them with piety. This is another experiment as to whose outcome we need not feel curious.

Thus, I must contradict you when you go on to argue that men are completely unable to do without the consolation of the religious illusion, that without it they could not bear the troubles of life and the cruelties of reality. That is true, certainly, of the men into whom you have instilled the sweet—or bitter-sweet—poison from childhood onwards.

But what of the other men, who have been sensibly brought up? Perhaps those who do not suffer from the neurosis will need no intoxicant to deaden it. They will, it is true, find themselves in a difficult situation. They will have to admit to themselves the full extent of their helplessness and their insignificance in the machinery of the universe. They can no longer be the center of creation, no longer the object of tender care on the part of a beneficent Providence.

They will be in the same position as a child who has left the parental house where he was so warm and comfortable. But surely infantilism is destined to be surmounted. Men cannot remain children forever; they must in the end go out into 'hostile life'. We may call this 'education to reality'. Need I confess to you that the sole purpose of my book is to point out the necessity for this forward step?

You are afraid, probably, that they will not stand up to the hard test. Well, let us at least hope they will. It is something, at any rate, to know that one is thrown upon one's own resources. One learns then to make a proper use of them. And men are not entirely without assistance. Their scientific knowledge has taught them much since the days of the Deluge, and it will increase their power still further.

As for the great necessities of Fate, against which there is no help, they will learn to endure them with resignation. Of what use to them is the mirage of wide acres in the moon, whose harvest no one has ever yet seen? As honest smallholders on this earth, they will know how to cultivate their plot in such a way that it supports them.

By withdrawing their expectations from the other world and concentrating all their liberated energies into their life on earth, they will probably succeed in achieving a state of things in which life will become tolerable for everyone, and civilization will no longer be oppressive to anyone. Then, with one of our fellow-unbelievers, they will be able to say without regret:

Den Himmel überlassen wir
Den Engeln und den Spatzen.
(We leave Heaven to the angels and the sparrows.)

"That sounds splendid! A race of men who have renounced all illusions and have thus become capable of making their existence on earth tolerable! I, however, cannot share your expectations. And that is not because I am the obstinate reactionary you perhaps take me for. No, it is because I am sensible. We seem now to have exchanged roles: you emerge as an enthusiast who allows himself to be carried away by illusions, and I stand for the claims of reason, the rights of skepticism.

"What you have been expounding seems to me to be built upon errors which, following your example, I may call illusions, because they betray clearly enough the influence of your wishes. You pin your hope on the possibility that generations that have not experienced the influence of religious doctrines in early childhood will easily attain the desired primacy of the intelligence over the life of the instincts. This is surely an illusion: in this decisive respect, human nature is hardly likely to change.

"If I am not mistaken—one knows so little about other civilizations—there are even today people who do not grow up under the pressure of a religious system, and yet they approach no nearer to your ideal than the rest.

"If you want to expel religion from our European civilization, you can only do it by means of another system of doctrines; and such a system would, from the outset, take over all the psychological characteristics of religion—the same sanctity, rigidity, and intolerance; the same prohibition of thought for its own defense. You have to have something of the kind in order to meet the requirements of education, and you cannot do without education.

"The path from the infant at the breast to the civilized man is a long one; too many human young would go astray on it and fail to reach their life-tasks at the proper time if they were left without guidance to their own development. The doctrines, which had been applied in their upbringing, would always set limits to the thinking of their riper years, which is exactly what you reproach religion with doing today. Do you not observe that it is an ineradicable and innate defect of our and every other civilization, that it imposes on children, who are driven by instinct and weak in intellect, the making of decisions which only the mature intelligence of adults can vindicate?

"But civilization cannot do otherwise, because of the fact that mankind's age long development is compressed into a few years of childhood; and it is only by emotional forces that the child can be induced to master the task set before it. Such, then, are the prospects for your *primacy of the intellect.*

"And now you must not be surprised if I plead on behalf of retaining the religious doctrinal system as the basis of education and of man's communal life. This is a practical problem, not a question of reality-value. Since, for the sake of preserving our civilization, we cannot postpone influencing the individual until he has become ripe for civilization (and many would never become so in any case). Since we are obliged to impose, on the growing child, some doctrinal system which shall operate in him as an axiom that admits of no criticism, it seems to me that the religious system is by far the most suitable for the purpose.

"And it is so, of course, precisely on account of its wish-fulfilling and consolatory power, by which you claim to recognize it as an illusion. In view of the difficulty of discovering anything about reality—indeed, of the doubt whether it is possible for us to do so at all—we must not overlook the fact that human needs, too, are a piece of reality, and, in fact, an important piece and one that concerns us especially closely.

"Another advantage of religious doctrine resides, to my mind, in one of its characteristics to which you seem to take particular exception. For it allows of a refinement and sublimation of ideas, which make it possible for it to be divested of most of the traces it bears of primitive and infantile thinking. What then remains is a body of ideas that science no longer contradicts and is unable to disprove.

"These modifications of religious doctrine, which you have condemned as half-measures and compromises, make it possible to avoid the cleft between the uneducated masses and the philosophic thinker, and to preserve the common bond between them that is so important for the safeguarding of civilization.

"With this, there would be no need to fear that the men of the people would discover that the upper strata of society no longer believe in God. I think I have now shown that your endeavors come down to an attempt to replace a proved and emotionally valuable illusion by another one, which is unproved and without emotional value."

You will not find me inaccessible to your criticism. I know how difficult it is to avoid illusions; perhaps the hopes I have confessed to are of an illusory nature, too. But I hold fast to one distinction. Apart from the fact that no penalty is imposed for not sharing them; my illusions are not, like religious ones, incapable of correction. They have not the character of a delusion.

If experience should show—not to me, but to others after me, who think as I do—that we have been mistaken, we will give up our expectations. Take my attempt for what it is. A psychologist, who does not deceive himself about the difficulty of finding one's bearings in this world, makes an endeavor to assess the development of man, in the light of the small portion of knowledge he has gained through a study of the mental processes of individuals during their development from child to adult.

In so doing, the idea forces itself upon him that religion is comparable to a childhood neurosis, and he is optimistic enough to suppose that mankind will surmount this neurotic phase, just as so many children grow out of their similar neurosis.

These discoveries, derived from individual psychology, may be insufficient; their application to the human race unjustified and his optimism unfounded. I grant you all these uncertainties. But often one cannot refrain from saying what one thinks, and one excuses oneself on the ground that one is not giving it out for more than it is worth.

There are two points that I must dwell on a little longer. Firstly, the weakness of my position does not imply any strengthening of yours. I think you are defending a lost cause. We may insist, as often as we like, that man's intellect is powerless in comparison with his instinctual life, and we may be right in this.

Nevertheless, there is something peculiar about this weakness. The voice of the intellect is a soft one, but it does not rest until it has gained a hearing. Finally, after a countless succession of rebuffs, it succeeds. This is one of the few points on which one may be optimistic about the future of mankind, but it is, in itself, a point of no small importance. And from it one can derive yet other hopes.

The primacy of the intellect lies, it is true, in a distant, distant future, but probably not in an infinitely distant one. It will presumably set itself the same aims as those whose realization you expect from your God (of course within human limits—so far as external reality allows it), namely the love of man and the decrease of suffering.

This being so, we may tell ourselves that our antagonism is only a temporary one and not irreconcilable. We desire the same things, but you are more impatient, more exacting, and—why should I not say it?—more self-seeking than I and those on my side. You would have the state of bliss begin directly after death; you expect the impossible from it and you will not surrender the claims of the individual.

Our God, Logox, will fulfill whichever of these wishes nature outside us allows, but he will do it very gradually, only in the unforeseeable future, and for a new generation of men. He promises no compensation for us, who suffer grievously from life. On the way to this distant goal, your religious doctrines will have to be discarded, no matter whether the first attempts fail, or whether the first substitutes prove to be untenable.

You know why: in the long run, nothing can withstand reason and experience, and the contradiction which religion offers to both is all too palpable. Even purified religious ideas cannot escape this fate, so long as they try to preserve anything of the consolation of religion. No doubt, if they confine themselves to a belief in a higher spiritual being, whose qualities are indefinable and whose purposes cannot be discerned, they will be proof against the challenge of science; but then they will also lose their hold on human interest.

Secondly: observe the difference between your attitude to illusions and mine. You have to defend the religious illusion with all your might. If it becomes discredited—and indeed the threat to it is great enough—then your world collapses. There is nothing left for you but to despair of everything, of civilization and the future of humankind.

From that bondage I am, we are, free. Since we are prepared to renounce a good part of our infantile wishes, we can bear it if a few of our expectations turn out to be illusions.

Education freed from the burden of religious doctrines will not, it may be, effect much change in men's psychological nature. Our god Logox is perhaps not a very almighty one, and he may only be able to fulfill a small part of what his predecessors have promised. If we have to acknowledge this we shall accept it with resignation.

On that account, we shall not lose our interest in the world and in life, for we have one sure support that you lack. We believe that it is possible for scientific work to gain some knowledge about the reality of the world, by means of which we can increase our power and in accordance with which we can arrange our lives.

If this belief is an illusion, then we are in the same position as you. But science has given us evidence, by its numerous and important successes, that it is no illusion. Science has many open enemies, and many more secret ones, among those who cannot forgive her for having weakened religious faith and for threatening to overthrow it. She is reproached for the smallness of the amount she has taught us and for the incomparably greater field she has left in obscurity.

But, in this, people forget how young she is, how difficult her beginnings were, and how infinitesimally small is the period of time since the human intellect has been strong enough for the tasks she sets. Are we not all at fault, in basing our judgments on periods that are too short? We should make the geologists our pattern.

People complain of the unreliability of science—how she announces as a law today what the next generation recognizes as an error and replaces by a new law whose accepted validity lasts no longer. But this is unjust and in part untrue.

The transformations of scientific opinion are developments and advances, not revolutions. A law, which was held at first to be universally valid, proves to be a special case of a more comprehensive uniformity, or is limited by another law, not discovered until later. A rough approximation to the truth is replaced by a more carefully adapted one, which in turn awaits further perfecting.

There are various fields where we have not yet surmounted a phase of research in which we make trial with hypotheses that soon have to be rejected as inadequate; but in other fields, we already possess an assured and almost unalterable core of knowledge.

Finally, an attempt has been made to discredit scientific endeavor in a radical way, on the ground that, being bound to the conditions of our own organization, it can yield nothing else than subjective results, while the real nature of things outside ourselves remains inaccessible.

But this is to disregard several factors which are of decisive importance for the understanding of scientific work. In the first place, our organization—that is, our mental apparatus—has been developed precisely in the attempt to explore the external world. It must, therefore, have realized in its structure some degree of expediency.

In the second place, it is itself a constituent part of the world that we set out to investigate, and it readily admits of such an investigation. Thirdly, the task of science is fully covered if we limit it to showing how the world must appear to us in consequence of the particular character of our organization.

Fourthly, the ultimate findings of science, precisely because of the way in which they are acquired, are determined not only by our organization, but by the things that have affected that organization. Finally, the problem of the nature of the world, without regard to our percipient mental apparatus, is an empty abstraction, devoid of practical interest.

No, our science is no illusion. But an illusion it would be to suppose that what science cannot give us we can get elsewhere.